Strategy IN THE 21st Century
SECOND EDITION

*A Practical Strategy Management Process –
Aligned to Baldrige Criteria for Performance Excellence
and IASP Global Certification Standards*

Lead Authors

RANDALL ROLLINSON
EARL YOUNG

Contributing Authors

Doug Maris, Robin Champ,
Jim Stockmal, Pierre Hadaya,
Richard Thayer, Tamera Parsons,
Sally Parker, William Zybach,
Richard Faulkner, and Don Ricketts

Editor

Lee Crumbaugh

LookingGlass Publishing

Strategy in the 21st Century, Second Edition

Copyright © 2024 Randall Rollinson

ISBN: 978-0-9841936-2-2

Library of Congress Catalog Number:

All rights reserved. No part of this book may be reproduced in any form or by any electronic means, including information storage and retrieval systems, without written permission from the authors, except by a reviewer, who may quote brief passages in a review.

Cover Photo 298574819 © Mykhailo Polenok | Dreamstime.com

LookingGlass Publishing

Chicago, Illinois, USA

www.lblstratgies.com

Dedication

In honor of Dr. Earl Young, Professor Emeritus at DePaul University and co-author of the first edition of *Strategy in the 21st Century*.

For nearly 40 years we collaborated, debated, and sometimes tangled on the content of this book. In the end, we listened and learned from each other. During our last meeting before his passing in August 2023, Earl, with characteristic resolve, imparted a final admonition that resonates as a guiding principle: "Stay the course."

The second edition of *Strategy in the 21st Century* stands as a testament to the life and memory of Dr. Earl Young. In dedicating this work to my dear friend and co-author, we celebrate his legacy, acknowledging the profound impact he had on this collaborative endeavor, and the countless lives he touched through his teachings. Earl's spirit, wisdom, and dedication will continue to inspire readers and guide future generations in the pursuit of strategic excellence.

Strategy in the 21st Century, Second Edition

Table of Contents

Figures and Tables i
Acknowledgements vii
A Word About Artificial Intelligence and Strategy Management ix
Preface xi
Introduction 1
    LBL Strategies, SMPS Framework 3
    SMPS Phases and Tasks 4
        Phase I – Initiating a Strategic Management System 4
            Task 1.1 – Assess Current Strategic Direction and Organizational Capabilities 5
            Task 1.2 – Design and Organize a Program Based on These Assessments 5
        Phase II – Complete an Environmental Assessment 5
            Task 2.1 – Practice Foresight When Conducting External Strategic Analyses 6
            Task 2.2 – Gain Insight by Conducting Internal Strategic Analyses 6
            Task 2.3 – Evaluate Results of Strategic Analysis Via SWOT/OTSW 6
        Phase III— Strategy Formulation 6
            Task 3.1 – Define the Strategic Direction of the Organization 7
            Task 3.2 – Establish HIGH LEVEL Strategy 7
        Phase IV – Strategic Planning 7
            Task 4.1 – Develop a Longer-Term Strategic Plan 7
            Task 4.2 – Develop a Shorter-Term Strategic Operating Plan 8
        Phase V— Strategy Execution 8
            Task 5.1 – Design and Transform the Operating Model 8
            Task 5.2 – Engage Stakeholders and Align the Team Behind the Strategy 9
            Task 5.3 – Implement the Strategic Operating Plan 9
        Phase VI – Performance Management 9
            Task 6.1 – Measure Performance 10
            Task 6.2 – Learn and Adapt 10
            Task 6.3 – Engage Stakeholders and Govern Strategy as an Ongoing Process 10

Crosswalk SMPS to Industry Standards 11
SMPS to the Baldrige Criteria for Performance Excellence 11
IASP Competency Model - Introduction 14
IASP Body of Knowledge 3.0 - Introduction 14
Crosswalk SMPS Framework, to IASP Competencies, to IASP BOK 3.0 17
Overview of Strategic Management as a Discipline 18
Strategy Vs. Strategic Management Definition and Timeline 19
Military Origins of Strategy 22
Strategic Management After World War II 24
SWOT Analysis 26
Other Strategic Management Contributors 27
Strategic Management Emerges as a Major Business Discipline 30
Contemporary Models 30
Strategic Management Competencies 44
Identifying, Articulating, and Developing a Core Set of Shared Values 46
Visioning 46
Strategic Thinking 46
Identifying and Developing Core Organizational Competencies and Capabilities 46
Converting Information Into Strategic Intelligence 47
Identifying, Evaluating, and Selecting Strategic Alternatives 47
Executing Strategy 48
Teamwork and Team Building 48
Phase I – Initiating a Strategic Management System 51
Task 1.1 – Assess Current Strategic Direction and Organizational Capabilities 52
An Assessment of the Organization's Current Situation and Strategy 54
An Assessment of the Organization's Portfolio of Offerings for Performance and Perceived Potential 58
An Assessment of the Longer-Term Vision of Key Leaders 60
An Assessment of Strategic Management Component Parts, a "Gap Analysis." 61
An Assessment of Available Strategic Management Competencies Required to Develop, Execute, and Improve Strategy 61
An Assessment of the Contextual, Situational, and Unique Features that Currently Exist in the Organization Including a Clarification of the Leadership Team's "Felt" Versus "Actual" Need 64
Task 1.2 – Design and Organize a Program Based on These Assessments 68
Design the Scope of the System 68
Understand Expectations of the Leadership Team 69

    Understand Critical Strategic Issues 69

    Modify Design Features 70

    Organize the System 71

Phase II – Complete an Environmental Assessment 79

  Task 2.1 – Practice Foresight when Conducting External Strategic Analyses 80

    Macro-Level Analysis 81

    Micro-Level Analysis 85

        Customers and Other Industry/Sector Stakeholders 86

        Competitors 87

        Scenario-Based Planning to Drive Strategic Foresight 91

  Task 2.2 – Gain Insight by Conducting Internal Strategic Analyses 94

    Core Competencies 95

    Work Environment 96

    Core Processes and Operating Model 97

    Resource Availability 98

    Generic and Specific Questions 102

  Task 2.3 – Evaluate Results of Strategic Analysis Via SWOT/OTSW 102

    Carefully Review the External Scan 104

    Compile a List of the Organization's Primary Market Opportunities and Threats and Document Assumptions 105

    Agree Upon the Organization's Core Competencies and Competitive Advantages 106

    Rank the Organization's Market Opportunities Using its Core Competencies and Threats Using Risk Assessment 107

    Carefully Review the Internal Scan 107

    Compile a List of the Organization's Primary Internal Strengths and Weaknesses 108

    Rank the Organization's Internal Strengths and Weaknesses Based on its Primary Market Opportunities 110

    Evaluate the Strategic Management System 110

Phase III – Strategy Formulation 113

  Task 3.1 – Define the Strategic Direction of the Organization 113

    Vision 115

    Mission 119

    Values (or Core Values) 121

    Policies 122

    Overarching Goal(s) 124

  Task 3.2 – Establish HIGH LEVEL Strategy 130

Use Conceptual Models Which Facilitate Strategic Thinking to Identify Strategy Alternatives 131
    Strategy Setting Frameworks..131
Develop a Well-Functioning Leadership Team 139
Identify Activities Already Underway Within the Organization that Will Impact Strategy.............140
Evaluate and Select High-Level Strategies 141

Phase IV – Strategic Planning 145

Task 4.1 – Develop a Longer-Term Strategic Plan 145
    Compare and Contrast Strategic Thinking and Strategic Planning...146
    Consider Strategic Planning as a Two-Stage Process 147
    Features of Effective Long-Term Strategic Plans 149
    Features of Effective Short-Term Strategic Operating Plans 151
    Identify Key Drivers of Success and Their Intended Results 152
    Translate Intended Results Into Realistically Achievable Strategic Objectives 156
    Adopt and Apply a Balanced Scorecard Mindset...157
    For Each Goal (or Set of Goals), Visualize the Cause-and-Effect Relationship Among Objectives Using a Strategy Deployment Map...160
    Identify and Evaluate the Various Types of Strategic Initiatives Currently Underway 163
    Provide for Contingency Plans..163
    Write a Summary Statement for the Longer-Term Strategic Plan 163
    Obtain Management Feedback, Revisions, Approval, and Authorization to Continue 165

Task 4.2 – Develop a Shorter-Term Strategic Operating Plan..166
    Identify Execution Planning Guidelines Up Front 168
    Select a Framework for the Strategic Operating Plan...171
        OKRs 171
        Hoshin Kanri 172
        Logic Model 173
    Identify Management Roles and Responsibilities Necessary to Align the Organization's Operating Model with the Strategy and Strategic Operating Plan 174
    Develop Implementation Plans for Strategic Objectives 175
    Identify Observable Evidence of Improvement, and then Translate Into Candidate KPIs 176
    Define and Establish a Target for Each Selected KPI...178
    Define Tactical Guidelines 179
    Define Tactics and Integrate Them into Strategic Initiatives and Projects to be Executed 180
    Comments on the Use of Project Management Tools and Concepts 186
    Develop Implementation Plans for Strategic Objectives in Non-Project Formats 187

  Reconcile Implementation Requirements of the Strategic Operating Plan with Available Implementation Resources 190

  Write a Summary Implementation Budget 191

  Obtain Necessary Governance and Management Approval and Authorization for the Strategic Operating Plan 191

  Distribute and Communicate the Strategic Operating Plan 192

Phase V – Strategy Execution 195

 Task 5.1 – Design and Transform the Operating model 196

  Evolution of Organization Design Approaches 198

  Emergence of Agile or Adaptive Design Methods 202

  Agile Organization Design Framework 206

   Principle 1: A North Star Provides Identity 207

   Principle 2: Organizations are Integrated Systems 207

   Principle 3: Co-Creation Activates Dormant Potential 209

   Principle 4: Use Agile Design Thinking to Embed Adaptive Capabilities 209

   Principle 5: Tailor the Approach to the Context 211

   The Agile Organization Design Cycle 213

  Business Capability Framework 216

 Task 5.2 - Engage Stakeholders and Align the Team Behind the Strategy 220

  Engage, Involve, Communicate, and Roll Out the Strategy and Strategic Operating Plan ... 220

  Create a Performance Culture 223

  Ensure Line of Sight to Strategy 224

  Align Individual Roles 227

   Increase Agility of Alignment 228

  For Agility, Manage With OKRs 230

 Task 5.3 – Implement the Strategic Operating Plan 231

  The Vital Role of Leaders 232

  Key Contextual Factors that Impact Implementation Processes 233

  Implementation Best Practices 235

Phase VI – Performance Management 239

 Task 6.1 – Measure Performance 239

 Task 6.2 – Learn and Adapt 248

 Task 6.3 – Engage Stakeholders and Govern Strategy as an Ongoing Process 253

  Role of Leadership in Stakeholder Engagement and Performance Management 254

  Role of Governance in Performance Management 257

    Strategy Management Calendar 261

    Strategy Management Office 263

    Strategy Management Information System 264

Epilogue 267

Appendix 1.1 – Crosswalk Strategic Management Tasks to 2023-24 Baldrige Builder & Results 269

Appendix 1.2 – Crosswalk Strategic Management Tasks to 2023-24 Baldrige Criteria & Results 271

Appendix 2 – 2023-24 - Baldrige Excellence Builder 273

Appendix 3 – SMP/SPP Competencies Included in Each Domain and Subdomain 297

Appendix 4 – SPP Content Outline and Knowledge Needed for Competent Performance 301

Appendix 5 – SMP Content Outline and Knowledge Needed for Competent Performance 307

Appendix 6 – Detailed Outline of IASP BOK 3.0 313

Appendix 7 – The Art of War, by Sun Tzu (Translated by Lionel Giles) 317

Appendix 8 – Nominal Group Technique 319

Appendix 9 – Differentiating Your Customer Value Proposition 331

Appendix 10 – Strategy Execution in the Public Sector 347

Appendix 11 – Robust Strategy Management Calendar 357

Glossary of Strategic Management Terms 359

Bibliography 375

Index 385

About the Authors 395

Figures and Tables

Figures

0.1 Six Phases of Strategic Management..3
0.2 Updated Strategic Management Performance System Framework...............................4
0.3 Baldrige Excellence Framework...19
0.4 BOK 3.0 Framework...15
0.5 Compare and Contrast Basic Strategy Concepts..19
0.6 Strategy Timeline...21
0.7 SWOT Analysis..26
0.8 Ansoff's Grid...29
0.9 The Boston Consulting Group (BCG) Growth Share Matrix..31
0.10 GE McKinsey Matrix...32
0.11 Porter's Five Forces..33
0.12 Value Chain Analysis..36
0.13 Balanced Scorecard..37
0.14 Red Ocean and Blue Ocean Strategy...39
0.15 The Hedgehog Concept..40
0.16 An Integrated Cascade of Choices...42

1.1 Initial Assessment of the Level of Development of the Current Strategic Direction.....57
1.2 BCG Growth Share Matrix – Apple 2022..58
1.3 Public Sector Growth Share Matrix..59
1.4 Gap Analysis Tool...61
1.5 Keys to Managing Strategic Performance..62
1.6 Scope of the Strategic Management System...69
1.7 Define the Strategic Planning Horizon...72
1.8 Core and Extended Planning Team..74
1.9 Example of an Organization's Planning Process..74
1.10 Sample Conceptual Models/Frameworks..75
1.11 Preliminary Two-Way Communications Planning..75

2.1 Key Dimensions to the Macro-Level Environment...80
2.2 Comparison of PESTLE and STEEPLE...82
2.3 Porter's Five Forces – Coca Cola Example..88
2.4 Red Ocean Strategy vs. Blue Ocean Strategy...88

2.5 Medellin Example..89
2.6 Planning for Increasing Uncertainty – Cone of Possibilities....................................92
2.7 Mastering Foresight: Scenario-Based Planning Framework...................................92
2.8 Framework for Internal Analysis..94
2.9 Three Factors of Core Competency..95
2.10 Why Amazon Succeeds..96
2.11 Organizational Agility Framework..97
2.12 Interwoven Processes and Functions Example..98
2.13 Evaluate and Prioritize Opportunities and Threats..103
2.14 OTSW Evaluation..103
2.15 Ansoff's Grid...105
2.16 Heatmap Exposure Matrix..106
2.17 Baldrige Criteria for Performance Excellence..108
2.18 Integrated Management System..110

3.1 The Vision is the Mountain Summit..115
3.2 Continuum of Vision Statements..116
3.3 Shared Vision is a Byproduct of Leadership Communications.............................119
3.4 The Overarching Goal is a Stop on the Climb...124
3.5 Strategy Alternatives Offer Routes for the Climb...130
3.6 Porter's Three Generic Strategies...132
3.7 Example Blue Ocean Strategy Canvas..133
3.8 Relationship of Customers and Stakeholders..134
3.9 Process to Sharpen Customer/Stakeholder Value Proposition............................135
3.10 Ansoff's Grid...137
3.11 Playing to Win...138
3.12 Business Model Canvas..139
3.13 Strategy Selection Filters...142
3.14 Strategy Selection Example..144

4.1a Strategic Operating Plan vs Strategic Plan..147
4.1b Two-Stage Process...148
4.2 An Example of Key Drivers of Success..152
4.3 Process Flow and Relationship...153
4.4 Balanced Scorecard..158
4.5 Cause and Effect Relationship Amongst Perspectives...159
4.6 Strategy Map Example..161
4.7 Strategy Map Rules...162
4.8 Strategic Altitude..166
4.9 Alignment..167
4.10 Hoshin X Matrix..173

4.11 The Logic Model Framework..174
4.12 2X2 Prioritization Matrix...182
4.13 Weighted Criteria Scoring..182
4.14 Paired Comparison Scoring..183
4.15 Example 2X2 Prioritization Matrix...183
4.16 Sample RACI Matrix..184
4.17 Sample Gantt Chart..185

5.1 Strategy Execution Gap...196
5.2 Strategy-Operating Cycle Model...197
5.3 Taylor's Scientific Management..198
5.4 Weber's Bureaucracy Theory..199
5.5 Galbraith's Star Model..200
5.6 Nadler-Tushman Congruence Model..200
5.7 Osterwalder's Operating Model Canvas...200
5.8 Operating Models and their Ecosystems..202
5.9 Organizations Are Becoming More Agile..204.
5.10 Integrated Organizational Systems...208
5.11 Components of an Integrated System..208
5.12 The Design Thinking Process...210
5.13 Organizational Life Cycle...212
5.14 Generic Business Ecosystems..212
5.15 Generic Business Cultures...213
5.16 Syngineering Solutions Design Cycle...214
5.17 Generic Methods...215
5.18 Generic Methods Flows...215
5.19 Target Business Architecture..218
5.20 Responsibilities of the Enterprise Architecture Team..219
5.21 Continuous Communications Throughout the Journey.....................................222
5.22 Sample Plan Rollout Agenda...222
5.23 Cascading – Ground Rule 1..225
5.24 Cascading – Ground Rule 2..226
5.25 Cascading – Ground Rule 3..226
5.26 Cascading Across Size and Complexity..227
5.27 Aligning Individual Roles...227
5.28 Aligned Objectives...228
5.29 Simple Example of Alignment...229
5.30 Agile Example of Alignment..229
5.31 Strategy Implementation Road Map..233
5.32 Key Contextual Factors..234
5.33 Cut Before You Add...236

6.1 From Measurement to Management...240

6.2	Performance Measurement Categories	240
6.3	Three Levels of Performance Measures	241
6.4	Example of Comparing Actual Results to Desired Results	243
6.5	Visualize Using Different Types of Charts	243
6.6	Adopt a "Percent to Target" Mindset for Effective Communications	244
6.7	Apply Performance Ranges and Color Indication	245
6.8	Sample Performance Review	246
6.9	Example of Guard Rails	248
6.10	Organizational Learning Definitions	249
6.11	Double-Loop Learning	249
6.12	Double-Loop Learning – Two Feedback Loops	250
6.13	Three Levels of Performance Measurement	251
6.14	Double-Loop Learning-Example	251
6.15	Stakeholder Focused Mindset Illustration	255
6.16	Strategic Management Roles and Responsibilities – Nonprofit Illustration	258
6.17	Governance and Engagement Operating Model	260
6.18	Basic Strategy Management Calendar	261
6.19	Roles and Responsibilities of the Strategy Management Office	263

Tables

0.1	IASP – SPP/SMP Certification Competency Domains and Subdomains	14
0.2	IASP BOK 3.0 – High Level Outline with Linkages to IASP Competency Domains	16
0.3	Crosswalk SMPS Framework, to IASP Competencies, to IASP BOK 3.0	17
0.4	Kenneth Andrews on Strategy as an Intellectual Process	28
0.5	Criteria for Becoming an Academic Discipline	30
0.6	Hamel and Prahalad	38
0.7	Misconceptions about Strategic Management	45
0.8	Rationale for Team-Based Leadership and Management	49
1.1	Components of an Initial Assessment	53
1.2	Components of Strategic Direction	56
1.3	Organizational Strategic Management Competencies Required	62
1.4	Assessment of Factors Influencing the Leadership Capability	63
1.5	Initial Assessment of Current Strategic Management Capabilities	66

Figures and Tables

2.1 Key Dimensions of the Macro-Level Environment 82
2.2 Key Dimensions to the Micro-Level Environment 90
2.3 Key Components of the Internal Dimension (Detailed) 98

3.1 Components of Strategic Direction 114
3.2 Characteristics of Effective Vision Statements 116
3.3 Examples of Vision Statements 117
3.4 Vision Statement Development Process 118
3.5 Characteristics of Effective Mission Statements 120
3.6 Example Mission Statements 120
3.7 Characteristics of Effective Values 121
3.8 Examples of Espoused Organizational Values 122
3.9 Examples of Policies with Strategy Implications 123
3.10 Examples of Effective Overarching Goal Statements 125
3.11 Characteristics of Effective Overarching Goal Statements 126
3.12 Major Aspects of Overarching Goal Setting 126
3.13 Criteria for Evaluating Current Goals 127
3.14 Sample Strategic Direction 128
3.15 Benefits to Identifying Activities with Strategic Impact That Are Already Underway ..140

4.1 Features of a Long-Term Plan 149
4.2 Sample Intended Results 154
4.3 Sample Strategic Objectives 156
4.4 Sample Objective Commentary 157
4.5 Key Drivers, Objectives, and Perspectives 160
4.6 Suggested Format and Content of the Written Strategic Plan 164
4.7 Sample Strategic Operating Plan Using the Balanced Scorecard Framework 168
4.8 Effective Implementation Guidelines 169
4.9 City Government OKR Example 172
4.10 Performance Measurement Exercise 177
4.11 Sample Set of KPIs with Targets 179
4.12 Sample Strategic Operating Plan with Initiatives 181
4.13 Useful Strategic Implementation Formats 187

5.1 Organizational Polarities 211

Acknowledgements

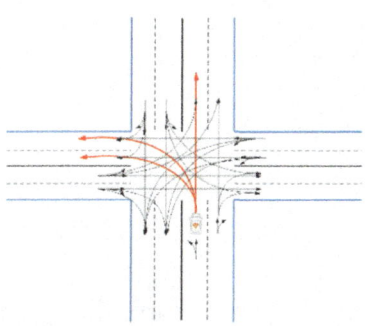

Since the first publication of *Strategy in the 21st Century* in 2010, my primary focus has been navigating the crossroads between abstract strategic management theories and concrete, practical applications. However, capturing this dynamic intersection in a holistic and accurate manner is best done by a team, rather than an individual.

My deepest respect and gratitude are extended to my LBL Strategies colleagues, Doug Maris, Robin Champ, and Richard Faulkner. Their collective intellect and efforts have been instrumental in creating and refining this work. Doug's wisdom, particularly about strategic planning and performance measurement, has been invaluable. Robin's effective insights clarified the practicality of strategic foresight, significantly improving the first edition's content. The realization of either iteration of *Strategy in the 21st Century* would not have been accomplished without Richard's tenacity, patience, and painstaking dedication.

My heartfelt gratitude is also extended to Tamera Fields Parsons, who has tirelessly devoted years of productive collaboration to this book's innovative second edition, primarily by illustrating the harmonious relationship between strategic management and the Baldrige Criteria for Performance Excellence.

I am thankful for the enormously beneficial contributions of Jim Stockmal (former IASP President) and Pierre Hadaya (current IASP Board Member). Their principal authoritative work on IASP Body of Knowledge 3.0, has been referenced liberally all through the book, particularly in association with the practice of Organizational Transformation and Governance of Strategy.

I am also grateful to our partners from Syngineering Solutions, Richard Thayer, William Zybach, and Sally Parker. They enlightened us about the approach to infuse agility into the core of any organization. They offer an illuminated pathway through the theory and practice of agile organizational design.

Similarly, Don Ricketts (a professional colleague and former IASP President with expertise in governance) added insightful depth to our discourse on the governance of strategy.

My special gratitude goes to Lee Crumbaugh, another former IASP president, who ensured veracity in strategic management throughout the publishing procedure as an editor.

Lastly, my sincere gratitude goes out to Mary Cummings, our exceptional business manager; Bob Webster, and Carrie Krakowski for their innovative graphic design work; Amy Hsieh for her timely leadership in aligning our Mastering Strategy coursework with this second edition; and Annika Tammiste, who has always been at the ready with timely and responsive social media support.

To all of you, I cannot overstate your invaluable contributions to this endeavor – without you, the complex interplay of strategic management would remain obscured and incomplete.

A Word About Artificial Intelligence and Strategy Management

The book you are about to read is a comprehensive overview of the strategy management discipline, from its earliest origins through December 2023. As the LBL Strategies team finalized this edition for publication, we were acutely aware of the acceleration of artificial intelligence (AI), and specifically generative AI, across all industries. It reminded us of similar excitement, fear, and uncertainty in 1993 when the world wide web entered use in the mainstream public. Like then, any attempt to predict the overall impact of this emerging technology on strategy management would be premature (if not outright fortune telling).

That said, the LBL Strategies team is committed to monitoring and leveraging the rapidly emerging AI applications, with a specific focus on strategy management. Even as this edition is released, we are working with the International Association for Strategy Professionals (IASP) and the Army Strategists Association on conducting an AI survey to further understand perspectives and usage in the industry. We will document how AI is aiding organizations with their overall strategy management system, as well as investigate its potential for future opportunities. To this end, we have created a landing page on our website for our readers to access the most current research and findings on AI and its advancements in strategy management. Please visit our AI and Strategic Management website:
https://www.lblstrategies.com/artificial-intelligence-and-strategy-management/

Strategy in the 21st Century, Second Edition

Preface

Beginning in the 1950s *strategic management* emerged as one of the most widely used (and often misused) terms in the business management lexicon. It has been the focus of a constant stream of articles, books, tools, concepts, and software; the primary product/service of many consulting firms; and a required capstone course in most MBA programs. Strategy-focused organizations are increasingly more common, as boards, owners, and executives globally seek out the advice of the latest crop of consulting gurus.[1] However, the actual practice of strategic management is limited to the innovators and adopters working on the forefront developing and applying it as a discipline.

For most organizations, including many large, growing, and profitable firms, strategic management is still considered an option, even a luxury. For the past 40 plus years executive level attention has been focused on functional management primarily in marketing, finance, operations, and technology, and more recently in digital transformation, data, and expanding use of Artificial Intelligence.

During this time, the emphasis overwhelmingly centered on making incremental improvements in systems and processes, while recognition of the need for a strategically aligned organization capable of responding to disruptive events and accelerating rates of change was not widespread. The latter remained the province of forward-thinking theorists, consultants, and leading-edge corporations while the former was occupied by organizations accustomed to incremental and predictable rates of change in a slow-growing economy.

It is not that management in these organizations consciously disregard the benefits attributed to corporate strategy. In fact, all too often they spend more time thinking about strategy than on its execution, leading to a gap in the system. Executives and managers in these organizations are not averse to change, nor are they unwilling to commit resources to developing new approaches. Their hesitancy is more often based on a healthy skepticism of the steady stream of new conceptual models and theories about strategy and strategic planning with scant consideration for the often more complex processes of strategy execution.

With these considerations in mind, we designed this book for those sitting for certification, along with busy executives, managers, owners, and professionals that want to accept the challenge of strategic management. In doing so they would like a grounded understanding of strategic management; a practical approach to selecting, developing, and implementing an appropriate strategy; and a means of implementing the strategic management process in their organization. They want to be empowered to

---

[1] Kiechel III, W. *The Lords of Strategy – The Intellectual History of the New Corporate World*, HBR, 2010.

take their organization to the highest level of their aspirations, consistent with the resources and capabilities of their organization and its members.

Accordingly, this book introduces the *strategic management process* including:

- Terminology
- An overview of the origin and development of strategic management
- Brief descriptions of selected strategic management models and theories
- A discussion of the emergence of strategic management as a comprehensive discipline
- A detailed set of core competencies deployed throughout all management levels and functions

Two assumptions guided the development of this second edition. First, there is a need to understand the entire set of processes necessary to develop, implement, and maintain an effective organization strategy. Until recently, strategy *formulation* has occupied the attention of academics with little emphasis on strategy *implementation*. This has reinforced the tendency of consultants to focus on strategic *planning*. Who does not know, or know of, a CEO with an expensive, beautifully rendered plan gathering dust on the shelf? Secondly, the proliferation of literature, be it research-based or practitioner distilled "wisdom," is quite confusing to strategy professionals let alone busy executives.

To quote Abraham Maslow, "If all you have is a hammer, everything looks like a nail." Strategy professionals need a robust toolbox of models, tools, and techniques to call upon when needed. Growing out of strategy's rich history of development comes a wide range of tools and techniques strategy professionals can use to facilitate their work. It is essential for strategy professionals to understand how and when to apply each of these tools to best meet the needs and priorities of the organization they serve. This book will introduce you to many of these proven tools and techniques. Beyond that, the IASP BOK 3.0 presents a broader set of tools; we encourage the reader to explore and tap into this resource.

Consequently, we developed a summary of key developmental events and trends in the rapidly emerging discipline of strategic management. As such, the book provides a framework for analyzing strategic management processes and to serve as a guide for strategy professionals, executives, and managers in the development and management of strategy within their organizations.

This book outlines the development of each phase of the strategic management process, described earlier, incorporating proven models and concepts of strategy where they can be most effectively utilized.

Introduction

Whether you are a strategy professional or business executive who purchased our book; are presently enrolled in our Mastering Strategy program sponsored by George Washington University (GWU), Center for Excellence in Public Leadership (CEPL); part of the College of Professional Studies; are preparing to sit for industry certification through the International Association for Strategy Professionals (IASP); are pursuing the Malcolm Baldrige National Quality Award; or are a professional wanting to learn more about strategic management, we welcome you to the second edition of *Strategy in the 21st Century*.

The contents of this book trace back to 1985, when we offered *a Certificate in Business Administration Program* to working professionals in partnership with DePaul University. In 1988, we expanded our program to the University of Illinois at Chicago. Edition one was published in 2010 as a hard copy textbook providing a holistic description of a "practical strategic management process" that melds understanding and application of best practices with strategic management "theory" and real-world "practice." As we share with our clients, LBL Strategies thrives at the intersection of theory and practice.

In 2010, we became active in the formation of the Association for Strategic Planning's professional certification program. Today the association is known as the International Association for Strategy Professionals (IASP). The development of the certification program was led early on by the late Stephen Haines, founder of the Haines Centre for Strategic Management®, Systems Thinking Press®, and the Global Association of Systems Thinking. Stephen led a team of association members to define the competency statements used to guide the original set of exams. He deserves great credit for his strategic and entrepreneurial leadership.[2] Over time we served as one of six primary authors of the association's second Body of Knowledge (BOK 2.0).[3] They were Stephen Haines, Howard Rohm, David Wilsey, Frank Mruk, Terry Schmidt, and Randall Rollinson.

When we published the first edition of our textbook in 2010, we became a leading *Certification Preparation Provider (CPP)* for the International Association for Strategy Professionals (IASP). Since then, we have been authorized to educate and train professionals as they prepare for professional certification as a Strategic Planning Professional (SPP) or a Strategic Management Professional (SMP).

In 2011, we renewed our partnership with DePaul University, offering a Certificate in Strategic Management Program. Late in 2015, we transitioned from DePaul University to George Washington University's Center for Excellence in Public Leadership (GWU CEPL), part of the College of Professional

---

[2] https://www.csm-asia.com/stephen_haines/
[3] https://www.strategyassociation.org/store/viewproduct.aspx?ID=4660938

Strategy in the 21st Century, Second Edition

Studies, where we now offer the *Mastering Strategy: Strategic Management Performance System (SMPS) Certification Program,* as well as other strategic management certification offerings.[4]

The program's 10 primary learning objectives align with the International Association for Strategy Professionals current certification competencies and Body of Knowledge (IASP BOK 3.0):

- Leading, engaging, facilitating, and governing all phases and tasks of effective strategic planning and management.
- Acquiring a foundation in principal developments in the study and practice of strategic management.
- Thinking strategically and screening for opportunities that best match the core competencies of the organization to deliver stakeholder value.
- Building strategic foresight to mitigate risk and position the organization for success.
- Aligning teams and individuals behind a common vision, strategy, and a strategic plan.
- Ensuring the organization's operating model, culture and strategic initiatives are aligned to strategy and designed to drive the right outcomes.
- Bridging the gap between strategy and execution via clear accountabilities, timely communications, and line-of-sight to strategy.
- Leveraging an agile performance management system to guide effective decision making and governance of strategy.
- Cultivating a strategy-focused organization to ensure purpose and governance drive strategy and strategy drives budgeting and deployment of efforts.
- Building professional credibility, including preparation for the International Association for Strategy Professionals (IASP certification exams).[5]

Edition two of *Strategy in the 21st Century* will remain at the heart of our professional development course work and learning processes. At the core of this book is a commitment to help our certification customers navigate the discipline of strategy management via our **Strategic Management Performance System (SMPS) Framework**. Additionally, it is designed to deliver maximum value as an IASP exam preparation book aligned with three relevant industry standards: **the Baldrige Excellence Framework; the IASP Competency Model; and the IASP Body of Knowledge 3.0**.

Following is a brief introduction to the **SMPS Framework** and to the three relevant industry standards.

---

[4] https://www.lblstrategies.com/training-and-certification/
[5] https://www.strategyassociation.org/page/StrategyCertificationProgram

Introduction

LBL Strategies, SMPS Framework

Central to understanding and applying the Strategic Management Performance System Framework is to understand the differences between strategic management and operations management. Strategic management is concerned with the processes, decisions, and actions a leadership team takes that determine the long-run performance of the organization. Sometimes this level of process, decision-making, and action is referred to as "working ON" the organization, while operations management focuses on day-to-day work, is referred to as "working IN" the organization.

Consequently, strategic management is about enabling an organization to recognize the need for change, to adapt quickly and navigate the tumultuous waters of constantly changing circumstances.

The following phases taken together, and completed, will move a management team and its organization through the necessary processes to fully analyze, formulate, plan, and implement a strategic management system.

Experienced strategic management professionals recognize commonalities in the practice of strategic planning and management. We see this as six fundamental, or generic, phases of strategic management activity. (See Figure 0.1.)

FIGURE 0.1: SIX PHASES OF STRATEGIC MANAGEMENT

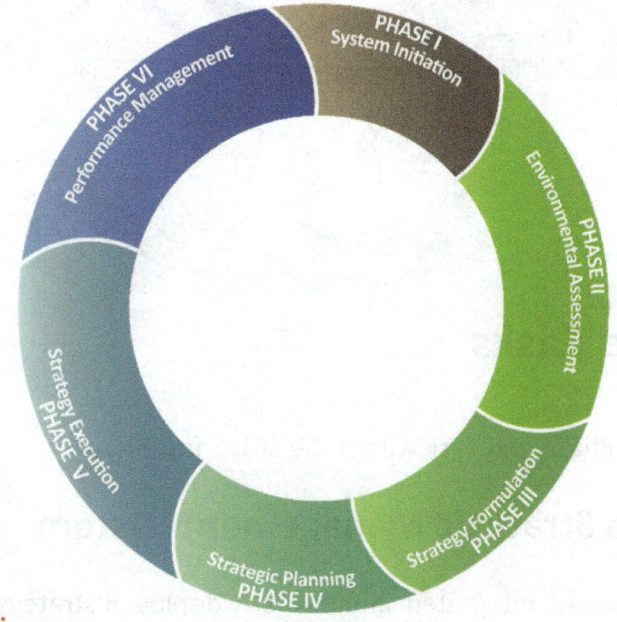

Building on this reveal (Figure 0.2) of common phases, we have realigned this textbook, and the Mastering Strategy Certification Program content, to align more closely with IASP's current certification model and Body of Knowledge BOK 3.0. In doing so, we now overlay 15 specific "team oriented" tasks, which include a new task in Phase V entitled **"Transform Organization."**

In addition, the SMPS framework now contains an expanded focus on **Engaging Stakeholders** and a new focus on **Governance of Strategy**. When viewed holistically, these phases and tasks give substance to a Strategic Management Performance System.

It is important to emphasize that while these common phases are presented as cyclical, they are in fact dynamic and continuous. It is the strategy professional who facilitates each phase and task within these sub-processes and works to optimize the overall system. (See Figure 0.2.)

FIGURE 0.2: UPDATED STRATEGIC MANAGEMENT PERFORMANCE SYSTEM FRAMEWORK

SMPS Phases and Tasks

Below is a summary of each Phase and Task within the SMPS framework.

Phase I – Initiating a Strategic Management System

To manage with a formally stated, integrated, and properly deployed strategy or set of strategies is a major challenge for any organization. To do so without the necessary preparatory steps will most likely result in wasted time, energy, misdirected efforts, and even potential failure. More important, management will be at the disadvantage of attempting the strategic journey without considering current aspirations and plans. To avoid this scenario, two important tasks/processes are required:

TASK 1.1 – ASSESS CURRENT STRATEGIC DIRECTION AND ORGANIZATIONAL CAPABILITIES

Before undertaking any significant effort to develop, improve, or manage strategy, there needs to be a shared understanding of the scope and depth of the change effort to be undertaken. This, in turn, needs to be grounded in a fact-based assessment of the strategic direction, organizational culture, and strategic management capabilities currently in place. This initial assessment and early-stage engagement, in large measure, will determine the basis for making changes. It is not a full-scope audit; that will come later. Strategy professionals play a critically important role in shepherding this task.

TASK 1.2 – DESIGN AND ORGANIZE A PROGRAM BASED ON THESE ASSESSMENTS

Once there is an agreement on the scope of the strategic management process and level of commitment required, a leadership and stakeholder team must be thoughtfully engaged and selected. In addition, decisions must be made specific to organization and governance structure; along with assigning organization-wide duties and responsibilities must be assigned to individual leaders and managers establishing their role and responsibilities in the process. Two primary responsibilities of the strategy professional are to 1) efficiently and effectively shape the process to fit the needs of the organization, and 2) ensure stakeholders are engaged throughout the entirety of the process.

Phase II – Complete an Environmental Assessment

Phase II builds on the Phase I foundation by outlining and describing the process of strategic assessment, the essential prerequisite for the development and implementation of an effective organization strategy. Conducting a comprehensive and thorough assessment at the outset of any significant effort to develop or simply to improve organizational strategy or strategic management capabilities is not an option; *it is the required and fundamental foundation upon which all subsequent strategic decisions are built.* Accordingly, Phase II is organized as follows:

TASK 2.1 – PRACTICE FORESIGHT WHEN CONDUCTING EXTERNAL STRATEGIC ANALYSES

In today's volatile, uncertain, complex, and ambiguous (VUCA) operating environment, a traditional approach to external analysis (i.e., PESTEL/STEEPLE/SWOT) [6] alone is not sufficient. New tools and approaches have emerged to provide the strategic foresight required to effectively inform today's strategic planning processes. The focus of external analyses is to gain foresight into the external factors, emerging signals of change, trends, possible scenarios, strategic opportunities, and threats that are, probably will, or may affect the direction, scope, and nature of the strategic management program the organization pursues.

TASK 2.2 – GAIN INSIGHT BY CONDUCTING INTERNAL STRATEGIC ANALYSES

Internal analyses work in compliment with external analyses by examining the organization's core competencies, internal factors, strengths, weaknesses, and resources to form understanding of capacities and capabilities required to pursue selected strategic objectives.

TASK 2.3 – EVALUATE RESULTS OF STRATEGIC ANALYSIS VIA SWOT/OTSW

The data and information collected and analyzed in the previous tasks are of little or no use until they have been evaluated in terms of relevance, applicability, and, most importantly, priority to the leadership team and to the strategic management process being developed. The process for conducting what we term an "OTSW" Evaluation (what is commonly referred to as a "SWOT" Analysis) is carefully examined.

Phase III— Strategy Formulation

Strategy formulation is a key to effective strategic management: It requires strategic thinking rooted in the resources and capabilities of the organization. It also requires an integration of organizational, functional, and project level considerations – all within the dual focus of the long-term vision and the realities of the present situation and contextual factors. Strategy formulation is an integrated process, which must adjust continuously to the emerging changes and disruptions in the environment.

This is challenging work. For the strategy formulation process to be successful it must be disaggregated into its component parts and facilitated carefully by the strategy professional. Over the years we have found the following tasks to be very useful in guiding this process:

---

[6] See glossary for definitions

TASK 3.1 – DEFINE THE STRATEGIC DIRECTION OF THE ORGANIZATION

This task, more than any other, requires balanced attention to long-term development of the strategic direction of the organization with near-term resources and capabilities available to pursue the chosen direction. This step requires consideration of the five key components of strategic direction, which are vision, mission, values, policies, and goals.

TASK 3.2 – ESTABLISH HIGH LEVEL STRATEGY

Once a strategic direction has been determined, the next task is to identify or develop a set of desired and feasible high-altitude strategy alternatives. Close examination of the external foresight, OTSW evaluation, and the strategic direction is basic to developing a useful set of alternatives.

A helpful place to begin is to clearly define your organization's competitive positioning and stakeholder value propositions, i.e., customer, owner, partner, and employee. The goal of this task is to agree upon a set of high-altitude strategic choices that leverage the organization's core competency and pursue available opportunities.

As these strategic choices are being made, the strategy professional and core planning team assess the impact of these choices on the organization's operating model.

Phase IV – Strategic Planning

Strategic planning is the process of translating the results of strategy formulation into a prioritized and actionable strategic plan. The output of the strategy formulation process from the preceding Phase contains the content of what will become the strategic plan. However, much needs to be done to translate it into an effective and efficient plan of action. As is the case with all other phases, leaders and key stakeholders must be able to adjust the strategic plan to the emerging changes and disruptions in their environment.

TASK 4.1 – DEVELOP A LONGER-TERM STRATEGIC PLAN

A comprehensive strategic plan is far more than a prioritizing and scheduling process. It will be the basis for leading and managing the organization in the future, while illuminating potential changes required to the organization's operating model. While always subject to modification, it is the best statement of the goals, strategies, key drivers of success, desired outcomes, measures, initiatives, and aspirations the leadership team embraces for the foreseeable future.

> *Importantly, the strategic plan should outline the changes required to provide added value in the future and include a high-level transformation plan to align the organization's operating model with the new strategy.*

TASK 4.2 – DEVELOP A SHORTER-TERM STRATEGIC OPERATING PLAN

Now the strategic plan must be converted into a blueprint for action. The longer-range strategic plan does not provide one. It contains the strategic direction of the organization, a high-level strategy, a balanced set of strategic objectives to achieve the desired future state, and a high-level plan to transform the organization's operating model to align with the new strategy.

There remains the task of carefully refining the transformation plan, further prioritizing the strategic objectives, identifying performance measures, and developing initiatives/projects to move the strategic plan into a coordinated set of actions (i.e., a strategic "operating" plan). This task also includes assigning roles and responsibilities for execution, committing the authorized resources, and determining the potential impacts on the organization's operating model.

The strategic operating plan typically covers a 12-month period, often the upcoming calendar or fiscal year, but sometimes for a shorter period such as the next six months or the next quarter.

Phase V— Strategy Execution

Execution of the strategic operating plan and ongoing management requires much more agility, time, commitment, and resources than the planning process ever consumes in planning *per se*. It is a continuous and integrated process, where collectively and individually, key stakeholders must adjust to the emerging changes and disruptions in their environment.

Moreover, the competencies required for execution and ongoing management are more complex and demanding than those required for planning. The common error is to value them less and give them less attention, often delegating them to lower management levels. *This is not a trivial matter; not valuing these competencies remains the most prevalent reason for faulty and incomplete execution of strategic plans.*

TASK 5.1 – DESIGN AND TRANSFORM THE OPERATING MODEL

To be effective at execution, a specific competency set all leadership teams MUST possess is the *ability to align the new strategy with an "operating model" that supports execution of the strategy*. If the goals of the organization are to be realized, designing, aligning, and transforming an organization's operational model to support the new strategy is a foundational requirement. This includes taking a fresh look at each major building block of the organization, including the functions, processes, units, technology, brands, knowledge, etc. as each is a primary determinant of strategy execution performance.

Furthermore, to be effective at execution requires understanding and designing an organization where each business/program unit, functional unit, department, team, and individual knows how their work fits into the organization's operating model and, by extension, the strategy. Here implementation of specific projects is required to bring desired transformations into reality.

Strategy practitioners play a coordinating role in working with the leadership team and human resources in translating strategy, execution processes, and performance/accountability language into an organization design to include employee job descriptions and individual development plans.

TASK 5.2 – ENGAGE STAKEHOLDERS AND ALIGN THE TEAM BEHIND THE STRATEGY

Transforming the operating model alone is not sufficient to ensure effective implementation of the strategic operating plan. *Aligning the organization's key stakeholders behind the strategy and related initiatives is required.*

Initially this means a heavy emphasis on multi-directional "team" collaborations and communications while delegating responsibility for various aspects of execution. This is the first hurdle. It is important to recognize that everyone involved may not fully understand or even accept the role they are being asked to play. This is a main reason for dealing with execution in three distinct, albeit, not easily differentiated tasks: transformation, alignment, and implementation. Each has its own communication and engagement challenges, all of which center on change. The importance of consistent team and stakeholder engagement cannot be overemphasized here. By achieving this engagement, a climate is established where a "line of sight" to strategy is created and maintained down and across the organization. This is especially true when strategic objectives are cascaded and aligned throughout the organization, and cross functional strategic initiatives are ready for launch.

TASK 5.3 – IMPLEMENT THE STRATEGIC OPERATING PLAN

It is common for managers and top executives (in particular) to believe their responsibility for strategic management ends when the plan is completed. In fact, their work has just begun. This is because the management processes needed to transform the operating model, align the organization, and implement the strategy require ongoing leadership, thoughtful governance, and management's careful attention to delegating responsibilities and providing continuous oversight that is both diligent and supportive.

Phase VI – Performance Management

Surely, the goal of any leadership team is to engage key stakeholders and govern strategic performance. This, more than any other strategic competency, requires team commitment, diligence, and continuous improvement. A strategic planning and management professional has a key role to play in building, operationalizing, and improving this ongoing phase of the strategic management system.

TASK 6.1 – MEASURE PERFORMANCE

Improvement in organizational performance will not occur unless leadership intentionally measures and manages strategic performance. The key to improved performance is to put in place strategic performance measures, most often known as Key Performance Indicators (KPIs), along with targets based on the strategic objectives, prior to defining initiatives and initiative measures. Both levels of performance measurement and management are important and should begin with the strategic objectives. Strategy practitioners must work closely with their leadership team to agree upon the appropriate KPIs with a realistic target for each.

A key supporting and complimentary process is effective data governance. Data governance is everything an organization does to ensure that its data is secure, private, accurate, available, and usable. Without effective data governance the value of measuring performance will be lost, as poor data quality often leads to poor decisions and ultimately poor performance.

TASK 6.2 – LEARN AND ADAPT

For organizational learning to take place, a reliable stream of valid performance information must be available on a timely basis to assess the effectiveness of the current strategy and strategic operating plan, and to adapt, accordingly.

Strategy practitioners must collaborate closely with their team to understand that performance measurement and management are integrated processes, not an event. Collecting, reporting, and visualizing performance information is the easy part. *Learning from the performance information to adapt to changing circumstances and continuously improve processes and systems is the hard part.* Strategy practitioners have a leading role to play in this regard.

TASK 6.3 – ENGAGE STAKEHOLDERS AND GOVERN STRATEGY AS AN ONGOING PROCESS

Engagement of stakeholders and governance of the strategic management process is required in all phases and tasks. It is a continuous and integrated process, where key stakeholders must adjust to the emerging changes and disruptions in their environment.

Effective leadership of the organization, provided by the owners and/or Board of Directors and executive management team, is required to productively engage key stakeholders and govern strategic management as an ongoing process. Failure to do so accounts for many of the difficulties encountered in organizations. Again, proactive leadership and governance of strategy must be at work in all phases and tasks of the Strategic Management Performance System (SMPS) Framework, particularly when it comes to Phase VI: Performance Management.

Tools to promote effective engagement and governance include the use of a strategic management calendar and engaging a strategy management office/officer, all supported by an efficient and practical strategic management information system.

Introduction

Crosswalk SMPS to Industry Standards

Each industry standard summarized below is fully aligned with the SMPS Framework, i.e., Baldrige Excellence Framework; IASP Competency Model; and IASP Body of Knowledge 3.0.

SMPS to the Baldrige Criteria for Performance Excellence

Over the past few years, we came to appreciate another discipline or standard strategy professionals may want to incorporate into their work. "The *Baldrige Excellence Framework* and its *Criteria for Performance Excellence* incorporate proven practices on current leadership and management issues <u>into a set of questions</u> that help you rise to challenges, leverage strengths, and manage all the components of your organization as a unified whole to achieve your mission, ongoing success, and performance excellence. This view of an organization is called a systems perspective." [7] The Baldrige Excellence Framework sets out *"Criteria to Meet"* in a non-prescriptive, systems approach. (See Figure 0.3.)

FIGURE 0.3: BALDRIGE EXCELLENCE FRAMEWORK

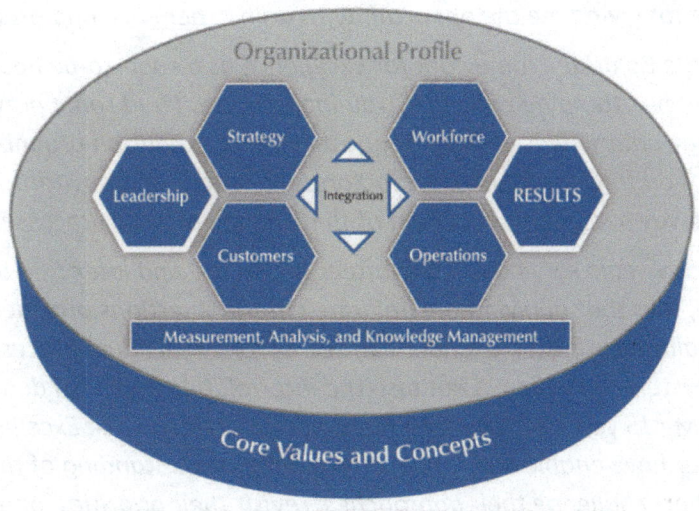

---

[7] 2023-2024 *Baldrige Excellence Framework*, p ii

Similarly, the discipline of Strategic Management enables organizations to systematically prepare for and overcome challenges to take advantage of market opportunities. Strategic Management is a **set of processes and competencies** required to specify an organization's strategy, execution plan, and management system to achieve success. The SMPS Framework outlines a *"Process to Achieve"* results via a semi-prescriptive, systems approach.

Below are the comments of our good friend and contributing author Tamera Fields Parsons. Tamera is a seasoned Baldrige Examiner. Here is her Baldrige story.

> *My respect and budding love of process probably had its start earlier than I recognize. As a teenager I frequently moved furniture around in my room, organized my clothing by article, color, or season, and oftentimes would walk through a version of a "dress rehearsal" if I were preparing for some type of special event or circumstance.*
>
> *Later, like most parents, I was constantly looking for ways to become more efficient with the daily activities associated with raising a family. While I was motivated to find efficiency so I could have more quality time either with my two children or on my own, I was also inspired to make things "better." This interest in making things better (which I learned had a real name and is Improvement!) showed up in the kitchen where I tried new ways to stretch groceries, prepare meals, store meals, and even reheat them so that they did not seem like leftovers. It showed up in the laundry process, the house cleaning process, the homework oversight process, and the weekly and monthly activity planning process.*
>
> *It was not until I was working as a quality manager for a very progressive leader at a Citigroup company that I was exposed to Process Management. I learned to create flowcharts using large rolls of paper, pencils, and a stencil. I learned about root cause analysis, Plan Do Check Act (PDCA), and Statistical Process Control (SPC). After completing several weeks of training in Process Management, my supervisor sent me to a course to learn how adults learn, and more importantly, how to design and deliver adult learning effectively. Some of my most rewarding hours as an employee were spent facilitating process improvement teams and training others how to use PDCA and performance measures. To this day, I am grateful to Pat Johnson for giving me the opportunity to gain experience and practice these skills.*
>
> *I was first exposed to the Baldrige Framework for Excellence as a soon-to-be healthcare executive. I was "voluntold" that I would be attending examiner training and that I had some prework to complete. I soon learned that the Baldrige criteria was a series of questions that guides an organization to define its key products and services, workforce and customer factors, challenges and advantages, and processes and measures. I was on my way to explore what kind of thinking lay beyond processes and measures.*
>
> *What I learned over many years serving as a volunteer examiner, and later as a team leader, trainer, and awards program judge, was that applying the Baldrige criteria questions provided a helicopter view of an organization. With a Baldrige mindset, a leader can see beyond individual processes to recognize not only the organization as a system (or systems) but also the interrelationships and dependencies across processes and results. My 15 years of service to the Baldrige Performance Excellence as an examiner, team leader, and trainer have enabled me to develop a deep understanding of the criteria questions, how to use them to help others challenge their approaches, revisit their priorities, and focus their efforts on the right things.*
>
> *In 2008, I was serving as a mid-level quality and performance improvement executive for a medium size healthcare organization in Northeast Tennessee and Southwest Virginia. Over a 36-hour period, the senior executive who I reported to left the organization, I was promoted to a Vice President position, my areas of responsibility doubled, and I had a flat tire on my way home from work. What a week!*

Introduction

While I received many congratulatory messages, I was also aware of the murmurings that I just catapulted into the position, didn't have the leadership experience yet, and wasn't qualified to lead clinical areas as I was not a nurse or a doctor (I had served as a paramedic several years prior and that was the extent of my clinical experience). After about two weeks of letting things keep operating on their own, I sat at my desk and realized that I was feeling quite overwhelmed and nearly paralyzed. Like any process thinker, I needed a plan! I did not have a mentor or a confidante to lean on at that time, and I was beginning to feel quite discombobulated.

What occurred next not only saved my career as a Vice President, but literally taught me to think like a leader. I opened the Baldrige Framework for Excellence and asked myself the basic criteria questions just as I had asked organizations as a Baldrige examiner. I started with "Who IS my customer (now)? I defined my customers in my new role as the other members of the executive team. The next questions were "What do they need or expect?" "How do I know?" I realized I needed to sit down and talk to my new set of customers, and I did. Six weeks later, I understood what they needed from my department to be successful.

From there I deployed the rest of the Baldrige Framework: based on what my customers needed, what was my purpose? How would I create a plan to deliver? How do I improve and manage processes to deliver what they need? How do I staff those processes? How do I know if the work we do is successful?" Answering these questions was challenging work, and it took months and years to get to a place of excellence, but we did it. The Baldrige Framework not only taught me to THINK like a leader, but it also gave me the right questions to ask to build a successful organization. Applying the Baldrige Framework in a time of desperation is not ideal, but it saved me in a sense, and was nothing short of a career-changing move.

Anyone that takes the time to read the Baldrige criteria questions will quickly realize that most of the questions begin with the word "how." The criteria are not a collection of best practices. In fact, a hallmark of the criteria is that it is not prescriptive, and because of that, applies to any organization in any sector, of any size, and at any stage along the journey to excellence. So then, what happens when a leader does not know the answer to the How questions, or if their answer falls short of excellence, or even adequate? This is where intentional, fact-based, forward-looking planning and design are key to success. It is not enough to ask the right questions (although it is a fantastic starting point!). It is crucial that an organization, and leaders of organizations, seek to identify best – not common – practices to learn from a process perspective, and to adopt a comprehensive, role model approach to planning and managing the culture, systems, workforce, operations, and results of the organization.

When linked, these two frameworks provide a holistic and practical approach to achieving organizational excellence and results. Their intersection and integration is documented via a crosswalk table. **See Appendix 1.1 – SMPS, Baldrige Builder Crosswalk and Results, and Appendix 1.2 – SMPS, Full Baldrige Criterion Crosswalk and Results.**

To facilitate understanding of the complementary nature of these two frameworks, we have inserted callouts in the right-hand column, *and italicized/bolded text* in Phases I through VI, to connect the dots between the many intersections of Baldrige Excellence Framework ("quality criterion to meet to be recognized for excellence") and the SMPS Framework ("a process to follow to achieve excellence").[8]

---

[8] https://www.nist.gov/system/files/documents/2021/01/29/2021-2022-baldrige-excellence-builder.pdf

IASP Competency Model - Introduction

In 2019, as part of a continuous improvement process, IASP invested in a professional "job task analysis" to understand and define what strategy professionals do and the competencies required. Once that research was completed, IASP's Certification Commission began the process to update the exams for each of the two certification levels to align with the newly crafted competency statements.

IASP's new and improved content, for both the Strategy Planning Professional (SPP) and Strategy Management Professional (SMP) certifications, centers on four required domains of competence and 10 subdomains of the strategic planning and management process. (See Table 0.1)

TABLE 0.1: IASP – SPP/SMP CERTIFICATION COMPETENCY DOMAINS AND SUBDOMAINS

Domain 1: Engagement
A. Culture of Strategy Management and Agility
B. Planning Team Expectations
Domain 2: Strategy Formulation
A. Internal and External Environmental Scans
B. Strategy Design and Formulation
Domain 3: Transformation
A. Alignment of the Organization Design with Strategy
B. Alignment of Operations with Strategy
C. Operational Planning for Implementation
Domain 4: Strategy Execution, Governance, and Evaluation
A. Strategy Execution and Transformation
B. Governance and Decision Making
C. Strategic Performance Management

Each subdomain is then broken down into the specific competencies required for an effective SPP and SMP. **See Appendix 3 for a breakdown of SPP and SMP competencies by subdomain.**

The IASP Competency Framework also includes specific knowledge needed for each domain. **See Appendix 4 for knowledge needed for competent SPP performance and Appendix 5 for knowledge needed for competent SMP performance.**

IASP Body of Knowledge 3.0 - Introduction

As part of IASP's continuous improvement process, beginning in early 2020 Dr. Pierre Hadaya and James Stockmal led the process of aligning and updating IASP's Body of Knowledge (BOK) with the new IASP

Introduction

competency domains and subdomains. This graphic depiction of this alignment work visually summarizes the BOK 3.0 Framework. (See Figure 0.4.)

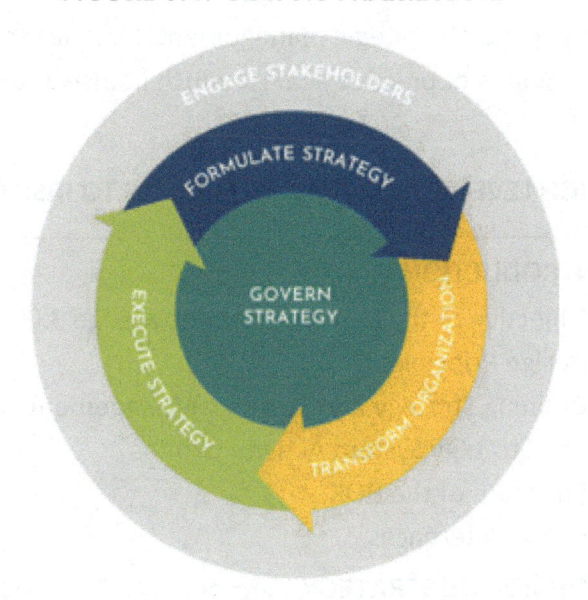

FIGURE 0.4: BOK 3.0 FRAMEWORK[9]

The five activity groups build on each other to form an iterative process. IASP defines each activity:

- *Formulate Strategy* is to develop the strategy. This entails analysis of the external and internal environments; the development of a shared vision; the formulation, analysis, and selection of appropriate strategy alternatives; and the preparation of the strategic plan.

- *Transform Organization* is to change the organization to align its operating model to the new strategy (Figure 1.2). This entails developing a plan detailing and sequencing projects to align the operating model to the new strategy and executing the projects properly at the appropriate time.

- *Execute Strategy* is to deliver value to the organization's stakeholders, as defined by the strategy. This entails ensuring alignment of the operational activities of the organization (e.g., human resources, marketing, finance, accounting, production, service delivery, sales, customer service, management, and information technology) to the new strategy.

- *Engage Stakeholders* is getting key participants to commit to making the new strategy work. This necessitates that leaders communicate and justify the importance of the new strategy and the activities required to make it work, as well as consider the feedback received from employees. This also requires building employee commitment, removing barriers to change, conducting training, developing the right employee objectives, and providing motivating incentives.

- *Govern Strategy* is to oversee the previous four activity groups. This involves monitoring the external environment, explicitly setting group and individual performance objectives, tracking, and evaluating deliverables and results, and learning from these activities and making adaptive decisions when needed. With clear role delineation, these governing activities may be performed

---

[9] *IASP BOK 3.0*, 1.4 Strategy System Activity Groups, pp 5-6.

Strategy in the 21st Century, Second Edition

by a Board of Directors, executive committee, change leadership team, the program and project sponsors and teams, or other governance bodies tasked with clearly defined roles.

The Body of Knowledge 3.0 Framework establishes high-level expectations of quality and consistency for working professionals in the discipline of strategic management. IASP has set a common language, required competencies, and standards of practice against which industry certification can be achieved and maintained. (See Table 0.2.)

TABLE 0.2: IASP BOK 3.0 – HIGH LEVEL OUTLINE WITH LINKAGES TO IASP COMPETENCY DOMAINS [10] [11]

Chapter 1 INTRODUCTION
- 1.1. Objective of the IASP Body of Knowledge 3.0
- 1.2. Design Principles
- 1.3. Defining Strategy and Strategy Management
- 1.4. The Strategy System Activity Groups
- 1.5. Structure of the BOK
- 1.6. Phase References

Chapter 2 FORMULATE STRATEGY (Competency Domain 2)
- 2.1. Key Concepts and Definitions
- 2.2. Key Activities
- 2.3. Tools

Chapter 3 TRANSFORM ORGANIZATION (Competency Domain 3)
- 3.1. Key Concepts and Definitions
- 3.2. Key Activities
- 3.3. Tools

Chapter 4 EXECUTE STRATEGY (Competency Domain 4)
- 4.1. Key Concepts and Definitions
- 4.2. Key Activities
- 4.3. Tools

Chapter 5 ENGAGE STAKEHOLDERS (Competency Domain 1)
- 5.1. Key Concepts and Definitions
- 5.2. Key Activities
- 5.3. Tools

Chapter 6 GOVERN STRATEGY (Competency Domain 4)
- 6.1. Key Concepts and Definitions
- 6.2. Key Activities
- 6.3. Tools

---

[10] Note IASP BOK 3.0 defines "Execution" and "Implementation" as two distinct terms. In this book, as there is no consensus on this point, the two terms are used interchangeably.
[11] See Appendix 6 for a detailed outline of IASP BOK 3.0.

Crosswalk SMPS Framework, to IASP Competencies, to IASP BOK 3.0

Critically important for leaders, managers, and working professionals seeking strategic planning and management credentialing is understanding the linkage between a particular preparation course and the competency statements driving a given certification exam. Below is a high-level crosswalk from the SMPS Program's Framework to the IASP Competency Model and IASP BOK 3.0 (see Table 0.3).

TABLE 0.3: CROSSWALK SMPS FRAMEWORK, TO IASP COMPETENCIES, TO IASP BOK 3.0

SMPS Framework Phases & Tasks	IASP Competency Domains & Subdomains	IASP BOK 3.0 Chapters
PI, T1.1 - Assess	D, 1B - Planning team expectations	Chapter 5 – Engage Stakeholders
PI, T1.2 - Organize	D, 1A - Culture of strategic management and agility	Chapter 5 – Engage Stakeholders
PII, T2.1 - External Foresight	D, 2A - External scan	Chapter 2 – Formulate Strategy
PII, T2.2 - Internal Insight	D, 2A - Internal scan	Chapter 2 – Formulate Strategy
PII, T2.3 - SWOT	D, 2A - Internal and external environmental scan	Chapter 2 – Formulate Strategy
PIII, T3.1 - Strategic Direction	D, 2B - Strategy Design and Formulation	Chapter 2 – Formulate Strategy
PIII, T3.2 - Establish Strategy	D, 2B - Strategy Design and Formulation	Chapter 2 – Formulate Strategy
PIV, T4.1 - Strategic Plan	D, 2B - Strategy Design and Formulation	Chapter 2 – Formulate Strategy
PIV, T4.2 - Strategic Operating Plan	D, 3C – Operational Planning for Implementation	Chapter 2 – Formulate Strategy
PV, T5.1 - Transform Organization	D, 3A - Alignment of the Organization Design with Strategy D, 3B - Alignment of Operations with Strategy	Chapter 3 – Transform Organization
PV, T5.2 - Alignment		
PV, T5.3 - Implementation	D, 4A - Strategy execution and transformation	Chapter 4 – Execute Strategy
PVI. T6.1 - Measure Performance	D, 4C - Strategic performance management	Chapter 6 – Govern Strategy
PVI, T6.2 - Learn & Adapt	D, 4C - Strategic performance management	Chapter 6 – Govern Strategy
PVI, T6.3 - Ongoing Management	D, 4B – Governance & Decision Making	Chapter 6 – Govern Strategy

Strategy in the 21st Century, Second Edition

The second edition of *Strategy in the 21st Century* represents the culmination of a journey that spans decades and a commitment to excellence in the field of strategic management. Today, as we find ourselves at the intersection of strategy theory and real-world application, *Strategy in the 21st Century* stands as a cornerstone in our journey. This book not only guides you through our SMPS Framework but also prepares you for the challenges and opportunities of the 21st-century strategic landscape. It is our hope that this book, aligned with industry standards such as the Baldrige Excellence Framework, the IASP Competency Model, and the IASP Body of Knowledge 3.0, continues to serve as an invaluable resource in your pursuit of strategic excellence.

Thank you for being a part of our story. We look forward to staying in touch with you on your own strategic adventures in the years to come.

Overview of Strategic Management as a Discipline

So, what is the purpose of strategic management? In the 1950's, writer, professor, and management consultant Peter Drucker helped us understand that strategy is about exerting influence over the operating environment to help shape it to an organization's benefit. We also know strategic management is about strengthening an organization's internal rhythms and capabilities to be successful.

In the end, strategic management is about enabling an organization to recognize and adapt quickly to navigate constantly changing circumstances. The phases of strategic management, taken together and completed, will move a management team and its organization through required processes to fully analyze, formulate, plan, and implement a strategic management program. It is important to emphasize that these phases and tasks require, while presented in a cyclical deterministic flow model, present ample opportunity for feedback to any preceding subprocess.

Of course, there will always be mitigating circumstances in which the processes outlined can and should be modified such as when an organization already has a well-established strategic management system in place or when selected subprocesses are functioning effectively and only well-defined changes, modifications, or additions are required. However, not fully considering outlined processes opens the door to management by individual, arbitrary guidelines, and domination of strategic management processes deployed to a single manager or small group of managers in key positions. *A fundamental premise of this book is that a team of leaders will outperform the "all-knowing leader" every time.*

Strategy professionals must also understand the difference between three basic strategy concepts... strategic thinking, strategic planning, and strategic management (see Figure 0.5):

FIGURE 0.5: COMPARE AND CONTRAST BASIC STRATEGY CONCEPTS

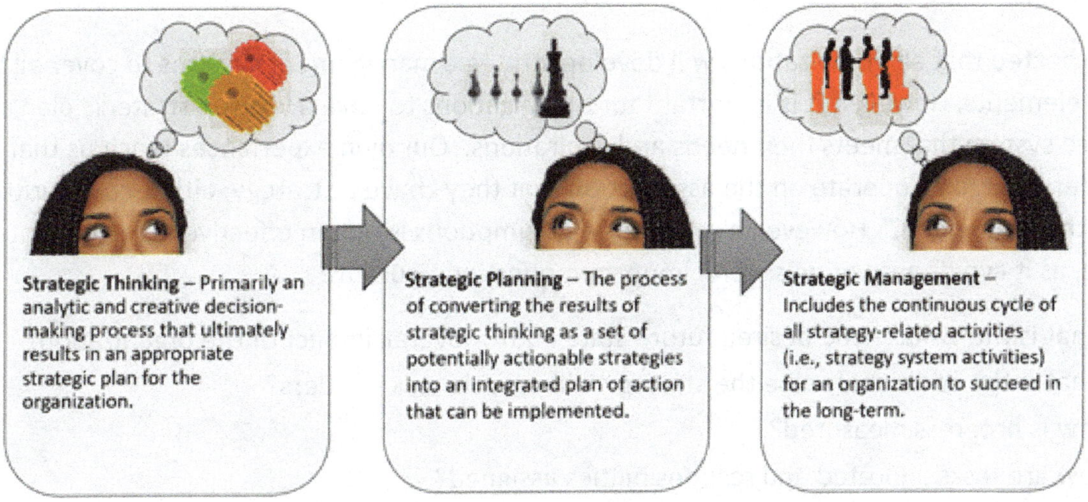

Strategic Thinking – Primarily an analytic and creative decision-making process that ultimately results in an appropriate strategic plan for the organization.

Strategic Planning – The process of converting the results of strategic thinking as a set of potentially actionable strategies into an integrated plan of action that can be implemented.

Strategic Management – Includes the continuous cycle of all strategy-related activities (i.e., strategy system activities) for an organization to succeed in the long-term.

Strategy Vs. Strategic Management Definition and Timeline

The term "strategy" is often defined as a plan of action to achieve a goal or goal set.[12] The International Association for Strategy Professionals (IASP) defines strategy as a "representation of the high-level guidelines an organization adopts to provide value to its stakeholders and/or gain an advantage over competitors. Whether these guidelines are deliberately designed and/or emerge in time, they determine how the rest of the efforts of the organization will be deployed."[13]

Strategic management is defined "as the set of processes required to specify the goals and objectives and develop the initiatives to attain them."[14] To be comprehensive, *strategic management* must undertake the following actions:

- Engage key stakeholders throughout the strategic management journey.
- Continually practice strategic foresight to scan for signals and trends, facilitate innovative thought, and develop creative scenarios that could affect the strategic direction.
- Build upon and leverage the unique core competencies of the organization.
- Identify, integrate, and formally state the vision, mission, values, policies, and goals of the organization.
- Transform the organization's operating model to align with the new strategy.
- Delineate, prioritize, and time-phase all significant actions required to achieve strategic goals and objectives.
- Provide guidelines for the acquisition and allocation of the resources and skills required to transform the organization and execute the strategy at all organizational levels.
- Precede and efficiently link with the annual budgeting and governance processes.

---

[12] Rollinson, R. and Young E. *Strategy in the 21st Century*, Edition #1, p 13, 2010.
[13] IASP, BOK 3.0, p4.
[14] Rollinson, R. and Young E. *Strategy in the 21st Century*, Edition #1, p 13, 2010.

- Measure progress, learn quickly, fail fast and fail forward, then govern strategy as circumstances warrant.

It is not expected that all organizations will develop strategic management systems to cover all the foregoing elements. However, it is important for organizations to have a written strategic plan and governance system that meets their needs and aspirations. Our own experiences teach us that all too often leadership teams operate on the assumption that they "have a strategy, although unwritten, and that is all that they need." However, a reliance on assumptions is not an effective management technique, as it avoids answering several important questions, such as:

- What is the vision – the desired future state and/or overall impact of the organization?
- What is the additional value the strategy will provide stakeholders?
- How is progress measured?
- How are tasks allocated and responsibilities assigned?
- How is the strategy communicated to key stakeholders?
- How are the management team and staff motivated to take ownership of, and for, organizational strategy and execution?
- How do you monitor and agilely adjust to changes in the environment?
- How do you move from an authoritarian management structure, and hierarchical organizational design, to a team approach, operating inside a co-created organizational design?

Many organizations, executives, owners, and managers prefer to operate without a written strategic plan, especially small businesses, family-owned businesses, small nonprofits, new ventures, and startups. This book is not written for them.

In the pages that follow we will present a basic timeline of the principal developments in the study and practice of strategic management. As presented in this section, a brief overview of the key developments in strategic management over the past 2,300 plus years will prove useful in three ways:

- Gaining a balanced overview of the discipline will offset the tendency to over commit to just one theory, model, framework, or paradigm.
- Knowing the availability and applicability of strategic management concepts and tools will aid in choosing the appropriate ones for any given situation an executive leadership team may face.
- Developing an interest in the history of strategic management and understanding the scope and depth of the discipline will reveal its necessity in sustaining long-term growth in uncertain and changing environments.

For a comprehensive, albeit brief, review of the primary strategic thinkers and their contributions to the field of strategic management, see Grundy (2003), Kiechel (2010), and Freedman, L. (2015). *Strategy: A history*. Oxford University Press. **What follows in Figure 0.6 are many of the primary building blocks of strategic management and their origins from ancient history through today.**

Introduction

FIGURE 0.6: STRATEGY TIMELINE

STRATEGY TIMELINE*

2300 - 2500 YEARS AGO
Alexander the Great, Strategos
Sun Tzu, Art of War

1500s
Machiavelli, The Prince
City-State Warfare

1800s
Napoleon & Clausewitz, Principles of War
Sylvanus Thayer, West Point

1850s
Frederick Taylor, Scientific Method
Industrial Revolution

1920s
Alfred Sloan, Analytics / Competition /
Strengths and Weaknesses

1940s
World War II, Ops. Res. / Linear Program /
Game Theory / Prioritize Allocations

1950s - 1960s
Peter Drucker, MBO
Igor Ansoff, Ansoff's grid / Popularized SWOT
Chandler, Strategy & Structure
Bridgestone Tire, Hoshin

1970s
Henderson, BCG Portfolio Matrix
GE McKinsey Matrix, Nine-box Matrix
Pierre Wack, Scenario Planning

1970s - 1980s
Henry Mintzberg, Organizations & Management
Chris Argyris, Double-Loop-Learning

1980s
Michael Porter, Porter's Five Forces / Value Chain Analysis
James Brian Quinn, Logical Incrementalism
Peters & Waterman, Seven S Model
Peter Senge, Learning
Rosabeth Kanter, Empowerment

1990s
Kaplan & Norton, Balanced Scorecard /
Applied Double Loop Learning
Jack Welch, GE

1900s cont.
Hamel & Prahalad, Core Competency /
Innovation / Competing for the future / Co-Creation

1991
Peter Schwartz, Art of the Long View
Scenario Planning

2000
Jim Collins, Hedgehog / Flywheel

2002
Bossidy & Charan, Strategy Execution
Robin Speculand, Implementation Compass

2005
Kim & Marborgne, Blue Ocean Strategy
Rich Horwath, Strategic Thinking

2010
Alexander Osterwalder, Business Model Canvas
Clayton Christensen, Innovator's Dilemma
Steven Haines, Lead Certification Pioneer

2012
John Kotter, Leading change (Updated from 1996)
Daryl Conner, Burning Platform

2013
Christensen & Raynor – Innovator's Solution
Lafley & Martin – Playing to Win

2016
Andy Grove, Intel; John Doerr, Google,
Strategic Agility (OKRs)
Niven & Laporte (OKRs)

2017
Hadaya & Gagnon, Business Architecture
Thayer & Team, Agile Organizational Design

2020
Mackey & Sisodia, Conscious Capitalism -
Balance Purpose & Profit

2021
Rita McGrath, Seeing around corners /
Innovation

2021
Peter Aiken, (Bad Data) + (Anything Awesome) = Bad
Results / Data Governance

2022
Hadaya & Stockmal, IASP, BOK 3.0
Transform, Engage and Govern Strategy

2023
Sam Altman, OpenAI – ChatGPT

*REPRESENTATIVE NOT COMPREHENSIVE

Military Origins of Strategy

The primary benefit of studying military strategy is understanding the competitive nature of strategic thinking and action. Adversaries must know the terrain; gather intelligence regarding their opponent, including estimating their relative strengths and weaknesses and measuring them against their own forces; form a plan of attack; and then lead their forces to engage the enemy. Sound familiar? This is strikingly similar to the situation that confronts competing organizations. In fact, it is so similar that it is amazing that it took until the 1980s to realize rich veins of knowledge and experience were there to be mined by studying military history. (McNeilly 1996; Michealson 2001; Tracy 2002.)

The military origins of strategy predate recorded history. The rivalries between competing tribes; clans; villages; city-states; and, ultimately, nations have been the natural resource for strategic thinking. The origin of the word *strategy* comes from *strategos* (a compound of two Greek words: S*tratos* which means "army" and *Agos* which means "leader"*)* and was used for military commander in histories of fifth-century B.C. Greek city-states (Diggle, J. *The Cambridge Greek Lexicon*, Cambridge University Press, 2021.) The commander's plans for battle, and more generally for waging war, were the first records of strategic thinking. In the ancient Western world, the city-state was the fundamental political unit of greatest significance. Rome, the most successful city-state of ancient times, developed the art of organized warfare to its highest level until the emergence of Italian city-states beginning in the 12th and 13th century.

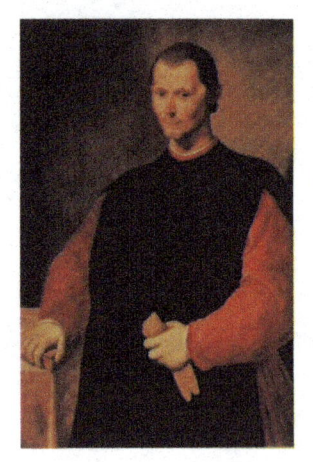

In the early 16th century, the Roman model was reintroduced by Machiavelli in his *Art of War* (Farneworth 2001) as the first model for modern warfare. Enormously popular in the Italian city-states of his day, Machiavelli became the guru on city-state warfare. Many of his precepts and principles, especially on the nature of war, are still incorporated in Western military thinking.

Military strategy continued to evolve incrementally during the next three centuries, but it took the military genius of Napoleon and Clausewitz (Farneworth 2001) to define new paradigms for modern military strategy that were nothing short of a revolution. The result was the emergence of innovations such as conscription; larger independent units that combined infantry, cavalry, and artillery; larger military staffs, both centralized and in military subunits; and, finally, the process of living off the land.

These innovations in both military strategy and structure combined to give commanders many strategic options. These options have continued to have great influence in warfare while becoming the subject of intense interest and study in business and commerce as well. However, the rewards of studying military history, not military history itself, are of key interest to this book.

Introduction

Western military strategy is but one pillar of the strategic management discipline. Another emerged 2,300 years ago in China when Sun Tzu is credited for having written *The Art of War*, a compilation of essays that might well be described as concentrated essence of wisdom on the conduct of war. There are several important themes developed by Sun Tzu still applied to the strategy challenges we encounter in business and organizational life today. **See Appendix 7, *The Art of War,* Sun Tzu.**

> *"Strategy without tactics is the slowest route to victory. Tactics without strategy is the noise before defeat."*
>
> —Sun Tzu (The Art of War)

However, the study of ancient and medieval military operations is not without its limitations. Its primary benefit is to provide an understanding of **strategic thinking** as conceived and conducted by a single military commander, such as Julius Caesar, Alexander the Great, or Napoleon, and perhaps a few trusted officers. This hardly qualifies as a model for modern strategic management in a large complex organization, or for that matter any organization.

Ironically, it was the introduction of a new method of instruction at the United States Military Academy (USMA), West Point, that ultimately provided the basis for a meta-model of strategic management that could be adapted to any organization operating in any environment. In fact, we know the exact year and the nature of the instructional innovations that laid the foundation for the development of modern strategic management—in both military and nonbusiness organizations. The magnitude and eventual impact of this event on the development of strategic management warrants summarizing here.

In 1817 Sylvanus Thayer, USMA Superintendent, introduced a revolutionary (at the time) method of running West Point, based on a detailed system of writing, examination, grading, and disciplining that covered **all individual and group activities** and maintained detailed permanent performance records.

Graduates immediately began to apply the system in both military and business organizations. Notable examples include the Springfield Armory, where Daniel Taylor, an 1819 graduate, developed single-unit factory management; the Western Railroad, where George Whistler, also an 1819 graduate, introduced a multi-unit system of administration; and the Pennsylvania Railroad, where Herman Haupt, an 1849 graduate, developed "a strategic reorganization, grounded in the collection and analysis of operating statistics and costs, and laid the foundations for the development of country's largest railroad" (Hoskin, Macve, and Stone 1997, 8.)

This approach spread during the Civil War with line and staff organizations becoming commonplace, especially in the Northern armies. Following the Civil War this method of managing organizations became widespread in the military and in business. The key point is that this comprehensive approach made it possible for a centralized command to develop and implement a **strategic plan of action** based on a fact-based, continuous record of the performance of an organization and its members.

This new system of writing, testing, grading, and correcting, now commonplace in all phases of modern organizations (business, military, government, nonprofit, and academic), does not determine strategic decisions *per se* but delivers the necessary inputs upon which they rest. This was a new power/knowledge relationship and focus on information experts to support and maintain this discipline.

The impact of the industrial revolution had a major impact on the emergence of strategic management as a discipline. "During the last half of the 20th century, the Industrial Revolution saw the emergence of the modern corporation, in which work, usually in a factory setting, was specialized, and coordinated by managers. Prior to the Industrial Revolution, goods and services lacked standardization and were produced at home in small batches. Work shifted from family-led home production to factory production. These factories could employ hundreds and even thousands of workers who produced mass batches of standardized goods more cheaply than they could be produced in homes. As factories grew in size, they provided chances for personal fulfillment." [15]

The impact of Alfred Sloane and his work at General Motors is another major development.

"In 1921, General Motors (GM) Corporation established a special product policy committee led by Alfred P. Sloan to develop a comprehensive repositioning strategy that would establish a series of products with corresponding price levels differentiating the existing GM automobile divisions. Prior to the development of this strategy, GM had a great deal of overlap in products and price levels across the various divisions that they manufactured and sold. The strategy developed in 1921 resulted in a segmentation scheme that created distinct target markets for the various GM divisions." [16]

Strategic Management After World War II

For the most part the development of strategic management following World War II was conducted without particular attention being paid to the military and nonmilitary developments in the previous century at West Point. In essence, the fundamental disciplines of information collection, analysis, and action (based on accounting and statistical data) managed by staff specialists had become second nature and their revolutionary introduction of a century ago long forgotten.

Notwithstanding these early origins of business strategy, much work remained to develop more comprehensive and nuanced models of strategic management: models that would take full advantage of the rapidly accelerating collection of organized information and intelligence. In essence, the foundation for the development of modern strategic management had been established long ago, but as conditions changed rapidly and radically for the postwar pioneers of strategic management, they began to think in terms of sailing toward new horizons.

---

[15] Wren, D. A., & Bedeian, A. G. *The evolution of management thought.* (6th ed.), New York: Wiley, 2009.
[16] Powers, T. L. & Steward, J. L. *Journal of Historical Research in Marketing*; Bingley Vol. 2, 4, 2010.

Before World War II, the need for strategic management was not so apparent with a great many unsolved business problems of organization and management still being answered in the military model. In fact, the management literature of the early 20th century is replete with examples of these borrowed concepts, for example: "line and staff," "command and control," "headquarters," "specialization," "functional management (that is, infantry, artillery, cavalry, etc.)." In the absence of new business specific models, military models and concepts were adopted and adapted to cope with the organizational and operational problems of large organizations.

After World War II strategic concepts and tools evolved to become the cornerstones of successful business management thinking and action. As large and complex organizations coped with the challenges of increasingly competitive and changing environments, they faced problems similar to those that had confronted military commanders. Many high-ranking officers became top managers of large firms. These new business leaders found it natural to apply the concepts of military strategy to business situations. The use of military-styled organization structures, combined with the infusion of military officers into top private-sector leadership positions, accelerated the focus on strategic management.

In succeeding decades, it became clear that neither the military command and control structures *nor* the military models of strategic leadership were well suited to the needs of the private sector. As competition increased and the scope and rate of change accelerated, new paradigms were needed. By the mid-1950s, it was no longer a matter of rebuilding a war-torn world; it was the beginning of a relentless, long-term competitive struggle for profit and market share. Strategic leadership and management were never more necessary, but their concepts needed to be rethought and applied within the situational context of each private sector organization.

A small group of business theorists, teachers, and consultants viewed this as a central management issue. In doing so, they recognized that the fundamental challenge of management was to develop plans of action to deal with a competitive and changing environment and then mobilize their organizations to implement these strategic plans. Three quarters of a century later we have a mature (and yet ever changing) discipline called strategic management.

Peter Drucker, "the" seminal thinker on management in the last half of the 20th century, wrote about "Management by Objectives" (MBO) in his classic *The Practice of Management* (1954). He further developed his ideas pertaining to strategy in *Management by Results* (1964). This latter work appeared just as strategy - as the central organizing concept for planning, structuring, and managing large-scale companies - was being developed and taught by leading theorists and scholars of the decade.

Drucker captured many ideas that were integrated in what became known as "classical strategic management." His essential message was that whatever an organization's strategy is, it must decide:

- What opportunities it wants to pursue and what risks it is willing and able to accept.

- What its scope and structure will be, and especially, the right balance between specialization, diversification, and integration.
- How it will balance the use of time and money to attain its goals, especially pertaining to owning versus buying or to sales, mergers, acquisitions, or joint ventures.
- What organizational structure will be most appropriate to the company's economic realities, opportunities, and performance programs.

SWOT Analysis

Strength, Weakness, Opportunity, Threat (SWOT) analysis has its origins in two institutions: Stanford Research Institute and the Harvard Business School. At the former, a research study funded by several Fortune 500 firms was conducted by a team of researchers directed by Robert F. Stewart from 1960 to 1969 (Humphrey, 2004, pp. 6-9). The study was prompted by the inability of these and other firms to implement the results of the strategic plans that they had been developing during the previous decade. The research included a 250-item questionnaire completed by more than 5,000 executives in 1,100 companies. Interviews were also conducted. Presumably, the results of this study were considered proprietary, at least in part, and therefore not immediately published in books or academic journals.

Parallel to this study, two Harvard Business School professors, George Albert Smith and C. Roland Christensen, were questioning the extent to which a firm's strategy matched its competitive environment. Other professors at Harvard expanded this inquiry at both the organizational and functional level, and several business cases were written, and courses developed. The SWOT framework was first described in detail in *Business Policy, Text, and Cases* (Learned et al, 1969).

With ongoing refinement and application driving continued development and application, SWOT analysis became popular throughout U.S. business firms and other types of organizations. Its use and popularity have spread throughout the world, as it continues to be developed as a tool by both consultants and academics, who adapt it to various types of problems and situations.

The essential components of the SWOT framework and approach follow (see Figure 0.7):

FIGURE 0.7: SWOT ANALYSIS

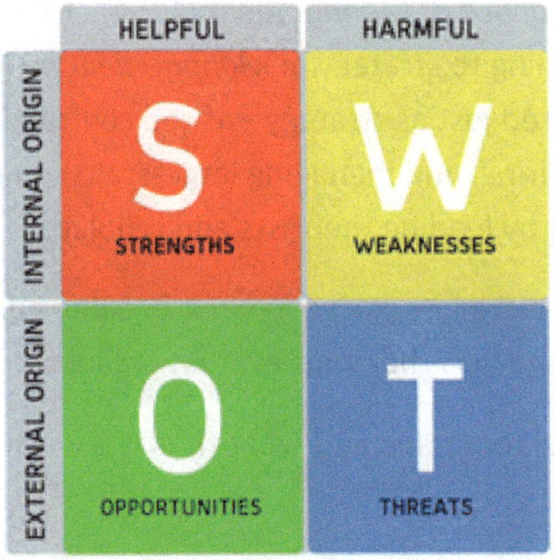

- **Strengths (S)** refers to the primary internal strengths of the organization. These attributes are essentially resources the organization can build on to move forward. Strengths can relate to any of the organization's products or services, or they may emerge from any function or process operating inside the organization.

- **Weaknesses (W)** refers to the primary internal weaknesses the organization has that may interfere with the organization moving forward. As with strengths, weaknesses can come from any of the organization's products or services or from the functions and/or processes operating inside the organization. Additionally, an organization may identify weaknesses within the organizational culture (capacity gaps, morale issues, undesirable behavior, psychologically "unsafe" work environment, lack of diversity, etc.) which need to be recognized and addressed strategically.

- **Opportunities (O)** Unlike strengths and weaknesses that are derived from the internal dimension of the organization, opportunities exist in the external dimension, that is, in the marketplace itself where customers make purchasing and/or other strategic decisions. They frequently emerge from changes in industry dynamics, customer buying behavior, new technologies, or from any other change that can give rise to a new business opportunity. Opportunities may exist in the "here and now," or they may relate to some future time frame.

- **Threats (T)** As with opportunities, threats are outside the organization itself. They are essentially storm clouds on the near-term or long-term horizon that could stand in the way of the organization moving forward. They can develop because of shifting industry trends, competitive actions of other industry players, changing customer buying behavior, and/or a host of other potential sources or disruptions.

As this "Cross-Impact Analysis" [17] technique grew in popularity, it became clear that to fully capitalize on this tool, organizations should build on the internal strengths that enable them to pursue high-priority external opportunities. Likewise, businesses learned to identify and eliminate the internal weaknesses hindering progress, as well as mitigate against high-priority threats in the external environment.

Other Strategic Management Contributors

The concepts of applying strategy to business were first defined and studied at Harvard by Alfred Chandler in 1962. From his studies of leading corporations, he concluded that strategy is the "determinant of the basic long-term goals of an enterprise, and the adoption of courses of action and the allocation of resources necessary for carrying out these goals" (Mintzberg, Quinn, and Voyer 1995, 2). Quinn noted that many scholars agree this was the first modern definition of business strategy. In 1980 Kenneth Andrews, former Commanding Officer in the US Air Force's Statistical Control Unit, while at Harvard, elaborated on Chandler's definition in *The Concept of Corporate Strategy* (see Table 0.4):

---

[17] "Cross-impact analysis **attempts to connect relationships between events and variables.** These relationships are then categorized as positive or negative relative to each other and are used to determine which events or scenarios are most probable or likely to occur within a given time frame." https://en.wikipedia.org/wiki/Cross_impact_analysis

> "Strategy is the pattern of objectives, purposes, or goals and the major policies and plans for achieving these goals stated in such a way to define what business the company is in or is to be in and the kind of company it is or is to be" (ibid., 2.)

TABLE 0.4 – KENNETH ANDREWS ON STRATEGY AS AN INTELLECTUAL PROCESS
• What a company might do in terms of environmental opportunity.
• What it can do in terms of ability and power.
• What the executives of the company want to do.
• What a company should do (ibid., 50-51).

More specifically, he defined *strategy* as the intellectual process of ascertaining what a company can and should do. (See Table 0.4.)

Andrews believed these processes must be brought into equilibrium. It is easy to see the military origin of this approach; it is exactly what a military leader does on the field of battle. The Andrews approach to strategy is similar to the other prescriptive approaches, but it differs in that strategy design is not viewed as a delegated and subdivided set of activities. The Andrews approach most often occurs in smaller and mid-sized organizations with a strong leader. The manager must:

- Determine what the firm *might do* to assess the firm's external environment for opportunities and threats and identify the key success factors of the industry.
- Determine what the firm *can do* by examining the internal environment for strengths and weaknesses and identify distinctive competencies.
- Determine what the firm's executives *want* to do.
- Determine what the firm *should do* - review the firm's social responsibilities. (ibid., 51.)

This definition of strategy became popular and spread in business schools throughout the world. It came to be what Mintzberg later called the "design approach" to strategy.

The second pillar of the classical school after the Western military strategic discipline is the "planning approach," as developed by Igor Ansoff in *Corporate Strategy: An Analytical Approach to Business Policy for Growth and Expansion* (1965). His view of strategy follows:

> "Strategy becomes the rule for making decisions: the 'common thread' would have four components—product/market scope; the growth vector (the changes the firm planned to make in its product market scope); competitive advantage; and synergy (a measure of how well the different parts of the firm could work together to achieve more than they could have by each working alone)" (ibid., 2).

Ansoff was a major contributor to the development of the conceptual foundations of strategic management theory and practice. As Grundy (2003) pointed out, in addition to establishing corporate planning as a formal management process, Ansoff also:

- Popularized SWOT analysis (referred to here as OTSW).

- Provided us with the Ansoff grid, which helps us to group similar opportunities and understand the degree of risk involved in diversification strategies (see Figure 0.8).
- Developed ideas of environmental scanning and detecting weak signals of disruptive environmental change.
- Repositioned "strategic planning" as "strategic management" as part of a continuing process rather than a once a year (or less frequent) planning process.
- Identified "gap" analysis—which looks at the gap between aspirations and the likely outcome of current strategies.

FIGURE 0.8: ANSOFF'S GRID

	CURRENT MARKETS	NEW MARKETS
CURRENT SERVICES / PRODUCTS	Market Penetration	Market Development
NEW SERVICES / PRODUCTS	Service / Product Development	Diversification

Increasing Risk (horizontal and vertical axes)

Andrew's design approach to strategy and Ansoff's planning approach dominated teaching and research on strategy for an entire generation. These models and all the variations that followed had four elements in common. They are:

- The firm must follow a set of external conditions. Some conditions are negative (threats) while others are positive (opportunities).
- The firm must establish goals and objectives, the highest level of which is the mission of the firm—a statement of the firm's reason for existence.
- The firm's management must perform a situational analysis to determine its posture in the environment and its level of resources. This analysis is often referred to as a SWOT analysis. (Here as OTSW.)
- The firm must plan how to use its resources to achieve its goals and get the best fit possible with its environment.

Strategic Management Emerges as a Major Business Discipline

The modern era conceptual foundations of strategic management were established in the 1950s and 1960s. In the decades to follow these concepts were discussed, analyzed, and refined; and strategic management emerged as an accepted business management discipline. Thus, strategic management became a recognized academic discipline among scholars and researchers (as well as the management community) when it met the criteria summarized below (see Table 0.5):

TABLE 0.5 – CRITERIA FOR BECOMING AN ACADEMIC DISCIPLINE
• A body of knowledge based on scholarly inquiry and research was established.
• Peer groups exchanged ideas and concepts, thus contributing to the development of this body of knowledge.
• Appropriate research methods were employed to validate propositions and findings.
• Contributors to this body of knowledge included scholars, theorists, researchers, teachers, practitioners, consultants, and the management community.
• The body of knowledge included prescriptive, descriptive, analytic, and research-based knowledge.

CONTEMPORARY MODELS

It is important to note Walter Kiechel's 2010 perspective outlined in The Lords of Strategy. "[Corporate strategy] didn't spring full blown from a single, godlike forehead but instead was assembled from the spoils of many an intellectual and business battle... There were and are many "lords of strategy," not just the original thinkers."[18]

Beginning in the 1970s and continuing through to present day, an increasing number of analytic models, concepts, and tools began to appear in response to the private sector's need for more effective approaches to the accelerating tempo of change and uncertainty in the environment. Management approaches that could be adapted to specific organizational contexts were required.

In the late 1960s and early 70s the Boston Consulting Group (BCG) developed an analytic model for managing a portfolio of different business units (or major product lines).[19] The first version had no graphics. The ultimate version and use of product portfolio analysis, the BCG Growth Share Matrix, displays the various business units on a graph charting market growth rate versus market share relative to competitors (see Figure 0.9):

---

[18] Kiechel, W. III. *The Lords of Strategy – The Secret Intellectual History of the New Corporate World*, p1, Harvard Business Press, 2010.
[19] Ibid.

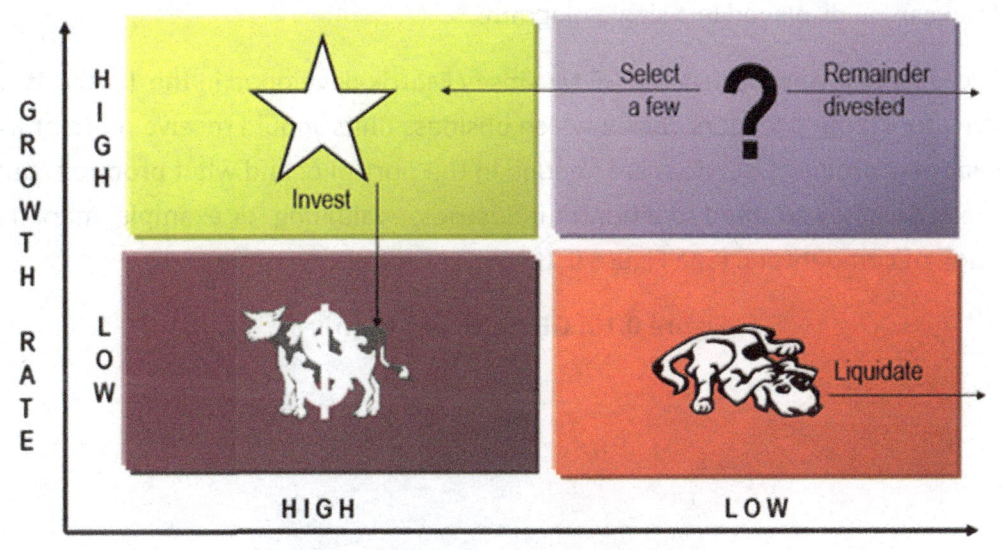

FIGURE 0.9: THE BOSTON CONSULTING GROUP (BCG) GROWTH SHARE MATRIX

Resources are allocated to business units based on where they are situated on the grid as follows:

- **Cash Cow** - A business unit that has a large market share in a mature, slow-growing industry. Cash cows require little investment and generate cash that can be used to invest in other business units.
- **Star** - A unit that has a large share in a fast-growing industry. Stars may generate cash, but because the market is growing rapidly, they require investment to maintain their lead. If successful, a star will become a cash cow once its industry matures.
- **Question Mark** - A business unit that has a small market share in a high growth market. These business units require resources to grow market share, but whether they will succeed and become stars is unknown.
- **Dog** - A business unit that has a small market share in a mature industry. A dog may not require substantial cash, but it ties up capital that could be better deployed elsewhere. Unless a dog has a strategic purpose, it should be liquidated if there is little prospect for it to gain market share.

BCG's basic strategy recommendation was to maintain a balance between "cash cows" and "stars," while allocating some resources to feed "question marks" (that is, potential stars). The BCG Growth Share Matrix allows one to compare many business units at a glance. However, the approach has received some negative criticism for the following reasons:

- The link between market share and profitability is questionable because increasing market share can be very expensive.
- The approach may overemphasize growth because it ignores the possibility of declining markets.
- The model assumes market growth. In practice, the organization may not be able to grow the market.

While originally developed as a model for resource allocation among the various business units in a corporation, the Growth Share Matrix can also be used for resource allocation among products within a single business unit. Its simplicity is its strength; the relative positions of an organization's entire business portfolio can be displayed in a single diagram.

A related but more flexible approach is the GE McKinsey Matrix developed in the 1970s. It is used as a portfolio planning tool to help leaders decide which business units should receive more or less investment; what new products/services are needed in the portfolio; and what products/services should be divested. It can be easily adapted to different industries, evaluating for example, market maturity and concentration of competitors. (See Figure 0.10.)

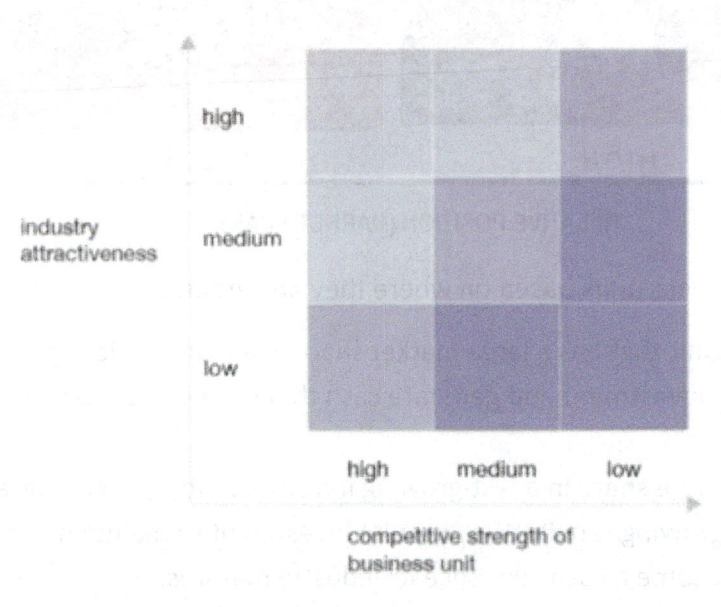

Figure 0.10: GE McKinsey Matrix [20]

Scenario-based planning is another example of a powerful strategic management framework rooted in military strategy. The work of Herman Kahn related to the possible scenarios associated with thermonuclear war in the late 1960's is the genesis of this discipline. Scenario-based planning in a business environment goes back to the 1970s with the work of Pierre Wack at Royal Dutch Shell whose use of scenarios helped the organization successfully navigate the oil crisis. [21]

Scenario-based planning is not about predicting the future, but rather it is about identifying what can possibly occur (i.e., different scenarios) and preparing accordingly. Scenario-based planning is a popular foresight tool that some organizations use to inform flexible long-term plans. Alternative scenarios can be developed from the assessments and analyses completed earlier, as well as by identifying trends and signals of change in the environment. These alternative scenarios will incorporate different assumptions about how the environmental factors could look in the future. Assumptions should be documented, so alternative scenarios can be reviewed periodically, and assumptions re-tested and validated against the evolving situation. Strategy practitioners play a major role in facilitating this process.

---

[20] Exhibit from "Enduring Ideas: The GE-McKinsey nine-box matrix", September 2008, McKinsey Quarterly, www.mckinsey.com. Copyright (c) 2024 McKinsey & Company. All rights reserved. Reprinted by permission.
[21] Schwartz, P. *The Art of the Longview*, Doubleday, 1991.

In 1980 the field of strategy made another leap forward with the work of Michael Porter. Porter developed a framework in which he used concepts developed in industrial organization economics to derive five competitive forces that determine the attractiveness of a market and the structure of the industry. Porter referred to these forces as the microenvironment to contrast it with the more general term macroenvironment. The microenvironment consists of those forces close to an organization that affect its ability to serve its customers and make a profit. A change in any of the forces normally requires an organization to reassess the marketplace. (See Figure 0.11.)

FIGURE 0.11: PORTER'S FIVE FORCES

The four forces—bargaining power of customers, the bargaining power of suppliers, the threat of new entrants, and the threat of substitute products—combine with other variables to create a fifth force, the level of competition in an industry. Each of these forces has several determinants. Understanding the nature of each of these forces gives organizations the necessary insights to enable them to formulate the appropriate strategies to be successful in their market.

- **Force 1: Bargaining Power of Customers**

Customer power is one of the primary forces that influence value created by an industry. The most important determinants of buyer power are the size and the concentration of customers. Other factors are the extent to which the buyers are informed and the concentration or differentiation of the competitors. Kippenberger (1998) states that it is often useful to distinguish potential buyer power from the buyer's willingness or incentive to use that power, willingness that derives mainly from the "risk of failure" associated with a product's use.

  o The risk of failure increases with a few large players in the market.
  o Risk is still present when there are a large number of undifferentiated, small players.
  o The risk is low when there is a low cost of switching between suppliers.

- **Force 2: Bargaining Power of Suppliers**

Supplier power is a mirror image of customer power. As a result, the analysis of supplier power typically focuses first on the relative size and concentration of suppliers relative to industry participants, and second on the degree of differentiation in the inputs supplied. The ability to charge customers different prices in line with differences in the value created for each of those buyers usually indicates that the market is characterized by high supplier power as well as by low buyer power (Porter 1998). Supplier bargaining power exists when:

- Switching costs are high (switching from one technical service provider to another).
- Brand power is high (McDonalds, British Airways, and Harvard).
- There is the possibility of forward integration of suppliers (beer brewer buying a bar).

- **Force 3: Threat of New Entrants**

Both potential and existing competitors influence average industry profitability. The threat of new entrants is usually based on market entry barriers. They can take diverse forms and are used to prevent an influx of organizations into an industry whenever profits, adjusted for the cost of capital, rise above zero. In contrast, entry barriers also exist whenever it is difficult or not economically feasible for an outsider to replicate the incumbents' position (Porter 1980; Sanderson 1998). The most common forms of entry barriers, except intrinsic physical or legal obstacles, are as follows:

- Economies of scale—benefits associated with bulk purchasing
- Cost of entry—investment in technology, infrastructure, and cost of talent
- Distribution channels—ease of access for competitors
- Cost advantages not related to the size of the organization—contacts and expertise
- Government legislation—introduction of new laws that might weaken an organization's competitive position
- Differentiation—certain brand that cannot be copied

- **Force 4: Threat of Substitute Products**

The threat that substitute products pose to an industry's profitability depends on the relative price-to-performance ratios of the different types of products or services to which customers can turn to satisfy the same basic need. The threat of substitution is also affected by switching costs—that is, the costs in areas such as retraining, retooling, and redesigning that are incurred when a customer switches to a different type of product or service. It also involves:

- Product-for-product substitution—based on the substitution of need
- Generic substitution
- Substitution that relates to something that people can do without

- **Force 5: Competitive Rivalry**

The intensity of rivalry, the most obvious of the five forces in an industry, helps determine the extent to which the value created by an industry will be dissipated through head-to-head competition. The most valuable contribution of Porter's five forces framework may be its suggestion that rivalry, while important, is only one of several forces that determine industry attractiveness.

- This force is located at the center of the diagram.
- It is most likely to be high in those industries in which there is a threat of substitute products and existing power of suppliers and buyers in the market.

The nature and structure of competition in an industry is strongly affected by the five forces. The stronger the powers of customers and suppliers and the stronger the threats of entry and substitution, the more intense competition is likely to be within the industry. However, these five factors are not the only ones that determine how organizations in an industry will compete – the structure of the industry itself may play an important role. In concentrated industries, according to this model, organizations would be expected to compete less fiercely and make higher profits than those in fragmented ones. That said, the histories and cultures of the firms in the industry also play a very important role in shaping competitive behavior.

In 2002 Preston McAfee advocated for a "Sixth Force" to be added to Porter's model known as "Complements."[22] Complements or Complementors are other organizations offering products or services in the same market that are complementary to the goods or services produced and sold in a given industry, e.g., Intel and Microsoft.

Porter's second major contribution to strategic management was his classification of *generic* strategies (see also Figure 3.6):

- **Differentiation**—when you add more value (real or perceived) than your competitors, evidenced by higher prices or discounts avoided.
- **Cost leadership**—when you achieve parity of value at a lower cost than your competitors.
- **Focus**—when you narrow your competitive strategy to concentrate only on your target customers and their specific need and potentially also only on your product range.

The attractiveness of the Porter model and analytic approach lies in its usefulness in understanding a specific organizational context by determining the relative impact of the five forces. This requires a certain amount of creativity – within the constraining forces. Porter's five forces model and his generic strategies were developed when there was a need to determine how to develop a competitive strategy. The focus was on identifying a competitive advantage. His two major works, *Competitive Strategy: Techniques for Analyzing Industries and Competitors* [23] and *Competitive Advantage: Creating and Sustaining Superior Performance,* [24] became immediately popular in academia and in major corporations.

From today's perspective, Porter's work on value chain analysis is particularly important as it dovetails nicely with the requirements for effective organizational design. The term value chain refers to the various activities and processes involved in developing a product or performing a service. A value chain can consist of the many stages of a product or service's lifecycle (see Figure 0.12).

---

[22] McAfee, R. Preston. *Competitive Solutions: The Strategists Toolkit,* Princeton University Press, 2002.
[23] Porter, M. *Competitive Strategy: Techniques for Analyzing Industries and Competitors,* Free Press, 1998.
[24] Porter, M. *Competitive Advantage: Creating and Sustaining Superior Performance,* Free Press, 1998.

FIGURE 0.12: VALUE CHAIN ANALYSIS

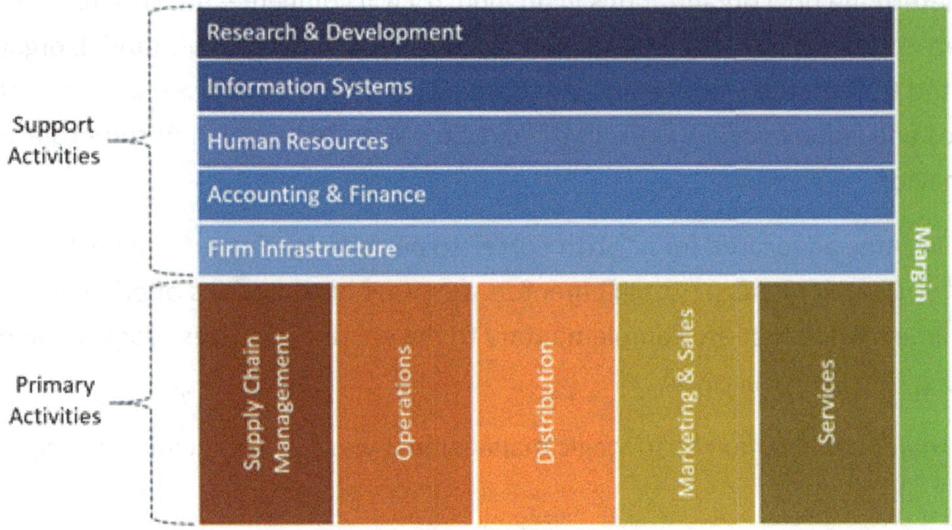

Support Activities:
- Research & Development
- Information Systems
- Human Resources
- Accounting & Finance
- Firm Infrastructure

Primary Activities:
- Supply Chain Management
- Operations
- Distribution
- Marketing & Sales
- Services

Margin

While many writers and researchers (primarily economists) continued to fine-tune, modify, and apply the Porter models, another major trend in strategic management was developing based on the works of such writers and researchers as Peters and Waterman (1982); Senge (1990); Kanter (1983, 1989, 1994); Kaplan and Norton (1992); and Hamel and Prahalad (1989, 1990, 1993, 1994). Taken together they build toward the creative, innovative, and shared roles and responsibilities of management (note: management *not* top management) in formulating, implementing, executing, and improving organizational strategy and strategic management processes. Their contributions follow.

In *In Search of Excellence,* [25] Tom Peters and Robert Waterman developed an organizational model called the "Seven S" model that puts strategic management within the context of a complex organizational network. The model includes:

- Strategy
- Structure
- Staff
- Skills
- Style
- Systems
- Shared values

These seven factors need to be described as currently developed and used within a given organization. However, describing them is only the beginning. Each needs to be properly aligned and balanced to achieve the most effective strategic management system. While the emphasis in this model is internally focused, it does strongly imply that each organization must give adequate attention to both internal and external factors. This was clear to the early strategic thinkers in the 1960s, but the specific factors both externally and internally are being more clearly identified and defined today.

---

[25] Peters, T. and Waterman, R.H. *In Search of Excellence,* Harper Business, 2006.

Peter Senge (1990) added to this internal focus by describing the impact of learning on both strategic and operational management. His concept of a learning organization is based on interactive learning and feedback loops. From this perspective, strategic management can be viewed as a formal and somewhat bureaucratic process. Organizational and individual learning and the feedback effects on strategic processes modify it.

R. M. Kanter (1989, 1994) had a major impact on strategic management primarily through her concepts of change management that include an emphasis on empowerment throughout the organization to implement and execute the strategy effectively.

Kaplan and Norton (1992) developed the concept of a "balanced scorecard" that stressed the need to measure and control performance based on measuring and monitoring four types of perspectives (see Figure 0.13).

FIGURE 0.13: BALANCED SCORECARD

The main value of the balanced scorecard model is its emphasis on forging a balanced approach to strategy development and measurement, pushing organizations to go beyond a single focus on financials. The assumption underlying the balanced scorecard is measuring drives performance and should be a prerequisite for an effective strategic management system. The metrics selected can be based on internal or external factors. It is the emphasis on balanced measures driving performance that make it an internal consideration, that is, a major determinant of management effectiveness.

Subsequent developments of the balanced scorecard model have moved from measurement to a more holistic tool for strategy development and execution aimed at generating tangible results. [26]

---

[26] Rohm, H., Wilsey, D., Perry, G.S., Montgomery, D. *The Institute Way: Simplify Strategic Planning and Management with the Balanced Scorecard*, The Institute Press, 2013.

Hamel and Prahalad (1989, 1990, 1993, and 1994) made several important contributions to the development of the strategic management field. Grundy (2003, 77-78) identifies the three as their most famous contributions to the field (see Table 0.6).

TABLE 0.6 – HAMEL AND PRAHALAD
• **Core competencies**— "these are a cluster of skills which either enables us to compete or give us a distinctive way of competing" (more on competencies is included in the following section). • **Competing for the future**—they do not see *any* industry as a given; instead, they are willing to consider a variety of possibilities. • **Innovation in strategy**—at the same time they emphasize innovation, they de-emphasize a bureaucratic approach to strategy.

Hamel and Prahalad also introduced the notions of "stretch" *and* "leverage" as means of how one can view what is possible. [27] Also, Prahalad's work around "co-creation" is of note. [28] Co-creation is the practice of collaborating with other stakeholders to guide the product design process.

Another recent leader in the field of strategic management is Rita McGrath. Her work on strategy and innovation ranks her among the top 10 management thinkers in the world and first for strategy, according to Thinkers50. McGrath's recent book on strategic inflection points is a must read for anyone serious about strategy. [29]

Taken together these writers and researchers expand the scope and depth of strategic management to include many internally generated strategies. However, in no case do they deny the impact of external forces on the organization. They counterbalance the tendency to rely too heavily on these forces and point to the new directions in strategic management that are based on development of the organization's human resources and supportive infrastructure.

One innovative example of thinking externally from a market perspective is demonstrated in the work of W. C. Kim and Renee Mauborgne (2005). They developed an imaginative and creative approach to gain an advantage in competing for the future. [30]

Based on a study of 150 strategic moves spanning more than 100 years and 30 industries, Kim and Mauborgne assert that "tomorrow's leading companies will succeed *not* by battling competitors in the 'bloody red ocean,' but by creating 'blue oceans' of uncontested market space ripe for growth." (See Figure 0.14.)

---

[27] Prahalad, C.K. and Hamel, G. *Stretch and Leverage*. Harvard Business Review, 1993.
[28] Prahalad, C.K. and Ramaswamy, V. *The Future of Competition: Co-Creating Unique Value With Customers*, Harvard Business Review Press, 1994.
[29] McGrath, R. *SEEING AROUND CORNERS: HOW TO SPOT INFLECTION POINTS IN BUSINESS BEFORE THEY HAPPEN*, Houghton Mifflin Harcourt, 2019.
[30] Kim, W.C. and Mauborgne, R. *Blue Ocean Strategy*, Harvard Business Review Press, 2005.

FIGURE 0.14: RED OCEAN AND BLUE OCEAN STRATEGY

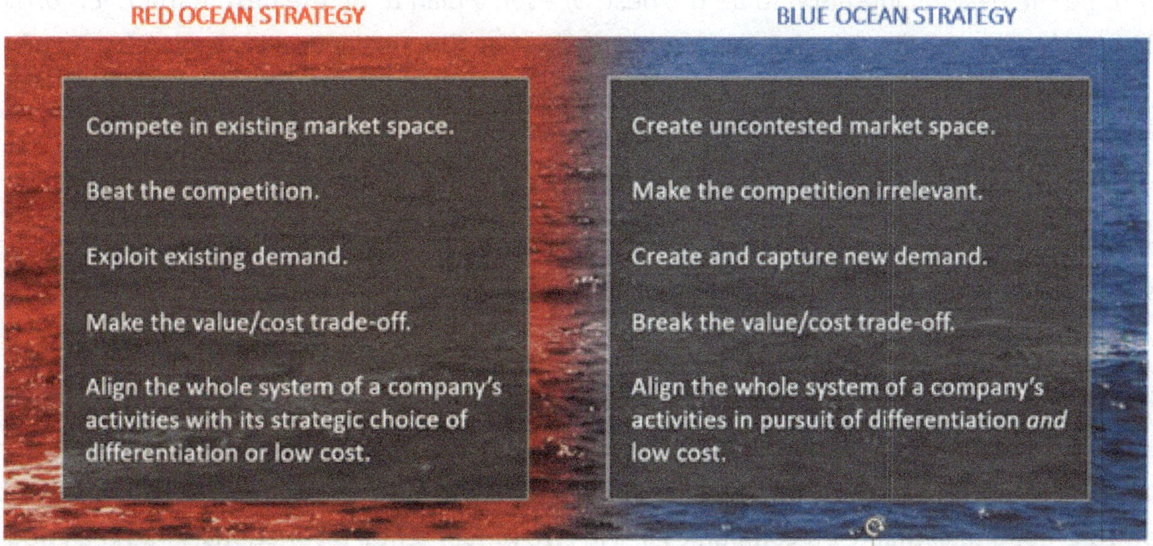

RED OCEAN STRATEGY	BLUE OCEAN STRATEGY
Compete in existing market space.	Create uncontested market space.
Beat the competition.	Make the competition irrelevant.
Exploit existing demand.	Create and capture new demand.
Make the value/cost trade-off.	Break the value/cost trade-off.
Align the whole system of a company's activities with its strategic choice of differentiation or low cost.	Align the whole system of a company's activities in pursuit of differentiation *and* low cost.

Blue Ocean Strategy (BOS) and, more recently, Blue Ocean Shift provide a systematic approach to making the competition irrelevant. Kim and Mauborgne present a tested analytical framework and the tools for successfully creating and capturing blue oceans. An effective Blue Ocean Strategy is about risk minimization, not risk taking. BOS highlights six principles that organizations can use to effectively formulate and execute blue ocean strategies. The six principles are:

- Reconstruct market boundaries
- Focus on the big picture
- Reach beyond existing demand
- Get the strategic sequence right
- Overcome organizational hurdles
- Build execution into strategy

There are several BOS tools that attempt to make the formulation and execution of BOS as systematic and actionable as competing in the red waters of known market space.

Four of the tools are as follows:

- The Strategy Canvas
- Three Tiers of Non-Customers
- Buyer Utility Map
- The Eliminate-Reduce-Raise-Create Grid

Kim and Mauborgne's conceptual model is further refined in their second book, *Blue Ocean Shift*. [31]

Emphasis on the creative and imaginative approaches to strategic management continues to receive attention by researchers and practitioners alike. In this regard, it is important to note the work of Jim Collins in developing the Hedgehog Concept. According to Jim Collins in *Good to Great: Why Some*

---

[31] Kim, W.C. and Mauborgne, R. *Blue Ocean Shift*, Hachette Books, 2017.

Companies Make the Leap and Others Don't, [32] the Hedgehog Concept is not a goal to be the best, a strategy to be the best, an intention to be the best, or even a plan to be the best. Rather, *it is arriving at a fundamental understanding of what you can be the best at*. The distinction is absolutely crucial.

In his famous essay "The Hedgehog and the Fox," Isaiah Berlin divided the world into hedgehogs and foxes, based upon an ancient Greek parable: "The fox knows many things, but the hedgehog knows one thing." Those who built good-to-great companies were, to one degree or another, hedgehogs. They used their focused hedgehog nature to succeed. Collins came to call this focused approach to growing a business the Hedgehog Concept. Those who led the comparison businesses tended to be foxes, scattered and inconsistent, rather than focused like hedgehogs.

Collins' study made paired comparisons of for-profit business in 15 industries. The comparison was between two similar companies in each industry, except that in each comparison one company had gone from simply being a "good" company to becoming a "great company." The strategic difference between the good-to-great and comparison companies lies in two fundamental distinctions. First, the good-to-greats founded their strategies on a deep understanding of three key dimensions – what Collins calls the three circles. Second, good-to-greats translated that understanding into a simple concept that guided all their efforts – hence the term Hedgehog Concept. More precisely, the Hedgehog Concept flows from a deep understanding of three issues illustrated by the following three circles (see Figure 0.15):

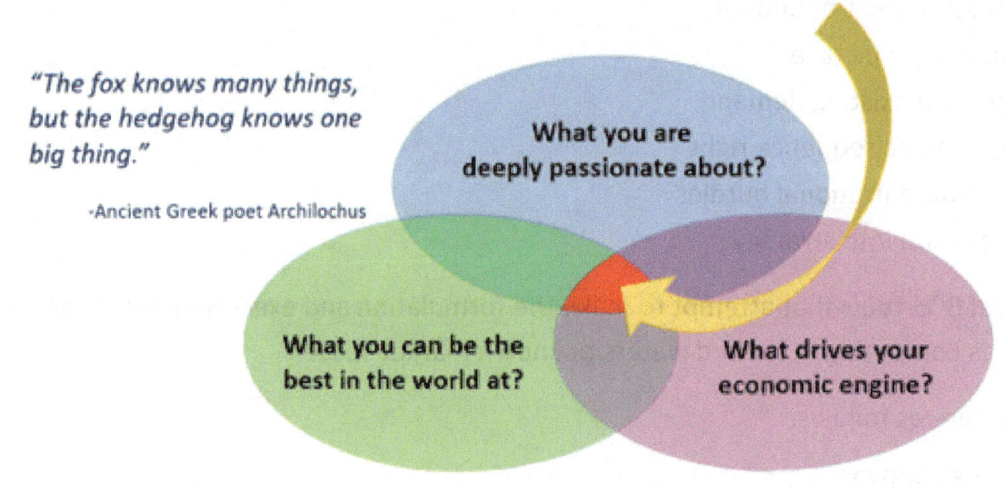

FIGURE 0.15: THE HEDGEHOG CONCEPT

"The fox knows many things, but the hedgehog knows one big thing."

-Ancient Greek poet Archilochus

- What you are deeply passionate about?
- What you can be the best in the world at?
- What drives your economic engine?

- **What can you do best in the world?** (And, equally important, what you cannot do best in the world). *This goes far beyond core competence*. Just because you possess a core competence does not necessarily mean you can be the best in the world. Conversely, what you can be the best at might not even be something in which you are currently engaged.
- **What drives your economic engine?** All the good-to-great companies attained insight into how to generate sustained, robust cash flow and profitability most effectively. They discovered the single denominator – profit per x – that had the greatest impact on their economies.

---

[32] Collins, J. *Good to Great: Why Some Companies Make the Leap and Others Don't*, HarperBusiness, 2001.

- **What are you deeply passionate about?** The idea here is not to create passion, but to discover what makes you passionate.

To have a fully developed Hedgehog Concept, all three circles must be integrated.

The work of Collins and Kim and Mauborgne bring us full circle to some of the points raised by early theorists, in particular the work of Kenneth Andrews (1980) who first clearly distinguished several issues with which management must grapple in determining strategy for their organization.

- What a company *might do* in terms of environmental opportunity
- What it *can do* in terms of ability and power
- What the executives of the company *want to do*
- What a company *should do*

Early this century emphasis began shifting from strategy formulation to strategy execution. When the transition from formulating strategy to executing strategy fails to take root, tangible results are not realized. According to Larry Bossidy, the highly acclaimed former CEO of Allied Signal, and Dr. Ram Charan, peerless advisor to senior executives and boards of directors, the processes of strategy execution must be organized, disciplined, and consistently discharged to be effective. In a book they co-authored entitled *Execution – The Discipline of Getting Things Done* [33] they emphasize the following:

- Strategies most often fail because they are not implemented well.
- Management does not recognize implementation as a management discipline.
- Execution is a discipline integral to strategy.
- Execution is the major job of the business leader.
- Execution must be a core element of an organization's culture.
- Everyone needs to understand and practice the discipline of execution and be involved in order for meaningful cultural change.

Bossidy and Charan's 2002 book is foundational reading for anyone interested in the emerging discipline of strategy execution. The more recent work of Robin Speculand [34] and Antonio Nieto Rodriguez [35] are also foundational to the discipline of strategy execution.

Another significant development occurred in 2013 with the publication of *Playing to Win* by A.G. Lafley, former CEO of Proctor and Gamble, and Dr. Roger Martin, former Dean of Toronto University's Rotman School of Management. They write, "Strategy can seem mystical and mysterious. It is not. It is easily defined. It is a set of choices about winning." [36] They go on to point out strategy is the answer to five interrelated questions which together function as an integrated cascade of choices (see Figure 0.16).

---

[33] Bossidy, L., and Charan, R. *Execution – The Discipline of Getting Things Done*, Crown Currency, 2002.
[34] Speculand, R. *Excellence in Execution: How to Implement Your Strategy*, Morgan James Publishing, 2017.
[35] Nieto-Rodriguez, A. *The Focused Organization: How Concentrating on a Few Key Initiatives Can Dramatically Improve Strategy Execution*, Routledge, 2012.
[36] Lafley, A. G., Martin, R. L. *Playing to Win: How Strategy Really Works*, Harvard Business Review Press, 2013.

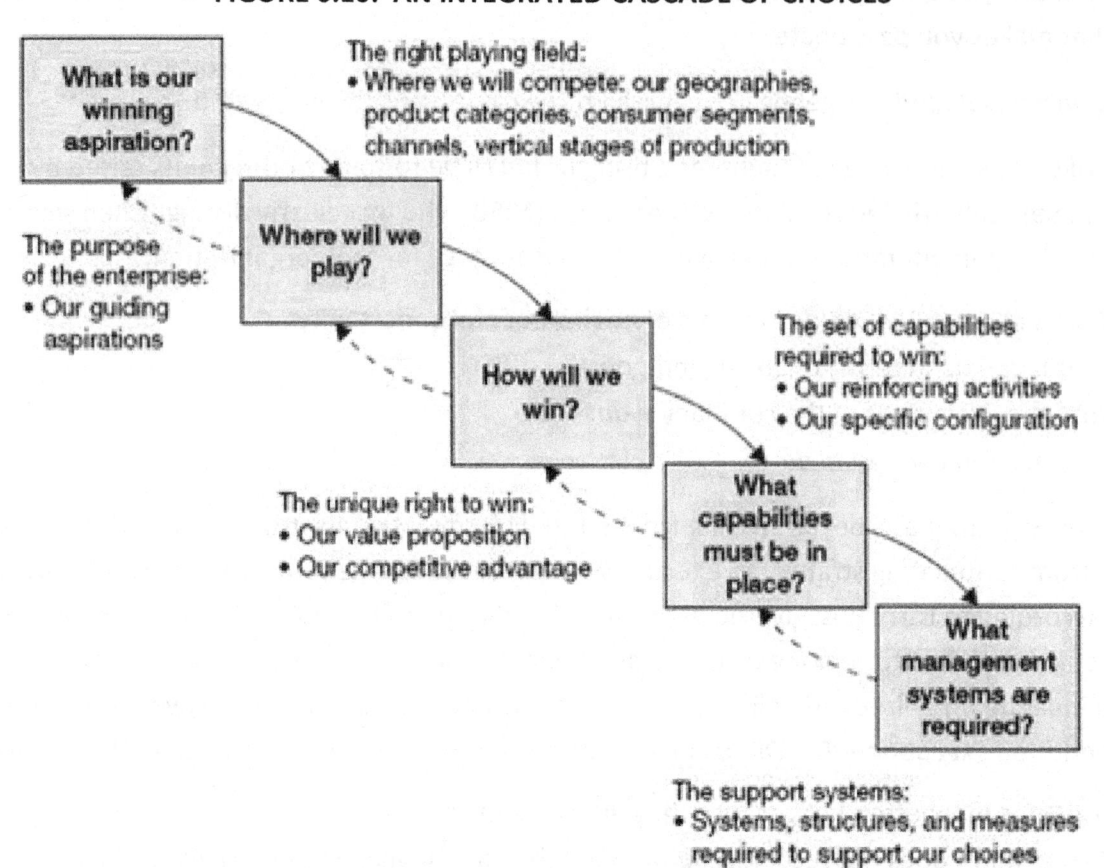

FIGURE 0.16: AN INTEGRATED CASCADE OF CHOICES

What is our winning aspiration?
The purpose of the enterprise:
- Our guiding aspirations

Where will we play?
The right playing field:
- Where we will compete: our geographies, product categories, consumer segments, channels, vertical stages of production

How will we win?
The unique right to win:
- Our value proposition
- Our competitive advantage

What capabilities must be in place?
The set of capabilities required to win:
- Our reinforcing activities
- Our specific configuration

What management systems are required?
The support systems:
- Systems, structures, and measures required to support our choices

More recently, an emerging management technique is for leaders and strategy professionals to facilitate agile objective setting by using "Objectives and Key Results" or OKRs. With roots back to Peter Drucker's "management by objectives," OKRs were first introduced by Andy Grove in his tenure as CEO of Intel Corporation, and then energized and popularized by John Doerr at Google. [37]

Others have contributed to OKRs' emergence including Niven and Lamorte (*Objectives and Key Results* [38] and *OKR Field Book: A Step-by-Step Guide for Objectives and Key Results Coaches* [39]) and, Dan Montgomery (*Start Less, Finish More: Building Strategic Agility with Objectives and Key Results*).

"Objectives" refers to where the organization wants to go – specific outcomes for a set period. "Key Results" refers to how far the organization has progressed in pursuit of achieving their objectives.

The primary benefits to utilizing OKRs are increased clarity of purpose, focus, alignment, agility, engagement, accountability, transparency, and most importantly, aligning short term results with stated objectives. OKRs will only deliver intended results when and where there is sustained team effort.

---

[37] Doerr, J. *Measure What Matters Most*, Portfolio, 2018.
[38] Niven, P. and Lamorte, B. *Objectives and Key Results, Wiley,* 2016
[39] Lamorte, B. *OKR Field Book: A Step-by-Step Guide for Objectives and Key Results Coaches,* Wiley, 2022

The purpose of OKRs is to connect organizational, department level, and personal (or small team) objectives to measurable results. All team members and leaders work together in one unified direction, making sure everyone in the organization knows what is expected of them. OKRs are visible to all as the organization moves towards the same overarching goal and enterprise objectives, ensuring people are aware of what others are working on. OKRs are typically part of a quarterly planning cadence.[40]

Another relatively new development in strategy management has been coined "Conscious Capitalism." Conscious Capitalism emphasizes creating sustainable value for all stakeholders, including customers, employees, strategic partners, suppliers, communities, and the environment. This contrasts with focusing solely on maximizing profits for shareholders. It is based on the belief that capitalism can be a force for good, and that businesses can serve a higher purpose beyond just making money. [41]

Major proponents of conscious capitalism include John Mackey, co-founder and CEO of Whole Foods Market, and Raj Sisodia, co-founder of the Conscious Capitalism movement. They authored *Conscious Capitalism: Liberating the Heroic Spirit of Business*, a seminal work on the topic.[42] Michael Porter has also written extensively on the importance of creating shared value in business. Conscious capitalism has gained traction as more businesses seek to balance purpose and profit. It is seen by many as a potential solution for some of the social, economic, and environmental challenges that we face.

Today these concepts and frameworks are still being examined in practice, but now organizations have an extensive body of knowledge and experience from which to draw. Moreover, while the early studies were largely prescriptive, studies now include descriptive, analytic, and research-based data as well.

All the preceding approaches to strategic management imply a strategic focus, that is, the deliberate intention to develop and implement an organization strategy. Alternative views of how strategy evolves have been set forth by Quinn and Mintzberg, two respected and well-known scholars who have spent many years studying and researching strategic management issues.

James Brian Quinn (1980) used "logical incrementalism" to express his view of the way strategy and strategic decisions evolve both randomly and logically. Grundy (2004, 116) notes that Quinn's very thoroughly researched work finds ample evidence of logical incrementalism in major U.S. corporations.

Henry Mintzberg's research (1973, 1979, 1983, and 1994) focused on organization structure and management. He viewed managers as primarily focused on operations, with little or no time for thinking about strategy. He viewed strategy as messy and haphazard; on occasion it could coalesce into an emergent strategy. This does not preclude *intended or deliberate* attempts by an organization to form and implement strategy; rather, the *emergent* strategies merge with and deflect the intended strategies into what he termed *realized* strategies.

---

[40] While OKRs are often done quarterly, it can be a challenge given other conflicting quarterly activities in large organizations. An "off cycle" schedule can help to maintain focus and is just as effective in terms of execution.
[41] https://medium.com/magnetic/a-short-history-of-conscious-capitalism-4aca5264746f
[42] https://www.amazon.com/Conscious-Capitalism-New-Preface-Authors/dp/1625271751

Both Mintzberg and Quinn believed that strategic management consists of deliberate processes that can be comprehensively analyzed, designed, planned, and implemented. However, strategic management does not exist without considerable randomness from trial and error and interrupted activity that may bear no relation to orderly strategic management processes.

As we participate in a global economy, there will be many new considerations, including:

- Research and analysis on strategic management in other countries made by contributing academics, practitioners, and managers in those countries.
- Studies of cultures, social, economic, political systems, and technologies of those countries.
- Studies of organizations operating in multicultural settings and having conflicting planning and control issues with the home office wherever it might be.
- Studies of the impact of globalization.

In essence, not only will strategic management have to cope with the dynamics of growth and development within each organization, but also it will be necessary to consider development in an expanded and increasingly competitive global context.

Strategic Management Competencies

It is the focus on strategy's formulation, transformation, and execution that distinguishes strategic management from simply managing day to day operations. It is not uncommon for the distinction between strategic and operational management to be blurred. When this occurs, operations management typically dominates management thinking and activities, while strategy receives occasional limited attention. This does not occur from intentional lack of concern about strategy, but more often because of misconceptions about strategic management. Table 0.7 summarizes these misconceptions.

TABLE 0.7 – MISCONCEPTIONS ABOUT STRATEGIC MANAGEMENT
• Strategic management does not deserve special attention; good business management automatically includes managing strategy.
• In our organization, we all know the organization strategy—it is our game plan.
• Strategic management is costly and time-consuming, and our energies are better focused on our main objective, that is, making money, satisfying customers, making superior products, and so forth.
• If we all do our jobs, we *are* managing strategy.
• Managing strategy is a top management responsibility. We are only required to do what they tell us to do.
• Strategy development is an academic pursuit. It is too theoretical and does not apply to us.
• If we followed the advice of these academics and consultants, we would never get anything done. Even worse, we would go broke in the process.
• The world changes so fast that we do not need a strategy. Rather, we need to be agile.

Introduction

Unfortunately, believing in these misconceptions about strategic management leads to the very end results they predict and precludes organizations from benefiting from employing a strategic focus and aligning all functions and processes with it.

Four primary reasons account for the above stated misconceptions:

1. The need for strategic management is not well-understood.
2. The process of strategic management is not understood as distinct from operations management, except that it is a top management responsibility.
3. The management competencies required to formulate and implement strategy are not well known or developed in most organizations.
4. Strategic management is an umbrella discipline complementary and not in contradiction to other fields (e.g., agility, business architecture, organizational design, change management, etc.).

To the best of our ability, we will try to address these misconceptions. However, a few comments are made here to highlight the need to acquire and/or strengthen the basic competencies that are required to achieve effective strategic management. These competencies should be placed high on management's list of basic training and development priorities.

While these competencies are necessary for effective strategic management, they are by no means exhaustive. There is a much longer list of both general management competencies that all organizations need to address, as well as a list of competencies that are necessary for specific types of organizations including those in given environmental configurations. However, even a brief consideration of this expanded framework of required management competencies is beyond the scope of this book where the focus will be on required basic strategic management competencies as summarized below.

IDENTIFYING, ARTICULATING, AND DEVELOPING A CORE SET OF SHARED VALUES

In part, all shared values evolve as the result of informal group processes. However, every organization needs a formal process that monitors and clarifies the emergence of its core set of shared values because ultimately, they provide the basis not only for guiding and directing the organization, but also for evaluating and rewarding performance.

Arriving at shared values is a significant and revealing process involving the contributions of many individuals. Articulating these values, and communicating them, is the work of a few individuals, usually members of top management and their staff. Through focus groups, surveys, crowd sourcing, or other methods, leadership can engage others throughout the organization for input. Arriving at a set of shared values is essential to strategic management as they provide a moral compass for developing the organization's strategic direction and function as the cultural "guideposts" to direct implementation of the strategy and operations of the organization.

VISIONING

Developing a clear and accepted vision for the organization is not an easily acquired competency, even among very successful managers. It requires the ability to arrive at a concise statement of a *desired future state* that is *grounded* in the core values of the organization, based on the current and future capabilities of the organization and its management. It must be *achievable*, albeit with effort, and with the improvement and possible acquisition of new resources and capabilities.

STRATEGIC THINKING

The ability to think strategically has always been essential to developing and executing new strategies, but only recently has it emerged as an essential skill that managers at all levels can and should acquire. As Richard Horwath describes the process, strategic thinking involves the generation of insights that drives business strategy development. Strategic planning involves the application of strategy. (Horwath, 11). Strategic thinking is a combination of skill sets that goes beyond simply generating insights and new directions for the organization. It includes the ability to incorporate these insights in the organization's strategic plan. In short, it is the synthesis of creative and action-oriented thinking applied in a specific organization. Strategic planning, essential for strategy development, requires strategic thinking.

IDENTIFYING AND DEVELOPING CORE ORGANIZATIONAL COMPETENCIES AND CAPABILITIES

With respect to core competencies, there is the need to distinguish between doing something new and doing something that already exists – but in a different way. In addition, it is important to distinguish between those things currently done in the organization, and then in which of those the organization excels. Unfortunately, it is the last of these competencies that tends to receive the most attention, as evidenced by the many attempts to improve quality, cost, and customer service. Sooner or later, this focus on operational excellence will result in widespread standard operational practices, with little lasting strategic advantage. <u>Consequently, it is immensely important to find those distinguishing and differentiating factors that separate an organization from its competitors and drive execution excellence</u>. This requires the constant attention of at least some of the top managers and staff personnel in an organization. Constant attention and the realization of the importance of differentiation are the two key drivers in developing this skill. *It is a skill primarily acquired through practice…not education or training.*

CONVERTING INFORMATION INTO STRATEGIC INTELLIGENCE

Information cannot be considered either strategic or competitive until it is processed in terms of its utility in the development or application of strategic direction. The process of providing guidelines for sifting information to find its strategic value is primarily, but not exclusively, the responsibility of top management. However, the main guidelines derive from the strategic direction that top management provides. Applying these guidelines in processing large amounts of information can be done by staff personnel so long as the results of this process are monitored and evaluated by top management.

The process of converting information into useful strategic intelligence requires the ability to spot trends and signals "still on the distant horizon," and to have some notion that they may ultimately be significant. Concentration on a few areas of importance to the organization will enhance the success of such scanning efforts, but ultimately success depends on an analytic ability based on tenuous and sometimes far-fetched reasoning. In the discipline of foresight, this is the ability to foresee third and fourth order effects. To illustrate, monitoring the products and services being generated in areas such as healthcare, retirement living, education and training, tourism, environmental concerns, technology development, telecommunications, and global trade provides many useful clues for future commercial opportunities. The skills involved include processing large amounts of information, retaining key items of interest, making imaginative and creative connections, and seeing the relevance to the organization and its future development.

IDENTIFYING, EVALUATING, AND SELECTING STRATEGIC ALTERNATIVES

Identifying, evaluating, and selecting strategic alternatives requires a combination of skills not usually found in a single individual. Hence, the customary solution is to break up the process among different individuals, or teams. This skill requires an ability to analyze the environment, generate feasible alternatives, evaluate each alternative, and select the most appropriate alternative (or group of alternatives) as the core strategy.

Why then should an individual manager try to acquire this multidimensional competency? Imagination, creativity, evaluation, and an action orientation underlie every step of the strategic management process in varying proportions depending on the process. Strategic management cannot conveniently be subdivided in the overall management of the organization, although specific strategic management projects can be singled out for development. Even then, projects of this sort are only valuable when integrated into the overall strategic management system of the organization.

In short, strategic management is a holistic process that transcends specialization and expertise as the dominant management skill. Consequently, it is incumbent upon any manager, especially those who consider themselves to be upwardly mobile, to build competency in this discipline.

EXECUTING STRATEGY

Transforming the organization's operations to align with a newly developed or refined strategy is fundamental to successful execution of any strategy and is a vital competency every leadership team most possess. Execution of strategy differs from simply implementing operational changes. Changes in the components of strategy: that is, vision, mission, values, policies, goals, strategies, objectives, initiatives, and measures of the organization's success/failure, reverberate through the existing organization structure and its operations. In contrast, planned changes originating at an operations level are usually conducted *within* the framework of a current strategic direction <u>and</u> operating plan. Having this competency is a primary key to the successful implementation of strategy.

TEAMWORK AND TEAM BUILDING

Strategic management consists of individual and collective processes. Every member of an organization will always have individual roles and responsibilities for which she or he is held accountable. However, it is increasingly clear that the new management and organizational paradigms of interdependent and interactive behavior of groups, committees, or teams are transforming these roles and responsibilities.

This has been evident for some time now at the operational level; organizations do not operate effectively without these structures and processes in place. However, with respect to *strategic management* it remains unclear in most organizations that *team structures and processes are the primary core competency underlying all other competencies*. This logic, the need to process individual inputs and outputs through collective processes, *especially through teams*, becomes a key organizational/behavioral competency required to develop effective strategic managers.

Table 0.8 summarizes the rationale for building a team-based leadership and management culture.

TABLE 0.8 – RATIONALE FOR TEAM-BASED LEADERSHIP AND MANAGEMENT

The challenges facing strategic management are increasingly beyond the scope of an individual, no matter how talented, experienced, or educated. For example:
 	
    o Internal and external factors are increasing and changing at an accelerating rate.
    o Second, third, and higher-order effects need to be taken into account, analyzed, and evaluated.
    o Organizations, management, processes, and technologies are ever more compelling, requiring multiple perspectives to identify and assess their impact and resultant need for innovative improvements and new actions.
 	
The aforementioned and other challenges facing management are best dealt with in a team format for a variety of reasons. More specifically, teams have a clear advantage over other approaches in the following ways by:
 	
    o Providing a synergy amongst team members that enhances and magnifies individual contributions.
    o Drawing on each team member's experience, skill, and ideas and incorporating them to develop a shared vision, strategy, and action plan.
    o Providing a multidimensional perspective on problems and issues.
    o Generating alternative courses of action.
    o Giving individuals an opportunity to grow in their commitment, skills, and contributions to the organization.

Note: The tasks and models introduced earlier in this section are often developed with many variations by different consultants, strategy analysts, and planners. In addition, an organization will often find reasons to make its own changes, modifications, and additions to meet unique situations or to emphasize a particular task that requires expansion and development. This is especially likely to occur in organizations with a great many strategic business/program units and/or organizations operating in several locations.

With these qualifications in mind, the balance of this book outlines the development of each of the SMPS Phases and Tasks described earlier, incorporating proven models and concepts of strategy where they can be most effectively utilized.

Appendices are included on those points that merit additional attention, but they can also be viewed as optional to those seeking an abridged overview of strategic management and an outline of the essential tasks in the strategic management process. The glossary and bibliography are organized to aid those seeking additional information on various aspects of the strategic management process.

Phase I – Initiating a Strategic Management System

Upon the drying of a lake, two frogs were forced to seek water elsewhere.

As they searched, they came upon a deep well.

Come, said one frog to the other, let's go in without looking any further.

Said the companion, you believe this fine, but what if the water should fail us here too?

How shall we get out again?

The Moral: 'Tis good advice to look before we leap.

– Aesop's Fables

All too often organizational leaders move into and through the strategy setting process without **building a common information base** upon which sound strategic decisions can be made. In a rush to define strategy and approve annual operating budgets, the judgments and decisions made fall prey to an uneven, and occasionally contradictory, understanding of the current strategic environment and its power to influence the future. This fundamental "knowledge gap" among senior leadership and down through the organization serves to undermine the strategic management process by:

2.1(2)

- Failing to leverage the existing strategic knowledge available via the workforce.
- Neglecting to consider accessible information resources inside and outside the organization.
- Decreasing the likelihood that an effective set of strategies will be selected and executed.
- Reducing the likelihood of workforce acceptance.
- Unintentionally creating work force resistance to change when reasons for the change are not clearly communicated and understood.

This phase presents two *preliminary* tasks that lay the groundwork for **a practical, systematic, sustainable, and repeatable strategic management system** within an organization:

2.1(2)

Systematic Approach

Task 1.1 – Assess Current Strategic Direction and Organizational Capabilities
Task 1.2 – Design and Organize an Appropriate Startup System Based on These Assessments

Strategy in the 21st Century, Second Edition

Task 1.1 – Assess Current Strategic Direction and Organizational Capabilities

To manage a formally stated, well integrated, and properly deployed strategy is a major challenge for any organization. To do so without completing the necessary preparatory tasks will likely result in wasted time, energy, and misdirected efforts. More importantly, management will be at a disadvantage by attempting to create a strategic direction without considering the organization's current aspirations and plans.

Before undertaking a significant effort to develop, improve, and/or manage strategy, there must be a shared understanding of the scope and depth of the change effort. The agreed-upon change effort must be grounded in a fact-based assessment of the organization's current strategic direction and strategic management capabilities in place.

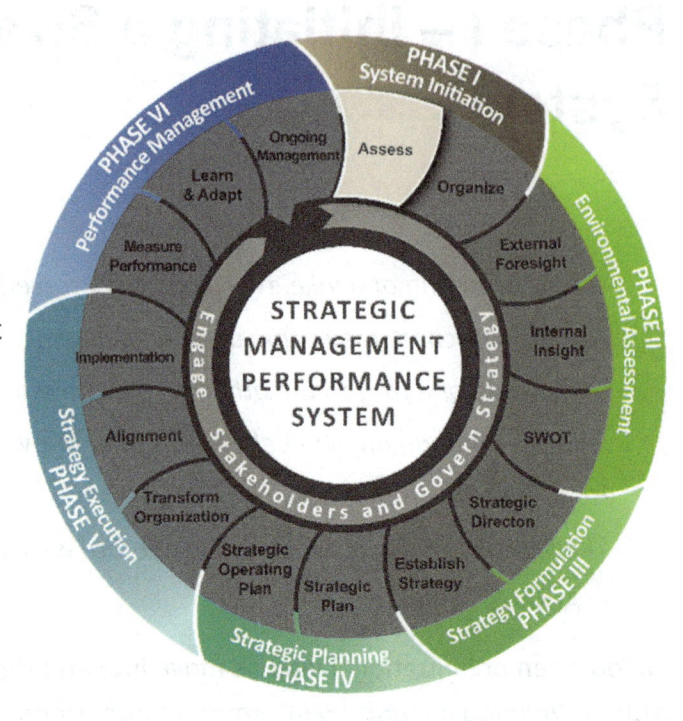

This initial assessment, in large measure, will determine the basis for making changes. To first build this shared understanding is an often-overlooked task in the strategic planning system.

A prerequisite to developing a strategy-focused management approach is a comprehensive assessment of the organization's current strategic direction, strategic management capabilities, prior success or failure in strategy implementation, and culture of agility. While this may seem obvious, many leadership teams begin by asking where they want to be without first understanding where they are (e.g., their performance on multicultural inclusion). Such an approach invariably proves ineffective, delivering results that fall short of expectations because leadership failed to consider the current state of organizational capabilities, competencies, and resources required to achieve high-level strategic goals they set.

The term *strategic direction* is used here, assuming all organizations have one either formally planned, ad hoc, or emergent from ongoing operations, to express where the organization is headed. The task at hand here in Phase I is to identify what leadership has in mind for a new strategic direction to drive the organization's activities.

P.1a(2)

It is equally important in Phase I to assess the organization's strategic management competencies along with financial and human resources available to pursue strategic level direction and goals. In doing this assessment, it soon becomes apparent what tangible competencies and resources will be necessary to initiate and sustain a strategy-based

2.1(2)

52

management system. The most critical and influential of these factors are noted below. A part of assessing the strategic management competencies is to take an honest "look in the mirror" at the *organization's past success and failures executing strategic plans*. It is important to identify and acknowledge where configuring and failing to execute a strategic plan has occurred. A well-written plan that goes unexecuted is simply "shelf ware" and a waste of valuable time and resources.

2.1(2)

In this book, the term *assessment* refers to two equally important and conceptually distinct processes: analysis and evaluation.

Analysis refers to an examination of data and information to understand its content, meaning, and significance for some purpose, in this case the strategic management of an organization. The processes of analysis are dependent on the nature of the data and information being analyzed. The information may be qualitative, quantitative and, in some cases, both. The information can be subjective, biased, fragmentary, and inconclusive. The important point is to recognize it for what it is and examine it as such in an objective manner.

Glossary

Evaluation refers to the process of comparing the information that has been analyzed in terms of some evaluation criteria, whether qualitative or quantitative. We live in an age where daily we drown in a sea of information. Evaluation is the process of reducing this literal explosion of information to useful and manageable proportions.

Analysis precedes evaluation in the assessment process. Analysis provides a solid information base that, in turn, can be evaluated to arrive at an assessment of needs, expectations, and capabilities of executive leadership and the organization. The overall body of assessment information will be valuable for planning team reference during identification and selection of the most effective organization strategies.

Table 1.1 summarizes six primary components of an initial assessment.

TABLE 1.1 – COMPONENTS OF AN INITIAL ASSESSMENT
• An assessment of the organization's current situation and strategy.
• An assessment of the organization's present portfolio of offerings as to performance and perceived potential.
• An assessment of the present longer-term vision of key leadership.
• An assessment of the organization's existing strategic management system and component parts, sometimes referred to as a "gap analysis."
• An assessment of the team's collective strategic management competency to develop, implement, and improve the organization's strategy.
• An assessment of the contextual, situational, and unique features that currently exist in the organization, including a clarification of the leadership team's "felt" need versus "actual" need.

Strategy in the 21st Century, Second Edition

These assessments are equally important whether the effort to develop strategy and strategic management capabilities is entirely an internal process or includes, to a greater or lesser extent, *external assistance*. Executive leadership must have a realistic assessment of what it takes to carry out a sustained change effort or run the risk of it becoming a "flavor of the month" soon to be forgotten initiative.

2.1(4)

In those cases where external assistance is used, individuals (such as strategic planning and management professionals) facilitating this effort will need the results of assessment work to calibrate and align their assistance with the needs of the organization and its leadership team.

There are different ways to listen to your organization in the strategy process. Investing in interviews, focus groups, surveys, crowdsourcing, and social media not only garners data that you may not otherwise have, but it begins to align the organization and can greatly hasten implementation and execution. Special efforts should be taken to listen to board members, executives, top managers, and staff members who are likely to be included in any effort to initiate a strategy-based management system.

Ideally, one senior manager who has some knowledge and experience with strategic management processes can be designated as the "strategy champion" to coordinate and consolidate (or oversee consolidating) the results of these assessments, as well as conduct and/or supervise interviews and other information gathering activities. In those cases where such an individual is not available, the services of a qualified and trusted outside strategic planning and management consultant or advisor may be required.

An important caveat: While more detailed information will be gathered in both the external and internal strategic analyses to follow, this assessment is an *overview* that will be a major determinant of what the leadership team ultimately wants the organization to become and the level of effort and commitment they are willing to undertake. Specifically, this means acquiring the following information.

An Assessment of the Organization's Current Situation and Strategy

Many factors impact the *"current situation"* faced by organizations. Take time to understand what is going on. Probe each of the questions below. Listen carefully and understand the implications for the proposed strategic management system.

P.1-P.2

- What is the organization's historical origin and reason for being?
- What are some of the events, major developments, and advancements that have shaped the organization?
- What are the successes, challenges, and the most pressing need(s) or problem(s)?
- What products and services does the organization offer and how are they performing?
- How effective is the organization's marketing effort?
- What is the organization's historical and current financial performance?
- What are the organization's key performance indicators? Is it achieving the desired targets?
- Who are the primary customers and key stakeholders? What are their needs and expectations?

Introduction

- Are there cultural factors or multicultural gaps in play that will need attention?
- How is talent meeting current organizational demands?
- How well is IT able to support operations"?

There are different ways to probe and gather information on these topics (i.e., interviews, focus groups, surveys, crowd sourcing, and social media). Every situation is different so choose the methods that best fit. If relevant information has already been created, review it first and then pursue chosen methods and ways to get a clear read on the important historical, performance, and situational factors to be considered during the planning, implementation, and evaluation processes.

To understand the organization's current strategy, ask questions such as these and then listen carefully:

- Does the organization have a written set of statements covering the organization's **vision, mission, values, policies, goals, and value propositions?**
- Is there a strategy for realizing these or is it ad hoc? Is it working? Why not?
- Has there been **major disruptions in the industry, sector**, or in the organization?
- Have **prior strategies and major change initiatives** been effectively communicated?
- Have **prior strategies been effectively executed**?
- Are there potential obstacles/objections that have been communicated by the team?
    - Wrong time of year
    - Planning is for larger organizations
    - Conflict between leaders
    - Dysfunctional organizational culture
    - Weak information systems
    - We have tried that before
    - Waste of time
    - Plans are never implemented
    - We aren't committed
    - Too expensive
    - We do not have time to plan
    - Today's crises trump tomorrow's planning

1.1(1)
2.2(2)

Carefully assess the current mission, vision, values, policies, and goals. For many organizations, these components exist as general statements that were not formally developed and approved as the basis for leadership planning and decision-making. A realistic assessment of the current strategic direction will set the tone and provide the basis for defining the scope of the strategic management system.

The following components of strategic direction, summarized in Table 1.2, provide a framework for organizing answers to these and similar questions and a basis for analyzing and developing strategy.

Strategy in the 21st Century, Second Edition

> **TABLE 1.2 – COMPONENTS OF STRATEGIC DIRECTION** [43]
>
> - *Vision— Inspirational statement that articulates the desired future state of an organization in terms of its strategic direction.*
> - *Mission—Actionable statement that identifies the organization's purpose and reason for existence.*
> - *Values— Fundamental beliefs, philosophies, principles, or standards that define the organization's character. They dictate correct behavior and guide the decisions and actions of an organization's leaders and workforce.*
> - *Strategic Policy— Requirement or guidelines developed for use in an organization to influence, instruct, and specify how leaders should act and govern when making decisions in given circumstances.*
> - *Goal—Long range, generally stated, directional aims to be achieved in alignment with the organization's vision and mission.*

Embedded Values

Glossary

The importance of reaching a common understanding of where the organization stands on the components of strategic direction cannot be overstated. Taken together, they provide the focus and rationale for all strategic management activities. Every organization has a strategic direction in some state of development. It need not be written to impact members of the organization. Paradoxically, in many organizations, some of its unwritten components are more widely shared and adhered to than those distributed in detailed documents and reports.

Once an organization embarks on developing a comprehensive strategic management system, it is no longer feasible to treat the components of its strategic direction informally: They form the foundation upon which all strategic management processes ultimately rest. No system can be effectively designed, managed/governed, or maintained without a clearly articulated, widely disseminated, and closely adhered to strategic direction. Consequently, the leadership team should clearly understand where it stands from the outset. Agreement is needed on how to develop its approach to strategy management.

It is useful to **assess each of the existing strategic direction components in terms of its level of development, whether right for the organization or not**. In organizations that have not formally designed their strategic direction, the level of development is an estimate of the extent of articulation, diffusion, understanding, and adherence to the components of the strategic direction in the organization. A realistic estimate of the level of development for each component is required. In Phase III, these components will be discussed in detail with guidance on how to develop a comprehensive statement of strategic direction. At this point, the following definitions provide enough guidance for reaching agreement on the level of development for each component:

L1-2

Approach

---

[43] See ASP BOK 3.0 precise definitions, Sections 2.1.1 through 2.1.4.

- *Level 1*—No clear articulation and diffusion of the component, although it may be well understood and used by the leadership to run the organization.
- *Level 2*—The component is written and disseminated but is recognized by the workforce as a passive announcement, a PR effort that leadership has little or no intention of using to orient, motivate, or otherwise influence the workforce.
- *Level 3*—The component is well documented and distributed, and leadership tries to ensure that all members of the organization understand and accept (hopefully internalize) the component; the level of development of the component still varies considerably from that of other components.
- *Level 4*—The component is documented, distributed, and used by leadership to make decisions, plan systems, and develop guidelines in managing all activities and in conducting relationships with customers, suppliers, and employees; the level of development of all components is beginning to approach the same level of articulation and utilization by management.
- *Level 5*—All components of the strategic management direction are at the same high level of articulation and utilization and are also integrated and synergistic; most of the board, management, staff, and the workforce understand, accept, and use them to guide their organizational activities.

L1-2 Approach

L3-5 Deployment

Integration

Estimates of these developmental levels can conveniently be summarized (see Figure 1.1):

FIGURE 1.1: INITIAL ASSESSMENT OF THE LEVEL OF DEVELOPMENT OF THE CURRENT STRATEGIC DIRECTION

Level of Development	Vision	Mission	Values	Policies	Goals
Level 1		◆			
Level 2	◆			◆	
Level 3			◆		
Level 4					◆
Level 5					

This assessment presents a picture of uneven development across the components of strategic direction. It is the product of participating stakeholder ratings and discussion to form a collective perception about the level of development of the strategic direction. Management needs to agree on this level; it is the best single indicator of the starting point for designing and developing the strategic management system.

Often, organizations set too many goals without a clear understanding of the time and resources required to achieve them. Sometimes organizations have purported values statements that in fact are just window dressing and play no role in guiding behavior or selecting initiatives. Finally, in many organizations a clear understanding of the vision and mission is not universally shared/effectively communicated throughout the organization, greatly impeding progress in managing strategically.

Strategy in the 21st Century, Second Edition

An Assessment of the Organization's Portfolio of Offerings for Performance and Perceived Potential

A fundamental component for any strategic management team is a base understanding of *how the organization's current offerings are performing and what their growth potential is*. It may be tempting to predicate future planning on a successful product or service, but strategically minded leadership must continually assess the realistic potential for either.

2.2(6)

As noted (see Figure 0.9), in the 1960s the Boston Consulting Group (BCG) developed an analytic model for for-profit companies to manage a portfolio of business units or product lines. (See Figure 1.2.)

EXAMPLE: NINTENDO
In the 1980's and 1990's Nintendo was the market leader in the video game industry with its Game Station and Game Cube products. Had Nintendo based its future strategy merely on these two products, it would have been annihilated by competitors PlayStation 2 and Xbox. However, Nintendo did not base future earnings growth on these products, but rather in 2006 launched the Wii, globally selling over 100 million units. A decade later they introduced Pokémon Go, which added billions of market value.
Learning from the low adoption of the Wii U in 2012, Nintendo announced the Nintendo Switch in 2017 that allowed gamers to enjoy both a couch and mobile handheld experience interchangeably without disrupting gameplay. Rather than focusing on building a console that could compete with the graphical performance of the Microsoft and Sony consoles, Nintendo focused on developing first-party exclusive titles that paired well with the Switch's mobility. They knew gaming technology was rapidly accelerating and that incremental increases to the existing product would not keep pace.

The BCG Growth Share Matrix displays business units on a graph charting market growth rate vs. market share relative to competitors. Resources are allocated based on where units are on the grid. BCG's basic recommendation was to balance resources between what they termed "cash cows" and "stars" and allocate some resources to feed "question marks" (potential stars). *Estimates of performance level versus potential can be plotted* to gain an understanding of the current state. (See Figures 0.9 and 1.2.)

4.1(3)(4)

FIGURE 1.2: BCG GROWTH SHARE MATRIX – APPLE 2022

Introduction

EXAMPLE: APPLE
Apple Inc. provides a good example of how to apply the BCG Growth Share Matrix. Based on 2022 market data and conditions, each of the four quadrants can be illustrated as following: • **Rising Star** - The iPhone continues to drive growth for Apple. Some argue it is gravitating into the "Cash Cow" quadrant, but because demand remains high and keeps growing, it continues to be a "rising star." Apple has also seen incredible growth in Apple Services and Software. • **Cash Cow** - The MacBook, Apple Watch, and Airpods may be the portables of choice. They generate huge profit and market share is high. However, the MacBook is losing growth as the iPhone and iPad become increasingly more capable. • **Question Mark** – Apple TV+ streaming service is still questionable, as it faces fierce competition from other streaming powerhouses such as Netflix, Hulu, and Amazon Prime. • **Dog** - iPods have been replaced by the iPhone (Apple has discontinued their production).

EXAMPLE: MICROSOFT
Microsoft provides another example of how to apply the BCG Growth Share Matrix. Based on 2022 market data and conditions, each of the four quadrants can be illustrated as follows: • **Rising Star** –Microsoft Cloud products such as Azure are growing due to cloud-based platforms need to move and warehouse massive amounts of data. • **Cash Cow** – Microsoft Windows and Office continue to remain an industry standard for local computing (i.e., operating systems and office applications). • **Question Mark** – Microsoft acquired Mojang Studies (known for the Minecraft multiplatform ecosystem) and XBOX (a gaming titan), which have great potential for wide-spread adoption. • **Dog** – Skype for Business was a market leader in video conferencing prior to the Coronavirus pandemic but was quickly disrupted by the more agile and user-friendly Zoom. Microsoft regained market share by imbedding Microsoft Teams in the MS suite.

An important technical skill for a strategy professional is the ability to adapt relevant conceptual models and frameworks to the nature and context of the organization they serve. An example is Montanari and Bracker's adaptation of the BCG Growth Share Matrix to the public sector.[44] (See Figure 1.3.)

FIGURE 1.3: PUBLIC SECTOR GROWTH SHARE MATRIX

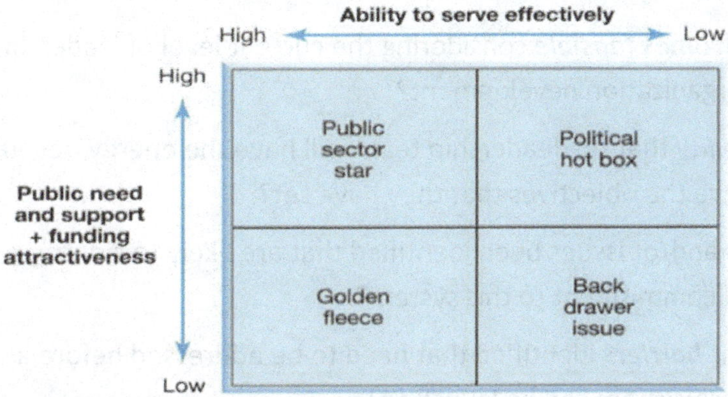

	Ability to serve effectively	
	High	Low
Public need and support + funding attractiveness High	Public sector star	Political hot box
Public need and support + funding attractiveness Low	Golden fleece	Back drawer issue

---

[44] Montanari, J.R., Bracker, J.S. *Strategic Management Journal*, V7, no. 3, 1986.

Strategy in the 21st Century, Second Edition

An Assessment of the Longer-Term Vision of Key Leaders

Often leaders have differing perceptions of the organization's longer-term vision of success. To borrow an example from U.S. history, two of George Washington's most trusted advisors, Thomas Jefferson and Alexander Hamilton, had conflicting visions of what the future of the United States should look like. Hamilton envisioned a nation fueled by a strong national bank that would promote business, manufacturing, and trade while Jefferson foresaw an agrarian-based economy made up of small independent farmers. Many scholars suggest their conflicting visions led to a "two-party system" of political representation that exists to this day.

2.1(2)

Examples of conflicting longer-term visions abound within the business world as well. The legendary conflict of vision between Steve Jobs (who envisioned Apple's future success to ride on sales of the Macintosh) and John Scully (who saw success primarily in the Apple II) exacerbated conflicts with the Apple Board resulting in the ouster of Steve Jobs from the very company he co-founded.

In both examples, two very smart, sincere, and capable leaders had differing views of future success. The wise strategy management professional is constantly attuned to detect differing longer-term visions of key leaders. If not, a major stumbling block can arise preventing the team from moving forward and being productive in the strategy formulation and execution processes. In fact, there are times when conflicting perspectives naturally leads to one or more leaders exiting the organization.

To avoid this stumbling block, make a concerted effort to understand where key leaders are coming from in terms of the organization's longer-term vision. Find ways to probe by using questions like these:

- What are the shared perceptions about the direction of the organization, its strategy for success, and its priorities?
- Are there any significant differences in these perceptions among senior leadership which need to be addressed?
- Does the board and/or management distinguish between long and short-term thinking and planning?
- Are the desired *outcomes feasible* considering the current level of leadership commitment and organization development?
- What is the *probability* that the leadership team will have the energy, resources, and willingness to achieve the objectives that they have set?
- Have any *problems* and/or issues been identified that are likely to sidetrack the leadership team's interest and commitment to this system?
- Were any significant *barriers* identified that need to be addressed before a viable strategic management process/system can be launched?

2.1(3)

Introduction

An Assessment of Strategic Management Component Parts, a "Gap Analysis."

Phase I should always include a gap analysis exercise. The point of this exercise is to identify all the major components of a robust strategic management system. Once they are identified, assess which components are in place and those in need of development.

2.1(1)

Figure 1.4 shows the *primary elements to include* in a robust strategic management system:

FIGURE 1.4: GAP ANALYSIS TOOL[45]

Strategic Management System Component	Developed	Partially Developed (Needs Work)	To be Developed	Comments
Environmental Assessment (External Foresight & Internal Insight)				
SWOT Analysis				
Core Competencies / Competitive Advantage				
Vision / Mission / Core Values				
High Level Goals (Strategic Results)				
Stakeholder Value Propositions (Customer, Partner, Owner, and Employees)				
High Level Strategies				
Perspectives (e.g., Balanced Scorecard)				
Strategic Objectives				
Strategy Map				
Key Performance Indicators & Targets				
Prioritized Strategic Initiatives				
Communications & Change Management Plan				
KPI Data Collection & Reporting (Automation)				
Implementation, Cascading & OKRs				
Strategy Management and Budgeting Calendar				

We recommend the strategic planning and management professional work with a staff member who can champion this assessment process from within as the work occurs to determine what pieces of strategy and strategy management are in place, partially in place, or need development. If system components are developed and functioning well, there is no need to start over: Build on the good work already done.

An Assessment of Available Strategic Management Competencies Required to Develop, Execute, and Improve Strategy

In the end, strategic management is about managing strategic performance. Success in managing performance (especially in turbulent times) requires *a thoughtful "strategic management system" to guide strategy development and agile execution*. However, having the system in place does not ensure success. Achieving an organization's vision requires "organizational capabilities" to deliver intended results.[46] (See Figure 1.5.)

Approach
Deployment
Evaluation
Learning

---

[45] Modified with permission - https://balancedscorecard.org/
[46] ASP, BOK 3.0, Section 2.1.5 - "organizational capability" is a set of resources that work together to enable the organization to produce a particular result.

SEE FIGURE 1.5: KEYS TO MANAGING STRATEGIC PERFORMANCE

Triangle diagram: "Manage Strategic Performance" with sides labeled "Strategic Management Process", "Organizational Capabilities", and "Strategy Management Competencies".

These capabilities must be built on a foundational set of team-based "strategic management competencies." (See Table 1.3) As a team's competency increases, organizational capabilities for effectively managing the process grow. Below are 10 strategic management competencies we believe every organization must possess to build the organizational capabilities necessary to guide their organization through an uncertain future.

TABLE 1.3 – ORGANIZATIONAL STRATEGIC MANAGEMENT COMPETENCIES REQUIRED	
• The foremost competency required is an ability to *think and act strategically*. It includes understanding how to engage, communicate, and lead a team to become strategy focused.	1.1(4,5)
• Teams must be able to identify, articulate, and live by *a core set of shared values*. This element is foundational for any organization.	1.1(1)
• Teams must be able to build strategic foresight by *converting alternative scenarios and emerging trends from interesting "information" into strategic intelligence* such that it facilitates decision making. This is critical to help the organization determine where it intends to go and how it intends to get there. A broad base of key leaders and managers must have the ability to assess and learn from the environment.	4.2(4) 4.1(2,3,4)
• Central to becoming strategy focused is *the ability to identify and develop an organization's core competencies* and/or competitive advantage(s). Any factor that differentiates an organization in the marketplace is a potential filter for screening relevant organizational opportunities.	P1a(2)
• Every organization (and team) must have the *ability to define a clear purpose* or mission statement. A mission statement describes why the organization exists. In parallel, a team must be able to define a desired future state (or vision statement) which engages a broad base of team members and guides key stakeholders.	

Introduction

TABLE 1.3 – ORGANIZATIONAL STRATEGIC MANAGEMENT COMPETENCIES REQUIRED	
• Leadership and management teams must be **able to identify, evaluate, and select one or more organizational goals**, a targeted set of high-altitude strategies and a balanced set of objectives. They must be able to align the operating model to the strategy and adapt as learning occurs and performance is managed.	2.2(5)
• Across the team there must be an **ability to practice a disciplined approach to selecting the right performance measures**, along with setting targets and time frames for measuring and reporting results.	2.1(5)
• Any team must be able to assess and **select the right strategic initiatives** to focus on. Far too often organizations try to do too much with too few resources. Selecting and prioritizing are critical competencies any team must possess.	
• Being able to **work as a team within a disciplined execution methodology** is central to success. Execution requires sustained effort and an ability to learn quickly and agilely adjust.	2.2
• Leaders, managers, and other team members must have **the ability to govern strategy by facilitating engagement** of key stakeholders in teamwork and in creating a culture focused on execution of strategy.	

The key competency required of a strategic planning and management professional is an **ability to design and develop flexible processes** any comprehensive strategic management system requires. Focusing initially on process management has its advantages. Since most strategic processes reside either at the organizational or cross-functional level, they foster the development of teamwork and an organizational perspective—while at the same time focusing on the detail of the processes being developed.

Table 1.4 provides a format for summarizing this assessment. The entries included here are for illustrative purposes only. Each organization will have its own unique profile of these and similar capabilities.

TABLE 1.4: ASSESSMENT OF FACTORS INFLUENCING THE LEADERSHIP CAPABILITY

Leadership and process capabilities	Comments on the status of the capability	Impact on a successful strategic management system
Board of Directors	Some members are experienced in strategic management processes.	To be effective a common nomenclature and process will need to be defined.
Executive Management	Owners and marketing manager closely control all management activities.	Executive education in strategic management is a top start-up prerequisite.
Middle Management	Little evidence of teamwork, silo management prevails.	All middle management requires functional strategic management education.
- Financial	Limited to budgeting and accounting duties.	Needs to develop financial strategic management capability.

Leadership and process capabilities	Comments on the status of the capability	Impact on a successful strategic management system
- Marketing	Dominate and most influential.	Needs to limit authority and power in non-marketing activities.
- Operations	Focused on new product development; operations management a secondary consideration.	Needs direct top management link; currently dominated by marketing.
- IT/Digital	Limited to financial and marketing systems development.	Need integration, documentation, control systems.
- HRM	Focused on routine personnel processes; no organized training function.	Not currently a top management concern. Weakest function. Needs integration in top management thinking.
System/Process Design and Development (PDD)	No organized capability for strategic PDD; acceptable PDD limited to accounting systems.	PDD capability will be a priority from the beginning.

The comments listed above are much too cryptic to be very helpful without a thorough understanding of the organization being assessed. However, they are meant to illustrate how the current leadership, management, and process capabilities will impact a strategic management system. *The key challenge is to gather enough information and insight into the current capabilities to develop a realistic plan, followed by gradual development of a competitive and integrated strategic management system* that meets both the needs of the organization and the aspirations of leadership.

2.1(2)

2.2

So far the emphasis on the strategic management direction, management, and system design capabilities does not identify factors that may prove to be even more critical. The next section considers contextual, situational, and unique factors that condition and configure the actual strategic management system.

An Assessment of the Contextual, Situational, and Unique Features that Currently Exist in the Organization Including a Clarification of the Leadership Team's "Felt" Versus "Actual" Need

Leaders, managers, strategic planning and management consultants, and advisors can easily overlook idiosyncratic factors that constrain, facilitate, or otherwise influence the strategic management decisions and actions of an organization. These are factors only the organization's leadership team can identify, since they alone have the knowledge and experience to develop a system designed to match the aspirations and resources of the organization.

Every leadership team needs to address the following and similar questions that, in answering them, will inform and influence how they go about strategic management in their organization. The relevance of

Introduction

these questions will vary greatly, depending on the unique circumstances in each organization. The objective is to find those key factors that will have significant impact.

- To what extent do the board and management understand the need for strategic management, its benefits, and the commitment and resources required to undertake and maintain a strategy-aligned approach to managing their organization?
- Is there a widely shared perception of the need for strategic management in the organization?
- Is there a widely shared desire to initiate a strategic management system, and, if not, what are the major concerns of the naysayers?
- Are there significant strengths and/or weaknesses in either the board, management, or staff skills and capabilities that will facilitate/impede a strategic system?
- Are there immediate or impending performance problems that must be addressed before any significant changes are made in the managerial system now in place?
- Are there key board members, managers and/or stakeholders (that is, unions, funders, regulators, stockholders, customers, other stakeholders) that have the power/influence to facilitate/impede a strategic management development system?
- *Has the organization undergone any major changes* and/or challenges that will significantly alter the functioning of a strategic management system, that is, a strike; merger/acquisition; loss of (or change in) leadership, a key manager, or staff member; loss of a key customer; or even loss of a key funding source?   2.1(2)
- What organizational features will impact the system such as multi-site locations, a highly centralized/decentralized organization structure, or a "one-man show?"
- What is the level of acceptance/resistance to managerial and organizational changes?
- Are there any impending or anticipated events/trends in the organization's environment that will impact a strategic management system, such as recession, a credit crunch, loss of a major customer, *entrance of a new competitor*, lacking   P.2a(2) multicultural inclusion, loss of a key supplier, a pandemic or geopolitical conflict?
- Are there any high priority problems not yet mentioned that currently occupy leadership's attention? If so, how longstanding is the problem? Is it a problem that can be leveraged as a starting point for a strategic management system?

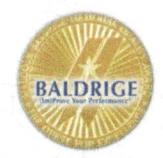

Only the significant factors need to be included in summary form as shown in Table 1.5. The entries included, as in the above assessments, are both illustrative and typical. Each organization will have its own unique profile. Here's an example:

TABLE 1.5: INITIAL ASSESSMENT OF CURRENT STRATEGIC MANAGEMENT CAPABILITIES

Factors to consider in designing a strategic management system	Comments on the status	Impact on a successful strategic management system
Management Posture		
Perceptions/attitudes	Realize must change, not sure of what to do.	Requires extensive emphasis on basic management.
Skills/competencies	Seeing new market opportunities.	May be able to use this competency to motivate development.
Performance	Few effective performance measures and controls.	A priority that could begin immediately with operational measures and controls.
Preferences/positions	Until recently, satisfied with slow growth and few changes.	Need to have specific reasons for each change. Need to have examples from other situations.
Availability	No major bottlenecks.	Good possibility of forming teams.
Organization design/development (ODD)	Recently established a new supplier system.	Need to emphasize horizontal relationships and minimize silo management.
Organization culture	Craft unions probably will resist.	Need clear agreement on conditions, and rates of change.
External Factors		
Economic conditions	Sector maturity.	Probably will require focus on cost savings, productivity, new products.
Competitive factors	International competition growing.	Explore international opportunities.
Supply network and service factors	Seeking new supplier.	Consider outsourcing and supplier consolidation.
Market conditions	Increasing price comp & customer demands.	Review customer service systems and processes.
Situation-Specific Factors		
High priority problems	Recent manufacturing acquisition focus of top management.	May require a rescheduling of a startup system or a scaling back of strategic startup activities.

Supply Network

Factors to consider in designing a strategic management system	Comments on the status	Impact on a successful strategic management system
Stakeholder positions	Family owner will stay in control.	Success hinges on how to work with the family without compromising focus.
Financial resources	Solvent but limited funding for new projects.	Need to develop strategic alternatives that require low or modest financial requirements. Projects must have quantifiable payback.

The comments in Table 1.5 are only meant to illustrate how current leadership and process capabilities will impact a strategic management system. As contextual, situational, and unique factors they will vary in their incidence and impact. At this point, the initial data and information collected, along with the insights and observations made by these individuals, should provide a good estimate of the status of the organization with respect to the overall strategic direction, strategic competencies, organizational capability, and strategic agility.

Toward the end of this task, a clear understanding should form within the leadership team of what their stated needs are versus what their actual needs appear to be. Why? Sometimes leaders focus too much attention on symptoms rather than root causes. A strategic planning and management professional's role and responsibility is to understand and manage this dynamic to help leaders differentiate between felt need and actual need.

Take time to explore each of these questions.

- Does the leadership team have a track record of effectively leading, managing, and executing strategy?
- Is there someone internally skilled enough to provide ongoing leadership to the strategy management system?
- What are the contextual and situational factors to consider?
- Is there a culture grounded in knowledge sharing and ongoing learning?
- What resources are available to effect change?

The focus now turns to consensus building on the current situation with respect to strategy, strategic management, organization capabilities, and need for agility. Once consensus is achieved by management regarding these assessments, they will become the basis for determining the scope and extent of the strategic system to be undertaken.

Strategy in the 21st Century, Second Edition

Task 1.2 – Design and Organize a Program Based on These Assessments

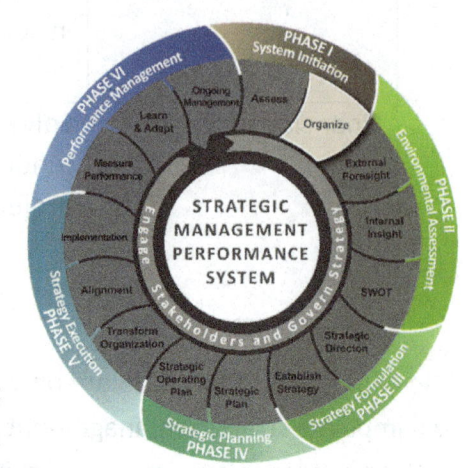

Sponsors of strategy development systems/processes and key stakeholders generally have a good idea of what they want to design and organize. However, expectations will not be the same for all involved. Strategy practitioners must listen and probe to clearly identify what these desired changes are and how they may differ across various stakeholders.

The preceding assessments and leadership discussions will shape the features of the startup initiative and ongoing activities in the strategic management system. There is no "standard approach" to kicking off a strategic management system, but the assessment work should yield enough information to design and organize a system that meets the expectations of the leadership team and organization. In all cases, the focus should be on designing a team-based approach that moves the system forward.

Do not rush through this task. Make sure top-level commitment is in place. Think carefully about *who should be on the core planning team and who should be recruited to give input into the system from outside the organization. Design a planning process* and use tools that will fit the needs of the organization and match the expectations of key leaders.

2.1(1)

Just because a leadership team wishes to have a strategy-focused organization does not mean it will happen. Change of this magnitude takes commitment to allocate the necessary time and resources in both the creation and execution of the strategy.

Any professional supporting a strategic planning and management system should *deliberately assess resource availability from the beginning*. Assessing resources is essential for designing a system that will meet the actual needs of the organization. This includes the financial resources necessary to develop an effective strategic plan along with commitment to invest in the strategic initiatives required to affect change.

2.2(3)

2.2(4)

Design the Scope of the System

While the strategic system of each organization will have its own unique and distinctive features, it is wise to first determine the level and scope of the system and then to modify it to meet the needs of the leadership team and the organization.

Build on the good work done earlier in Phase I. The level and scope of the initial system should reflect the best use of management capabilities and, equally important, leadership preferences on how to initiate strategic management activities — regardless of the ultimate level and scope of the strategic management system aspired to and eventually realized. (See Figure 1.6.)

FIGURE 1.6: SCOPE OF THE STRATEGIC MANAGEMENT SYSTEM[47]

Strategic Management System Component	Developed	Partially Developed (Needs Work)	To be Developed	Time Frame
Environmental Assessment (External Foresight & Internal Insight)		✓		Q1
SWOT Analysis			✓	Early Q2
Core Competencies / Competitive Advantage	✓			Revalidate in Early Q2
Vision / Mission / Core Values	✓			Revalidate in Q2
High Level Goals (Strategic Results)		✓		Q2
Stakeholder Value Propositions (Customer, Partner, Owner, and Employees)			✓	Late Q2 & Q3
High Level Strategies			✓	Q3
Perspectives (e.g., Balanced Scorecard)		✓		Q3
Strategic Objectives			✓	Q3
Strategy Map			✓	Q3
Key Performance Indicators and Targets		✓		Q3 and Q4
Prioritized Strategic Initiatives			✓	Q3 and Q4
Communications and Change Management Plan			✓	Q1 – Q4
KPI Data Collection and Reporting (Automation)			✓	Q4
Implementation, Cascading, and OKRs			✓	Q4
Strategy Management and Budgeting Calendar			✓	Q4

In this case most components need to be refined or created. In different situations a number of elements might require little or no attention.

Understand Expectations of the Leadership Team

In any strategic effort, vigilant attention must be paid to the expectations and goals of the sponsor(s) of the proposed strategic planning system. These expectations and goals are best determined by meeting with the sponsor(s) to explore the reasons behind launching the effort. Careful listening and probing are essential to identifying these goals and expectations.

Sponsors of strategy development processes (ultimately a system) and *key stakeholders* generally have a good idea of how they want to improve the organization. However, their expectations for what should change will likely differ. Strategy practitioners must *listen and probe to clearly identify* what these desired changes are and how they differ across sponsors and stakeholders.

3.1 (1)

Understand Critical Strategic Issues

Understand what the sponsor(s) believe are the critical strategic issues to be addressed. Issues highlighted by the sponsor(s) may ultimately be determined to be symptoms rather than root causes. Careful listening and probing are essential to identifying critical strategic issues including the

---

[47] Modified with permission - https://balancedscorecard.org/

organizational culture [48] along with drivers, pressures, and factors causing the planning process to be launched. Gain a base understanding about the direction of the organization, its strategy for success, and its priorities.

A helpful method for initially exploring critical issues is to selectively use the "5 Whys" analysis technique in which the facilitator repeatedly asks, "why?" in response to a specific leadership concern. This technique was developed in the 1930's and popularized by Sakichi Toyoda,[49] the Japanese industrialist, inventor, and founder of Toyota Industries. It became popular in the 1970s, and Toyota, to this day, still uses it to solve problems. The concept is simple: By repeating the question "why" five or more times, the nature of the problem, as well as its solution, becomes progressively clearer.

Remember to note significant differences in perceptions among senior leadership and identify problems and/or issues that could sidetrack the leadership team's interest and commitment to the strategy system.

Modify Design Features

These preliminary insights always require further adjustment to the contextual, situational, and unique factors that *modify the direction and types of strategies that the organization is able to pursue effectively*. Many of the observations and comments made in the assessments above translate directly into design features. Others are implicit in leadership attitudes, preferences, and capabilities.

2.2(7)

In all cases, the key task is to determine what the leadership team wants, is capable of, and needs to do to launch a strategic management system. The following design modifications are illustrative of decisions to be made, but certainly not exhaustive:

- Desired level of development
- Desired scope and rate of development
- Development priorities
- Strategy preferences
- Strategy deployment potential at the functional level
- Strategic projects currently underway
- *Acceptable risk level* of new strategies
- Acceptable scope and rate of change
- Expected benefits and outcomes
- Profile of the initial strategic management team
- Resource requirements and availability of management and staff
- Education and training capabilities and requirements
- Perceived need for outside assistance

4.2(6)

---

[48] IASP BOK 3.0, 5.1.2 Organizational culture defined, p 95.
[49] https://www.toyota-industries.com/company/history/toyoda_sakichi/

- Time horizon
- Initial schedule for the first quarter of the system
- Expanded schedule for the first year of the system
- Key leverage point(s)
- Cost estimates

Organize the System

This task includes several subtasks that must be accomplished before an organization can undertake any significant effort to develop strategy as outlined earlier. Where the previous task was focused on the assessment process to determine *what* should be included in the system, this task refers to *how* the system should be organized to ensure achieving the desired outcomes. The subtasks required to organize the system are the following:

- **Get commitment from the top.** Before effective strategic management can take place, organizational leaders[50] (including the board of directors) must embrace the need for a disciplined approach, *both strategically and operationally*. By accepting this fundamental premise, coupled with the *willingness to allocate the resources (time, skills, and money) necessary* to clarify the direction of the organization and its implementation, a successful effort can be launched.

  2.2(3)
  2.2(4)

  Commitment to the effort must come from all levels of leadership and management since strategic management is an organization-wide responsibility. Before this or, for that matter, any major change system is undertaken, *this commitment must be communicated to all levels* of the organization. It is top management who must take the lead, not only in making this commitment but also in ensuring the commitment is understood and prioritized throughout the organization.

  1.1(2)
  1.1(3)

- **Outline how to organize and manage the system.** Organizations, even ones the same in size performing the same functions, will vary greatly with respect to organizational structure, management authority and responsibilities, degree of specialization, levels of agility, and management style. Therefore, it is only feasible to offer general guidelines and suggestions to organize and manage in a manner that fits the organization while respecting comfort levels and familiar patterns to those involved in the system. It is difficult enough to deal with new tools and concepts without also having to adopt new management styles and systems.

  Based on this organization and management approach, it is important to assign responsibility for various aspects of the strategic management system. Obviously, many members of the leadership team will be involved in all parts of the system; however, as the system progresses, new roles and responsibilities will be identified and need to be assigned. At the end of the strategic planning process (covered in Phase IV), the leadership team may choose to adjust the planning team

---

[50] Leadership - The people who successfully marshal human collaborators to achieve particular ends. IASP BOK 3.0, 5.5.1, p 92

membership to best monitor execution of the plan and refine the strategic management system on an ongoing basis.

At this point, the following determinations should be made:

- **Define the planning horizon.** The planning horizon is the period of time covered by a strategic plan. Sometimes it is referred to as the organization's planning cycle. In general, the length of time is influenced by the degree of uncertainty in the external environment: the higher the uncertainty…the shorter the planning horizon. For most organizations the time horizon is 3 to 5 years. *The planning horizon can also be defined based on the pace an organization needs to change* to deliver customers economic and/or system value. Finally, it can be dictated by an organization's "strategy cadence" which takes its cue from the operating environment it finds itself in. In some operating environments change occurs at a snail's pace. In others, change is constant, and agility is critical. (See Figure 1.7)

2.1(1)

FIGURE 1.7: DEFINE THE STRATEGIC PLANNING HORIZON

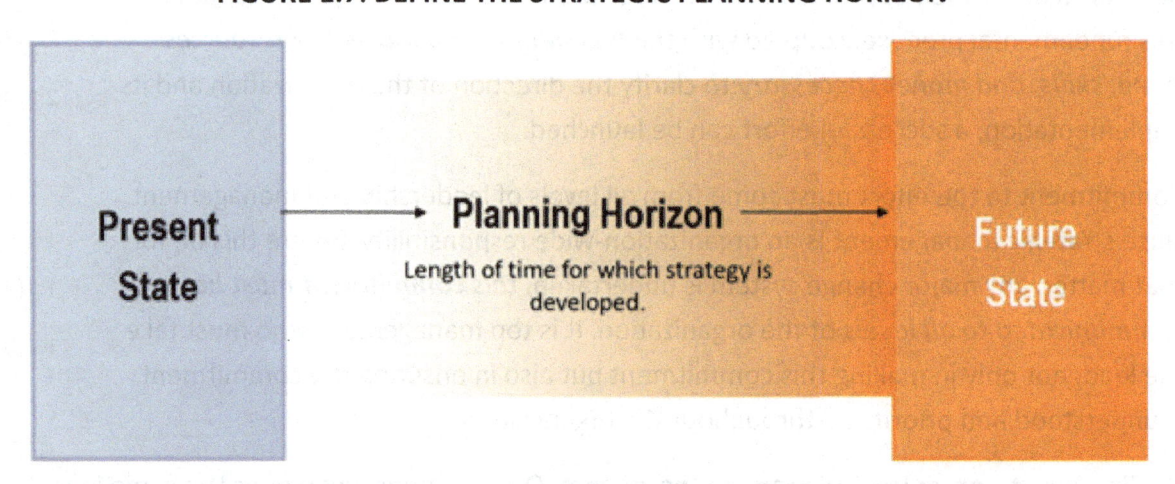

Present State → Planning Horizon (Length of time for which strategy is developed.) → Future State

- **A strategy development champion should be selected.** This is usually a senior member of the management team, but it could also be a board member, the owner, the founder, or in some cases an outsider brought in to set a new strategic direction. Within the last two decades, larger organizations have introduced a Chief Strategy Officer role. This "C-suite" executive typically reports directly to the CEO and is responsible for the entirety of the strategy management system. Today other roles are being defined included Chief Transformation Officer and Chief Execution Officer.

- **A core strategic management leadership team** should be carefully identified and recruited to provide stakeholder representation, guidance, motivation, and continuous monitoring and evaluation. *This "team-oriented" working committee* should remain engaged for the duration of the strategy "formulation" and "planning" phases of the system. Depending on the nature and culture of the organization, the strategic management leadership team should consist of board members, executive managers, strategic business/program unit managers, and

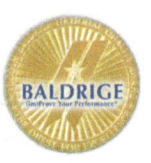

2.1(1)

functional managers, including areas such as marketing, finance, operations, human resources, and information systems in business organizations. In other types of organizations, such as government agencies, nonprofit organizations, and associations, the main functional areas may be different. In general, a core planning team of 8-15 individuals is recommended.

Each major functional area should be represented on the strategic management team. This is true even where few changes in strategy in an area are contemplated. As members of top management, functional managers have a major responsibility for organization-wide strategic management.

- **An extended group** can also be included depending on the organization. These extended team members can include the following:
  - **Strategy analysts**—Many organizations have staff analysts—perhaps not full-time strategy analysts but nevertheless analysts who can carry out the analyses required in this system. They should be a part of the planning team because they will be better able to conduct studies without a lot of time spent in "getting up to speed." Also, as they gather more information, they become a valuable strategic management resource.
  - **Relevant specialists**—At times strategy development requires the expertise of specialists that were not identified or anticipated at the outset. This is especially important in high-tech and digital transformation areas and when making decisions about entering new global markets. These industry experts can come from within the organization or from the outside. They need not become permanent members of the planning team but only participate so long as their expertise is required.
  - **Customers/members** – While there are many voices to which a strategic management team must listen, it is the voice of the customer that is most important to the organization and what the organization should focus on. Clearly customer input must be balanced against the voices of the organization's governance and employees, but it is still the dominant voice.
  - **Other stakeholders**—Input from individuals and/or organizations that have a significant impact on, or are influenced by, the organization can also be included in the process. They may include employees, customers, strategic partners, suppliers, major shareholders, investors, and funding bodies. Whether or not they should be members of the strategic management team is a judgment call made by each organization.
  - **Outside consultants and advisors**—Consultants brought in specifically for this study should become members of the strategic management team.

Below is a representative example of a "core" and "extended" planning team (see Figure 1.8):

Strategy in the 21st Century, Second Edition

FIGURE 1.8: CORE AND EXTENDED PLANNING TEAM

- Ideal size: 8-15
- Consisting of board members, executive leaders and senior managers
- Responsible for leading and guiding the strategic planning process

Core Strategic Planning Team

Extended Strategic Planning Team

- Ideal size: 10-50
- Consisting of key staff, customer representatives, industry experts and other stakeholders
- Responsible for providing input to environmental scan

You may recruit outside experts to accelerate the process

- **Define a process that fits the needs of the organization.** One size does not fit every situation. *Design a planning process that fits* the needs of the organization and the expectations of key leaders. (See Figure 1.9)

2.1(1)

FIGURE 1.9: EXAMPLE OF AN ORGANIZATION'S PLANNING PROCESS

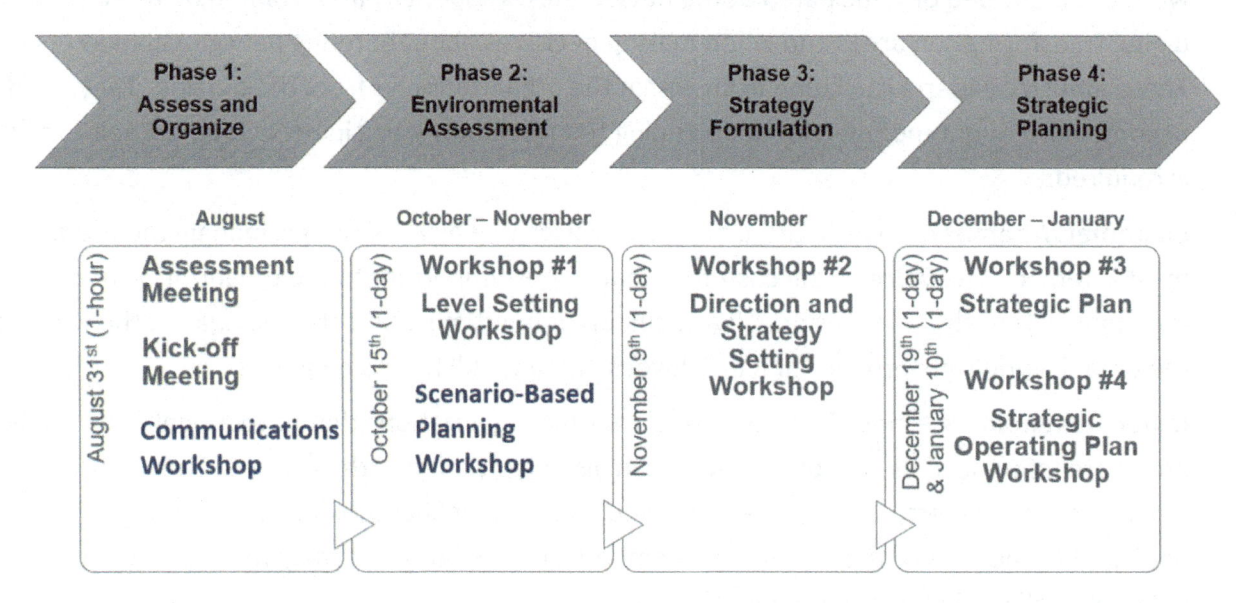

Phase 1: Assess and Organize → Phase 2: Environmental Assessment → Phase 3: Strategy Formulation → Phase 4: Strategic Planning

August	October – November	November	December – January
August 31st (1-hour)	October 15th (1-day)	November 9th (1-day)	December 19th (1-day) & January 10th (1-day)
Assessment Meeting	Workshop #1 Level Setting Workshop	Workshop #2 Direction and Strategy Setting Workshop	Workshop #3 Strategic Plan
Kick-off Meeting			
Communications Workshop	Scenario-Based Planning Workshop		Workshop #4 Strategic Operating Plan Workshop

Figure 1.9 depicts a small-scale planning process. That said, organizations vary greatly with respect to size, complexity, organization structures, management authority and responsibilities, degree of specialization, style of managing, and so forth. Take time to carefully organize the process to meet the specific needs of the organization you are serving.

Also, be sure to use conceptual models (such as those covered in the introduction) and tools that fit the situation. (See Figure 1.10.)

Introduction

FIGURE 1.10: SAMPLE CONCEPTUAL MODELS/FRAMEWORKS

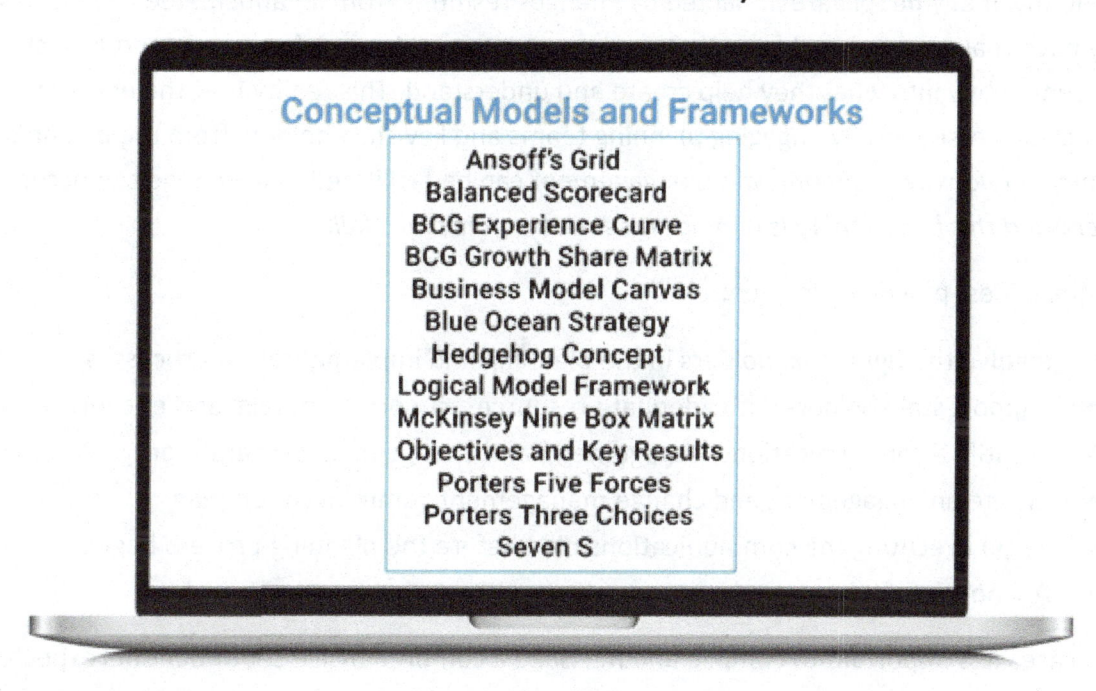

Conceptual Models and Frameworks

- Ansoff's Grid
- Balanced Scorecard
- BCG Experience Curve
- BCG Growth Share Matrix
- Business Model Canvas
- Blue Ocean Strategy
- Hedgehog Concept
- Logical Model Framework
- McKinsey Nine Box Matrix
- Objectives and Key Results
- Porters Five Forces
- Porters Three Choices
- Seven S

The key for strategy professionals is to be proficient in a wide range of strategic planning and management tools/frameworks and only use those that align with the needs of your client/customer/team. *For a broader look at the tools and frameworks currently being used, see IASP's Body of Knowledge 3.0.*

- **Design a Preliminary Communications Plan**

It is important to think through, implement, and *regularly update an engaging stakeholder communications plan especially if the change required centers on the organization's culture*. Culture change is one of the most difficult and complex outcomes to achieve; it takes time, patience, and persistence. Strategy professionals should carefully consider and facilitate the deliverables required to be effective in two-way communications. (See Figure 1.11.)

BALDRIGE

2.2(2)

FIGURE 1.11: PRELIMINARY TWO-WAY COMMUNICATIONS PLANNING

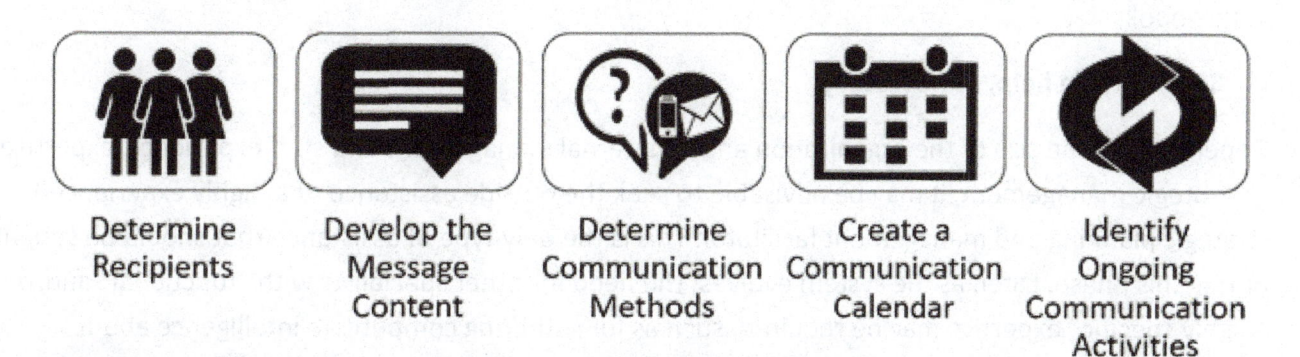

| Determine Recipients | Develop the Message Content | Determine Communication Methods | Create a Communication Calendar | Identify Ongoing Communication Activities |

(Two-way communications required)

75

Frequently, many people are impacted by changes resulting from an anticipated change in strategy. They have real concerns and fears that are important to address. A fundamental rule in strategy is that people buy into what they help create and understand. This reality is at the heart of our work as strategy professionals. By engaging planning teams and key stakeholders from the beginning of the journey in two-way communication, engagement can be facilitated, and change can occur. *Failure to understand this basic reality is a major reason strategic plans fail.*

Marquee "best practices" include:

- Involve the right stakeholders in the planning and implementation processes
- Support stakeholders with adequate resources, support, training, and encouragement
- Identify a communications, engagement, and change management team
- Create an engagement and change management communication plan
- Begin executing the communications plan before the planning process begins
- Anchor the change into the organization's culture

In all cases it is important to compile and message a comprehensive set of benefits expected from the system and a list of anticipated concerns to be addressed before the process begins. The team must agree upon and communicate a reasonable work plan that includes a timeline highlighting anticipated report-out events and listening activities.

It is vital to maintain top leadership involvement and participation throughout the development and subsequent execution of the communication plan. This cannot be emphasized too strongly. Determining strategic direction, defining strategy, planning for execution, and implementing strategy throughout all functions and at all levels of the organization remains the primary responsibility of top management. *These realities must be communicated and modeled by leadership.*

Although it depends on the size of the organization, cascading from and contributing to the organization's plan, those divided into strategic "business" or "program" units should have their own integrated strategy development process, communications plan, and execution system. In addition, there needs to be a relationship between each strategic business/program unit and the organization's strategic management leadership team. Our guidance here is to follow and adapt the tasks outlined in this book.

- **Seek outside help, as necessary**

Depending on the size of the organization and its internal management and staff experience/expertise in strategic management, it may be advisable to seek the outside assistance of a highly experienced strategic planning and management facilitator. This is the only type of assistance that should be sought during this phase. Later, as the system evolves, the need for other specialists with "functional" and/or "highly specific" expertise may be required, such as for gathering competitive intelligence about rapidly changing industries, process improvement, privately held businesses, nonprofit governance, or governmental and political nuances.

Introduction

Careful attention to selecting a team manager/facilitator and to forming the system's oversight team is extremely important as the resultant composition of same will determine the system's scope as well as manage expectations. It is critical to keep the scope realistic and achievable. If key members of the leadership team or the professional staff are omitted, the success of the system may fall short of its deliverables. It is all too easy to make assumptions about a function, process, or strategic business/program unit when its key manager(s) is not on the team.

The effort to complete these prerequisite activities will be well-rewarded from the moment the strategic management system is initiated to continuously improve management of the organization. In the next phase, the first strategic management processes are outlined for strategic analysis and evaluation.

In summary, Phase I lays the foundation for the remaining five phases of the Strategic Management Performance System framework. *Before the work of crafting strategy begins,* it is imperative for a leadership team to assess the current strategic direction and organizational capabilities, and then design and organize a start-up system which fits the needs of the organization.

Phase II – Complete an Environmental Assessment

Once the scope of the strategic management process/system has been determined, as outlined in Phase I, the process of strategic management moves into thoughtful analysis and evaluation of the strategic environment facing the organization.

Effective consideration of the strategic landscape is premised on the availability and robust analysis of team and stakeholder input regarding the organization's external and internal environments. From a "best practices" perspective this information should be consolidated and maintained by the strategy professional and continuously made available to the planning team. This is particularly important in today's disrupted operating environment requiring timely decision making and aligned actions.

A leadership team should first engage key stakeholders and collect strategic information and then consolidate it as a "first generation" snapshot of the organization's strategic operating environment. This will give leadership a shared understanding about the nature of the strategic information for the organization. Building on this understanding, the planning team can develop and maintain a repository of information for use in the current and future cycles of the strategic planning and management process.

Three sequenced tasks are required to effectively analyze an organization's environment, as follows:[51]

Task 2.1 – Practice Foresight When Conducting External Strategic Analyses
Task 2.2 – Gain Insight by Conducting Internal Strategic Analyses
Task 2.3 – Evaluate Results of Strategic Analyses

Note: Throughout the book we emphasize the Strategic Management Performance System (SMPS) phases and tasks. While presented in a cyclical model, they are quite dynamic, allowing feedback to other phases or tasks occurring at any time. As described in Phase I, "analysis" and "evaluation" should be separate processes within a strategic management system, in accordance with the following definitions:

> **Analysis of strategic information** refers to the *processing of relevant data and information* into useful information of potential relevance in subsequent tasks in the strategic management process. There are two primary foci to be considered in analyzing strategic information, that is, external information and internal information. This type of information will be made clear in each task.

2.1(3)

---

[51] See ASP BOK 3.0, Key Activities, Sections 2.2.1 and 2.2.2

Strategy in the 21st Century, Second Edition

Evaluation of strategic analyses refers to the *process of comparing the information that has been analyzed in terms of some evaluation criteria*, whether qualitative or quantitative. In this case, it refers to an evaluation of analyses and classifying the results into external opportunities and threats and internal strengths and weaknesses. Further clarification of these bodies of information takes place during the final task in Phase II, i.e., SWOT Analysis.

Task 2.1 – Practice Foresight when Conducting External Strategic Analyses

This critical task focuses exclusively on gathering and analyzing *external* information to gain foresight. Analysis of *internal* information will be covered next. This division of the process is based on a fundamental premise of all organizational strategies: they are contextual. They seek the best fit between an organization and its external environment. Thus, it is most appropriate to mirror this distinction in classifying information.

Many external forces, dynamics, and constraints must be considered to arrive at the most desirable and effective strategy. Analysis begins with a comprehensive understanding of these forces and constraints and how they interact to allow a *strategic direction* to emerge within a specific organizational context. (See Figure 2.1.)

FIGURE 2.1: KEY DIMENSIONS TO THE MACRO-LEVEL ENVIRONMENT [52]

---

[52] Wheelen; *Strategic Management Business Policy*; © 1986, pgs. 79, 93. Reprinted with permission of Pearson Education, Inc., Upper Saddle, NJ 07458.

Phase II – Complete an Environmental Assessment

We begin by breaking the external analysis into two parts: a macro-analysis (global/domestic level) and a micro-analysis (industry/organizational level).[53]

There is no standard format for making these analyses since organizations vary in the type and level of information that are significant to their needs. However, several recurrent dimensions at both levels have been found useful in most organizations.

The following lists will serve as a guide for the macro-level forces. In time, the leadership of each organization will be able to develop a more focused list, adding and deleting forces as they are determined to be relevant. A discussion of micro-level analysis follows this section.

Macro-Level Analysis

Macroenvironment forces can be conveniently considered in terms of global, domestic, and sometimes even local, broad-based trends that impact and/or influence the overall performance of the organization. In this regard it is useful to distinguish between current, short-term, urgent impacts and/or influences and future, long- or medium-term trends and their cumulative impacts.

Many factors in the macro-environment affect management decisions on strategies to pursue to satisfy customers and stakeholders, including existing, structural, and newly emerging trends along with weak signals at work in any organization's external operating environment. A major role of the leadership team and strategy professional is to engage key stakeholders to capture and process this critical information. A "traditional approach" to macro-analysis is sometimes referred to as a PESTLE or STEEPLE analysis.

The history of PESTLE Analysis is vague. Francis Aguilar, an American scholar whose expertise was in strategic planning, is often given credit. In the late 1960s, he published a book titled *Scanning the Business Environment* in which the PESTLE tool was first identified.[54] A STEEPLE analysis is a variant of this very popular and simple method for analysis of an organization's external environment. (See Figure 2.2.)

---

[53] *Guide to the Strategic Planning and Strategic Management Body of Knowledge*, (2nd ed) (BOK 2.0), IASP, 2015.
[54] Aguilar, F.J. *Scanning the Business Environment*, The Macmillan Company, 1967.
https://www.researchgate.net/publication/26387525_Scanning_The_Business_Environment_For_Information_a_Grounded_Theory_approach

FIGURE 2.2: COMPARISON OF PESTLE AND STEEPLE

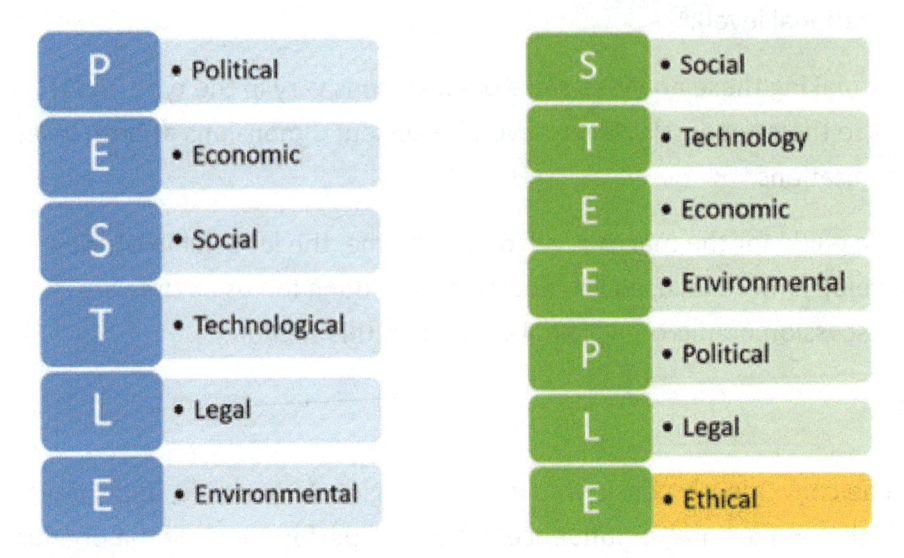

PESTLE	STEEPLE
P • Political	S • Social
E • Economic	T • Technology
S • Social	E • Economic
T • Technological	E • Environmental
L • Legal	P • Political
E • Environmental	L • Legal
	E • Ethical

Table 2.1 summarizes the *key dimensions* in the Macro-level environment linked to relevant topics and questions to consider within each STEEPLE dimension.

2.1(3)

TABLE 2.1 – KEY DIMENSIONS OF THE MACRO-LEVEL ENVIRONMENT

• **Social and cultural forces** What social and cultural trends are driving change in your sector, market, and organization?
    o Changes in how and where people work
    o Online learning and technology in education
    o Demographic changes
    o Racial and ethnic disparities
    o Generational differences and issues
    o Changing class structure
    o Ethnic and religious factors
    o Enclave cultures within a mainstream culture
    o Necessary vs. discretionary spending patterns
    o Shifting lifestyles
    o Changing work patterns, attitudes, and behaviors
    o Regional and local differences in all of the preceding factors
    o Immigration patterns
    o Educational issues
    o Healthcare issues
    o Security and safety issues
• **Technological and scientific forces** What trends in technology and science are driving change in your sector, market, and organization?
    o Cybersecurity implications for an increasingly digital world
    o Evolving health technologies

TABLE 2.1 – KEY DIMENSIONS OF THE MACRO-LEVEL ENVIRONMENT
<ul><li>o Science, emerging technologies, and the innovation economy (e.g., AI, Synthetic biology, and Nanotechnology)</li><li>o Information and communication technology</li><li>o Commercial "E-commerce" use of the Internet</li><li>o Consumer use of the Internet</li><li>o Technology licensing and patents</li><li>o Intellectual property issues</li><li>o National research and development expenditures</li><li>o National rates of innovation and patent production</li><li>o Technology legislation</li><li>o Manufacturing infrastructure</li><li>o Science and engineering issues</li></ul><ul><li>**Economic forces** What economic trends are driving change in your sector, market, and organization?<ul><li>o Workforce</li><li>o Fiscal stability and debt</li><li>o Global supply chains</li><li>o Home country economic situation and trends</li><li>o Taxation regulations (general and product specific)</li><li>o Seasonality and climate factors</li><li>o Market, product, and trade cycles</li><li>o Exodus of industries and services</li><li>o Energy issues</li><li>o International economic situation and trends</li><li>o International trade financing and distribution infrastructure</li><li>o Interest and exchange rates</li><li>o Trade and monetary issues</li><li>o Banking stability</li></ul></li><li>**Environmental forces** What environmental trends are driving change in your sector, market, and organization?<ul><li>o Environmental policies, legislation, and regulations</li><li>o Tracking, reporting, and managing carbon.</li><li>o Sustainable development movement</li><li>o Impact of biological species</li><li>o Impact of global warming</li><li>o Changing climate patterns</li><li>o Climate migration</li><li>o Home country national, regional, state, and local level environmental issues</li></ul></li></ul>

TABLE 2.1 – KEY DIMENSIONS OF THE MACRO-LEVEL ENVIRONMENT

- o International environmental issues
- o Public awareness concerning environmental issues
- o Industry/sector pollution impact and control
- o Pollution control technology
- o Energy consumption/environmental impact relationships
- o Development patterns vs. nature preservation
- o Catastrophic viral or biological events (endemic/pandemic)
- **Political forces** What political trends are driving change in your sector, market, and organization?
    - o Misinformation, and disinformation, e.g., a false flag
    - o Political division
    - o Global and domestic threats, e.g., war, terrorism, conflict
    - o Geopolitics
    - o Change in administrations
    - o Pending home country legislation/regulations
    - o International, regional, bilateral agreements
    - o Future legislation
    - o Government policies, e.g., climate change, labor, trade, subsidies, safety, health care, immigration, etc.
    - o Government funding, grants, and contracts
    - o Lobbying and advocacy groups
- **Legal forces** What legal trends are driving changes in your sector, market, and organization?
    - o Zoning laws
    - o Health and safety laws
    - o Civil rights laws (discrimination)
    - o Employment laws
    - o Intellectual property laws
    - o Consumer protection laws
    - o Privacy and data protection laws
    - o Antitrust laws
    - o Banking laws
    - o Tax laws
    - o Industry-specific regulations
- **Ethical forces** What ethical forces are driving changes in your sector, market, and organization?
    - o Ethical issues and corporate social responsibility
    - o Expectations of stakeholders regarding social issues
    - o Ethical practices in sales and advertising

TABLE 2.1 – KEY DIMENSIONS OF THE MACRO-LEVEL ENVIRONMENT
o Discrimination
o Standards with accounting, management, and marketing
o Attitudes toward honoring copyrights or breaking patents
o Recruitment process and the standards of employment
o Respecting religious and social values of employees, customers, and partners
o Negligence in informing shareholders about company's situation
o Insider trading, hiding information about mergers, acquisitions, and investments
o Consequences of physical and verbal harassment in the workplace
o Avoiding processes and technologies that jeopardize employee and public safety.
o Preferring fair trade products, over low-priced products produced unethically (bad working conditions, low wages, etc.)

Each dimension can be analyzed using *generic* and *specific* questions to prompt team thinking and input. Generic questions relate to all or most dimensions, while specific questions pertain to each dimension or subtopic and are best formulated by members of the organization undertaking the strategic analysis. These questions should be developed and then reviewed by the champion of the strategic management process. Doing so will focus the task of gathering and presenting the information in a useful format.

Examples of generic questions follow:

- How much information is available from core and extended planning team members?
- Which forces (or factors) should receive the greatest attention?
- How sensitive is the organization to changes in a particular force?
- Does it therefore warrant closer scrutiny?
- At the international level, can the focus be narrowed to specific countries of interest?
- At the national level, can the focus be narrowed to states and metropolitan areas of interest?
- What is the rate of change of these forces?
- What is the cost of acquiring this information versus the benefits of its potential use?
- Are there alternative sources for acquiring the information?
- Have the relevant factors been identified within each dimension before beginning the analysis?
- Do any of the forces or factors need to be subdivided or specified in more detail?

Micro-Level Analysis

It is useful to break the micro-level environment analysis of forces and trends into two parts: an "industry" or "sector" analysis and an "organizational" analysis. Industry or sector analysis is a high-level profile that can be made without considering the organization except as a statistical unit in the industry/sector. An organizational level analysis is concerned with the specific external relationships of the organization, including those within the industry/sector that have been profiled.

Strategy in the 21st Century, Second Edition

CUSTOMERS AND OTHER INDUSTRY/SECTOR STAKEHOLDERS

During this level of analysis, the organization clearly defines, understands, and articulates who its primary customers are, and what they need and value from the organization. Stakeholder engagement in understanding existing and potential customers is often the most critical element in developing the insight needed to support complex, strategic decision-making by better understanding market needs, wants, expectations, growth projections, technology, product changes, and the organization's performance, as well as *competitors' plans and performance*.

P.2a(1)

Identifying customers is both a critical and challenging exercise. *Customers are defined as the direct beneficiary of the organization's products or services. Customers can be segmented into "primary" and "secondary" customers.* Primary customers are the subset of customers that the organization is targeting with its strategy. According to IASP, BOK 3.0, Section 2.2.1, "not every customer provides equal benefit to the organization, and, as such, not all potential customers should be specifically targeted." Secondary customers, in turn, are a subset of stakeholders, which include anyone who has an interest, positive or negative, in the outcome of the organization.

3.1(3)

If quality work has already been done to gain understanding from customers, there is no need to start over. Rather, build on what has been done. *Different means exist for collecting input from customers*, including surveys, focus groups, interviews, social media, and AI tools. Each has limitations.

3.1(1)

- A **Survey** is usually conducted online. It can reach the broadest audience, but the response rate is often poorer than other means.

- A **Focus Group** is a form of qualitative research consisting of one or more facilitated group interviews. Group members are asked about their perceptions of a product, organization, or something else of interest in guided or open discussions. The information collected is used to determine the reactions that can be expected from a larger population. A successful focus group study requires time to recruit the best representative group, and an experienced facilitator to guide and document group discussions. Another version of the focus group is a Town Hall or other organizational meeting to which all members of or participants in group are invited to provide input or feedback on a topic. Like a survey, it promotes buy-in to the resulting plan because everyone has been asked for their thoughts.

- An **Interview** is the most effective means to collect input from one or more customers, but not necessarily the most effective means to reach all customer segments. It often requires a significant amount of time and resources to collect a broad set of representative data.

- **Social Media** is a popular means to learn valuable insights into customer experience and how products and services are being used. However, social media is all about interaction, and

Phase II – Complete an Environmental Assessment

customers expect your organization to be standing by, ready to help. It can be difficult to control for organizations who do not have the right processes and capacity in place.

- Use of a **Generative AI tool** is another option. AI tools are available to collect customer and stakeholder input and data. Careful monitoring and diligent review of outputs are required.

Additionally, it is important to *identify, engage, listen to, communicate with, and think carefully about each key stakeholder* during this task, i.e., customers, owners, partners, and employees. The goal is to obtain strategic intelligence and actionable insights that serve to inform the strategy formulation processes. This assessment should be done for any stakeholder who has a significant impact on the organization's strategic success. Take time to understand and respect their needs, wants, and expectations.

3.1(1)

COMPETITORS

In parallel, strategic planning and management professionals must ensure due diligence in the competitive environment takes place. Whether competition is direct or indirect, organizations of all types (with few exceptions) face competitive forces. Even public sector entities have factors which, while not "competition" in a traditional sense, are competitive in nature and form an obstacle to future success.[55] Thoughtful leaders will want to define their organization's competitive advantages versus those of its primary competitors. A clear identification of the factor's driving competitiveness is essential to any micro-level analysis. You can begin this analysis by asking questions like these.

- *Who are our competitors?*
- What are their competitive advantages?
- What are our competitive advantages?
- What are the competitive factors?

P.2a(1

Useful for most for-profit companies, and for many mission-driven organizations, are two conceptual models for competitive analysis that are widely accepted and valued. As highlighted in Introduction (See pp 33-37), in 1980 Michael Porter developed his model, **Porter's Five Forces**,[56] in which he applied concepts developed in industrial organization economics to derive five competitive forces that define the attractiveness of a market. (See Figures 0.11 and 2.3 – Coca Cola Example.)

---

[55] See ASP BOK 3.0 Section 2.2.1, Step 3 for a discussion of "Customers in Government and Nonprofit Sectors"
[56] Porter, M.E. *Competitive Strategy: Techniques for Analyzing Industries and Competitors.* New York: Free Press, 1980.

FIGURE 2.3: PORTER'S FIVE FORCES – COCA COLA EXAMPLE

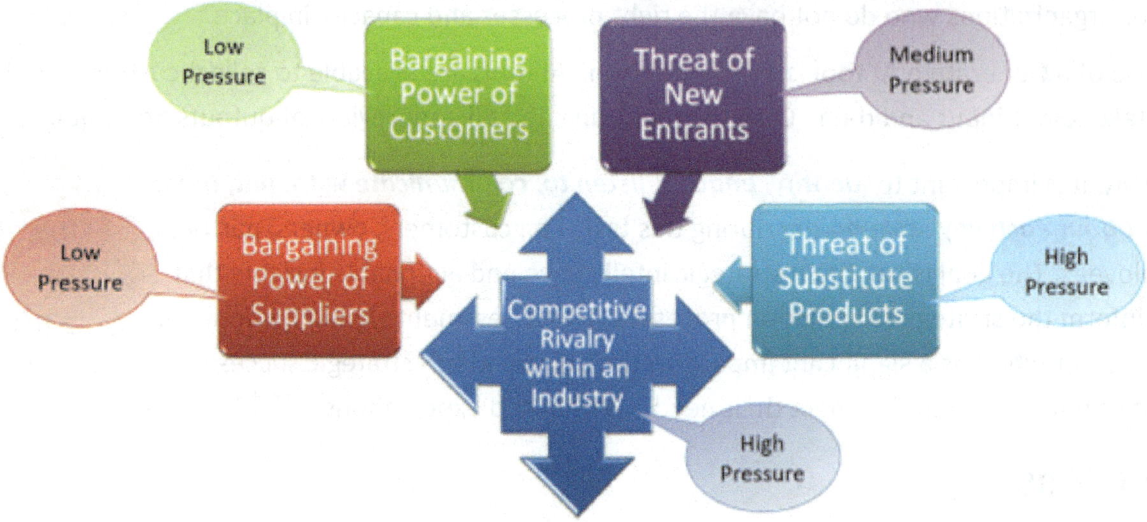
Low Pressure
Bargaining Power of Customers
Threat of New Entrants
Medium Pressure
Low Pressure
Bargaining Power of Suppliers
Competitive Rivalry within an Industry
Threat of Substitute Products
High Pressure
High Pressure

The five forces are:

- The bargaining power of customers
- The bargaining power of suppliers
- The threat of new entrants
- The threat of substitute products
- The level of competition in an industry

Understanding the character of each of these forces gives the necessary insight to allow for the formulation of appropriate strategies in response to competitive market conditions.

In 2005, W. C. Kim and Renee Mauborgne offered the **strategy canvas** as part of their **Blue Ocean Strategy** framework. They stressed that organizations competing in a "Red Ocean" are seeking to outperform their competitors to gain a larger share of the market by aligning organization resources and activities to be the low-cost provider *or* by offering a different value proposition. (See Figure 2.4.)

FIGURE 2.4: RED OCEAN STRATEGY VS. BLUE OCEAN STRATEGY

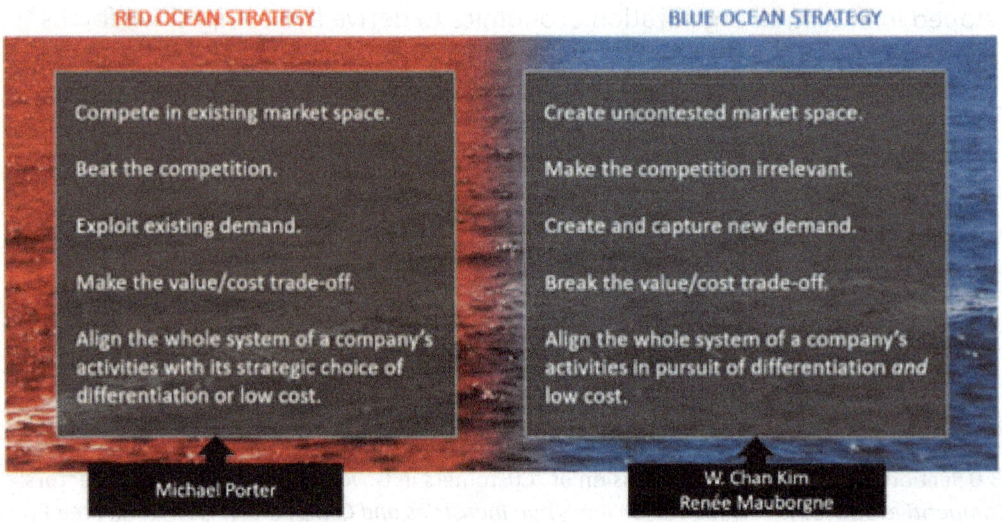
RED OCEAN STRATEGY
BLUE OCEAN STRATEGY
Compete in existing market space.
Beat the competition.
Exploit existing demand.
Make the value/cost trade-off.
Align the whole system of a company's activities with its strategic choice of differentiation or low cost.
Create uncontested market space.
Make the competition irrelevant.
Create and capture new demand.
Break the value/cost trade-off.
Align the whole system of a company's activities in pursuit of differentiation and low cost.
Michael Porter
W. Chan Kim
Renée Mauborgne

Phase II – Complete an Environmental Assessment

On the other hand, organizations seeking to make the competition irrelevant are attempting to *access untapped "Blue Ocean" market space and create new demand*. By aligning all their resources and activities in pursuit of differentiation *and* low cost, the organization aspires to create a Blue Ocean of market opportunity.

A strategy canvas exercise seeks to graphically depict key competitive factors of an ***organization's value proposition to customers, compared to other organizations*** operating in the same market space. A strategy canvas is the central analytic and action structure for identifying and building a Blue Ocean Strategy. (See Figure 2.5 – Medellin example.) [57]

3.1(4)

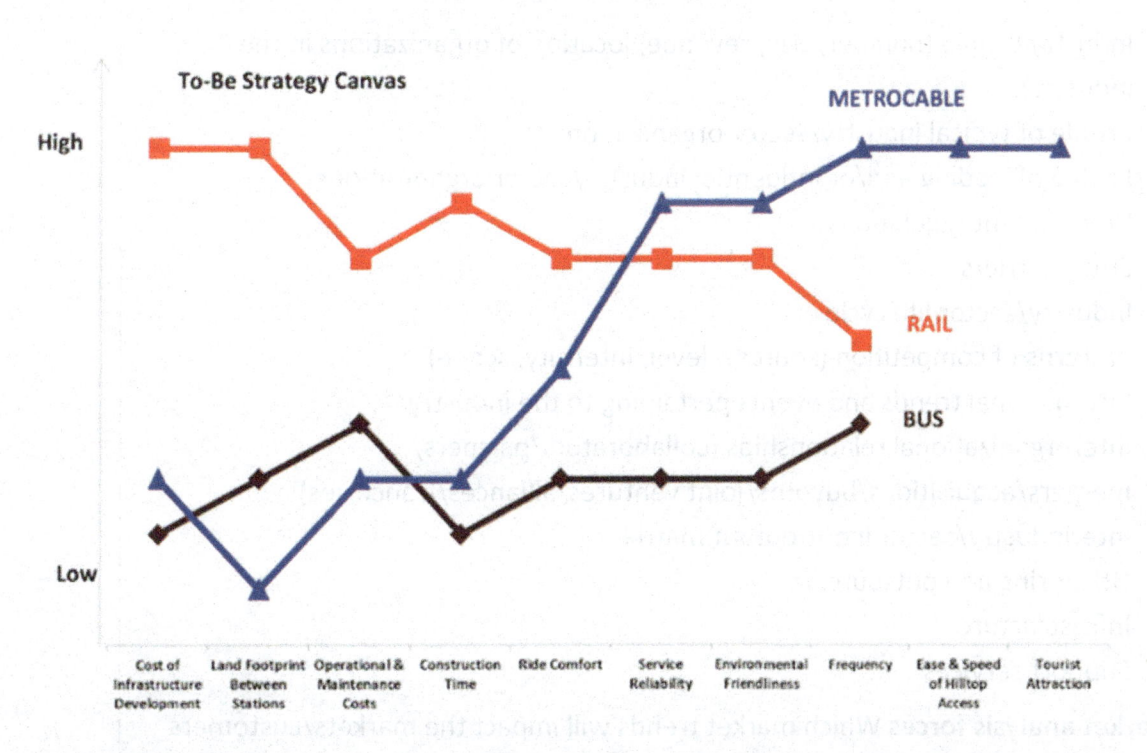

FIGURE 2.5: MEDELLIN EXAMPLE

© Chan Kim & Renée Mauborgne, *Blue Ocean Shift: Beyond Competing – Proven Steps to Inspire Confidence and Seize New Growth.*

In 1991, Colombia's second-largest city, Medellin, had one of the highest homicide rates in the world, averaging 16 murders a day. It was dubbed "Murder Capital of the World." Fast forward to today: The crime rate is 80% lower than it was in 1991 and poverty has dropped by more than 96%. Medellin's "Blue Ocean Strategy" resulted in a metro cable system of transportation, enabling workers to travel to the city center more safely and tourists to explore the city from a novel perspective. It has created a blue ocean of uncontested market space, transforming itself into a model city of innovation.

---

[57] https://www.blueoceanstrategy.com/blog/medellin-from-murder-capital-of-the-world-to-most-innovative-city/

Strategy in the 21st Century, Second Edition

More generally, Table 2.2 summarizes the **key dimensions** in the Micro-level environment with relevant subtopics and micro-level questions to consider.

TABLE 2.2 – KEY DIMENSIONS TO THE MICRO-LEVEL ENVIRONMENT
• **Industry/sector analysis forces** What is the overall state of your industry/sector *and your organization's position relative to competitors* and those who influence the industry/sector?   P.2a(1)   P.2a(2) <ul><li>Products/services<ul><li>Standardized versus customized products/services</li><li>Product life cycles</li><li>Complementary and/or substitute products/services</li></ul></li><li>Industry profile (number, size, revenue, location of organizations in the industry)</li><li>Profile of typical industry/sector organizations</li><li>Profile of leading and/or influential industry/sector organizations</li><li>Government regulations</li><li>Entry barriers</li><li>Industry/sector life cycle</li><li>Patterns of competition (sources, level, intensity, scope)</li><li>International trends and events pertaining to the industry</li><li>Interorganizational relationships (collaborators/partners, mergers/acquisitions/buyouts/joint ventures/alliances/franchises)</li><li>Interindustry/sector input-output matrix</li><li>Offshoring and outsourcing</li><li>Infrastructure</li><li>Support services</li></ul>
• **Market analysis forces** Which market trends will impact the markets/customers we serve and the needs that we fill? <ul><li>Market segmentation and need</li><li>Market niche and need</li><li>Market position</li><li>Market portfolio</li><li>Market life cycle</li></ul>
• **Customer analysis forces** What is the profile of our customer, and what customer needs do we fill? <ul><li>Usage/consumption/service/buying patterns</li><li>Demographics</li><li>Product/service expectations</li></ul>

Phase II – Complete an Environmental Assessment

TABLE 2.2 – KEY DIMENSIONS TO THE MICRO-LEVEL ENVIRONMENT
<ul><li>Changing profiles of current customers.</li><li>Potential new customers</li><li>Business to Business (B2B) versus Business to Customer (B2C)</li></ul>**Competitor analysis forces** What is the profile of our competitors, and what is our competitive advantage?<ul><li>Competitive factors (price, service, unique product/service features)</li><li>Level, type, and intensity of competition among industry members</li><li>Barriers to exit</li><li>Barrier to entry</li><li>Profiles of key current competitors (including competitive advantage)</li><li>Cross-industry competition</li><li>New sources of competition</li><li>Changing competitive forces</li><li>Proximity to customers</li></ul>**Supply chain analysis forces** *What is the nature of our supply chain*, and where are the bottlenecks that need to be addressed?<ul><li>Suppliers</li><li>Distributors</li><li>Strategic partners</li><li>Transportation</li><li>Logistics</li></ul>

P.1b(3)

Micro-level forces and factors can be analyzed from generic and specific perspectives in the same manner as macro-level concerns. Macro-level generic questions (listed earlier) can apply equally well to micro-level factors. Also, from the perspective of a given context, questions will always gain relevance when generated by members of the organization.

SCENARIO-BASED PLANNING TO DRIVE STRATEGIC FORESIGHT

Scenario-based planning is an effective approach to provide foresight to inform the strategic planning process - providing multiple alternative futures to consider, along with traditional approaches of environmental scanning such as interviews, SWOT analysis, focus groups, etc.

Scenario-based planning is a creative way of engaging key stakeholders in evaluating the external environment to gain strategic foresight throughout an organization. By exploring alternative "plausible" futures, then identifying key capabilities required to navigate within and across those possible futures, a collective innovative and agile mindset can be established within an organization.

Strategy in the 21st Century, Second Edition

As noted, scenario-based planning is not about predicting the future but about identifying what can possibly occur (i.e., different scenarios). It explores many possible alternative future outcomes to help organizations identify the capabilities necessary to prepare for an uncertain future. These alternative scenarios incorporate different assumptions about how the environmental factors may be realized. Plausible trends and other assumptions should be documented so alternative scenarios can be reviewed periodically and assumptions re-tested and validated against the evolving situation. (See Figure 2.6.)

FIGURE 2.6: PLANNING FOR INCREASING UNCERTAINTY – CONE OF POSSIBILITIES

Additionally, the output of this approach adds valuable input into the "traditional" environmental analysis and evaluation processes. Strategy practitioners play a major role in facilitating this entire set of processes.

LBL Strategies offers the following scenario-based planning framework in its *Mastering Foresight: Scenario-Based Planning Certification* program (see Figure 2.7):

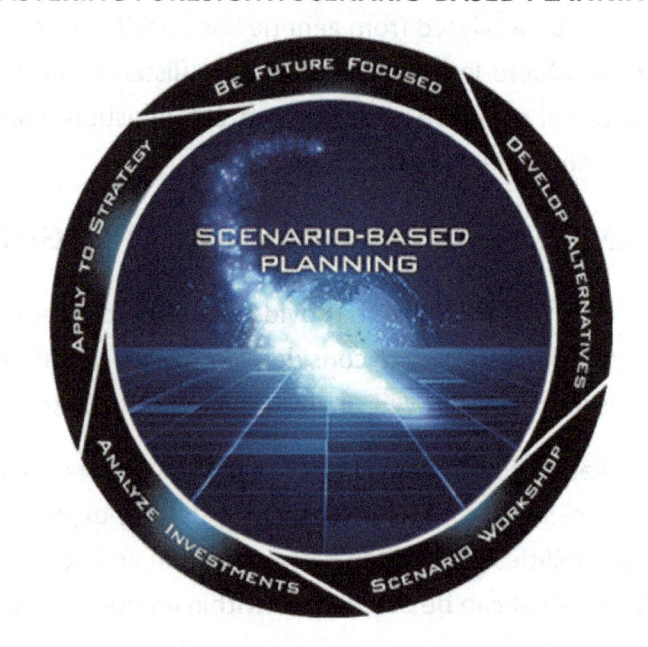

FIGURE 2.7: MASTERING FORESIGHT: SCENARIO-BASED PLANNING FRAMEWORK

Phase II – Complete an Environmental Assessment

Foresight expert Robin Champ offers these remarks about the value of scenario-based planning:[58]

> *"Albert Einstein said the definition of insanity is doing the same thing over and over again and expecting a different result. We can apply the same adage to strategy. If we always use the same input and thought processes when developing strategy, will we really get a different result? How do we prepare ourselves for an uncertain future, when we are often unaware that we are chained to our usual beliefs?*
>
> *A solution widely used by organizations such as Shell oil company, and the United States Coast Guard, is scenario-based planning. This is a tool to exercise strategic foresight, but it is not the same as forecasting. And the difference is an important one. Forecasting is predicting. This is often the track we find ourselves in as organizations. We often pick the most anticipated future, predict what might happen, and plan only around that one event. We tend to use the same subject matter experts, the same background, and the same tools.*
>
> *Contrarily, scenario-based planning as a foresight tool is intended to cast a wide net to the unknown future. It helps us break outside of our conventional thinking, pushing the boundaries of our thought to examine the possible, but not necessarily popular ways the future could unfold. By doing so we accept that the future is inherently uncertain and prepare accordingly. We are not trying to develop one particular future, but rather explore many possible futures so that we are prepared for, as opposed to predicting, what we will need to stay relevant in the years ahead.*
>
> *By pushing boundaries, we expand our thought process, fuel innovation, and stay ahead of our competition. While doing our operations well keeps us relevant today, we require innovation and strategy to keep us relevant tomorrow. I challenge everyone to get truly creative to stay relevant in the future. Scenario-based planning is a proven technique to help embrace uncertainty!"*

Whether an organization chooses to use a more traditional framework such as PESTEL or a less traditional scenario-based planning framework or both, the point is to gain shared insight into the forces at work which will shape the near- and long-term future of the organization.

The importance of this task cannot be overemphasized. When leaders hold differing points of view on the external factors influencing their organization, effective strategic planning and management is impossible. A leadership team that has attained shared insight on the forces that will shape the organization's future has taken a major step toward achieving its goals. This time investment enables the team to build its strategy based on a shared understanding of the external environment.

---

[58] Robin Champ is VP of Strategic Foresight with LBL Strategies and is the lead instructor for LBL Strategies' Mastering Foresight: Scenario-Based Planning Certification program. See https://www.lblstrategies.com/scenario-based-planning-bootcamp/

Strategy in the 21st Century, Second Edition

Task 2.2 – Gain Insight by Conducting Internal Strategic Analyses

This task builds on the assessment of strategic direction in Phase I.

It is time to collaborate with key stakeholders to develop a comprehensive understanding of and insight on the organization's internal capabilities and gaps as they relate to current performance and, ultimately, to the achievement of the anticipated new strategy.[59]

To guide this analysis, understanding how internal analysis fits within the environmental assessment, foresight building, and strategy-setting framework is important. (See Figure 2.8.)

FIGURE 2.8: FRAMEWORK FOR INTERNAL ANALYSIS[60]

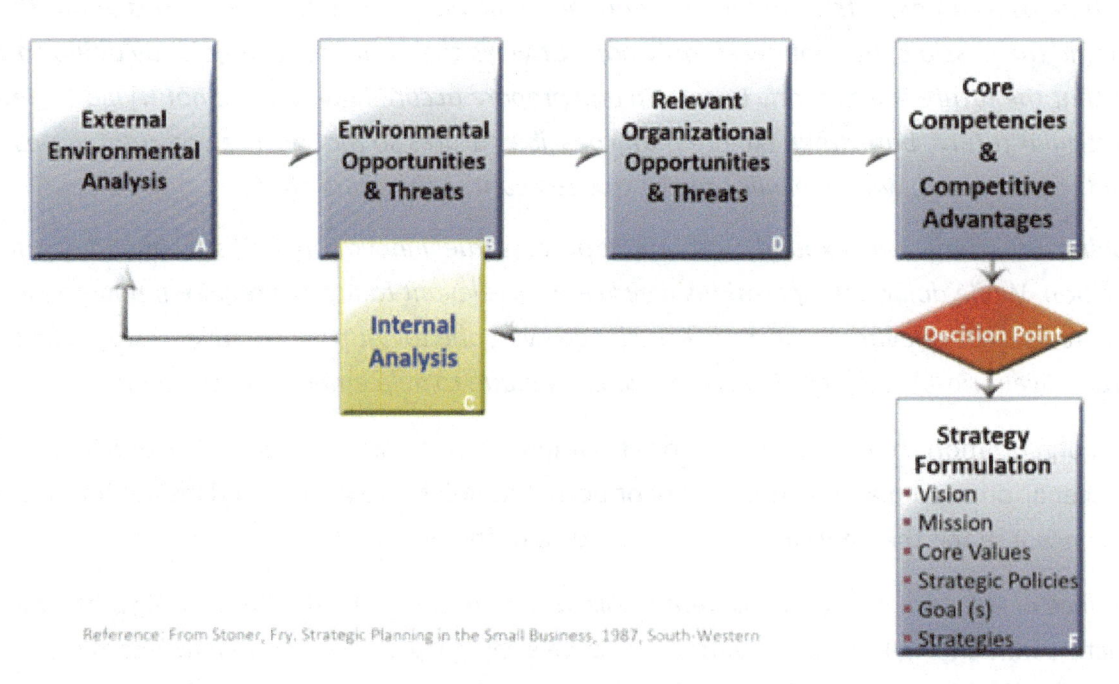

Reference: From Stoner, Fry. *Strategic Planning in the Small Business*, 1987, South-Western

Internal forces, dynamics, and constraints must be considered to arrive at the most desirable and effective strategy. Many of these forces are detailed in *Table 2.3 – Key Components of the Internal Dimension*. Each of these forces should be given the appropriate level of consideration.

Of particular importance is for the strategy professional to enable key stakeholders and the core planning team to "level set" their understanding of the organization's core competencies, work environment, core processes, and resource availability.

---

[59] See ASP, BOK 3.0 Section 2.2.2 - Conduct Internal Environmental Scan
[60] Stoner, Fry. *Strategic Planning in the Small Business*, South-Western, 1987.

Phase II – Complete an Environmental Assessment

Core Competencies

Central to any internal analysis is an exploration of an organization's core competencies. *A core competency is any area, factor, or consideration perceived by the customer to differentiate the organization by providing a sustainable competitive edge over its rivals.*[61] Often an organization's core competency becomes the focus for choosing relevant opportunities and defining strategic direction.

To start to understand core competency, recognize that competition between organizations is as much a contest for competence mastery as it is for market position and market power.

The concept of core competence was posed by C. K. Prahalad and Gary Hamel.[62] In the 1990s, they recognized that, over time, organizations develop key areas of expertise that are both distinctive and critical to their long-term growth. They further recognized these key areas of expertise are most likely to develop within areas of the organization where the most value is added to its products or services.

Core competencies are not fixed; **they should change in response to fluctuations in the organization's environment**. They are flexible and evolve over time. As an organization adapts to new circumstances and opportunities, new core competencies will have to be identified, developed, and exploited to make growth possible.

2.1(4)

Prahalad and Hamel suggest three factors that help to identify core competencies in any organization (see Figure 2.9).

FIGURE 2.9: THREE FACTORS OF CORE COMPETENCY

Hamel and Prahalad suggest three factors to help identify core competencies:

- Provides access to a wide variety of markets
- Is difficult for competitors to imitate
- Makes a significant contribution to the perceived customer benefit

A core competency must be "competitively unique." In all industries, skills are required for competent participation and do not provide any significant competitive differentiation. For an attribute to be a core competency, it must be valued by the customer and one that competitors wish they had in their own

---

[61] Hamel, G. and Prahalad, C.K. *The Core Competency of the Corporation*, HBR, May-June, 79-91, 1990.
[62] Ibid.

organization. A competency central to the organization's operations yet not exceptional in some way is not a core competency since it does not differentiate the organization from its competitors.

Amazon's mission is to be "Earth's most customer-centric company." (See Figure 2.10.)

FIGURE 2.10: WHY AMAZON SUCCEEDS

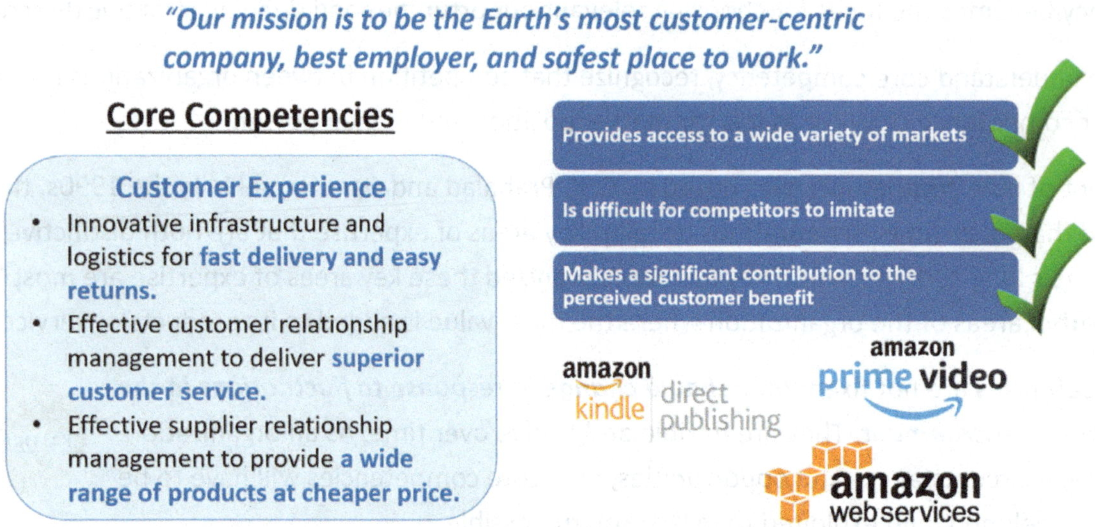

"Our mission is to be the Earth's most customer-centric company, best employer, and safest place to work."

Core Competencies

Customer Experience
- Innovative infrastructure and logistics for **fast delivery and easy returns.**
- Effective customer relationship management to deliver **superior customer service.**
- Effective supplier relationship management to provide **a wide range of products at cheaper price.**

- Provides access to a wide variety of markets
- Is difficult for competitors to imitate
- Makes a significant contribution to the perceived customer benefit

amazon kindle direct publishing
amazon prime video
amazon web services

In this case study we see Amazon's core competency is centered on providing a premier customer experience via fast delivery, easy returns, superior customer service, and access to a wide range of products at a lower cost. These capabilities taken together provide access to a wide range of markets, are difficult for competitors to imitate, and make a significant contribution to the perceived customer benefit. Amazon's ability to build, leverage, and reconfigure core competencies into sustainable competitive advantages exemplifies why it is positioned to continually expand what they offer, and succeed in a rapidly changing external environment.

Work Environment

Another crucial factor is the organization's work environment. The work atmosphere between the Board and management, within management, and between management and staff is critically important. Central to a productive working environment is a **culture of mutual respect, accountability, and agility.** Such a culture exists when staff members feel safe and free to openly discuss their concerns and ideas without fear of reprisal or a belief that their communications will be ignored. *This notion, referred to as "psychological safety," is an indispensable ingredient in enabling an agile organizational culture.*

5.2(3)

Miller and Kirkpatrick highlight the importance of psychological safety for governmental organizations in their Organizational Agility Framework.[63] (See Figure 2.11)

---

[63] Miller, S.C. & Kirkpatrick, S.A. *The Government Leader's Field Guide to Organizational Agility: How to Navigate Complex and Turbulent Times.* Oakland, CA: Berrett-Koehler, 2021.

Phase II – Complete an Environmental Assessment

FIGURE 2:11: ORGANIZATIONAL AGILITY FRAMEWORK

Organizational Levers:
- Organizational Structure
- Knowledge Sharing and Experimentation
- Decision-Making
- Leader Actions
- Process Management
- Roles
- Norms and Expectations

External factors (around the wheel): Technology, Social Trends, Customer/Citizen Expectations, Political Changes, Naturally Occurring Events, Internal Changes

Routines: Sensing and Interpreting, Responding

Agile organizations engage the levers to support the routines:

- **Norms:** Psychological safety
- **Leader Actions:** Setting agility norms
- **Structure:** Stable structure; response teams
- **Knowledge Sharing:** Sharing information across organizational boundaries
- **Decision Making:** Decisions based on expertise
- **Roles & Processes:** The right mix of stability and flexibility

Other crucial factors to *understand are whether the skills, incentives, resources, and attitudes* are in place to accomplish the work required. Finally, the team should take time to consider if there is a record of taking desired action on a timely basis. When these capabilities are in place, one can expect positive organizational performance.

5.1(1)

Core Processes and Operating Model

When doing an internal analysis, it is important to *systematically analyze the internal operational and value creation processes* of the organization, i.e., the "operating model." [64] In many cases this is where differentiation from competition occurs. It is critical to do a good job of securing quality inputs to the model to provide valuable tangible outputs that, taken together, are foundational to long term competitive advantage. Key to possessing this important advantage is alignment between the organization's strategy and its operating model (discussed further in Phase V).

5.1(1)
6.1(2)
6.1(3)

Within most organizations, the *basic "functions"* and *operational "processes"* are inextricably interwoven (see Figure 2.12). Therefore, these organizational building blocks should be identified conceptually, examined closely, and used to analyze an organization's internal strategic performance and current operating model.

6.1(2)
6.1(3)

---

[64] See IASP BOK 3.0, Chapter 3, Transform the Organization, 2021.

FIGURE 2.12: INTERWOVEN PROCESSES AND FUNCTIONS EXAMPLE

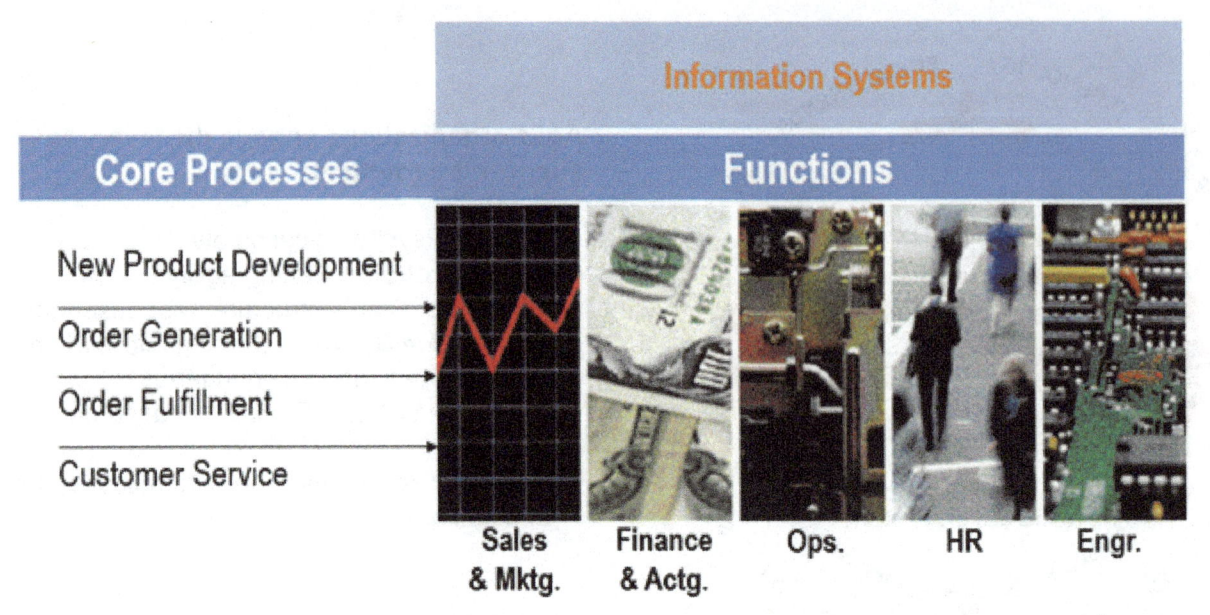

An integrated approach to examining the efficiency and effectiveness of core processes and functions results in an objective fact-based analysis of the internal capability of the organization. A robust understanding of these facts enables the leadership team to make modifications and improvements in the organization's strategy, operational effectiveness, and strategic management capabilities.

Resource Availability

Lastly, internal analysis is not complete until a thorough analysis of the organization's available resources is conducted. If required resources (time, skill sets, management capability, money, ecosystem, bandwidth, etc.) are not available to pursue market-based opportunities, then the organization will be ill-equipped to adopt new strategies.

Table 2.3 presents a more detailed reveal of key components that, taken together, shape the internal environment and drive organizational capability in most organizations (relevant subtopics and questions to consider are included).

TABLE 2.3 – KEY COMPONENTS OF THE INTERNAL DIMENSION (Detailed)
• **Core competency** What makes you special in the eyes of your customers? What internal capabilities do you have within your organization that give you a competitive advantage? Below are typical areas where core competency can be found: 　○ Quality of product or service high above industry/sector standards 　○ Fill a special niche 　○ Strong consumer orientation leading to a high degree of customer intimacy 　○ Service levels high above industry/sector standards 　○ Operational efficiency that leads to becoming the low-cost provider 　○ Reputation/brand image established over years of outstanding performance

P.1a(2)

Phase II – Complete an Environmental Assessment

TABLE 2.3 – KEY COMPONENTS OF THE INTERNAL DIMENSION (Detailed)

- o Site selection (location, location, location)
- o Flexibility and adaptability meeting customer needs that can change quickly
- o Special and unique technical skills of one or more people on the team

- **Pending issues** What other pending internal issues require the organization's attention? Below are several illustrative examples:

    - o Management and Board leadership do not agree on how to move the organization forward
    - o The organization does not produce timely financial statements that accurately track performance
    - o The organization does not know what customers value most
    - o A defined marketing and sales process that operates effectively to generate new customers does not exist
    - o A defined research and development process does not exist to produce high quality products to meet emerging needs on a consistent basis
    - o A process is not in place for leadership development within the organization
    - o Staff members are not motivated to produce at levels to help the organization reach and exceed its goals
    - o A staff development process does not exist to meet the organization's needs across all departments and business/program units
    - o The organization does not recruit and develop the membership of the board of directors to provide visionary leadership
    - o One or more senior executives will be leaving the organization, and succession planning has not taken place
    - o Layoffs have just occurred and the organization has not adjusted.

- **Culture and general work atmosphere** How would you characterize or describe the culture/general work atmosphere between the board and management, within management, and between management and staff?

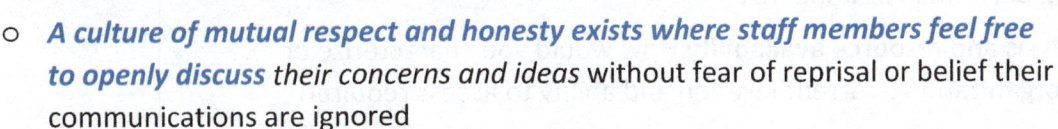

    - o *A culture of mutual respect and honesty exists where staff members feel free to openly discuss their concerns and ideas* without fear of reprisal or belief their communications are ignored   1.1(3)
    - o *Skills exist to accomplish the work required*   5.1(1)
    - o Effective incentives are in place
    - o Resources are available in sufficient quantity to succeed
    - o Desired actions are taken by the leadership team on a timely basis
    - o A history of positive organizational performance exists

- *Core Processes.* Below are core internal processes   6.1(3)

    - o *New product/service development* What issues within your organization impact your ability to *develop and deliver new products and/or services to customers?*   3.1(4)

Strategy in the 21st Century, Second Edition

TABLE 2.3 – KEY COMPONENTS OF THE INTERNAL DIMENSION (Detailed)

- o **Securing new customers** - What issues within your organization impact your ability to *grow your customer base*?
- o **Product/service delivery** - What issues within your organization impact the *quality and timeliness of product and service delivery*?
- o **Customer service** - What issues within your organization impact your *delivery of customer service*?

For each core process review the following checklist.

- o Employee experience
- o The entire process is defined, detailed, and communicated to all employees
- o A performance baseline is established against which improvement can be measured
- o Total cycle time is within appropriate limits
- o The process is consistent, and outputs are regular
- o Workflows in unison between the external suppliers, the internal providers of the product or service, and the targeted customers
- o The process can quickly produce work outputs in response to changing customer needs
- o The process produces what is needed when it is needed
- o The process is flexible, responsive, and readily accommodates changes while remaining in balance
- o *Problems are identified and eliminated on a systematic basis*
- o Problems identified with the process are solved on the first attempt
- o Changes to the process are well thought out and carefully implemented.
- o Managers of the process correct problems instead of rationalizing them or blaming others
- o Providing value to the customer is the overriding reason for the process
- o Employees have a thorough understanding of the process and are committed to meeting performance standards

- **Location analysis and resource availability** How would you characterize or describe the organization's current location and ability to access required resources?
    - o Financial Resources— savings, banks, investors, i.e., access to growth capital
    - o Human Resources—employment patterns for management versus staff
    - o Physical Resources and Raw Materials
    - o Logistical Resources—online, air, rail, and port
    - o Professional Services—legal, accounting, cyber, public policy, social media

- **Prerequisites for effective strategic management** - How would you characterize your organization's strategic management competencies and overall strategic management system?

6.1(6)

TABLE 2.3 – KEY COMPONENTS OF THE INTERNAL DIMENSION (Detailed)
o Our organization is driven by a clearly articulated vision, mission, and core values
o Our organization puts the right amount of emphasis on strategic management.
o Shared perceptions exist about the direction of the organization, its strategy for success, and its priorities
o Significant differences in these perceptions exist among senior leadership, which need to be addressed
o The Board and/or management distinguish between long- and short-term thinking and planning
o Our board and senior leadership regularly review our strategy
o Our strategic plan guides the decision-making and behavior of managers
o Our desired outcomes are feasible in light of the current level of leadership commitment and organizational development
o The probability is high that the leadership team will have the energy, resources, and willingness to achieve the objectives that they have set
o Problems and/or issues that are likely to sidetrack the leadership team's interest and commitment to this project have been identified
o Significant barriers have been identified that need to be addressed before a viable strategic management process can be launched
o We are consistently moving towards achieving our organizational goals
o We know the key drivers of our success and we know how to measure them
o We regularly track our performance toward longer-term goals, and our current data shows good performance towards achieving our longer-term goals.
o Managers at all levels of the organization clearly understand our strategy
o We have an information technology structure in place that meets our strategic management needs

Do not rush. Take your time (and overtime) to understand what the internal environment is telling you. Listen, learn, and build a shared understanding of the environment across your planning team. Explore each of the relevant items before defining organizational direction and strategy. Keep in mind the singular focus here is to analyze the organization's current "internal" operating environment.

The rationale for this approach is simple and straightforward: Developing and implementing strategy is an evolving process. To be successful one must first complete the analysis of organization issues and capabilities presently in place. *Any attempts to evaluate the current strategy—especially in terms of strengths and weaknesses—are premature.* Also, efforts to develop a new strategic direction or to formulate alternative strategies are tasks that should be avoided at this point in the process. These tasks will be addressed in Phases IV and V.

Generic and Specific Questions

As stated in the dimensions for external analysis, each of these nine internal focused dimensions can be analyzed using a combination of generic questions and specific questions. Generic questions are universally applicable to all or most categories while specific questions are custom configured to relate to an organization's specific circumstances. These questions should be reviewed and further developed by the strategy champion and the strategic management leadership team. This will help to focus the team on the task at hand, that is, gathering and presenting the information in a useful format.

Examples of generic questions:

- Do analyses/reports/documents already exist on any of the forces or factors requiring analysis?
- Is each factor strategically significant to the accomplishment of the current organization strategy?
- Has there been a tendency to shift from a strategic to an operational focus?
- Do any of the factors need to be subdivided or specified in more detail?
- Which factors should receive the greatest attention?
- Which factors have the greatest impact on the organization, that is, which ones are driving it?
- How sensitive is the organization to changes in a particular factor? Does it therefore warrant closer scrutiny?
- What is the rate of change of these factors?
- What is the cost of acquiring this information versus the benefits of its potential use?
- How much information needs to be collected and for what purpose?
- Are there alternative sources for acquiring the information?

Task 2.3 – Evaluate Results of Strategic Analysis Via SWOT/OTSW

An "assessment" was defined as having two components, that is, an analysis and then an evaluation based on the analysis.

So far, in Phase II the emphasis has been on the analysis. The objective of these analyses has been to develop a fact-based understanding of the current situation faced by the organization from a strategic perspective. This includes analysis of the external environment and of the internal dimensions and dynamics of the organization. The remaining task in Phase II attends to evaluating the combined external/internal analysis work.

The end result should be a comprehensive assessment of the environment from a strategic organizational perspective and its potential for developing and improving strategic management. (See Figure 2.13.)

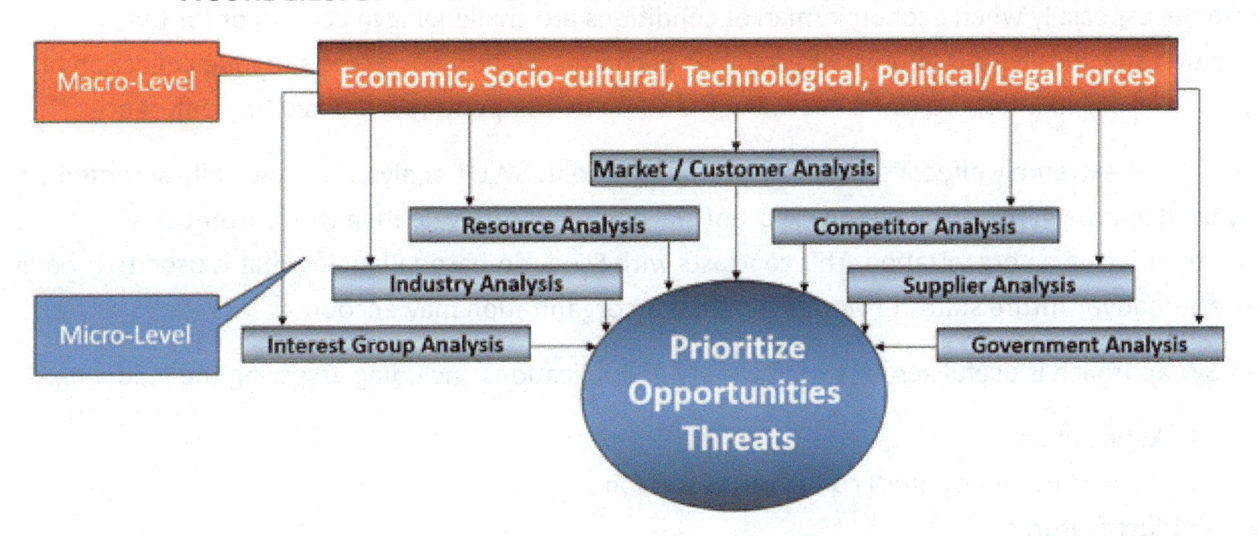

Phase II – Complete an Environmental Assessment

FIGURE 2.13: EVALUATE AND PRIORITIZE OPPORTUNITIES AND THREATS

Here the work of the planning team centers on evaluating what has been learned about primary opportunities and impending threats facing the organization. Mindful of this, the team will assess the organization's internal capacity and capabilities to take them on and identify gaps the organization has that would prevent the organization from being successful. Careful attention must be taken here to first identify and prioritize the opportunities and threats within the external operating environment, followed closely by a prioritization of the organization's internal strengths and weaknesses. Taken together, a snapshot of organizational priorities essential for effective strategy formulation comes into focus.

The most frequent way to conduct this evaluation is through a Strengths, Weaknesses, Opportunities, and Threats (SWOT) Analysis (see pp 26-27). From our perspective, this tool is better identified as an "OTSW" Evaluation. We believe in most cases external opportunities and threats should be determined *before* internal strengths and weaknesses (see Figure 2.14). A strategy should be based on the realities of the current and future market and customer needs, not the day-to-day operating needs of the organization. It certainly is the case that internal strengths and weaknesses can be strategic in nature, but in most cases, we believe that they should be identified after analyzing the external environment.

FIGURE 2.14: OTSW EVALUATION

Strategy in the 21st Century, Second Edition

Note that there are situations where a "strengths-based" or resource-based prioritization approach is preferrable, especially when economic/market conditions are challenging in general or for the organization specifically. This approach recognizes each organization possesses a unique collection of resources and capabilities; the key is not doing the same as competitors but exploiting differences.[65]

This method is extremely effective for strategic management. SWOT analysis is universally accepted and widely used approach that provides an excellent starting point for evaluating the "current state" environment facing an organization. This contrasts with Scenario-based Planning that is used to broadly assess alternative "future state" environments that an organization may encounter.

The OTSW approach is useful across a wide variety of applications, including assessing the following:

- Market position
- The current (or anticipated) competitive position
- Product features
- A new venture
- A strategic option, such as launching a new product or service
- An opportunity to acquire
- A potential strategic partnership
- Changing a supplier
- Outsourcing a service, activity, or resource
- An investment opportunity

Included in this task are eight specific sub-tasks:

- Review the external scan carefully
- Compile a list of the organization's primary market opportunities and threats, and document assumptions
- Agree upon the organization's core competencies/competitive advantages
- Rank the organization's market opportunities and threats in light of its core competencies and risk assessment
- Review the internal scan carefully
- Compile a list of the organization's primary internal strengths and weaknesses
- Rank the organization's internal strengths and weaknesses in light of its primary market opportunities
- Evaluate the overall strategic management system

Carefully Review the External Scan

In all cases, the strategic evaluation process is most effective when conducted after completing a thorough external environmental scan and careful consideration of the findings. The external scan

---

[65] Grant, R.M. *Contemporary Strategy Analysis – Text and Cases*, 9th Edition, Chapter 5, pp 116-119., 2016.

Phase II – Complete an Environmental Assessment

information should be reviewed and discussed by all planning team members. In most situations the team is advised to meet with a skilled strategy facilitator to review and consider the external scan report.

Senior leadership and management's investment of time in this phase allows the organization to build out its strategy based on the team's shared understanding of the external environment.

Compile a List of the Organization's Primary Market Opportunities and Threats and Document Assumptions

Following a thorough review of the external scan, team members should be invited to share their perspectives on the primary market opportunities and threats facing the organization. Once this information is collected, it should be consolidated and categorized.

Be sure to document assumptions the team is making about a given opportunity. This information will be extremely valuable as a base "reference point" once implementation related to the opportunity begins. Identify the assumptions made for each primary opportunity by discussing these three questions.

1. How will your solution help customers and stakeholders achieve their desired outcomes?
2. How will customers/stakeholders perceive your solution as viable and take advantage of it?
3. How can your team feasibly overcome your biggest political, technical, economic, and regulatory challenges?

To maximize effectiveness of the evaluation process, the facilitator should categorize each market opportunity using Ansoff's Grid (see Figure 2.15). In general, every market opportunity can be categorized as a market penetration, market development, product/service development, or *diversification opportunity with increasing levels of risk as the organization moves beyond market penetration opportunities.* [66]

1.1(4)

2.1(3)

FIGURE 2.15: ANSOFF'S GRID

	CURRENT MARKETS	NEW MARKETS
CURRENT SERVICES / PRODUCTS	Market Penetration	Market Development
NEW SERVICES / PRODUCTS	Service / Product Development	Diversification

Increasing Risk →

↓ Increasing Risk

---

[66] Ansoff, Igor H. *Corporate Strategy*. New York: McGraw Hill, 1965.

Strategy in the 21st Century, Second Edition

As in the process for evaluating opportunities, evaluate threats by having each team member list those they believe should be prioritized. External threats should be consolidated and categorized as longer-term, medium-term, or short-term in nature. Those defying categorization by time can be labeled "general."

After consolidation, the team can categorize each threat by using a Heatmap Exposure Matrix. A Heatmap Exposure Matrix is a chart that plots the severity of impact of an event occurring on one axis, and the probability of it occurring on the other (see Figure 2.16).

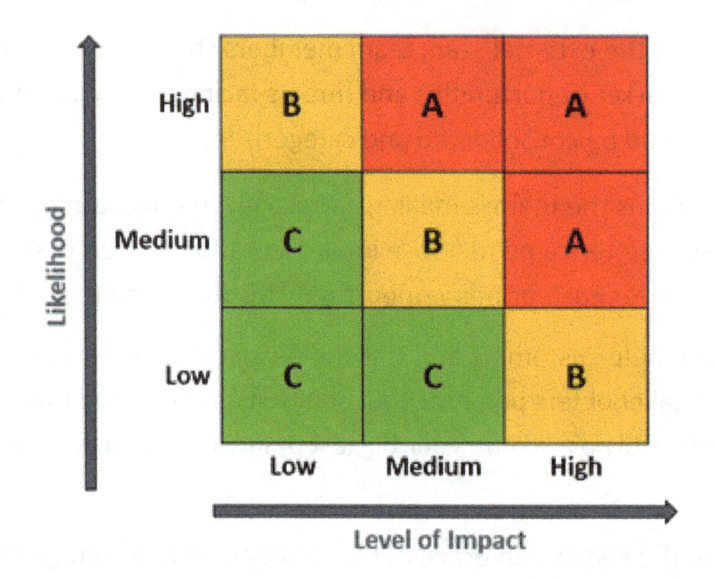

FIGURE 2.16: HEATMAP EXPOSURE MATRIX.

Likelihood \ Level of Impact	Low	Medium	High
High	B	A	A
Medium	C	B	A
Low	C	C	B

By visualizing existing and potential threats in this way, the team can assess their impact and identify which ones should be considered as potential priorities. From there, the team can create a plan for responding to the risks they believe need most attention.

In considering strategic threats, five questions should be considered.

- Are there threats which were previously identified as opportunities?
- Which threats can be converted into opportunities?
- Which threats require mitigation strategies?
- What are the assumptions the team is making regarding any potential threat?
- What is the organization's overall appetite for and tolerance of risk?

Agree Upon the Organization's Core Competencies and Competitive Advantages

Fundamental to this process is to agree upon the differentiating capabilities the organization possesses that enable it to maintain a competitive advantage. *Core competencies and competitive advantages* are closely related. Both help organizations achieve greater market/mind share, customer satisfaction, loyalty, and greater returns on their investments.

P.1a(1)

P.2b

Core competencies generally lead to competitive advantages, although this may not always be the case. Core competencies and competitive advantages help an organization to stand apart from the competition.

A competitive advantage occurs when an organization achieves a competitive edge over its competitors. There are three types of competitive advantage: cost leadership, product/service superiority or differentiation, and customer service. [67] A competitive advantage helps the organization stand out from its competitors. Competitive advantage can be achieved through serving an untapped market, intellectual property, first mover position, convenience in location, access to cheaper raw materials, etc.

Rank the Organization's Market Opportunities Using its Core Competencies and Threats Using Risk Assessment

The number of strategic opportunities facing an organization can sometimes be overwhelming and therefore difficult to prioritize. By using the organization's "core competencies" as a filter for evaluating each opportunity, potential priorities will naturally emerge. (See Figure 2.8.)

The goal of *the opportunity-ranking process* is to *select* those market opportunities that best leverage the core competencies of the organization and therefore enhance its overall competitive advantage.

The goal of *the risk ranking process* is to prioritize the list of threats, paying close attention to threats having a high likelihood of occurring and high negative impact.

One approach to prioritizing market opportunities and threats is to use the *nominal group technique, sometimes called N/3 voting*. The nominal group technique is a decision-making and prioritization method that delivers an efficient well-structured voting process that engages full participation of the planning team in a nonthreatening way. The nominal group technique provides this by ensuring anonymity for participant involvement in the evaluation process.

This is a very structured process that involves full participation by the entire planning team. This method ensures a broad-based input into the evaluation process. A complete set of instructions and scoring sheets are included in *Appendix 8: The Nominal Group Technique*.

Carefully Review the Internal Scan

As with the external scan, the strategic evaluation process is most effective when conducted following completion of a thorough internal environmental scan and careful consideration of the findings. The internal scan information should be reviewed and discussed by all planning team members. In most situations it is advisable for the team to meet with a skilled strategic planning and management facilitator to review and consider the internal scan report.

---

[67] Treacy, M., Wiersma, F., *The Discipline of Market Leaders*, Basic Books, 1995.

Strategy in the 21st Century, Second Edition

Senior leadership and management's investment of time in this phase of the process will serve to "level the strategic playing field" for all team members and enable the organization to build shared understanding of the internal environment.

Compile a List of the Organization's Primary Internal Strengths and Weaknesses

Following a thorough review of the internal scan, team members should be invited in advance to write down their views,[68] then share (anonymously if necessary) their perspectives regarding the internal strengths and weaknesses of the organization. This is a critical stage in the process, one that allows team members the opportunity to communicate their unvarnished insights into the operational capabilities and limitations of the organization. This information is then consolidated and categorized as necessary by the strategic planning and management professional or a designated team member.

We recommend an organization-wide assessment of the type that the *Malcolm Baldrige Quality Award for Performance Excellence* provides. The Malcolm Baldrige Criteria are part of the **Malcolm Baldrige National Quality Award** which recognizes U.S. organizations for performance excellence. Recipients are selected based on achievement and improvement in seven areas, known as the *Baldrige Criteria for Performance Excellence*. See Figure 2.17 and Appendix 2 – 2023-2024 Baldrige Excellence Builder.[69]

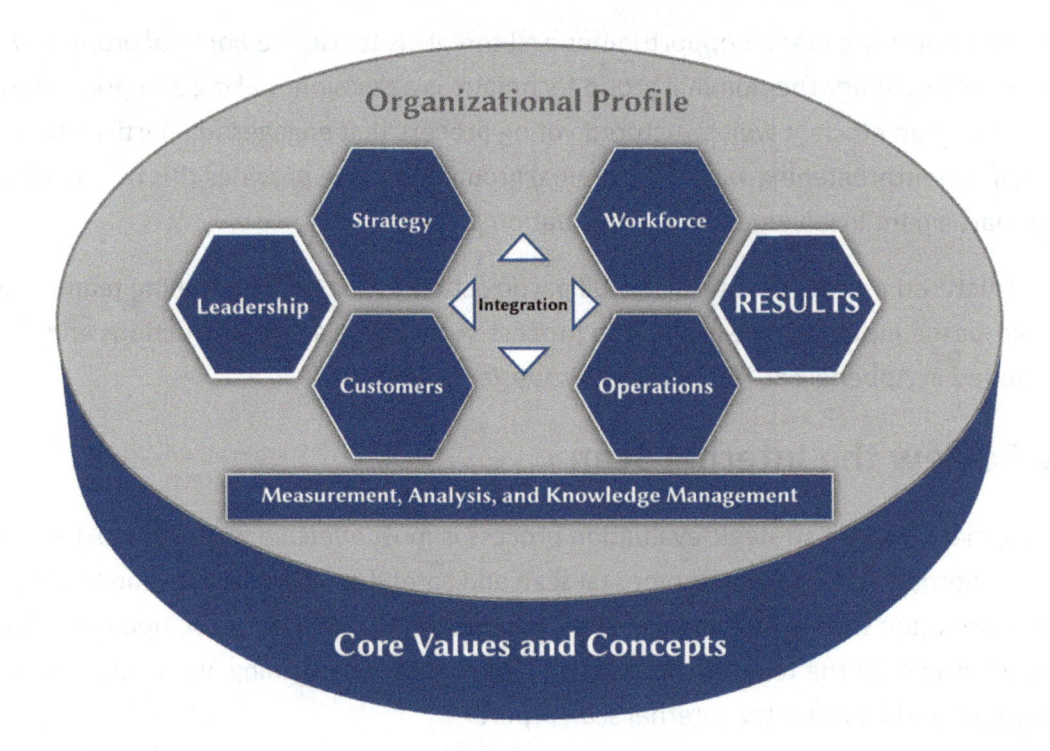

FIGURE 2.17: BALDRIGE CRITERIA FOR PERFORMANCE EXCELLENCE

---

[68] Crumbaugh, L. *BIG DECISIONS*, Forrest Publishing, 2022.
[69] Baldrige Performance Excellence Program, *2023–2024 Baldrige Excellence Builder*, Gaithersburg, MD: U.S. Department of Commerce, National Institute of Standards and Technology. https://www.nist.gov/baldrige, 2023.

Phase II – Complete an Environmental Assessment

In general, every organizational strength or weakness can be categorized into one of the following dimensions:

- **Leadership:** How upper management leads the organization, and how the organization leads within the community.
- **Strategy:** How the organization establishes and plans to implement strategic directions.
- **Customers:** How the organization listens to and learns from customers to build and maintain strong, lasting relationships with customers.
- **Measurement, analysis, and knowledge management:** How the organization measures and improves organizational performance and manages information and knowledge data to support key processes and manage performance.
- **Workforce:** How the organization engages and involves its workforce.
- **Product and Process Results:** How the organization performs in terms of customer satisfaction, finances, human resources, supplier and partner performance, operations, governance, and social responsibility, and how the organization compares to its competitors.

Using the Baldrige Criteria is an effective way for leadership teams to sort and categorize strengths and weaknesses.

In some cases, leadership teams may be more comfortable categorizing their strengths and weaknesses by organization function and/or core process (see Figure 2.12).

By function:

- Board of Directors
- Management
- Marketing
- Finance
- Operations
- Human Resources
- Information Technology

By core process:

- Governance throughout
- Order generation or business development
- New product/service/program development
- Order fulfillment or delivering value
- Customer service before, during and after

Strategy in the 21st Century, Second Edition

Rank the Organization's Internal Strengths and Weaknesses Based on its Primary Market Opportunities

The process used to rank opportunities and threats is now replicated to rank the planning team identified/leadership team categorized internal strengths and weaknesses. A complete set of instructions and scoring sheets are included in Appendix 8: The Nominal Group Technique.

Evaluate the Strategic Management System

Finally, the team should take time to evaluate the organization's ability to manage its strategy. Effective strategic management does not require a separate management system. Quite the contrary, the most effective strategic management systems are embedded in a holistic integrated management system—one with well-articulated and linked strategic and operational processes. (See Figure 2.18.) This is due to the nature of strategic management itself. It is intended to direct and activate all systems and processes as well as motivate, coordinate, and direct management and staff.

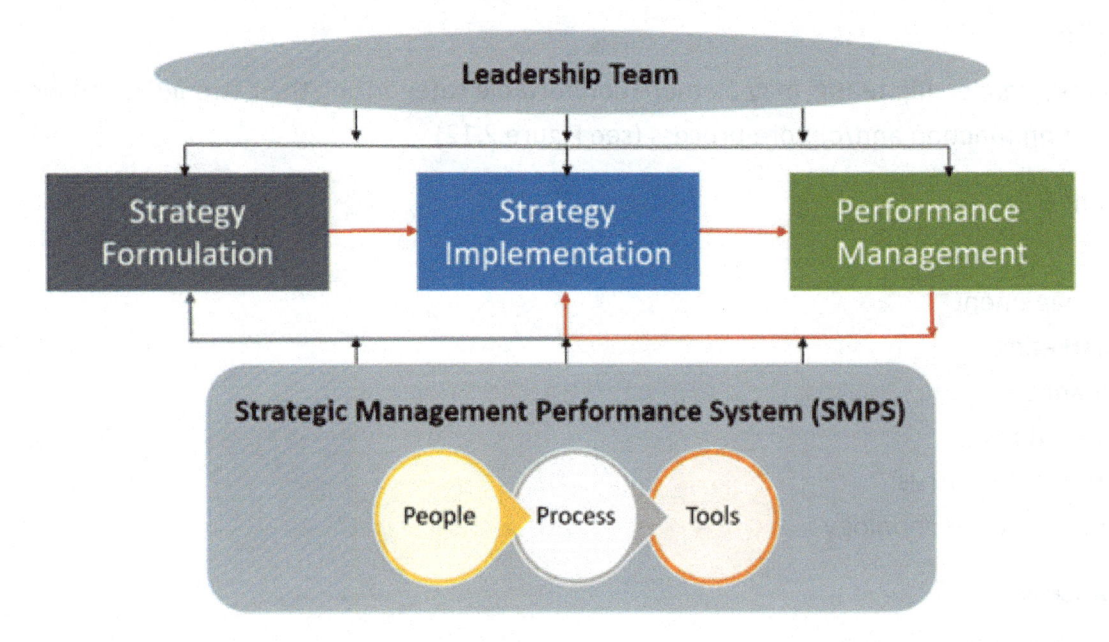

FIGURE 2.18: INTEGRATED MANAGEMENT SYSTEM

For those organizations embarking on a significant effort to improve their strategic management system, it is helpful to consider the following questions:

- Is the current strategic management process well designed?
- Is it being managed effectively?
- How can it be improved with respect to flow, variability, and documentation?
- Do board members, management, and/or staff need training in its operation?
- Are there effective performance measures in place?
- Do these performance measures include measures of strategic management performance?

- Is performance being measured with respect to operations? With respect to personnel responsible for the process? With respect to operating staff personnel?

In addition, the planning team should separately consider (as appropriate to the organization) the strengths and weaknesses of the following strategic management processes:

- Governance of Strategy
- Stakeholder Engagement
- Budgeting
- Analysis and Evaluation
- Planning
- Implementation
- Performance Measurement
- Ongoing Management
- Project Management
- Process Design and Improvement
- Change Management
- Organizational Design
- Developmental Learning Organization
- Benchmarking

In making these evaluations, keep in mind the terms *strength* and *weakness* are both general and relative; that is, they only have meaning within a given organization. As mentioned, they are building blocks. A rating of strength also implies that the strategic management processes (listed above) are well developed processes. A rating of weakness implies that a particular process needs further development to manage the organization strategically in an effective manner.

Remember that these are not technical evaluations; rather, they are intended to provide an understanding of the existing system from a strategic perspective to better direct and design subsequent efforts to improve organization strategy and strategic management capabilities.

Phase III – Strategy Formulation

Strategy formulation covers the processes necessary to articulate the overall strategic direction of the organization as well as the high-level strategies the organization pursues to arrive at the desired destination. From a team perspective, building and managing strategies in tandem with engagement and change management processes is necessary for strategy formulation.

In this phase, the team must:

>   **Task 3.1** – Define the Strategic Direction of the Organization
>   **Task 3.2** – Establish HIGH-LEVEL Strategy

Many top managers are accustomed to setting the strategic direction of their organization in an intuitive and subjective manner. However, the premise of this book is that strategic planning, as a fundamental strategic management process, is most effectively executed using a team-based approach. Therefore, strategic planning tasks are an orderly process that is team driven.

While the strategy formulation tasks laid out in Phase III are presented in a cyclical sequence, they are, in reality, non-linear and dynamic. For example, the *organization's strategic direction should remain flexible and responsive to changing stakeholder needs and events* to adjust when a new opportunity is identified, a new threat appears, or an existing threat intensifies. Any strategic management process should continuously seek new opportunities, monitor threats, and then adjust the organization's strategies and tactics. This can only be done within *a system designed with enough flexibility to adjust whenever is desired or required.*

2.1(6)

Task 3.1 – Define the Strategic Direction of the Organization

Initially identifying and documenting the components of an organization's strategic direction can be arduous and time consuming. However, because of its fundamental importance in the strategic management process, the value of the time and energy spent in this task cannot be overestimated. In short, *a substantial investment is required.*

Developing a comprehensive strategic plan requires the ability to differentiate between strategic versus operational plans and to apply the appropriate procedures to develop them. Unfortunately, the tendency in planning is to adopt a "one size fits all" approach and treat strategic planning the same as operational planning. It is true that strategic plans will later deploy into operational activities, but a starting focus on strategy formulation is necessary. Otherwise, it will be only a matter of time before the entire process becomes a meaningless and disconnected top-management exercise yielding a set of fragmented and isolated operational activities lacking strategic focus.

During Phase I, the components of the organization's current strategic direction were assessed as to their relative strengths or weaknesses and the extent to which they could be used to develop new ones. Based on this evaluation, the leadership team can begin the strategic planning process with the assumption they will convert the current strategic direction into a new or refined strategic direction, supported by well-crafted guidelines for strategy formulation, implementation, and, ultimately, transformation.

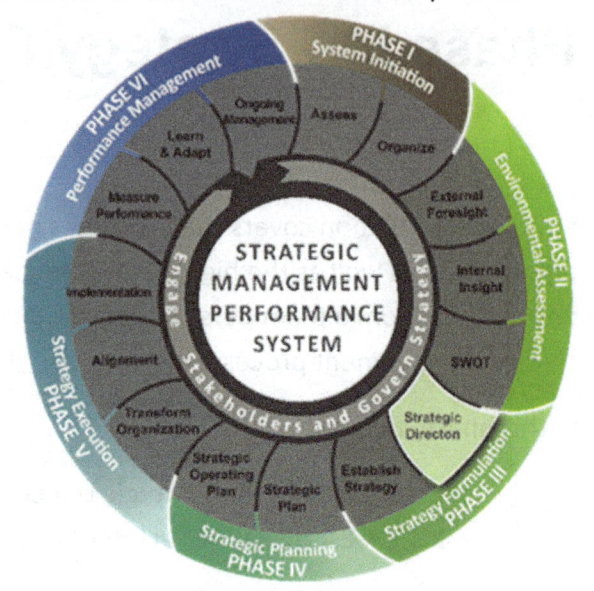

This task has two primary objectives:

- Provide an understanding of the components of the organization's strategic direction.
- Provide guidelines to the leadership team by which to formulate these components and establish a strategic direction.

The purpose of a strategic direction is to set a course that 1) is sufficiently explicit to guide and motivate the organization's board of directors, executive leadership, management, and staff, and 2) is sufficiently general to use for identification and consideration alternative strategies consistent with it. As such, the strategic direction is a selection filter that allows for removal of strategic alternatives that do not meet the leadership's consensus thinking.

Table 3.1 summarizes the components of strategic direction that must be examined and defined.

TABLE 3.1 – COMPONENTS OF STRATEGIC DIRECTION[70]
- Vision – destination or desired future state - Mission – purpose or reason for existing - Values – fundamental beliefs - Policies – high-level decision-making guidelines - Overarching Goal(s) – directional aims or long-term results to be achieved to realize the organization's vision

---

[70] It is recommended that the reader, especially if preparing for IASP certification, also review IASP BOK 3.0 Chapter 2 – Formulate Strategy. The terms are defined slightly differently but are consistent with those used in this book.

The components are interdependent. Every effort should be made to identify and record each as an integral piece to the composite strategic direction. The order in which the components are listed and defined can be changed, but the order in which they are presented here is a useful sequence to follow.

Vision

A vision statement is central to an organization's strategic direction. It is a concise, thoughtful, and inclusive statement of where the organization is going and what it looks like when it reaches the desired destination. Vision statements can paint an inspiring picture of the greater impact the organization wants to have in the future (e.g., *A world without hunger*).

The vision statement, in essence, is an "engagement and change management tool" that describes a desired future state of what the organization will look like and where it will be in the accepted long-range planning horizon of the organization. It seeks to align the organization's focus, actions, resource allocations, and operations.

Visualize a shared vision as being a mountain's summit representing the vision of success – desired future state – to be reached by the organization's team over a defined period of time. (See Figure 3.1.)

FIGURE 3.1: THE VISION IS THE MOUNTAIN SUMMIT

Similarly, the base of the mountain is analogous to the "current state" of the organization.

The anticipated length of time needed to reach the summit is defined as the "planning horizon."

Vision statements generally are written in two formats. The first describes an organization's future state including what must be achieved to realize it. The second type expresses the greater impact the organization provides to those it serves. Both formats are equally valid.

Vision statements of either format can be organized along a continuum, with some vision statements being very concrete, tangible, and achievable over the course of the organization's planning horizon. Other vision statements are more abstract, inspirational, and motivational, and may extend beyond the planning horizon. (See Figure 3.2)

FIGURE 3.2: CONTINUUM OF VISION STATEMENTS

Concrete / Tangible / Achievable *(Same as the planning horizon)* ←→ Abstract / Inspirational / Motivational *(beyond the planning horizon)*

A well-crafted vision statement is best discerned and then defined *after building a common information base*, as outlined in previous tasks. It grows out of a set of shared values and beliefs of the members of the organization, a common understanding of marketplace needs, and confidence that organizational capabilities and individual competencies can successfully align to meet those needs.

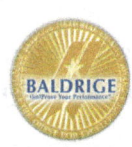

2.1(2)

If the current vision statement is essentially that of the founder, leader, president, or some key stakeholder, it should be transformed into a shared and accepted vision statement. The most effective vision statements are developed by a team, with all team members contributing.

Table 3.2 summarizes characteristics of effective vision statements.

TABLE 3.2 – CHARACTERISTICS OF EFFECTIVE VISION STATEMENTS
• Aspirational, and yet presented as what the organization can realistically expect to achieve, based in part on past experience, and also with provision for "stretching" to new levels of achievement and value for those served.
• Presented as sustainable and the basis for continuous expansion and advancement.
• Written in terms that will clearly communicate to all stakeholders how achieving the vision will benefit them.
• Written in present tense and in a style that will energize and mobilize the various units of an organization and give the board, management, and staff a sense of direction.
• Written in terms that are clear, concise, distinctive, and easy to remember.

Table 3.3 presents generic examples of "externally oriented" and broadly defined vision statements.

Phase III: Strategy Formulation

TABLE 3.3 – EXAMPLES OF VISION STATEMENTS
• *Mastercard* – A world beyond cash.
• *Nike* – Bring inspiration and innovation to every athlete.
• *Ben & Jerry's* – Making the best possible ice cream, in the nicest possible way.
• *Feeding America* – A hunger free America.
• *Project Hood* - Ending violence and building communities, one neighborhood at a time.
• *Microsoft* – (At its founding) A computer on every desk and in every home.
• *Heritage College of Osteopathic Medicine* - A healthier Ohio, empowered by compassionate osteopathic physicians.
• *Cleveland Clinic* - To be the best place for care anywhere and the best place to work in healthcare.
• *National Geospatial-Intelligence Agency* - Know the Earth… Show the Way… Understand the World.
• *National Council on Weights and Measures* - Making every marketplace transaction fair and equitable.
• *DC City Government, Department of Employment Services* - Ensure a competitive workforce, full employment, life-long learning, economic stability, and the highest quality of life for all District residents.
• *Missouri SBDC* - The preferred partner for entrepreneurship and business solutions in Missouri.
• *LBL Strategies* - Valued across the globe for strategy management education, certification, and leadership.

For internal communications, we recommend supplementing a concise vision statement with a more descriptive statement that provides added detail on the destination and stakeholder benefits. A more descriptive statement, written in present tense, conveys the scope of the gap between the present state and the desired future state. It further provides a sense of strategic intent to focus available resources to attain the desired future state and, in turn, is the basis for designing and developing actionable programs.

Here is an example of a great vision statement from Heritage College of Osteopathic Medicine:

> *VISION: A healthier Ohio, empowered by compassionate osteopathic physicians.*
>
> *With our graduates and partners, we advance care and knowledge to improve the health of our communities. Our culture is built upon resiliency, courage, and compassion. Our physicians humanize each patient encounter, bridging the gap between therapeutics, medical technologies, health systems, care delivery and disparity.*[71]

---

[71] Used with permission of Heritage College of Osteopathic Medicine.

Producing an effective shared vision requires team-based development and decision making. Arriving at a shared vision can be a challenge, especially for organizations emerging from command-and-control cultures with autocratic, top-down management philosophies.

Table 3.4 summarizes an effective process to overcome these challenges.

TABLE 3.4 – VISION STATEMENT DEVELOPMENT PROCESS
• Begin with a group of five to ten members who have been immersed in the process (Phases 1-2). Fewer members may not be representative, more than 10 can result in difficulties in communication and domination by the more vocal unless carefully facilitated.
• Develop ground rules on process and meeting frequency, record-keeping, agenda preparation, individual assignments, and use of existing organization documents and reports.
• Ask members to think about the future and how the organization can deliver more value to stakeholders.
• Collect the key ideas and visionary language the organization is currently using and finds effective.
• Ask individuals or subgroups give input into a "straw man" statement for consideration by the team before drafting a shared vision.
• Have the process facilitator use the team's input to draft a small set of vision statements for the team to review.
• Ask team members to critique the initial draft(s) and note suggestions for improvement.
• Ask the process facilitator to redraft a vision statement for further team consideration.
• Distribute the final draft for review, refinement, and approval by senior leadership or the board of directors, depending on the organizational type.

The process we have outlined is a practical approach to developing a shared vision statement. Variations to it can easily be adapted to fit the specific needs of the organization.

The value of having an effective, well-crafted vision statement cannot be overstated. Its development may be frustrating and time consuming, especially if the organization has never tried to develop a vision statement. In that case, remember that the process of strategic management requires formulating a clear vision (and mission) before proceeding with development of the components of strategic direction. (See Figure 3.3.)

Phase III: Strategy Formulation

FIGURE 3.3: SHARED VISION IS A BYPRODUCT OF LEADERSHIP COMMUNICATIONS

Mission

A mission statement defines an organization's purpose and reason that it exists. It describes what the organization does and how (in general terms) it does it. Recognize that a vision addresses the future, and the mission statement addresses the here and now. However, they are related. A mission statement should describe activities that, collectively, pave the way to the fulfillment of the organization's vision.

An important functional difference between mission and vision is that a vision statement can be revised and refocused with comparatively little effort, since it lives in the future. A mission statement cannot: It communicates the organization's purpose "here and now" and provides high-level direction to its intended actions.

A mission statement's development benefits from the vision statement. Articulating a mission statement is challenging to leaders who spend much of their time immersed in the micro-detail of managing day-to-day activities of the organization. It can become a case of "not seeing the forest for the trees," a challenge to be overcome. With the vision statement in place, a framework exists for thinking about and developing the mission statement at a "strategy-focused" level.

Whatever the reason, every organization needs to clearly state its mission, linking its human capital, systems, and processes to keep the organization from straying from its shared commitment. A process analogous to the formation of a vision statement (see Table 3.4) can be employed to identify and write a mission statement. Do not be surprised if a consensus is not arrived at easily in the first meeting. More likely the mission will emerge from informal discussions with members of the strategic management team as ideas are shared and developed.

As with writing a vision statement, having a facilitator or a small group of two or three team members write the agreed-upon key components of the mission statement is most effective. Drafts of the mission statement should be circulated to the strategic management team for review, refinement, and eventual approval by senior leadership.

The consequences of a poorly conceived or incomplete mission statement can be a major barrier to effective strategy management. Conversely, a well-crafted mission statement serves to energize and focus the team while providing a major reference point for making longer-term strategic decisions.

A useful and effective mission statement is not "cast in stone" since missions change over time, as organizations grow, evolve, and respond to change in their environment. An example of this is found in the petroleum industry where oil companies now include finding and developing alternative sources of energy as part of their mission.

Leadership teams should recognize the characteristics of good mission statements, summarized in Table 3.5, and use them for reference/guidance in crafting their own mission statement.

TABLE 3.5 – CHARACTERISTICS OF EFFECTIVE MISSION STATEMENTS
• Communicates a sense of purpose.
• Clearly states what the organization does.
• Identifies, in broad terms, how the organization pursues its mission.
• Establishes boundaries within which the organization operates.
• Affirms the direction set forth in the vision statement.
• Avoids broad statements that are of little use to leadership in guiding the organization.
• Is action oriented, to the point, and easily remembered.
• Can be divided into functional mission statements, as necessary.

Table 3.6 presents examples that illustrate how organizations have crafted their mission statements.

TABLE 3.6 – EXAMPLE MISSION STATEMENTS
• *Walmart* - Saving people money so they can live better.
• *ComEd, Energy Efficiency Department* - Develop and deliver energy management solutions that improve quality of life and the environment in which we live, work, and play.
• *US Secret Service* - Protect our Nation's Leaders and Financial Infrastructure.
• *Dow Chemical* - To deliver a sustainable future for the world through our materials science expertise and collaboration with our partners.
• *U.S. State Department* - Create a more secure, democratic, and prosperous world for the benefit of the American people and the international community.
• *Heritage College of Osteopathic Medicine* - Training osteopathic primary care physicians to serve Ohio.

> - *Kiva* - To connect people through lending to alleviate poverty.
> - *McDonalds* - To make delicious feel-good moments easy for everyone.
> - *LBL Strategies* - We help our clients focus, make better decisions, and grow by leveraging foresight to think and act strategically.

Values (or Core Values)

Organizational values (lived and enacted vs. desired and espoused) [72] are the fundamental beliefs, philosophies, principles, or standards that dictate correct behavior and guide the decisions and actions of an organization's leaders and workforce.[73] They are the qualities that directors, managers, and staff strive to incorporate into their production of goods and delivery of services.

Values play an important role in determining the strategic direction and culture of an organization. In large measure, this is a result of more inclusive managerial styles, organizational structures, and operating processes. A corollary of a "flat organization" is the need to include a wide variety of ideas, opinions, and values. Including diverse views is critical. Even if the process of arriving at a consensus is made more difficult by including diverse views, the result is a set of widely shared espoused values that, when enacted, form a solid foundation for strategic management.

To be major factors in determining strategic direction and influence culture, values must share several characteristics. Table 3.7 summarizes these important characteristics.

TABLE 3.7 – CHARACTERISTICS OF EFFECTIVE VALUES
• Espoused and enacted.
• Represent organizationally relevant core beliefs.
• Held over the long-term and subject only to slow, incremental changes.
• Widely shared among members of the organization.
• Believed to be central to the development and maintenance of corporate culture.
• Defined as substantive beliefs, not slogans, soundbites, or superficial statements made for promotional or public relations purposes to enhance the organization's image.
• Developed to be sufficiently specific to translate into actions and transactions.
• Incorporated in the way the organization acts and reacts with its stakeholders.

Values are the foundation of strategic direction, providing stability to the process of selecting core strategies. For example, if "protecting the environment" and "conserving energy" or "improving diversity, equity, and inclusion" are held (espoused) as organizational values, they should figure heavily into the consideration and decision-making process (enacted) for developing strategies and deploying tactics.

---

[72] Schein, E.H. Organizational Culture and Leadership, 2010.
[73] IASP, BOK 3.0, 2.1.3

The objective is to articulate the (shared) values that the leaders and staff will proactively commit time and resources to honor.

Espousing core values to enact helps determine a strategic direction consistent with the highest aspirations of the organization. At the same time, core values must have the capacity to translate into meaningful actions, processes, services, and products if the culture is to be strengthened. They must be shared, as they impact the strategic direction of the organization.

Table 3.8 illustrates examples of what some organizations identify as core values.

TABLE 3.8 – EXAMPLES OF ESPOUSED ORGANIZATIONAL VALUES

- Ethical behavior
- Integrity
- Commitment to diversity, equity, and inclusion
- Environmental responsibility
- Commitment to customers, employees, shareholders, and community
- Teamwork
- Trust
- Openness
- Accountability
- Social responsibility/corporate citizenship
- Innovation/entrepreneurship
- Customer focus

Having a written set of values is best practice. If the values are not recorded in black and white, how do they get inculcated into the organizational culture? Without written values, how the organization aspires to behave will be more amorphous and open to interpretation. Just because senior management can generate a value set after discussion does not mean that the entire organization knows and aligns around the desired set of values.

When necessary, new values to inculcate into "team" leadership thinking need to be identified, articulated, and enacted as a team. Over a few meetings in which organizational values are discussed, the core values that are deeply held and shared by the Board of Directors, management, and staff should begin to emerge. Each value statement should be succinct, well defined, and resonate with employees. Recognize that without the commitment of the leadership to enact the espoused values, the values will become "window dressing" and easily dismissed.

Policies

Policies are "high altitude" guidelines that instruct members of the organization how to act in various circumstances. Policies – not to be confused with policy manuals – are also key components of strategic direction. However, the role policies play in strategic management is often not considered. This can be traced, in part, to two primary factors. First, many of the most important policies of an organization have been a part of the organization's culture for so long that they are taken for granted. And second, most policies govern the design and use of operations, processes, systems, and procedures, not strategies. Thus, it is easy to overlook the inclusion of policies as components of strategic direction.

Observe the illustrative strategic policies, used in organizations, in Table 3.9. When they were adopted, the impact they could have on facilitating or constraining the future strategic direction the organization was likely not considered. Many of these policies are common and easily recognized; others are more recent and less known. But in no case are they being cited as examples of "good" or "bad" policies.

TABLE 3.9 – EXAMPLES OF POLICIES WITH STRATEGY IMPLICATIONS

- We will always promote from within our organization.
- We will prioritize diversity, equity, and inclusion in all aspects of our work.
- We will pursue international opportunities only when in support of our domestic customers.
- Our debt-to-equity ratio will never be lower than 0.5 or greater than 1.5.
- Our policy on retained earnings versus dividends will be determined by the Executive Committee on an annual basis.
- Our family will always retain control of the organization.
- We will outsource whenever possible.
- Our professional staff must make partner in three years or leave the firm.
- "All our businesses must be number one or two in the industries in which they operate." – Jack Welch, former President of General Electric
- "You can have any color you want as long as it is black." — Henry Ford, regarding the Model T

These strategy impacting policies may be facilitative and expansive or, conversely, limiting, even severely limiting, in creating strategy. However, they must be recognized and considered when setting strategic direction for the organization.

The aim here is to identify all the policies, written and unwritten, that will have an impact on formulating a strategic plan of action. Some policies may simply need to be identified and considered while others may be due for review by leadership.

All told, the result of this work should be a list of agreed-upon policies with strategic impact. If policy creation is being done for the first time, a finalized list may not be complete, but the value of assessing the impact of current policies and establishing new ones will be evident when a strategy is implemented.

Once policies have been reviewed, assessed for strategic impact, documented, and put into effect, a periodic review process needs to be established. As organizations evolve, policies will become more or

Strategy in the 21st Century, Second Edition

less relevant, requiring assessment. It is more effective and less disruptive if this is done on a consistent basis, rather than reactively in crisis situations.

Overarching Goal(s)

An Overarching Goal is the long-range, directional theme defined after developing the organization's vision and mission statements. It *energizes and motivates the Board of Directors, management, staff, and key stakeholders*. An overarching goal, while high in strategic altitude, is more narrowly focused than the vision and mission statement. In fact, lower-level managers and staff often find it easier to focus their efforts on a well-stated overarching goal than on loftier, more general vision and mission statements.

1.1(5)

For most organizations seeking to align stakeholders behind a chosen strategic direction, we recommend identifying *only one* high-altitude overarching goal. Articulating one overarching goal will create focus and energy for the strategic planning process. In some cases, such as very large organizations or organizations with a bifurcated mission, more overarching goals may be required.

In our mountain metaphor, the overarching goal is a major achievement or result which moves the organization up the mountain, closer to the summit, its ultimate vision of success. (See Figure 3.4.)

FIGURE 3.4: THE OVERARCHING GOAL IS A STOP ON THE CLIMB

In this book, the term overarching goal is distinctly separate from the term objective. There are no hard and fast rules governing the use of these terms related to strategy, which has led to a major source of confusion in management literature. In fact, many authors use the terms interchangeably. However, in this book they arise from two different development processes serving two very different purposes.

Overarching goal setting is included as part of the process of establishing the strategic direction of an organization. An overarching goal may or may not be derived from the previously discussed components of strategic direction, that is, vision, mission, values, and policies. However, if the resources and capabilities of the organization are to be focused on the central thrust of the strategic direction, the overarching goal(s) must be consistent with the other components of the strategic direction.

In contrast, objective setting is part of defining strategy and guiding strategy implementation. Objectives are established before specific measures, initiatives, processes, and projects are designed or integrated into an overall operating plan and model. Suffice it to say that objectives are set after a specific strategy has been selected. They are achievable, assignable outcomes to be used to manage ongoing operations.

Table 3.10 presents examples of effective and useful overarching goal statements.

TABLE 3.10 – EXAMPLES OF EFFECTIVE OVERARCHING GOAL STATEMENTS
• Stabilize and increase yield.
• Facilitate a culture of innovation and collaboration.
• Enhance compliance with environmental laws .
• Protect and grow the core business.
• Position and invest for the future.
• Strengthen the foundation of the organization.
• Reduce environmental footprint.
• Reduce childhood illnesses.
• Grow member value.
• Attain self-funding.

Setting an overarching goal's target(s) is the final task in defining strategic direction. The value of setting overarching goal targets is to provide clarity regarding the primary results the team is working towards. With targets defined, the scope of the challenge comes into focus and sets the mark for the key measures of success.

Example:

- **Overarching Goal = Reduce environmental footprint**
    - Target 1 = CO_2 emissions reduced by 25% by _____.
    - Target 2 = Nutrient and organic pollutants reduced by 50% by ___.

These examples incorporate many of the more important features of effective overarching-goal setting. Table 3.11 presents features of effective overarching goals.

TABLE 3.11 – CHARACTERISTICS OF EFFECTIVE OVERARCHING GOAL STATEMENTS
• Are high-altitude, but may not encompass all of the organization's vision and mission statements.
• Validate that an organization is progressing toward the vision.
• Imply values but as qualities incorporated in a goal; they are not value statements per se.
• Are not policies that guide action; they are the actions.
• Imply a completion date at some point in the future but not always defined at this point.
• Are measured via a small set of (one to three) targeted results.
• Provide guidance in setting high level strategy.
• Can be divided into key drivers of success and milestones that, in turn, can be translated into achievable, assignable, and measurable objectives.

Table 3.12 presents five major aspects of the goal-setting process that need separate consideration.

TABLE 3.12 – MAJOR ASPECTS OF OVERARCHING GOAL SETTING
• In most cases one overarching goal statement is recommended for an organization's strategic direction.
• Current goal(s) should be reviewed and evaluated and, as needed, dropped, or revised in light of the new or modified strategic direction being formulated.
• In rare cases, such as very large organizations or organizations with a bifurcated mission, more overarching goals may be required. Limiting the number of goal statements will provide focus and enhanced alignment.
• Identifying new overarching goal(s) that should be pursued to realize the vision, fulfill the mission, and activate the espoused values and policies of the organization.

Unfortunately, because of the predominant focus on short-term results and ongoing operations in many organizations, overarching goals are often not explicitly stated, updated, and reviewed periodically from a strategic perspective. This is a legacy of the outdated practice of top managers setting organization goals but not communicating them to other members of the organization or educating colleagues on their significance to the future growth and development of the organization.

An effective strategy review process should begin by identifying current goals, regardless of their state of acceptance, utility, or attainment. Once assembled, each should be subject to close scrutiny.

Table 3.13 presents a series of questions to ask when evaluating current goals.

TABLE 3.13 – CRITERIA FOR EVALUATING CURRENT GOALS
• Is this goal consistent with the new strategic direction being developed?
• How does this goal reinforce, enhance, or otherwise contribute to the new vision, mission, values, and policies?
• Is this goal widely shared?
• Do the benefits of pursuing the goal significantly outweigh its costs?
• Is this goal in conflict with other goals (current or new)? If so, how?
• Is this goal synergistic with other goals (current or new)?
• What will be the impact of eliminating this goal?
• Do we have the resources to pursue this goal effectively and efficiently?
• What results can be realized as a result of pursuing this goal?
• Has this goal been translated into achievable objectives? If so, with what results?

Modifying current goals is a relatively straightforward process. In fact, the questions listed above can be used to examine extensions and modifications of current goals. This approach to overarching goal setting should never be overlooked because current goals are usually in the leadership's "comfort zone" and are more easily modified when setting a new strategic direction.

The downside to this approach is that it may prove to be too easy, that is, leadership may feel that it has made some changes — enough to avoid the more difficult process of setting a new overarching goal to define the strategic direction in a sufficiently challenging manner.

When setting a new overarching goal, an organization is often entering new terrain with little or no experience to guide it. A useful approach is to examine each of the preceding components of strategic direction, that is, vision, mission, values, and policies, and derive an overarching goal that will fulfill them.

The goal-setting process will vary depending on the leadership style, organization structure, and organizational context. However, as with the other components addressed in setting strategy, the processes outlined for developing vision statements can also be used to develop an overarching goal.

There are times when strong and logical reasons exist for having more than one overarching goal. For example, the scope and size of enterprises such as Amazon, the United Nations, and the U.S. Department of Defense demand multiple goals to deliver on their missions and achieve their visions. Other organizations may need several overarching goals to adhere to differing time frames required by regulatory and funding requirements.

The key point is to focus! Restricting the number of overarching goals (preferably to one) helps keep the strategy within the capabilities and resources available. It will also help prevent overreach and the creation of unnecessary expectations.

Strategy in the 21st Century, Second Edition

Before continuing to the next task, each component of the strategy-setting process should be written and formally approved. The task of formulating the upcoming strategic plan is directly dependent on the care and attention given to the process of setting the strategic direction.

In essence, strategic direction is the core of the strategic plan. Certainly, there may be necessary changes in its component parts as the process of strategy formulation unfolds, but this first draft serves as the starting point from which to embark on the process of developing a new or revised strategy.

Table 3.14 presents a sample strategic direction summary Heritage College of Osteopathic Medicine.

TABLE 3.14 – SAMPLE STRATEGIC DIRECTION	
\multicolumn{2}{c}{OHIO **Heritage College of Osteopathic Medicine**}	
\multicolumn{2}{c}{*Used with permission*}	
Vision	**A healthier Ohio, empowered by compassionate osteopathic physicians.** With our graduates and partners, we advance care and knowledge to improve the health of our communities. Our culture is built upon resiliency, courage, and compassion. Our physicians humanize each patient encounter, bridging the gap between therapeutics, medical technologies, health systems, care delivery and disparity.
Mission	**Training osteopathic primary care physicians to serve Ohio** Our medical school educates physicians committed to practice in Ohio, emphasizes primary care, engages in focused research, and embraces both Appalachian and urban communities. Integral to this mission, our college community commits itself to provide a clinically integrated, learning-centered, osteopathic medical education continuum for students, interns, residents, and primary care associates; embrace diversity and public service; and improve the health and well-being of underserved populations.
Values	• Wholeness and balance within each person • Integrity • Community of mutual respect • Acceptance of others and embracing diversity • Pursuit of excellence • A climate of scholarship • Commitment to service • Generosity • Compassion
Policies	*Written:* • HCOM will focus on training primary care physicians for Ohio • A review of the Heritage College strategic plan and its mission will be conducted at least every five years. Heritage College internal and external stakeholders,

	TABLE 3.14 – SAMPLE STRATEGIC DIRECTION
	Heritage College of Osteopathic Medicine *Used with permission*
	students, faculty, and staff will have the opportunity to contribute to the strategic planning and mission review processes. This policy ensures Commission on Osteopathic College Accreditation (COCA) Standard 1 on Mission and Governance accreditation requirements are met for program mission and strategic planning. • Policies from COCA, our accrediting body: • A COM must produce and publish a current strategic plan addressing all core aspects of the COM mission. Faculty and students must be included in the strategic plan development, review, and revision. • A COM must have a written mission statement that: 1) explains the overall purpose of the COM's program; and 2) serves as a guide for program planning and assessment. Where the COM is part of a larger educational institution or parent institution, the COM's mission must be consistent with the institution's mission. The COM must review its program mission at least once every five years and upon review, if the COM deems it to be appropriate to do so, the COM should revise its mission to meet the COM's growth and continued development. The COM must consider the input of its faculty, staff, and students when reviewing and revising its mission. • A COM must have a governing body or be part of a parent institution with a governing body, which defines the mission of the COM and/or institution, approves the strategic plan, provides financial oversight, and approves requisite policies. *Unwritten:* • Great universities have great medical colleges, great medical colleges have great clinical partners. • Student affordability is a paramount concern • Success depends on continually investing in our people
Overarching Goal	**Our graduates are highly sought after and indispensable members of Ohio's healthcare teams.** o Measure: Residency match rate

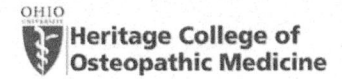

Strategy in the 21st Century, Second Edition

Task 3.2 – Establish HIGH LEVEL Strategy

Once the components of the strategic direction have been constructed and sufficient time has been taken to think strategically about implications and possibilities, the next task is to identify and evaluate alternative strategies necessary to achieve the organization's overarching goal(s).

In Edition 1 we defined a **strategy** as *a plan of action to achieve an overarching goal and move the organization towards its shared vision of success.*

The IASP BOK 3.0 defines strategy as a "representation of the high-level guidelines an organization adopts to provide value to its stakeholders and/or gain an advantage over competitors. Whether these guidelines are deliberately designed and/or emerge in time, they determine how the rest of the efforts of the organization will be deployed."[74] We agree with this definition.

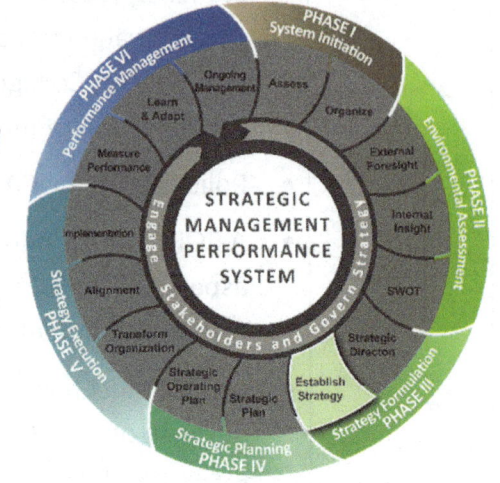

The notion of **alternative strategies** suggests that there is almost always a variety of ways to pursue an overarching goal. Like any other challenge, there is almost *always* a range of ways to climb a mountain or pursue a goal. Sometimes we must make "either/or" choices, at other times "both/and" choices, and yet at other times "now/later" choices.

It is important to take time to evaluate each option before selecting a course of action. (See Figure 3.5.)

FIGURE 3.5: STRATEGY ALTERNATIVES OFFER ROUTES FOR THE CLIMB

---

[74] IASP, BOK 3.0, 1.3, p4

Phase III: Strategy Formulation

The output of this task is a set of potentially actionable strategies developed by the strategic leadership team. Arriving at a small set of high-level strategies is a pivotal accomplishment requiring both analytic and creative thinking – and focus. Analytically, this task requires identification of alternatives that flow from a study of the strategic direction and the capabilities, competencies, and resources of the organization to achieve them. Creatively, innovative thought is required to develop alternatives that will counter traditional direction to produce transformational strategies.

Analytical and creative thought processes are inextricably entwined in our minds and can be difficult to separate. Yet, for the best results, they should be separated during team-based strategy development.

The task of developing alternative strategies demonstrates the benefits of a team approach to strategic management. Accordingly, in this task we offer suggestions and considerations that have been found useful when employing a team-based approach to identifying, creating, and selecting high-level strategies. Specifically, the component sub-tasks are as follows:

- Use conceptual models which facilitate strategic thinking to identify strategy alternatives
- Identify activities underway within the organization that can have a positive impact on strategy
- Evaluate and select high-level strategies

Use Conceptual Models Which Facilitate Strategic Thinking to Identify Strategy Alternatives

Before a team begins identifying alternative strategies to move the organization forward, leaders should think at an "ecosystem level" [75] about the implications of their chosen strategic direction. Leaders rarely have enough time to consider differing perspectives required for this creative process. Sometimes referred to as divergent thinking, it grows from a thought process or methods used to generate creative ideas by exploring alternative approaches to strategy setting and competitive positioning.

Strategy professionals play a vital role in facilitating divergent thinking, by helping their organization's core planning team apply **one or more of the strategy-setting frameworks** summarized below.

STRATEGY SETTING FRAMEWORKS

There are many conceptual frameworks and approaches to facilitate this often-needed input into strategy formulation. A helpful place to begin this process is to clearly define how you will position and *"differentiate" your value in the marketplace,* e.g., via operational excellence, product leadership, customer intimacy, or value innovation.[76]

---

[75] An ecosystem is the network of organizations — including suppliers, distributors, customers, competitors, government agencies, and so on — involved in the delivery of a specific product or service through both competition and cooperation. https://www.investopedia.com/terms/b/business-ecosystem.asp

[76] Kaplan, R. S., and Norton, D. P. *The Strategy-Focused Organization: How Balanced Scorecard Companies Thrive in the New Business Environment.* Boston, MA: Harvard Business School Press, 2000.

Strategy in the 21st Century, Second Edition

In commercial settings particularly, "**Competitive positioning** is about carving out a spot in the competitive landscape, putting your stake in the ground, and winning mindshare in the marketplace. In short, it is about being valued for a certain something."[77]

Here are five primary frameworks for established organizations, and an early-stage ventures framework.

- **Porter's three generic strategies**

Depending on the organizational context, this clarity can be gained in several ways. In the business sector it may be helpful to begin by reviewing Michael Porter's *three generic strategies* and choosing which strategy best positions the business in the market. [78] (See Figure 3.6.)[79]

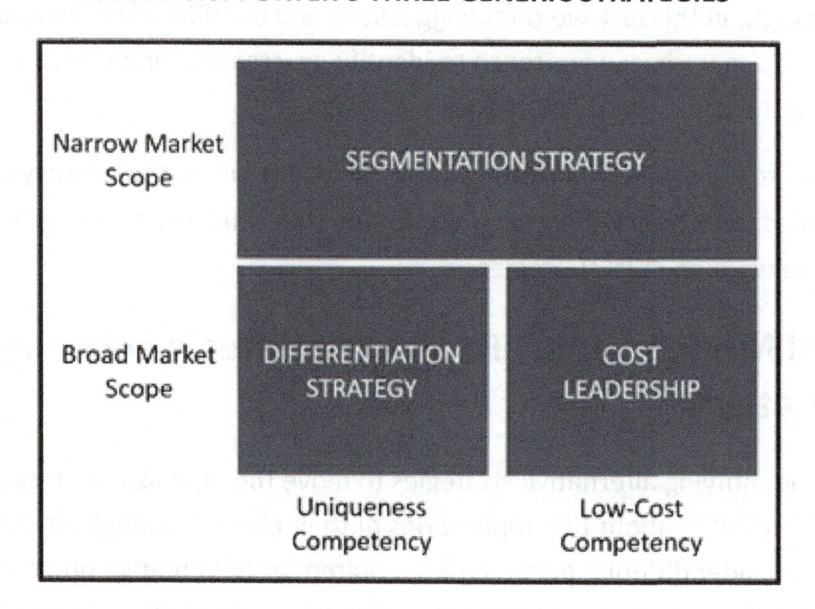

FIGURE 3.6: PORTER'S THREE GENERIC STRATEGIES

Narrow Market Scope	SEGMENTATION STRATEGY	
Broad Market Scope	DIFFERENTIATION STRATEGY	COST LEADERSHIP
	Uniqueness Competency	Low-Cost Competency

In 1980 Porter described three generic strategies that a business of any size can choose from to build a competitive advantage and focus its strategy: cost leadership, differentiation, and segmentation.

A business can choose one of two types of *competitive advantage*; having lower costs than its competitors or differentiating itself in ways valued by customers to command a higher price. A business also chooses one of two types of *market scope*, a narrow focus by offering its value proposition to a niche segment or a mass market approach, offering its value across many market segments.

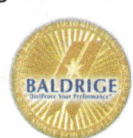

P.2a(1)

P.1b(2)

Examples:

  o *Cost leadership strategy*: Walmart is an American multinational retail corporation that operates a chain of hypermarkets, discount department stores, and grocery stores offering "low price leadership."

---

[77] http://www.marketingmo.com/strategic-planning/competitive-positioning/
[78] A Harvard Business School professor, Porter is a founder of the field of modern strategy and one of the world's most influential thinkers on management and competitiveness.
[79] Porter, M. E. *Competitive Strategy: Techniques for Analyzing Industries and Competitors*. New York: Free Press, 1980.

Phase III: Strategy Formulation

- o *Differentiation strategy*: Whole Foods is an American supermarket chain which exclusively sells products free from artificial colors, flavors, preservatives, sweeteners, and hydrogenated fats. It focuses on offering natural and organic foods and the highest quality standard food products.
- o *Segmentation strategy*: Happy Foods is a family owned and operated supermarket located in Chicago that serves the community of Edgebrook with fresh deli, bakery, and European grocery selection.

- **Strategy Canvas**

Developing a strategy canvas for competitive positioning was introduced in Phase II as a diagnostic tool to analyze the competitive environment. It can also be used by any sector as a strategy-setting tool to further define market positioning as well as to differentiate between "current state" positioning versus "future state" positioning.

W. Chan Kim and Renée Mauborgne [80] developed the strategy canvas in 2005 as a tool to build a compelling "Blue Ocean" strategy. In one simple chart, the canvas graphically depicts an organization's current strategic landscape and the prospects within it (see Figure 3.7).

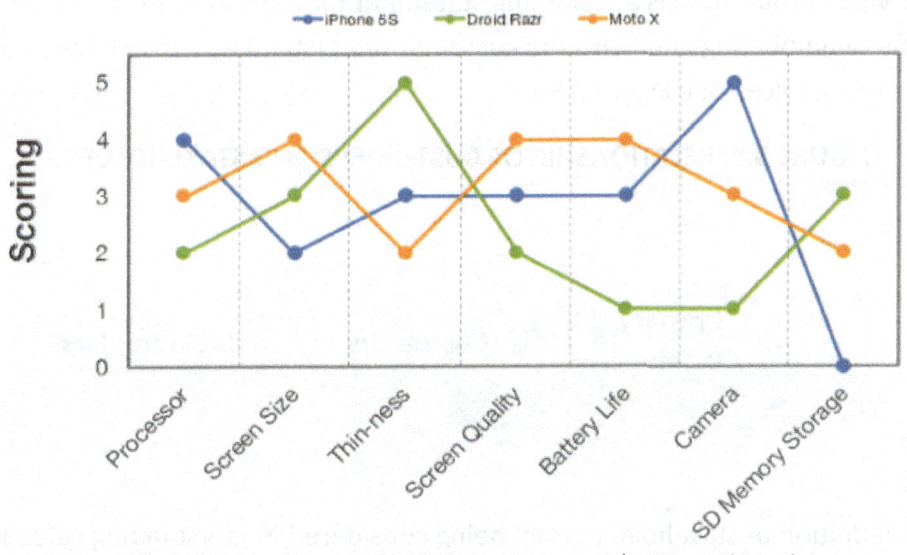

FIGURE 3.7: EXAMPLE BLUE OCEAN STRATEGY CANVAS

Note: This drawing was created by LBL Strategies, not by Kim and Mauborgne.

- **Customer/Stakeholder Value Propositions**

A central component of any strategy is to describe the value the entire organization or a part of the organization wants to provide to its stakeholders, i.e., customers, owners, employees, and partners.[81]

---

[80] Kim and Mauborgne are Professors of Strategy at INSEAD and co-directors of the INSEAD Blue Ocean Strategy Institute in Fontainebleau, France.
[81] Hadaya, P., and Gagnon, B. *Business Architecture: The Missing Link in Strategy Formulation, Implementation and Execution.* Montreal: ASATE Publishing, pp 25-29, 2017. Cited in the ASP BOK 3.0, 2.1.4.

- o **Customer Value Proposition** describes the value the organization wants to provide its customers in exchange for purchasing/utilizing its products/services.

- o **Owner Value Proposition** describes the value the organization wants to provide its owners to justify their participation in its ownership.

- o **Employee Value Proposition** describes the value the organization wants to provide its employees in exchange for its employees' work, skills, and experience.

- o **Partner Value Proposition** describes the value the organization wants to provide its partners who contribute to the organization's customer value proposition, to justify the time and money they invest to build and maintain a relationship with the organization. Partners can include suppliers, distributors, wholesalers, complementors, etc.

In 1982, Michael Lanning of McKinsey was the first to write about a "value proposition" applying to customers as stakeholders.[82] By 2006, James C. Anderson, James A. Narus, and Wouter Van Rossum of Northwestern University's Kellogg School of Management found that "Customer Value Proposition" was one of the most widely used terms in business. However, their research revealed there is no universal agreement as to what constitutes a customer value proposition, let alone owner, employee, or partner value proposition.[83]

The Customer Value Proposition is a marketing statement that summarizes the tangible and intangible value of an offering and helps the customer understand why they might want to buy the product or use the service. (See Figure 3.8.)

FIGURE 3.8: RELATIONSHIP OF CUSTOMERS AND STAKEHOLDERS

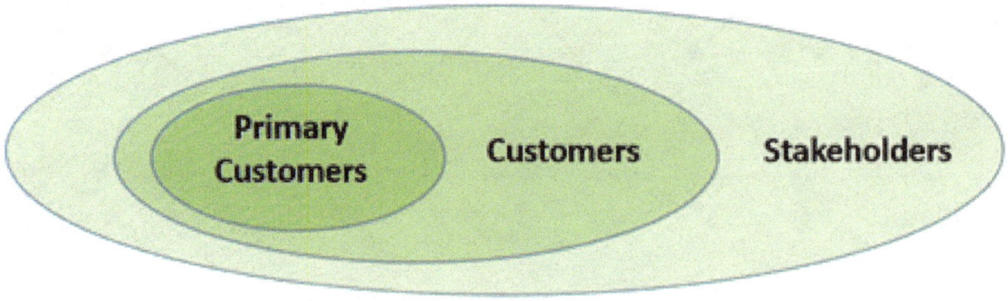

Regardless of definition or stakeholder group being considered, understanding value is in the eye of the beholder. When setting strategy, planning team members must think about value from the perspective of their primary customers, secondary customers, and key stakeholders, e.g., owners, partners, employees, and community.[84]

Gail Stout Perry and her colleagues at Credera emphasize the importance of establishing the customer value proposition. "In today's ever-evolving business landscape, organizations face the

---

[82] Interview with Michael J. Lanning on Value Proposition (& Value Delivery), *Journal of Creating Value*, V5(2), 237-241, 2019.
[83] Anderson, J. C., Narus, J. A., & van Rossum, W. *Customer value propositions in business markets. Harvard Business Review*, 84(3), 90–149, 2006.
[84] See ASP BOK 3.0 – 2.1.4.

daunting task of crafting and refining robust strategies for growth, transformation, and competitive advantage. The backbone of any such strategy is a clear understanding of one's Customer Value Proposition (CVP) and Competitive Positioning – critical elements that define how a business leverages its capabilities to connect with its customers and to differentiate from its competition. And yet, too few organizations dedicate the requisite time and effort to defining their CVP, using it to shape their strategy, and aligning their enterprise to it." A detailed description of Credera's [85] innovative approach to defining CVP is included in Appendix 9.

Here are examples of customer value proposition statements.

- Uber - *The Smartest Way to Get Around*
- Amazon - *Low price, wide selection with added convenience anytime, anywhere*
- Google - *Providing very targeted advertising globally*
- U.S. Homeland Security - *Keeping America safe*
- American Dental Association - *Personalized one-on-one help with provider issues; the latest in clinical information and student debt solutions*

Below is a process to sharpen your stakeholder value propositions (see Figure 3.9):

FIGURE 3.9: PROCESS TO SHARPEN CUSTOMER/STAKEHOLDER VALUE PROPOSITION

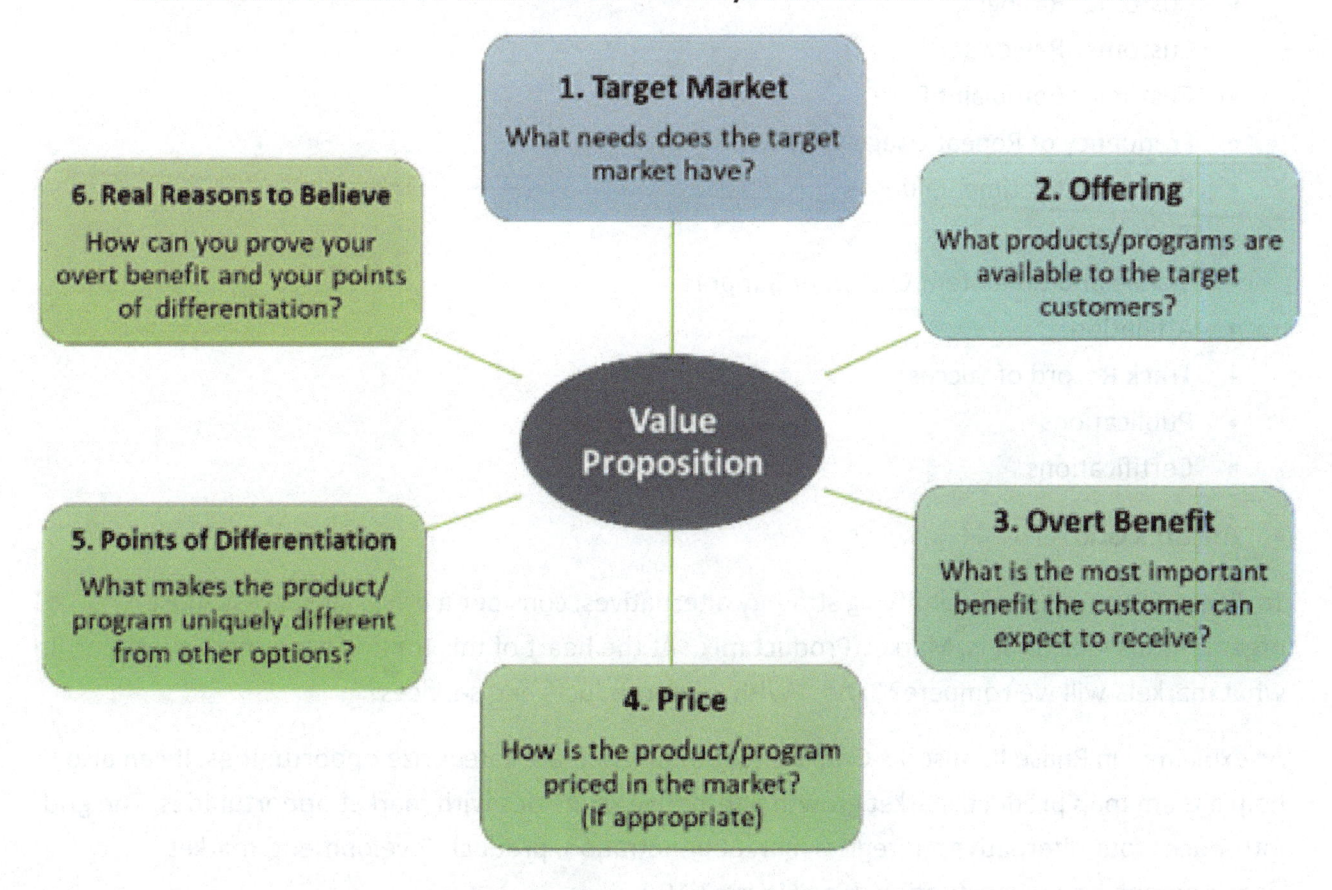

1. Target Market — What needs does the target market have?

2. Offering — What products/programs are available to the target customers?

3. Overt Benefit — What is the most important benefit the customer can expect to receive?

4. Price — How is the product/program priced in the market? (if appropriate)

5. Points of Differentiation — What makes the product/program uniquely different from other options?

6. Real Reasons to Believe — How can you prove your overt benefit and your points of differentiation?

---

[85] https://www.credera.com/insights/strategically-essential-but-frustratingly-elusive-differentiating-your-customer-value-proposition.

As your team works to sharpen and articulate the *Customer/Stakeholder Value Propositions*, take time to consider these fundamental questions.

- What is the urgent customer/stakeholder and market need?
- What products, services, and options for these products and services are available to the targeted customer/stakeholder?
- What is the most important benefit the customer/stakeholder can expect?
- How is the product or service priced in the market?
- What makes the product or service unique or different and valued by customers/stakeholders?
- How can we *prove* our overt benefit and the points of differentiation?

3.1(1)

3.1(2)

Of primary importance is the ability to *prove* that each of your value propositions is valid. We call this "Real Reasons to Believe." When we give customers/stakeholders "real reasons to believe," our desired competitive positioning is reinforced. In most cases, proof positive comes from performance data and is demonstrated via operating practices.

Examples of proof include:

- Customer Satisfaction
- Customer Ratings
- Customer Reviews
- Customer Complaint Rate
- Frequency of Repeat Usage
- Customer Lifetime Value
- Testimonials
- Visible and Consistent Customer Support
- Affiliations
- Track Record of Success
- Publications
- Certifications

- **Ansoff's Grid**

To illustrate the value of identifying strategy alternatives, consider a driver of success most organizations face, that is, Market/Product mix. At the heart of this topic is a two-part question: "In what markets will we compete?" and, "With what products and services?"

As explained in Phase II, Ansoff's Grid is a tool to help a team categorize opportunities. It can also help a team map product/market growth alternative strategies with market opportunities. The grid introduces four alternative strategies: market penetration, product development, market development, and diversification. (See Figure 3.10.)

FIGURE 3.10: ANSOFF'S GRID

	CURRENT MARKETS	NEW MARKETS
CURRENT SERVICES / PRODUCTS	Market Penetration	Market Development
NEW SERVICES / PRODUCTS	Service / Product Development	Diversification

- o As organizations go deeper into their existing markets with their existing products or services, they are pursuing a *market penetration strategy*.
- o Organizations launching existing products or services into new markets are pursuing a *market development strategy*.
- o When organizations develop new products or services for existing markets, they adopt a *product or service development strategy*.
- o Finally, when organizations introduce new products or services into new markets, they are implementing a *diversification strategy*.

Each strategy alternative comes with different risk implications. A market penetration strategy is generally understood to be of least risk as both the market and product line are known. A diversification strategy is considered to carry the greatest risk as the market and product line are generally unknown.

- **Playing to Win**

Playing to Win is an integrative approach to competitive positioning and strategy setting developed by Roger Martin and A.G. Lafley. [86] (See Figure 3.11.)

---

[86] Martin is former Dean of the Rotman School of Management at the University of Toronto and Lafley led consumer goods maker Proctor & Gamble (P&G) as chairman, president, and CEO.

FIGURE 3.11: PLAYING TO WIN

An integrated cascade of choices

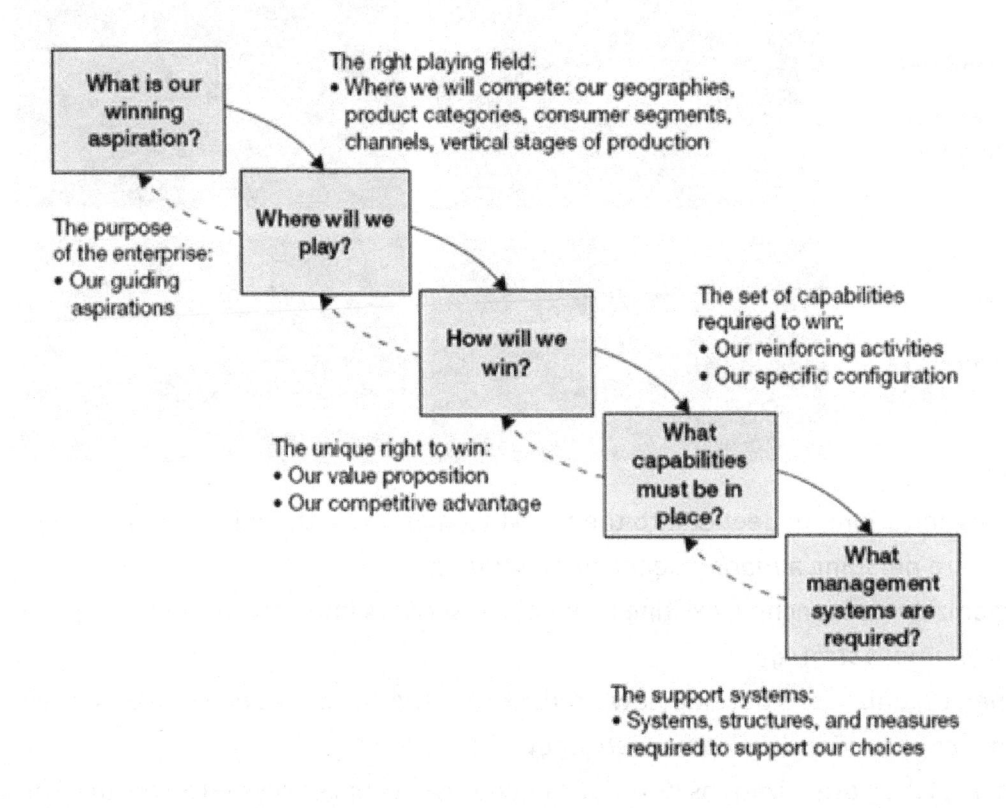

- **What is our winning aspiration?**
  - The purpose of the enterprise:
    - Our guiding aspirations
- **Where will we play?**
  - The right playing field:
    - Where we will compete: our geographies, product categories, consumer segments, channels, vertical stages of production
- **How will we win?**
  - The unique right to win:
    - Our value proposition
    - Our competitive advantage
- **What capabilities must be in place?**
  - The set of capabilities required to win:
    - Our reinforcing activities
    - Our specific configuration
- **What management systems are required?**
  - The support systems:
    - Systems, structures, and measures required to support our choices

Their fundamental point is that strategy can seem mystical and mysterious. "It is not. It is easily defined. It is an integrated set of choices about winning."[87] To this end, they cascade these five strategic choices. The third choice – "How will you win?" – surfaces strategy alternatives.

- o   What is your winning aspiration? (or purpose)
- o   Where will you play? (to achieve your purpose)
- o   *How will you win?* (the way you will win or your strategy)
- o   What capabilities must be in place? (capabilities required to win)
- o   What management systems are required? (systems and measures to support winning)

- **Business Model Canvas**

As noted throughout this book as well as in our *Mastering Strategy* certification program, the discipline of strategic management is context specific. Where planners are strategizing a new startup or the launch of a product or service, a more simplified approach to strategy setting is likely required.

The Business Model Canvas (BMC) is a strategic management tool to define and communicate a business idea or concept quickly and easily. It is a one-page document which works through the fundamental elements of a business or product, structuring an idea in a coherent way.

---

[87] Lafley, A. G., and Martin, R.L. *Playing to Win*, Harvard Business Review Press, 2013.

Alexander Osterwalder [88] proposed the Business Model Canvas in 2004. It is a visual chart using nine building blocks or elements to describe an organization's value proposition, infrastructure, customers, and finances. This straightforward tool helps strategic leaders, especially entrepreneurs, to clarify their business model and strategy.[89] (See Figure 3.12.)

FIGURE 3.12: BUSINESS MODEL CANVAS

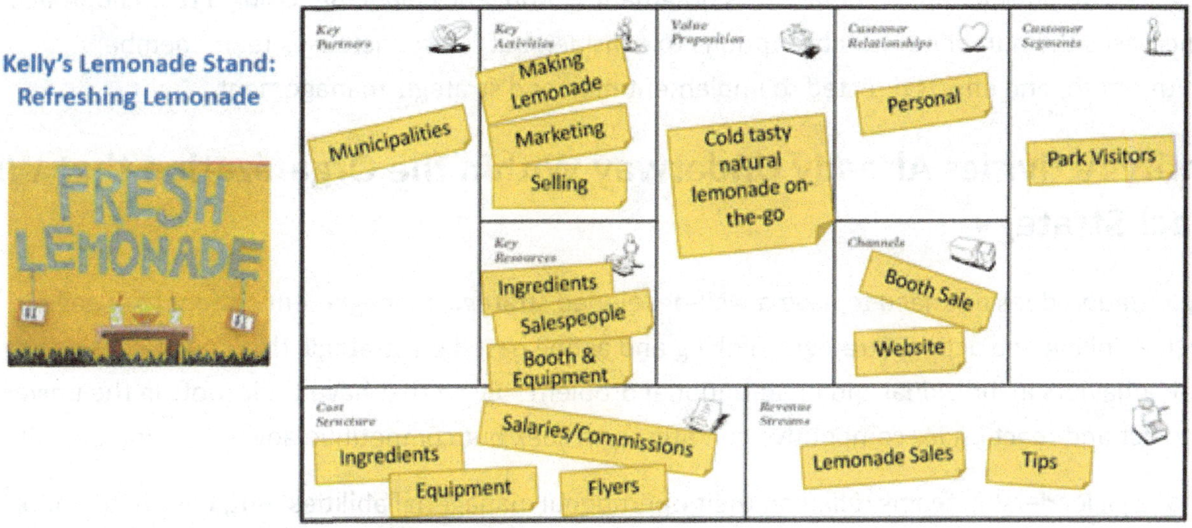

Develop a Well-Functioning Leadership Team

In summary, a well-functioning leadership team can discern the best strategies to implement as part of their ongoing strategic thinking and communication processes. These processes should flow from a collective, ongoing study of the environment rather than following a set of linear activities and requirements.

To become a well-functioning leadership team is no easy task. Leadership teams become effective in identifying and creating effective and sustainable competitive strategies by incorporating rigorous disciplined thinking with open inquiry, team discussions, regular feedback, and interaction.

In contrast to a team-based approach, strategies developed based solely on the perceptions of an "all knowing leader" severely limit the development of multiple approaches to moving forward and – more importantly – block the opportunity to build a multilevel strategic leadership team. Organizations pursuing the old model of top leadership formulating strategy and then relegating implementation to lower levels of leadership are destined to lose. We strongly advocate that all levels of leadership – the team – be continuously involved throughout the strategy process.

Using a team approach helps to ensure that strategy formulation and execution are more likely to be incremental processes that build on the existing capabilities, competencies, and current strategic

---

[88] Osterwalder is a Swiss business theorist, author, speaker, consultant, and entrepreneur, known for his work on business modeling.
[89] See video for a more detailed overview. https://www.youtube.com/watch?v=2FumwkBMhLo.

direction. Thus, deciding on a small number of carefully selected high-level strategies to develop and implement strategic change is usually more effective than attempts to make sweeping changes.

The essence of team-based strategy setting consists of developing options for realizing the overarching goal(s) and, ultimately, the vision. The goal is a repertoire of feasible responses to deal with the ever-changing environment and unexpected events. Developing a set of strategy alternatives, even if most are not selected for current implementation, is pragmatic contingency planning. Using a team approach not only increases the number of feasible options to consider, but it also increases team members' commitment to, and efforts directed to implementation and strategic management.

Identify Activities Already Underway Within the Organization that Will Impact Strategy

An organization does not need to have a well-developed strategic management system to engage in strategic thinking and action. Strategic thinking and acting based on strategic thinking are basic and natural behaviors in individual and organizational problem solving that have their roots in the universal need to act and react under competitive conditions, to seek out competitive advantage and prevail.

Traditionally, leadership teams relied on their operational managerial abilities. But, over time, more comprehensive strategic management models and approaches have been defined, developed, and adopted to focus leaders on the strategic level as opposed to the operational, day-to-day, level.

In any case, whether an organization has a well-developed strategic management system or operates on an ad hoc basis, there is no denying that a basic strategy formulation task remains: identifying activities that currently have, or will have, an impact at the strategic level.

Table 3.15 presents three primary benefits for identifying activities underway that have strategic impact.

TABLE 3.15 – BENEFITS TO IDENTIFYING ACTIVITIES WITH STRATEGIC IMPACT THAT ARE ALREADY UNDERWAY
• They indicate where leadership is currently placing its time, energy, and resources.
• They provide leadership with a realistic assessment of the level of strategic management capabilities presently used within the organization.
• They provide a starting point and a platform for making changes to strategy that are based on a realistic understanding of the baseline situation.

Two major sub-tasks can be undertaken to identify current activities likely to impact the organization's strategic direction, proposed strategy, or subsequent strategic planning and implementation.

- The first sub-task is to identify all *high-impact activities* underway that may or may not have resulted from a previous strategy formulation process. Many of these activities evolve incrementally over time and even the initiators of these activities may not recognize them as "strategic." This is important to understand because these strategies can be a double-edged sword. They may be the basis of a new and rewarding approach or they may be counterproductive to the new strategic direction. Key at this stage of the strategy formulation process is to highlight and recognize strategies and activities now being pursued and then to begin to monitor and evaluate them to determine their place in the strategic plan.

- The second sub-task is to identify the *strategy-support processes*, that is, operational capabilities that are essential systems and/or processes needed so a strategic alternative can be executed. These prerequisite processes are dictated by the strategies selected for implementation and vary depending on the organization and its capabilities, resources, and competitive conditions.

Organizations entering a new market or offering a new service often are disappointed to discover that they cannot compete. Having the necessary processes in place is of fundamental importance. For example, entering a market may be desirable but may only be possible if the organization's product development process incorporates customer expectations about quality, delivery, price, and competitive value. Being competitive in any of these areas may not be possible or be in the best strategic interests of the organization to pursue until the required operating model, skills, and capabilities are in place.

Conversely, the prerequisite processes may eventually be honed to a such high level that they become strategies for success. For example, the Japanese automobile industry used quality as a primary strategic advantage when they took the United States auto market by storm.

A downside for the innovator is that competitors eventually adopt their strategies. The innovator loses the initial competitive advantage.[90]

At this point, it is not necessary to catalog all the prerequisite processes, but it is important to identify those that are known and obvious to the leadership team. Later, for each strategy selected for inclusion in the organization's strategic plan, specific prerequisite processes can be developed in more detail.

Evaluate and Select High-Level Strategies

Every leadership team knows that time, money, and human resources are limited. This fundamental reality demands that leaders choose a small number of carefully selected strategies rather than attempt sweeping change. The decision-making process begins by evaluating each strategy alternative and ends with selecting a small set of strategies that the organization will proactively pursue.

Evaluation and selection processes play a key role in helping to ensure that the strategies provisionally identified will be the ones most likely to contribute to achieving the organization's vision, mission, and over-arching goal(s).

The term "evaluation" as used here refers to the process of examining strategic alternatives to determine the extent to which a given alternative meets specific criteria.

---

[90] Christensen, C. M. The Innovator's Dilemma: When New Technologies Cause Great Firms to Fail. Boston, MA: Harvard Business School Press, 1997.

Strategy in the 21st Century, Second Edition

The criteria should be created based on the potential impact each strategy will have on the organization and achieving its desired future state. Any list of potential criteria will likely include the following:

- Specific benefits and advantages to the organization
- Alignment with the new strategic direction
- Linkage to current strategies
- Consistency with management perspectives and organizational espoused values
- Risks incurred
- Feasibility
- Ease of implementation
- Duration

Ultimately the leadership team will develop its own set of evaluation criteria that are consistent with the management system, style, and capabilities of the organization.

Our recommendation is to make the strategy evaluation process explicit by using *strategy selection filters.* These filters will help narrow the number of choices to the vital few strategies that will best move the organization forward. (See Figure 3.13)

2.1(3)

FIGURE 3.13: STRATEGY SELECTION FILTERS

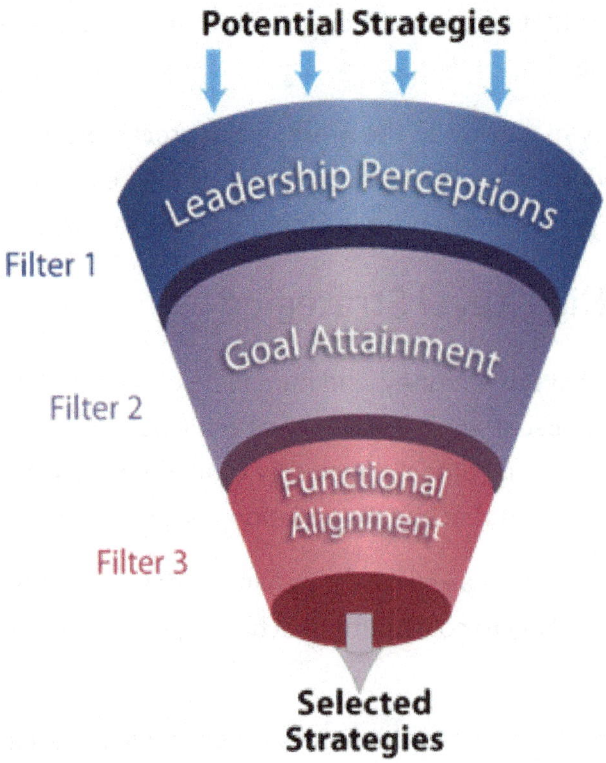

Here is a description of each **primary filter**:

Filter 1: Consistency with leadership perceptions

Phase III: Strategy Formulation

A key determinant for identifying potential strategy alternatives is the set of perceptions the leadership team has about its abilities, managerial skills, capabilities, and organizational resources. With respect to strategic management there are three critical perceptions:

- The perceived *need to change* any of the current strategies or to adopt new/revised strategies. The origin, focus, and urgency of this perceived need factor into the decision-making process of each leader and guide their decision making. However, no matter how nuanced or provisional the decision, each leader, and collectively the leadership team, will adopt or reject a strategy based on perceived need. The level of satisfaction (or dissatisfaction) with the current situation will be a key determinant of this perception. The questions that must be addressed are: Do we need to undertake this alternative? If so, how urgently?

- The *willingness to change* any of the current strategies or to adopt new or revised strategies. This perception has its roots in a set of complex factors, including the leadership's assessment of risks, costs, benefits, impact on the organization, competitive threats, and similar factors. The strategic management team must ask: Are we willing to undertake this alternative?

- The perceived *feasibility of changing* any of the current strategies or of adopting new or revised strategies. The perception of feasibility of an alternative is rooted in factors such as those listed above, but ultimately leadership is governed by its own estimate of the feasibility of undertaking an alternative. The perception of feasibility rules: Does the leadership believe that the organization can undertake and implement this alternative successfully?

Filter 2: Expectation of goal achievement

Goals, in effect, are summary statements of leadership expectations. They encapsulate the best expression of what leadership expects to accomplish during their tenure. It follows that if a strategy is viewed as having a significant impact on achieving a goal (or goals), it will be a strong candidate for inclusion in the strategic plan. Keeping this criterion in mind while identifying and generating strategic alternatives will make the process more effective and efficient.

Filter 3: Linkage/synergy/impact across core functions

This criterion differs from the two preceding criteria in a significant way: It does not originate with leadership perceptions or preferences. It has its basis in the characteristics of the most effective types of organizational strategy --- promoting significant and balanced contributions from across the organization, including finance, marketing, operations, information technology, human resource management, and governance.

Initially, identifying or creating strategic alternatives may seem to be a deceptively easy process. After all, it is the chief purpose of a leadership team to set the strategic course and to pursue it effectively. While this is true, it is not simple. Becoming a strategy-focused leadership team that can successfully chart and follow a new course of action is no easy matter.

The rationale for using detailed evaluation and selection processes stems from the need to ensure that the strategic initiatives in place, along with newly proposed ones, are necessary, feasible, and desired.

A proven approach is for team members to propose strategies in a brainstorming session. And a best practices way to initiate the brainstorming process, to avoid group think, is to have the participants consider and write down their initial ideas before the group session. The ideas and approaches proposed should not be analyzed or judged until *after* the brainstorming session, lest the generation of ideas be inhibited. The purpose here is for ideas to flow from the team so that others may build on them.

While identifying feasible strategies, an alternative that is the consensus view might come to light and should be undertaken as soon as possible. This demonstrates that these processes do not always proceed in the linear fashion. However, for organizations engaging in a disciplined approach to strategic management for the first time, it is usually best to follow a sequential analytic approach and then modify the approach as experience, intuition and judgment suggest. (See Figure 3.14.)

FIGURE 3.14: STRATEGY SELECTION EXAMPLE

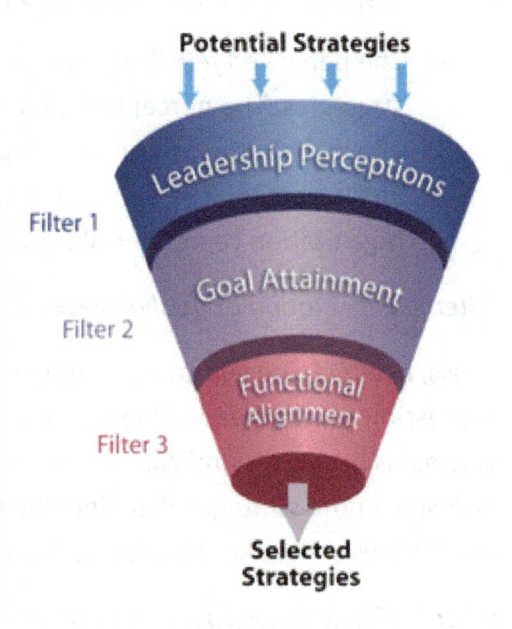

	Windy City Shoes Strategy Alternatives:	Market Penetration — Add 4 more stores	Market Development — Add shoe stores throughout St. Louis Region	Product Development — Introduce new line of socks/gloves	Diversification — Launch new stores in Western Europe – socks/gloves
Filter 1	Leaders don't want to develop Europe market	✓	✓	✓	✗
Filter 2	Windy City Shoes: To be the No.1 *shoe* store in Midwest US.	✓	✓	✗	
Filter 3	Acceptable risk and returns	✓	?		
	Meets customer needs	✓	?		
	Operationally feasible	✓	✓		
	Workforce capacity exists	✓	✓		

Potential Strategies → Leadership Perceptions (Filter 1) → Goal Attainment (Filter 2) → Functional Alignment (Filter 3) → Selected Strategies

The evaluation and selection processes counterbalance the more creative processes of identifying or generating feasible strategies. What may seem desirable and necessary when developing feasible strategy alternatives may not prove to be so if a particular strategy does not meet the tests of profitability, cost, feasibility, growth, and more. Evaluation and selection play a key role in helping to ensure that the strategies provisionally identified are those most likely to contribute to the achievement of the organization's vision, mission, and goals.

As these strategic choices are being made, the strategy professional and the core planning team should strive to assess the impact of these choices on the organization's operating model. In the end, the day-to-day operations of the organization must align with its strategy.

Phase IV – Strategic Planning

The result of the work in Phase III "Strategy Formulation" is a set of preferred strategies to include in the strategic plan. Developing strategies is an exercise in strategic thinking. It includes setting the strategic direction, generating candidate strategies, and selecting a subset for inclusion in the strategic plan.

Strategic planning requires a distinctly different set of activities that will transform the organization's strategic goals and selected strategies into a balanced set of objectives linked to key performance measures and prioritized initiatives. The process for strategic planning occurs in two tasks:

> **Task 4.1** – Develop a Longer-Term Strategic Plan
> **Task 4.2** – Develop a Shorter-Term Strategic Operating Plan

Implementation (in general) does not occur in the strategic planning phase. Rather, actions are planned to pave the way for implementation of a "strategic operating plan" in Phase V – Strategy Execution.

At the conclusion of this phase, special emphasis should be placed on transforming the organization's operating model to align with the new strategy and strategic plan. This process will be detailed in Phase V but begins here with a clear-eyed discussion and summary of what will be required to gain alignment.

Task 4.1 – Develop a Longer-Term Strategic Plan

Developing a longer-term strategic plan requires the ability to differentiate between *strategic* versus *operational* planning, and to apply the appropriate procedures to develop them. Here we caution not to adopt a "one size fits all" approach to all planning assignments.

In the case of strategic planning, an all too frequent result is to treat strategic planning the same as operational planning. Strategic plans should eventually deploy into operational activities. This requires the appropriate links and alignment so that the strategic plan does not become a meaningless and disconnected top-management exercise yielding a set of fragmented and isolated operational activities lacking strategic focus. Therefore, we begin with a few preliminary observations on planning per se as we outline the process of developing a longer-term strategic plan. The objectives of this task are the following:

- Compare and contrast strategic thinking and strategic planning.
- Consider strategic planning as a two-task process.
- Recognize the features of effective long-term strategic plans.
- Recognize the features of effective short-term strategic operating plans.
- Identify key drivers of success and their intended results.
- Translate intended results into a realistically achievable set of strategic objectives.
- Adopt and apply a balanced scorecard mindset.
- For each goal, visualize the cause-and-effect relationship among objectives via a strategy deployment map.
- Identify and evaluate the various types of strategic activities currently underway.
- Provide a contingency plan.
- Write a summary statement strategic plan.
- Obtain governance/stakeholder feedback, revisions, approval, and authorization.

Compare and Contrast Strategic Thinking and Strategic Planning

As noted, *strategy formulation* is primarily an exercise in strategic thinking, which is both analytic and creative. It includes developing a thorough understanding of the organization's capabilities and resources and setting the strategic direction based on these resources and capabilities filtered through the perceptions and preferences of leadership. Strategic thinking requires active questioning about strategy:

- What did we do?
- What are we doing?
- What do we want to do?
- What can we do?
- What are we willing to do?
- What do we need to do?
- What should we do?
- What will happen if we do?

Questions such as these may remain reality-based or can include hypothetical premises. They may be intensive and/or extensive and, taken together, form a strategy-focused thought process that provides the basis for strategic planning.

The primary deliverable from strategic thinking (covered in Phase III) is a big-picture direction and viable strategies to achieve success. However, these strategies are not a comprehensive long-term strategic plan or short-term operating plan, and certainly not a set of detailed deployable implementation instructions.

Phase IV: Strategic Planning

In contrast, *strategic planning* includes the set of activities that will develop these strategies into a balanced set of strategic objectives with instructions for implementation. Strategic planners are concerned with a more constrained set of questions, such as the following:

2.1

- What is the set of potentially actionable strategies that are to be included in the plan?
- How do we prioritize which strategies to act on?
- How do we scope strategies for planning purposes?
- How do we select the strategies that are to be included in the next annual operating cycle as policies, enterprise-wide initiatives, department-level projects, or individual assignments?
- How do we write a strategic plan for governance and/or management approval?

Consider Strategic Planning as a Two-Stage Process

The farther that a planning horizon extends into the future, the more a strategic plan will be subject to revision as conditions change, causing new opportunities and challenges to arise. In contrast, the shorter the planning horizon, the more fixed plans become with implementation activities selected and formally established in the strategic operating plan. This program then becomes operational as funding begins, staff commitments are made, and the implementation process is initiated. Therefore, strategic planning is best considered as a two-task process: 1) Longer-term strategic plan, and 2) Shorter-term strategic operating plan.

Characteristics of the Strategic Operating Plan and the Strategic Plan are summarized below (see Figure 4.1a):

FIGURE 4.1A: STRATEGIC OPERATING PLAN VS STRATEGIC PLAN

Strategic Operating Plan	Strategic Plan
Shorter Time horizon	Longer planning horizon
More structured	Less structured
More certainty	Less certainty
Reversible decision impact	Irreversible decision impact
Means oriented	Ends oriented
Focused on the part	Focused on the whole
Detailed analysis required	Analysis required
Micro level focused	Macro level focused

147

These two processes should be viewed as a continuum extending from the present into the future. However, for managerial and organizational purposes, they are best included as a two-stage process meeting the needs of both long-run and short-run approaches. (See Figure 4.1b.)

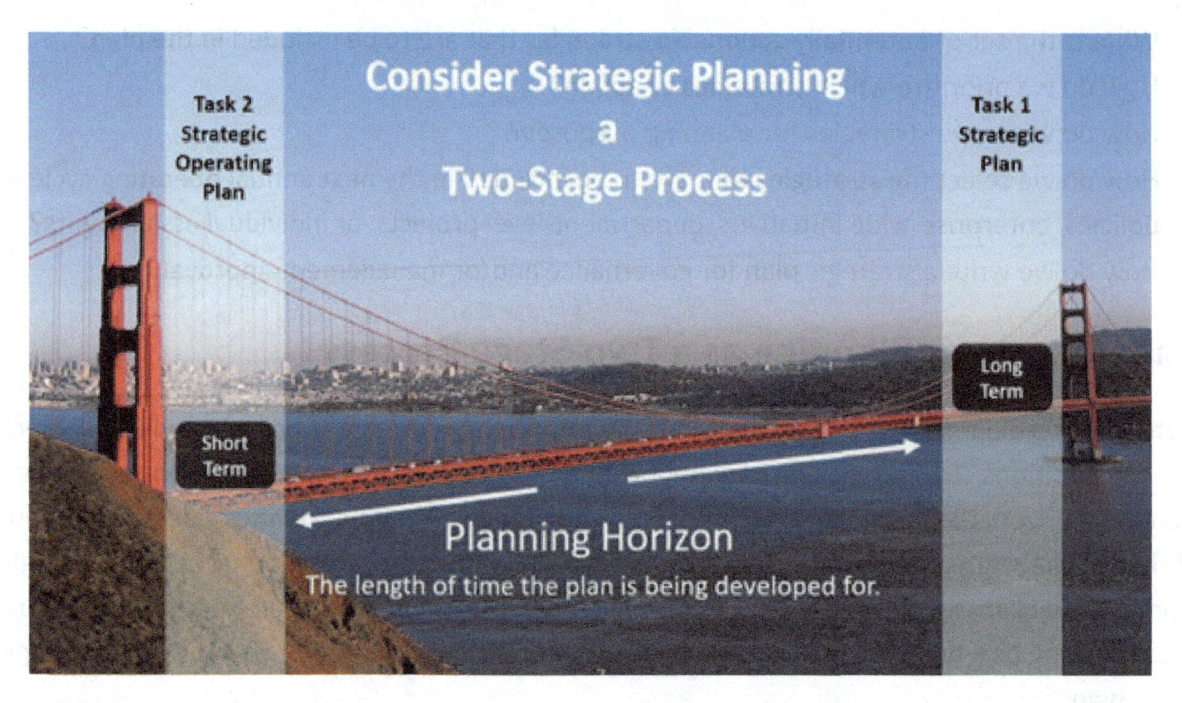

FIGURE 4.1B: TWO-STAGE PROCESS

With respect to the long-term, a small set of potentially actionable strategies are needed, giving management the ability to act either proactively or reactively as conditions and opportunities emerge. These strategies must already have been selected for their potential to realize the strategic vision, mission, and overarching goal(s) of the organization.

In contrast, the short-term strategic planning process should include evaluating strategies and initiatives that were implemented in the previous period, *still being implemented in the current operating period*, and possibly continued in future periods. These are "in-process initiatives" that have impact on newly formed strategies because they compete for the capabilities and resources available for implementing new and/or revised strategies.

Long- and short-term planning cannot be effectively combined into a single process, even though both are central components to planning the organization's future course of action.

Accordingly, this task focuses on developing a longer-term strategic plan, while the next task further develops the short-term plan (hereafter referred to as the strategic "operating" plan) by designing specific implementation plans for each strategic objective.

Throughout this phase, special consideration and emphasis are placed on transforming the organization's existing operating model to align with the new strategy. Two alternative approaches to accomplishing this end are detailed early on in Phase V.

Features of Effective Long-Term Strategic Plans

The result of the long-term planning process is *a small set of actionable strategies* for each strategic goal that will be implemented at some point over the organization's planning horizon.

Long-term plans should be designed so management can use them to accomplish these objectives:

- A basis for informed long-term strategic decision-making.
- A basis for planning by the strategic management team.
- Linkage between long-term goals and strategies and the nearer-term objectives and initiatives.
- A set of evaluation criteria for evaluating performance.
- A document that can be revised, if required by extenuating circumstances.

To accomplish these objectives, long-term plans should incorporate specific features in their design. (See Table 4.1.)

TABLE 4.1 – FEATURES OF A LONG-TERM PLAN

- *The primary focus is on successful deployment of an aligned operating model and integrated organization strategy.* This begins at the highest governance and management levels and includes the deployment of strategy throughout all levels of management and all functions.

- *It addresses the longest planning period that is being used in the organization.* Strategic planning reaches into the future as far as leadership is accustomed to laying out plans and making decisions. It needs to have the *flexibility to make changes, modifications, and additions to strategy in an integrated, systematic way*.

- *It provides an up-to-date information base* for management discussions on strategic planning. It should be regarded as a "work in progress" wherein all strategies *and assumptions* are subject to change as circumstances warrant.

- *Strategies are provisionally prioritized.* All strategies are not equally important so they should be prioritized in terms of need, feasibility, cost, and benefits. Most leadership teams know how to prioritize a given list of options – the real challenge was addressed during Phase III development and evaluation of an *initial set of alternatives* for inclusion in the strategic plan.

- *Sequencing, relationships, and interactivity between strategies are identified.* It is easy to overlook the impact that various strategies have on each other and the collective impact they can have on the organization. The way strategies build on each other is often overlooked as are precedence relationships that *require* sequencing.

2.2(7)

2.1(5)

TABLE 4.1 – FEATURES OF A LONG-TERM PLAN

- *Goals and strategies are then "road tested"* by specifying the overarching goal(s) and strategies into a small set of key drivers of success, their intended results, the strategic objectives the organization will work toward to achieve its goal(s) and, ultimately, the overall strategic direction.
- *Roles and responsibilities are identified.* At this point, the focus is on assigning overall responsibility for overseeing the strategic plan (not detailed implementation responsibilities). This includes the following:
    o Overall authority and responsibility for executing each strategic objective. A single individual should be assigned this responsibility for each strategic objective.
    o Overall responsibility coordinating the process of compiling, writing, obtaining approvals, editing, and distributing the plan.
    o Developing and maintaining a schedule to complete the strategic plan, including reviews, revisions, and approvals.
- *Provision is made for contingencies.* The strategic plan is incomplete until the leadership team (including strategy professionals) considers how the organization will respond to unforeseen events by curtailing initiatives, starting others, and modifying existing initiatives. A Plan B or Plan C is not needed for every contingency. However, alternative scenarios need to be identified for major concerns. Externally, these concerns may relate to changes in economic conditions, geopolitical unrest, domestic political unrest, pandemics, climate concerns, competition, customers, suppliers, and new technologies. Internally, the primary concerns relate to products/services and process development that does not always go according to schedule. Another important internal consideration is the turnover of key managers or professional staff.
- *Long-term strategic plans are different from operating plans.* One common mistake of management is to combine strategic and operational planning. Therefore, it is useful to consider their differences. Many so-called strategic plans are actually operating plans based on, for example, five-year marketing, operations, and financial projections of current operations.
Operating plans differ from strategic plans in the following ways:
    o They focus on programmed action plans, that is, the multitude of activities and milestones needed to complete initiatives. These initiatives together make progress to accomplishing the strategic objectives.
    o They do not require the close involvement of top management that formulating strategic initiatives requires. This includes explaining the rationale for the new initiatives, motivating the organization to accept

TABLE 4.1 – FEATURES OF A LONG-TERM PLAN
them, and closely following their progress throughout the strategic management process. <ul><li>Operational planning may include projects and programs that are several times larger than some strategic initiatives. It is not a matter of size; it is a matter of content and impact on a change or modification in the strategic direction that requires new and/or modified capabilities and competencies.</li><li>An operating plan's primary focus is on the annual budget cycle, not the long-run strategic direction.</li></ul><ul><li>*Long-term strategic plans require performance evaluation.* A particular strategy may be executed efficiently and still come up far short of achieving the leadership's desired objectives and expected results. Thus, provision for performance evaluation must be included in the strategic planning process. In this task, strategies started, and assumptions made in the previous operating cycle need to be evaluated before starting the new implementation program. These "legacy strategies" must also be evaluated periodically during and after implementation as part of ongoing operations management.</li><li>*Long-term strategic plans should highlight the required changes to the organization's operating model.* Alignment of the organization's strategy and operating model are a must for successful implementation of the strategy to occur.</li></ul>

These features, taken together, convey an understanding of the essential structure and format of a long-term strategic plan. How they get combined is left to the individual(s) charged with writing the plan, since this is a matter of the organization's planning policies and procedures combined with the writing style of those charged with producing the plan.

Features of Effective Short-Term Strategic Operating Plans

Short-term strategic planning refers to the following processes that are described in this task.

- Selecting strategic initiatives and operational projects, which are *necessary to transform the organization in alignment with the strategy*. These include:
  - Initiatives and operational projects started in previous planning cycles but not yet completed.
  - Initiatives and operational projects selected for implementation in a future cycle requiring some initial action due to long lead times.

- Writing the "short-term" portion of the comprehensive strategic plan that will be submitted to governance and/or management for approval *before* preparing detailed implementation plans.

- Preparing a detailed implementation plan for each objective selected from the long-term plan. Activities required to do this are covered in the remaining portions of this phase.

Strategy in the 21st Century, Second Edition

Identify Key Drivers of Success and Their Intended Results

Before identifying a tight set of strategic objectives, a critical step in operationalizing the strategy is defining where explicit continuous improvement and organizational focus are needed. This establishes a cohesive infrastructure, or scaffolding, around which strategic objectives can be thoughtfully articulated to achieve the organization's goals.

We refer to these as "key drivers of success." (See Figure 4.2 for an example.) *A key driver of success is an explicitly stated component or dimension of the organization where tangible results must be achieved for the shared vision, mission, overarching goal(s), and value propositions to be realized.* Key drivers can be external or internal in their focus. For example, an externally focused key driver of success might be "Stakeholder Relations," while an internal counterpart might be "Process Improvement."

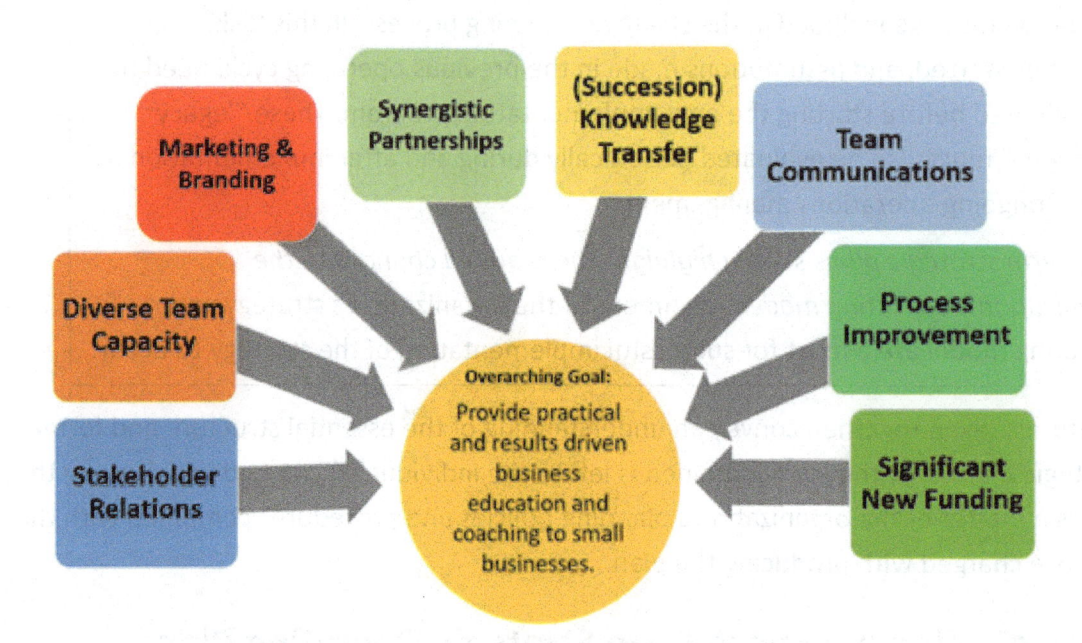

FIGURE 4.2: AN EXAMPLE OF KEY DRIVERS OF SUCCESS

Note: The figure components in this section (Tables 4.2, 4.3 and 4.5, along with Figure 4.6) maintain the same colors so that readers can easily see how the process unfolds across this example.

It follows that the task at hand is to identify critically important key drivers of success and intended results, which should receive priority attention. The basis for identifying them is grounded in the experience and judgment of the leadership team and considers the outputs of the strategic management process completed to this point. There is no standard set of key drivers of success that should be included. This work remains a collaborative and contextual process based on the needs, structure, resources, capabilities, and strategic direction of the organization.

To identify an organization's key drivers of success, start by asking the leadership team to review the results of work completed. Re-examine the results of the OTSW evaluation, earlier team conversations, and the results of any scenario planning work the team has completed.

Planning teams should pay particular attention to their already defined overarching goal(s) and strategies. Goal(s) and high-level strategies are primary inputs into this process. The strategy professional is responsible for facilitating a discussion to identify drivers of success, their intended results, and derive the strategic objectives to be included in the strategic plan.

The figure below summarizes the process flow and relationship between goals, strategies, key drivers, and strategic objectives (see Figure 4.3):

FIGURE 4.3: PROCESS FLOW AND RELATIONSHIP

*Note: In Phase III the organization's overarching goal(s) are **defined**. Informed by the goal statement, a small set of high-level strategies to achieve the goal(s) are **selected**. Now the team is challenged to keep these two primary inputs in mind as they **identify** key drivers of success and their intended results, from which a balanced set of strategic objectives can be **derived**.*

By leading the team to process this information individually and as a team, a skilled facilitator can guide the team to identify potential key drivers of success. After the necessary input is collected and consolidated, the team comes together to discuss and agree on seven to 12 key drivers of success. This can be achieved through brainstorming or through a more robust affinity-grouping exercise.

Here is a sample approach:

Pre-workshop assignment: Ask the leadership team to review the results of work completed for earlier tasks (i.e., OTSW evaluation, team conversations, results of any scenario planning work, and other assessment and strategy formulation work the team did). Each member is asked to make a short list of key performance areas requiring attention to achieve the overarching goal.

During the workshop, pose three questions for team consideration.

Q1. **What dimensions of performance** (or Key Drivers of Success) did you identify where tangible results must be realized to achieve the **defined** goal.

Collect each team members' input and create an affinity group team list of a set of 7-12 potential key drivers of success.

Once the affinity grouping exercise is complete, ask a second question.

Q2. **What are the intended results** the team seeks for each preliminary key driver of success?

Once the intended results discussion is complete, ask a third question.

Q3. **Will (and how will) the strategies** previously selected by the leadership/planning team **positively impact each potential intended result**?

Validate the alignment of the strategies with the intended results and identify and fill the gaps.

Finalize the Key Drivers of Success and Intended Results in a simple table (see Table 4.2).

TABLE 4.2: SAMPLE INTENDED RESULTS

#	Key Drivers of Success	Intended Results
1	**Stakeholder Relationships**	• Establish mutual understanding, trust, and communication with stakeholders. • Develop a pipeline of potential and diverse stakeholders. • Sustain stakeholder relations. *Keep them happy!* • Accomplish a win-win relationship. *Achieve goals!*
2	**Diverse Team Capacity**	• Team reflects demographics of the population. • Clients become more diverse. • Key stakeholders are more diverse. • Ability to meet the needs of clients with diverse backgrounds.
3	**Marketing & Branding**	• Create a clear understanding of our brand identity. • Create statewide voice. • Development of a statewide streamlined, consistent, annual marketing campaign that can be utilized by all offices. • A marketing capacity exists for centers to leverage.
4	**Synergistic Partnerships**	• Generate indirect dollars through partnerships. • Increase partnership referrals. • Potential partners proactively come to us. • Strategic partnerships begin to serve as a pipeline for future stakeholders. • Jobs, sales, loans, and program income rise. • DEI-specific partnerships in place and working.

Phase IV: Strategic Planning

#	Key Drivers of Success	Intended Results
		• Partnerships are being managed effectively. • Our referral network is expanding.
5	Knowledge Transfer	• Have a place where staff can efficiently store and find data/resources. • Cross training occurs. • Succession plans in place. • Onboarding process is effective and efficient. • Active mentoring occurring across centers. • Technology leveraged to support KT. • Expanded collaboration – sharing contacts
6	Team Communications	• Less isolation of employees in the field and more teamwork resulting in less burnout. • Information sharing enables new employees to better understand and do their job quicker. • Hearing from a larger diversity of team members and flattening the communication pyramid. • Mechanisms to support communication working. • Less redundant content is communicated. • We are practicing "intentional communications."
7	Process Improvement	• Processes are more consistent. • Processes are documented. • SOPs are improved with more "how to." • We have fostered a positive culture. • Silos are eliminated. • Administration is streamlined.
8	New Funding ($15,000,000 target)	• More financial independence • Corporate contributions grow. • State and local government are investing directly in small business development. • Foundations are actively involved. • Individual contributions are growing.

Translate Intended Results Into Realistically Achievable Strategic Objectives

When translating intended results into strategic objectives, *they should always be stated as outcomes, not activities*. Only objectives stated as outcomes provide a stable foundation for execution of the strategic operating plan. While objectives can evolve over time, the organization should be thoughtful about the need to change them. Both the strategic plan and the strategic operating plan need to be stable and understood by all. At this point, emphasis is not placed on creating measurable and quantifiable objectives. This occurs later in the process.

To translate intended results into a small set of objectives, a three-step process is recommended.

- Reflect on the intended results for each key driver of success. Then articulate one predominant outcome (or objective) statement for each driver. Larger organizations may find it helpful to identify other major outcomes within each key driver and consolidate them as much as possible into a smaller set of outcome statements.

- Each objective should describe the outcome the leadership team seeks to achieve. Each outcome should be stated in "verb-object" form, if possible, using a change verb that implies improvement, such as: Improve, Increase, Reduce, Decrease, or Strengthen.[91] (See Table 4.3.)

TABLE 4.3 – SAMPLE STRATEGIC OBJECTIVES

Key Driver	Strategic Objective (Predominant Outcome)
Stakeholder Relations	Strengthen & diversify stakeholder relationships
Diverse Team Capacity	Build diverse team capacity to meet and satisfy needs
Marketing & Branding	Improve marketing and branding
Synergistic Partnership	Expand strategic partnerships
Knowledge Transfer	Capture and transfer institutional knowledge
Team Communications	Improve team communications
Process Improvement	Improve internal operational processes
Significant New Funding	Grow new and existing sources of funding

These "future oriented" outcomes should be built to last and serve the organization for several years. To facilitate this process, practitioners must work with the leadership team to help them understand the outcomes they seek for each key driver.

- The final step is to document the essence of the team's discussion about strategy and strategic objectives into an "objective commentary."[92] Documentation should cover these questions:

---

[91] Rohm, H., Wilsey, D., Perry, G.S., Montgomery, D. *The Institute Way - Simplify Strategic Planning and Management with the Balanced Scorecard*, 127-135, 2016.
[92] Ibid, p137-138, 2016.

Phase IV: Strategic Planning

- What does this objective mean?
- What does it include and not include?
- What are the intended results?
- How can we measure its success?
- What is the linkage of this objective to other objectives?
- How will attaining this objective help us to be successful?

The purpose for documenting objective-level commentary is for future reference by the leadership team in the planning and execution of the strategy. (See Table 4.4)

TABLE 4.4 – SAMPLE OBJECTIVE COMMENTARY [93]

Objective Commentary Worksheet	
Objective	*Improve knowledge, skills & abilities*
Description	*Attract and retain skilled experienced leaders, technical and construction professionals. Improve recruiting strategies to ensure we recruit people that are highly motivated and share our core values. Reduce the recruiting cycle and increase our ability to meet the rising needs of our organization as we grow. Improve candidate assessment, screening and selection process.*
Intended Results	• *Skills match needs* • *Lean, versatile, committed and loyal workforce* • *Labor pools that fluctuate with workload* • *'Right size' recruitment time and cost* • *A diverse work force*
Linkage to Other Objectives	*This objective lays the foundation for success of objectives in "Internal Process" perspective. Without organizational capacity and staff competencies, we cannot operate efficiently, satisfy customers nor meet our financial expectations.*
Priority Level (Year 1)	*Since this objective is foundational to all other objectives, it should be put as high priority to be focused on first next fiscal year.*
Objective Champion	*Jennifer Courtney* **Working Team** *Mark Cutter, Casey Hanks*
Candidate KPI(s)	• *Short-term turnover rate* • *Certifications*
Candidate Initiative(s)	• *Redesign & refocus recruiting process*

Adopt and Apply a Balanced Scorecard Mindset

While there are many ways to build a strategic operating plan, we recommend adopting and applying a balanced-scorecard mindset when working on the longer-range strategic plan. (See the following task - *Select a framework for the strategic operating plan, p 171.*)

---

[93] ibid, p. 137, 2016.

Strategy in the 21st Century, Second Edition

Among the first thought leaders to recognize the importance of linking strategic objectives to operations were Drs. Robert Kaplan and David Norton in their pioneering work on the balanced scorecard. (See Figure 4.4.)

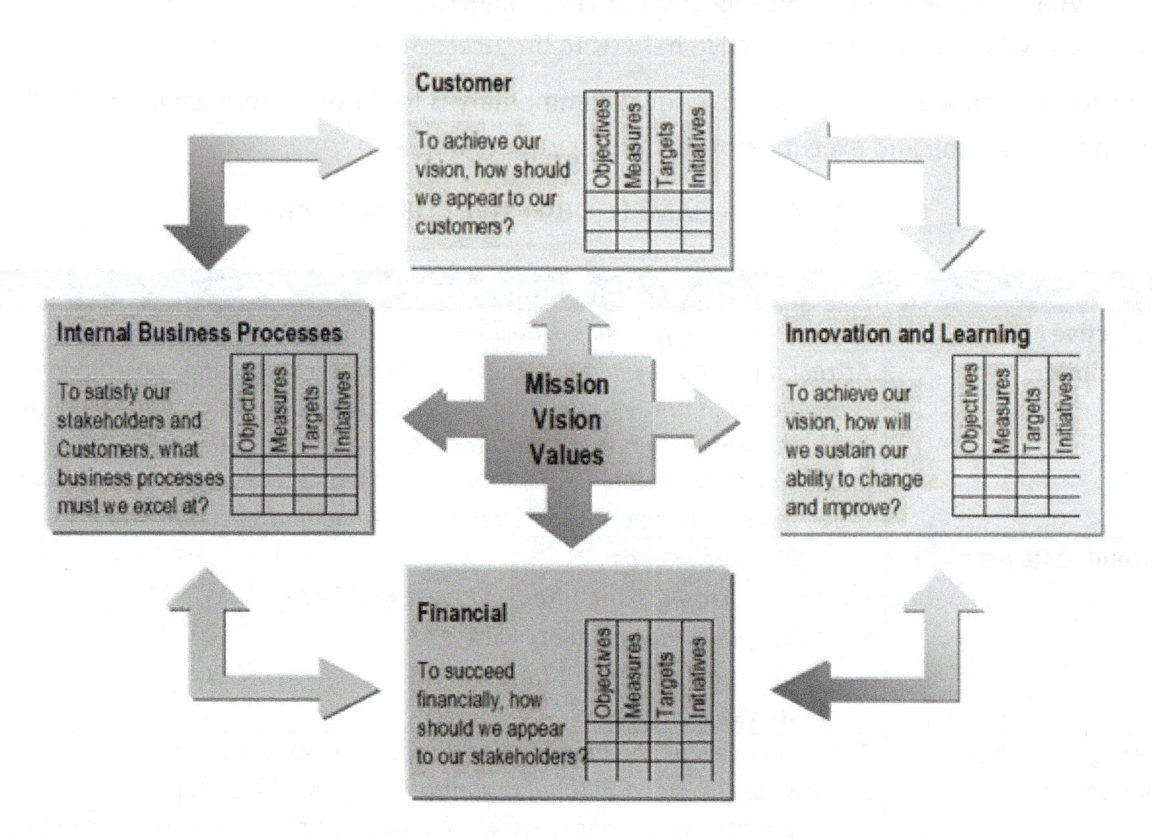

FIGURE 4.4: BALANCED SCORECARD

Kaplan and Norton stressed the importance of approaching strategy through a balanced approach to objective setting. They recognized four "strategic perspectives" involved in executing any strategy: *Financial, Customer, Internal Business Processes*, and Learning and Growth (or capacity building).

Further, these perspectives are linked in a synergistic, "cause and effect" relationship that enables a leadership team to translate the strategy into operations (see Figure 4.5).

7.1
7.2
7.5

FIGURE 4.5: CAUSE AND EFFECT RELATIONSHIP AMONGST PERSPECTIVES [94]

Tangible Outcomes ← Financial Perspective ← Customer Perspective | **Objectives & Outcomes**

Intangible Assets ← Internal Perspective (Processes) ← Learning & Growth Perspective (People) | **Actions**

Robert Kaplan and David Norton (2004) *Strategy Maps: Converting Intangible Assets to Tangible Outcomes*

Financial perspective objectives are desired outcomes that often lead to a myopic short-term focus on financial performance. Objectives in this perspective answer the question, "What are the desired financial outcomes we must achieve to satisfy our stockholders and/or other key stakeholders?" Financial objectives need to be complemented by the three other perspectives which are performance drivers contributing to financial achievement.

The **Customer** perspective examines business success through the lens of the customer. Objectives in this perspective answer the question, "What customer needs, desires, and expectations must we meet in order to meet our financial expectations?" This in turn drives a *need to improve current processes, and many times drives identification of new processes*.

Learning

The **Internal Process** perspective helps organizations identify and monitor outcomes related to their internal operations. Often these objectives include quality, process effectiveness, and efficiency improvements.

Objectives in the **Learning and Growth** perspective answer the question, "Where must we learn and grow as individuals and a team to operate efficiently, satisfy customers, and meet our financial expectations?"

---

[94] Depending on the organization type (i.e., B-Corp, nonprofit, mission driven, governmental, association) the sequencing of perspectives and the cause-and-effect relationship may differ from how they are presented by Kaplan and Norton in their original for-profit approach.

The answers to these questions become key to developing the strategic operating plan. The leadership team should carefully consider each question and document the results. Then, they should be restated as clear and concise strategic objectives.

The strategic objectives derived earlier in this Phase can be refined (as necessary) and categorized in one of the four balanced scorecard perspectives (see Table 4.5).

TABLE 4.5 – KEY DRIVERS, OBJECTIVES, AND PERSPECTIVES

Key Driver	Predominant Outcome Statement	Objective Name	Perspective
Stakeholder Relations	Relationships with all stakeholder groups have grown, strengthened, and expanded overall impact of our organization	Strengthen stakeholder relationships	Customer
Diverse Team Capacity	Our team comprises of coworkers from many backgrounds and experiences to best meet our customer needs	Increase diverse team capacity	Learning & Growth
Marketing & Branding	Our brand is recognized globally increasing our lead pipeline	Improve marketing and branding	Internal Process
Synergistic Partnership	Our relationship with partners is so valuable that neither party could image doing business without the other	Expand value to our strategic partners	Customer
Knowledge Transfer	Newer employees have access to the wealth of experience and information from those closer to retirement	Improve capture and transfer of institutional knowledge	Learning & Growth
Team Communications	Every member of our team has the information they need, when they need it.	Improve team communications	Internal Process
Process Improvement	Our processes continue to be streamlined for greater efficiency and overall team productivity	Improve internal operational processes	Internal Process
Significant New Funding	We need to add new revenue streams in creative ways while growing core business	Grow new and existing sources of funding	Financial

NOTE: For larger organizations, it may be helpful to identify other major outcomes within each key driver and consolidate to a small set of outcome statements

For Each Goal (or Set of Goals), Visualize the Cause-and-Effect Relationship Among Objectives Using a Strategy Deployment Map

The strategy map was developed by Kaplan and Norton and serves as a graphic representation of the cause-and-effect relationships among strategic objectives. This visualization process is at the heart of the balanced scorecard.

Developing a strategy map provides the strategic management team with a way to check for imbalances and/or ineffective linkages among the strategic objectives. It provides a summary view and facilitates communications about the plan, providing the basis for the operating model.

An important consideration for "mission driven" organizations (such as non-profits, associations, and many government-sector agencies) is whether to reverse the top two perspectives. (See Figure 4.6.) Often government agencies and nonprofits choose to put the Customer (in this case labeled Stakeholder) Perspective on top, to demonstrate their value to customers/stakeholders. Most for-profit organizations have the Financial Perspective on top to emphasize financial performance.

Phase IV: Strategic Planning

The strategy map depicted below, illustrates the result of translating an overarching goal statement (for this same mission-driven organization) into a balanced set of objectives arrayed across each strategic perspective with cause-and-effect relationships identified between objectives (see Figure 4.6):

FIGURE 4.6: STRATEGY MAP EXAMPLE

Overarching Strategic Goal:	Provide practical and results driven business education and coaching to entrepreneurs, business owners, and workforce.
Stakeholder Perspective	Strengthen and Diversify Stakeholder Relationships
Financial Perspective	Grow New and Existing Sources of Funding
Internal Process Perspective	Capture and Transfer Institutional Knowledge — Improve Network Communications — Expand Strategic Partnerships; Improve Internal Operational Processes — Enhance Brand Identity
Capacity Building Perspective	Build diverse team capacity to meet and satisfy our state's small business development needs (rural & urban)

A strategy map serves as a powerful visual communications tool. It is a versatile tool that communicates in different ways to different audiences in your organization. For instance, for front-line staff you can easily read a strategy map from the bottom up, by asking "Why?" while senior leaders and a board of directors read the same map from the top down by asking "How?"

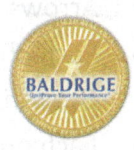

BALDRIGE

2.2(2)

Take a moment to follow the cause-and-effect linkages displayed in the example above, reading it in both directions.

There are four rules[95] to guide a team in constructing a strategy map (see Figure 4.7):

---

[95] Rohm, H., Wilsey, D., Perry, G.S., Montgomery, D. *The Institute Way - Simplify Strategic Planning and Management with the Balanced Scorecard*, p147-153, 2016.

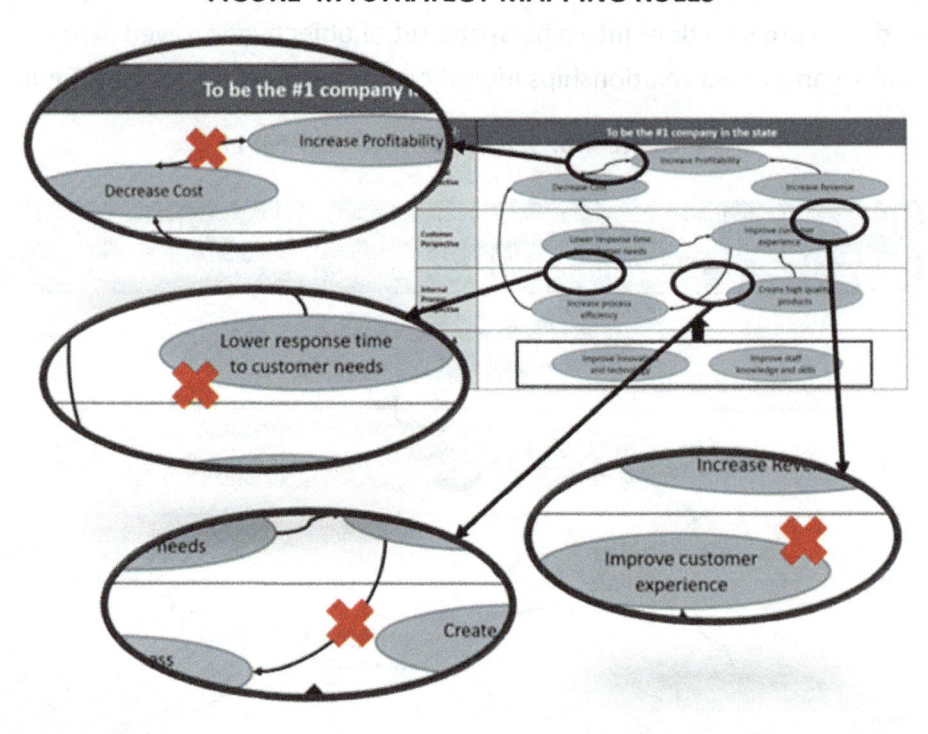

FIGURE 4.7: STRATEGY MAPPING RULES

The rationale for these rules is to ensure that the strategy map clearly communicates an accurate "value creation story," showing the predominant cause-effect linkages that drive positive performance in achieving objectives within your plan. To this end, the Balanced Scorecard Institute recommends:

- Avoid using arrows that point in two directions.
- Arrows should not flow/point downward.
- Each objective should be driven by at least one other objective (except for the Learning and Growth objectives).
- Each objective should drive at least one other objective.

Once a strategy map has been drafted, "stress test" it before communicating the results. This stress testing can be accomplished by asking fundamental questions:

- Does the team see any gaps in the map?
- Are our objectives worded clearly?
- Do we agree (as a team) with the cause-and-effect arrows?
- Do we see any objectives that are too tactical in nature?
- Do we see where we might combine objectives?

For more information on strategy maps, we refer you to Kaplan and Norton's 2004 book, *Strategy Maps, Converting Intangible Assets into Tangible Outcomes*,[96] and the work of the Balanced Scorecard Institute on strategy mapping.[97]

---

[96] Kaplan, R.S., Norton, D.P. *Strategy Maps - Converting Intangible Assets Into Tangible Outcomes*, 2004.
[97] Rohm, H., Willsey, d., Perry, G.S., Montgomery, D. *The Institute Way* - Chapter 9. 145-157.

Identify and Evaluate the Various Types of Strategic Initiatives Currently Underway

Organizational leaders are continuously making decisions that can have an impact on strategy — ones that may not have been considered "strategic" at the time. Decisions made implicitly or explicitly, intuitively, or formally as part of a process are what James Brian Quinn refers to as "incrementalism" (1980).

These decisions need to be evaluated periodically, especially when a strategic plan is written. Planning for new strategic initiatives should not start until legacy strategies are evaluated. The main reasons are:

- To ascertain the costs of continuing implementation and, therefore, *the funding level available for strategic initiatives for the next budgetary cycle*.
- To assess relationships with, and the impact on, proposed new/revised alternatives.

2.2(3)

Provide for Contingency Plans

Strategic initiatives are not always realized according to plan. Strategic planning is often experimental since it deals with untried initiatives in new and uncertain circumstances. This points to the need for leadership (facilitated by strategy professionals) to engage in a basic level of contingency planning before it becomes clear that a new or modified strategy is required. Unfortunately, contingency planning often does not occur until initiatives are underway.

The purpose of introducing contingency planning here is to underscore the importance of alternative courses of action and the need to include alternative courses of action in consultation with the strategic management team.

Consider contingencies with respect to size, scope, cost, and duration of strategic initiatives. For example, ask questions such as the following:

- Can this initiative be reduced in size?
- Can its scope be altered?
- Can you reduce the cost of the initiative?
- Can you adjust the length or temporarily stop the initiative's implementation?

Write a Summary Statement for the Longer-Term Strategic Plan

Writing a summary statement provides an expanded explanation of the longer-term strategic plan. It outlines the primary assumptions and key points of the plan for both the long- and short-term in an integrated overview.

Table 4.6 summarizes suggestions on the format and content of this written plan.

TABLE 4.6 – SUGGESTED FORMAT AND CONTENT OF THE WRITTEN STRATEGIC PLAN

The written plan serves both instructional and motivational purposes. In this "single summary" document the organization's leadership can provide an overall perspective on an integrated strategic plan to motivate and unite the broader team toward the achievement of shared goals.

While the written plan is a plan of action, it is technically a proposed plan of action, a precursor to the real action that is delineated in the strategic operating plan. However, the written strategic plan serves another purpose: it sets forth the vision, the mission, and the pathway for achieving them.

- *Introduction.* Corporate annual reports are a good example of how leadership can make a summary introduction that includes salient features of the organization's progress, problems, prospects, and plan. The reader has an overall perspective of the state of the organization and its future direction. In writing an introduction to the strategic plan, leadership has a similar responsibility and can use a similar format with a few modifications. First, the strategic plan is primarily written for internal consumption by the organization. It should briefly cover key points regarding the existing plan with respect to progress, problems, and prospects already identified in the more detailed evaluation of the existing strategic plan (outlined in the sections above).

- *Outline of the new (or revised) strategic direction.* A recommendation in the previous task was that all components of the strategic direction be included in summary form and approved by the board or leadership team. This statement should be included in the strategic plan to set the stage for all that is to follow and provide the rationale for revising or setting a new strategic direction. When members of the organization are given information that helps them understand the new direction and the implications of the organization's current operating model (needs connected to benefits), they are more likely to buy in and be motivated to implement the required changes.

- *Description of the organization's strategic plan,* including at least the following:
   - *A summary statement of the organization's strategy.* This statement covers the planning horizon. It should include the description of high-impact strategies in broad terms. These descriptions set the stage for the subsequent "immediate" strategic initiatives that will be introduced during the next budget cycle.
   - *Significant strategic outcomes.* There must be some salient, easily identified outcomes that further reinforce the need for the new strategies. These should be highlighted.

- *Deployment of the organization strategy.* The objective of describing strategy deployment is to show how the strategy cascades into the functional areas. It does this without going into the details of each strategic objective/initiative – that is the function of the strategic operating plan and subsequent implementation program.

- *Preliminary identification of strategic initiatives that are to be implemented in the next iteration of the operating plan.* These initiatives will become components of the strategic operating plan considered in the following task. This is the pivotal link between strategic planning and implementation, making the transition to initiative execution.

> - ***Scope and nature of the implementation program.*** Every significant strategic activity should be scoped properly to develop a feasible implementation plan. Therefore, attention to the following factors is advised:
>   - Primary changes required in the organization's operating model.
>   - The risks, uncertainties, and potential obstacles that might delay or otherwise impede the implementation process.
>   - The amount of training and education required.
>   - Resources that need to be acquired.
>   - Resistance, even opposition, is likely to occur.
>   - The time it takes to reach expected returns on the investments.
>   - New (to the organization) implementation processes.
>
> These and related factors need to be considered to establish a feasible strategic operating plan and cost-effective implementation program. The difficulty is that these estimates must be made at the outset when the necessary information is often not available. Nevertheless, an effort is required to make careful estimates based on current, albeit incomplete information, to help offset the all-too-common tendency to attempt to do too much ineffectively and/or inefficiently. Doing this helps avoid over commitment and underachievement and falling prey to the planning fallacy, our tendency to underestimate task-completion times, due to optimism bias and the ease of imagining a successful outcome versus all the things that could go wrong.

Obtain Management Feedback, Revisions, Approval, and Authorization to Continue

Leadership involvement in the strategic management process does not obviate the need for a formal approval process. Once the plan is finalized, it needs the approval of the Board, leadership, and/or executives.

The approval process has the following objectives:

- Ensure that the members of governance and management included in the strategic planning process have reviewed the plan and suggested additions, modifications, and/or deletions.
- Ensure that the members of management who are responsible for approving plans, authorizing expenditures, and acquiring resources have approved the plan.
- Allow time to revise the plan until all suggestions have been accepted, modified, or rejected.

This approval process does not entail a detailed budget review, nor is it a request for funds and other resources. This is the time to ensure that the plan has leadership approval so that the team can proceed to the next stage of planning, where budgetary, scheduling, and resources are addressed.

As this task ends, special emphasis should be placed on identifying the transformations required in the organization's existing operating model to align with the new strategy.

Task 4.2 – Develop a Shorter-Term Strategic Operating Plan

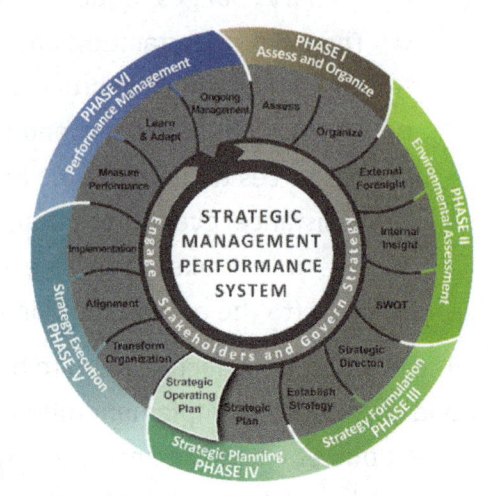

In many situations, translating a strategic plan into an effective strategic operating plan is difficult. Often a gap develops between the strategy as it comes down from the top of the organization *and* the level of employee understanding of how their daily activities contribute to achieving the vision.

This gap appears because a strategic plan is longer term, while most managers are trained to gauge their progress by assessing achievement in meeting operations-level "here and now" demands. Further, the strategy itself means change. After all, it is about transforming the organization to provide added value in the future. This will require a shift not just in actions, but sometimes in culture and knowledge as well.

Central to building an effective strategic operating plan is understanding the concept of "strategic altitude." Remember, the organization's overall "enterprise" level strategic direction sits at the highest altitude in the planning and management hierarchy. The strategies and objectives to achieve are at mid-altitude. Implementation initiatives along with management measures and budgets sit at ground level. (See Figure 4.8.)

FIGURE 4.8: STRATEGIC ALTITUDE

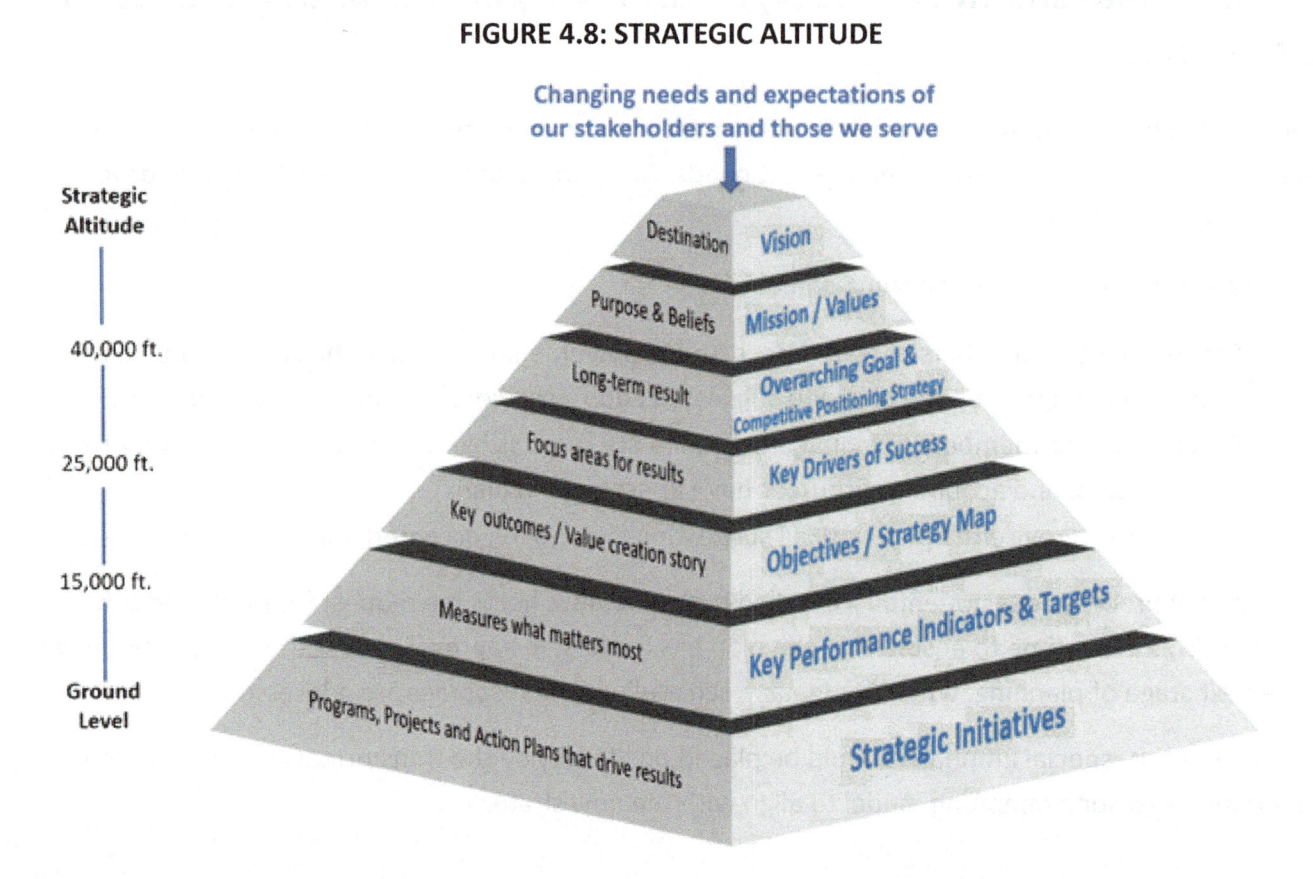

Phase IV: Strategic Planning

The purpose of a *strategic operating plan* is to move from higher-altitude strategic outcomes to lower-altitude tactical execution. At this lower altitude, more specific and narrowly focused language is used to empower teams to engage and achieve results.

The strategic operating plan is an integrated and deployable set of marching orders detailing exactly *what* will be done to transform strategies into operational level activities with measurable results. It includes *implementation of selected and approved strategies into operations level activities.* It is tactically focused: It includes objectives, responsibilities, measures, and initiatives/projects. (See Figure 4.9.)

2.2(1)

2.2(3)

2.2(4)

FIGURE 4.9: ALIGNMENT

Strategic Direction
- Vision
- Mission
- Values
- Policies
- Overarching Goal(s)

Strategic Plan
- Strategies
- Key Drivers
- Strategic Objectives
- Strategy Map

Strategic Operating Plan
- Strategic Objectives
- Strategy Map
- Key Performance Indicators / Targets
- Strategic Initiatives / Projects

Execution
- Organizational and Individual Alignment
- Annual Budgets
- Activities and Tasks

Performance Management
- Performance Measurement
- Ongoing Performance Management
- Double-loop Learning

Alignment begins to form as strategy professionals guide a planning team through development of each component while helping them stay mindful of the needs, wants, and expectations of their customers and key stakeholders. This is particularly true when it comes to development of the organization's strategic operating plan.

Translating the big-picture strategic direction and strategic plan into everyday operational activities has been the desired end result of strategic planning from its earliest manifestation on the American corporate scene. To front-line workers, the organizational strategy can seem highly irrelevant to their daily existence. Their sense of disconnection and powerlessness to affect the outcome can be overwhelming. They often feel, "Why should this matter to me? Success at the top never reaches us down here." *To avoid this problem, careful attention must be placed on the development of a practical strategic operating plan.*

To illustrate the balanced scorecard as a framework for a strategic operating plan, let us review a fictitious small business example, Chicagoland Gas. The owners of the business set their vision as becoming "Chicagoland's #1 gas and convenience store provider," with a target of "doubling sales of convenience store products and gasoline dispensing services in three years." The Chicagoland Gas leadership team then defined a balanced set of objectives, key performance indicators with defined targets, and initiatives to establish the strategic operating plan's focus on implementation.

Take a moment to review the illustration below depicting the use of the balanced scorecard framework to articulate a strategic operating plan, the example being Chicagoland Gas (see Table 4.7):

TABLE 4.7 – SAMPLE STRATEGIC OPERATING PLAN USING THE BALANCED SCORECARD FRAMEWORK

Goal: Chicagoland's #1 gas and convenience store provider

Perspective	Objectives	KPI/Target	Initiatives/Projects
Financial	Ensure sufficient liquid assets to add locations when the opportunity arises.	Quick Ratio | Target: 1.4 Days Cash on Hand | Target: 180 Pre-tax profit | Target: +2%	• Evaluate and select banking alternatives • Benchmark existing cost structure against industry leaders
	Lower operating costs	Operating Costs per Employee | Target: -2%	
	Increase sales	Sales | Target: +10%	
Customer	Improve facility appearance and cleanliness	Customer Rating Score | Target: 90% Very Satisfied	• Determine which communities to target and begin building new sites • Work with contractors to remodel existing store (to enhance safety and cleanliness) • Design, develop and deliver a "Safety First" program
	Make access to each facility easy.		
	Improve the appearance and safety of every facility	Worker Compensation Claims | Target: 0	
Internal Perspective	Improve marketing & brand image	New Customers | Target: +2% per month Customer Rating Score | Target: 98% Very Satisfied	• Expand sponsorship and partnership opportunities • Provide customer service training for all employees • Create a new employee orientation program • Do a location by location assessment and establish benchmarks and baselines per store
	Improve employee customer service performance		
	Improve our operational efficiency	Inventory Turns | Target 50% monthly	
Learn & Grow (capacity)	Improve retail management skills of employees	Staff Retention | Target: 85% stay 5 or more years Employee Satisfaction Rating | Target: 90% Very Satisfied	• Conduct a competency gap analysis for all management positions • Implement a cross training program (hire a consultant)

The work to develop the strategic operating plan includes:

- Identifying execution planning guidelines (upfront).
- Selecting a framework for the strategic operating plan.
- Identifying management roles and responsibilities required to align the organization's operating model with the strategy and strategic operating plan.
- Developing implementation plans for strategic objectives.
- Reconciling aggregate strategic operating plan implementation requirements to available implementation capabilities and resources.
- Writing a summary statement of the strategic operating plan.
- Obtaining governance approval and authorization for the strategic operating plan.
- Distributing and communicating the strategic operating plan.

Identify Execution Planning Guidelines Up Front

Think ahead! Significant time and effort have been invested by the organization and its leadership team in the planning process up to this point. Be mindful that much of the expected return on work already completed can be "lost in translation" when moving from planning to execution. Stories abound about professionally facilitated planning processes resulting in beautifully bound and presented calls to arms that never get implemented. Too often plans are approved only to remain in limbo waiting for the day

Phase IV: Strategic Planning

when "best intentions" meet "when things slow down." Such an experience does great damage to the organization's collective psyche, ratcheting up the level of employee cynicism toward the value of strategic planning.

Another frequent pain point occurs when those charged with executing the strategy do not understand how their day-to-day work supports the overall strategy. Again, confusion occurs, and the strategic management capacity of the organization is undermined.

To avoid these and other pitfalls, heed the "golden oldie" universal truths in implementation management. These basic management principles have stood the test of time and are good to revisit as strategy execution takes center stage. (See Table 4.8.)

TABLE 4.8 – EFFECTIVE IMPLEMENTATION GUIDELINES

Guideline 1: Strategic Operational Planning

- In many cases, it is smart to focus on the overarching goal(s) to begin the execution planning process. Detailed implementation planning will inevitably expand the requirements and demands on management and staff beyond initial considerations.
- Before implementation occurs, think through where and how to transform the organization's operating model to align with the new strategy (see Phase V).
- Evaluate strategies/initiatives implemented in previous planning periods before continuing them into the current planning period.
- Select initiatives/projects to implement that that will best close the performance gap while remaining consistent with leadership aspirations, deploy across all core functions, contribute to the development of those functions, and contribute significantly to goal attainment.
- Carefully select and scope the tactics and strategic initiatives that will deliver the greatest benefit.

Guideline 2: Organization

- Select an appropriate format and structure for the strategic operating plan.
- Deploy the operating plan in the core functions of the organizations.
- Make explicit any external relationships required for a given strategy.

Guideline 3: Operations

- *Develop implementation procedures and tactics required to implement a given strategy.*
- Clarify relationship between ongoing operations and strategic implementation activities.

Guideline 4: Management

- Assign and align the roles and responsibilities at all management levels required to implement a given strategy. (See Phase V.)

2.2(2)

TABLE 4.8 – EFFECTIVE IMPLEMENTATION GUIDELINES	
<ul><li>Obtain leadership approval of the implementation plan and its budget.</li><li>Thoughtfully communicate the implementation plan to organization members and relevant stakeholders.</li><li>Explain the importance of the strategic plan and sustain interest in its implementation.</li></ul>**Guideline 5: Management Systems**<ul><li>Provide efficient management systems for the implementation plan, including:</li><li>*Performance monitoring, measurement, evaluation, and learning.*</li><li>Engagement of subject matter expertise as required.</li><li>Scheduling, milestones, assignment of personnel.</li><li>*Acquisition and allocation of resources.*</li><li>*Budgetary controls, approvals, authorizations, and top management oversight.*</li></ul>**Guideline 6: Staffing**<ul><li>*Select the people who have the ability to do the job* and:</li><li>Confirm that they clearly understand what is expected.</li><li>Let them know that you believe in their ability to achieve the planned implementation.</li><li>Negotiate a deadline and secure their commitment on following through.</li><li>Provide latitude so that they can use their own imagination and initiative.</li><li>Reinforce the need for accountability by letting each person know in the beginning you will follow up on agreed upon commitments and then do it.</li><li>Do not do the job for them.</li><li>Recognize and reward them commensurate with the results they produce.</li><li>Include implementation, engagement, and change management responsibilities in job descriptions and performance evaluations.</li><li>Assign non-management personnel to implementation tasks to broaden the effort and develop wider interest in the plan's success.</li><li>Ensure that the required personnel are made available for new/revised strategies being implemented through recruitment, promotion, transfer, training, job restructuring, and/or reassignment of duties.</li></ul>**Guideline 7: Resources**<ul><li>Provide for the acquisition and allocation of required resources.</li><li>Ensure the efficient and effective utilization of resources.</li></ul>	2.2(5) 2.2(3) 2.2(4)

Phase IV: Strategic Planning

TABLE 4.8 – EFFECTIVE IMPLEMENTATION GUIDELINES
• *Provide for the development and upgrading of current resources as a consequence of introducing new strategies and the resultant changes required.*
Guideline 8: Report and Documentation
• *Record and report significant events, problems encountered and solved, barriers overcome, and suggestions for future implementation processes.*
• *Document this experience in a way to facilitate development of effective implementation processes.*

2.2(4)

Learning

Select a Framework for the Strategic Operating Plan

A strategic operating plan can be built in multiple ways and decisions about what should be included are context specific. In general, fundamental components consistently included in most strategic operating plan frameworks include:

- List of strategic objectives
- Accountabilities
- KPIs and targets
- Initiatives
- Initiative workplans and schedule
- Strategic operating plan budget

Earlier in this phase we introduced the balanced scorecard. However, there are times when a different model should be utilized. The role of the strategy professional is to work with the management team to pick the framework that best meets the needs of the organization. Here are three additional models: Objective & Key Results (OKRs), Hoshin Kanri, and Logic Model Framework.

OKRs

If the strategy management cadence in a particular organization requires strategic agility, then the leadership team may want to consider the use of OKRs.

The term "Management by Objectives" (MBO) was first coined by Peter Drucker in *The Practice of Management* (1954). It was Andrew Grove (the CEO of Intel) who upgraded MBO with the OKR concept in *High Output Management* (1983) and thus became the father of the OKR framework. [98]

---

[98] Grove, A. *High Output Management*, 1983, updated 1995.

In 1999, John Doerr introduced the OKR Framework to Google. Doerr defines OKRs as "a management methodology that helps to ensure that the company focuses efforts on the same important issues throughout the organization."[99] Niven and Laporte define OKRs as "a critical-thinking framework and ongoing discipline that seeks to ensure employees work together, focusing their efforts to make measurable contributions that drive the company forward."[100] Dan Montgomery defines OKRs as "a formula for quantifying enterprise-wide vision and strategies, or shorter term-level goals."[101]

OKRs consists of two parts: Part 1 are the Objectives or the intended "outcomes" the organization, unit, or individual seeks to accomplish in a short period time, let us say 90 days. Part 2 are the Key Results or the measures the organization, unit, or individual will use to document progress made toward achieving those most important objectives. (See Table 4.9.)

TABLE 4.9 – CITY GOVERNMENT OKR EXAMPLE

Tier One	Tier Two (Department or Functional Unit)		Tier Three (Individual Role)	
Enterprise Wide Strategic Objective	Function/Department Objective	Key Result	Individual Objective	Key Result
Increase environmental awareness and environmentally responsible practices across all of city government	Child and Family Services: Increase recycling compliance within agency offices . . .	. . . by 25% by Q2	Case Worker: Make case data available electronically . . .	. . . 50% by Q2
	Hire Vehicles: Decrease carbon monoxide emissions for all hire vehicle services . . .	. . . by Q2 all vehicles emission level established	Director of Hire Vehicles: Complete emissions baseline training . . .	. . . to 90% of drivers by Q2
	Education Agency: Decrease unrecyclable garbage in all grade schools . . .	. . . by 1% by Q2	Dir of Environmental Services: Conduct facility audits . . .	. . . to 35% of facilities by Q2

For each objective included on the organization's enterprise level strategy map, organizational units, teams, and individuals put in place a cadence to define and transparently report OKRs. The primary benefits are clarity of purpose, accountability, transparency, and, most importantly, aligning short-term actions with short-term objectives. OKRs will only deliver intended results with sustained team effort.

More detail on OKRs is provided in Phase V.

HOSHIN KANRI

Hoshin Kanri, also called Policy Deployment, is a method to ensure that an organization's strategic goals drive progress and action at each level in the organization by eliminating waste from inconsistent direction and poor communication. It is a systems approach to the management of change in critical business processes. This proven technique helps organizations focus efforts and achieve results. [102]

---

[99] Doerr, J. *Measure What Matters: How Google, Bono, and the Gates Foundation Rock the World with OKRs*, 2018.
[100] Niven, P. and Lamorte, B. *Objectives and Key Results: Driving Focus, Alignment, and Engagement with OKRs*, 2016.
[101] Montgomery, D. *Start Less, Finish More - Building Strategic Agility with OKRs*, 2018.
[102] Kesterson, R.K. *The Basics of Hoshin Kanri*, 2015.

Phase IV: Strategic Planning

Originally, Hoshin Kanri planning was developed in Japan during the 1960s from Quality Management practices used at Bridgestone Tire, Toyota, Nippon, Denso, Komatsu, and Matsushita. It was strongly influenced by the "Plan-Do-Check-Act" management method introduced by W. Edward Deming and the "Management by Objectives" process developed by Peter Drucker.

The Japanese words **hoshin kanri** can be generally interpreted as direction setting. The words **nichijo kanri** can be interpreted as daily fundamental management. The blending of these two methods is key to the success of the hoshin process summarized in the X Matrix. (See Figure 4.10.)

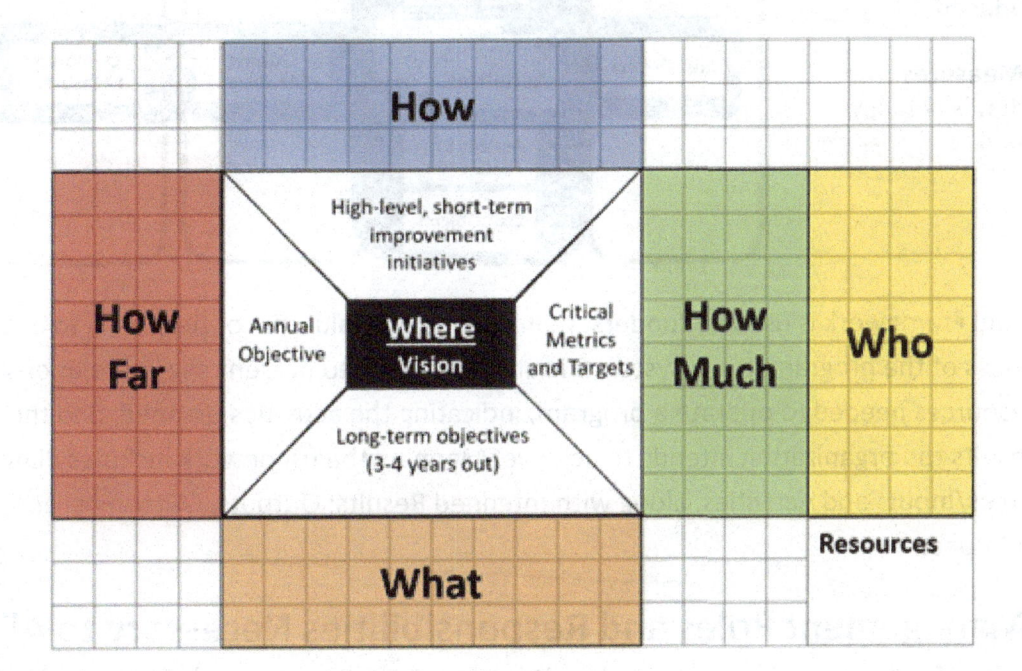

FIGURE 4.10: HOSHIN X MATRIX

LOGIC MODEL

Logic models graphically depict the logical relationships between the resources/inputs, activities, outputs, and outcomes of a program. Logic models can be presented in many ways. The purpose of the logic model is to assess the "if-then" relationships between the elements of the program.

Logic models were first described over 35 years ago by Joseph S. Wholey of USC.[103] Several years later the value, evolution, and use of the logic model was clarified by consultant John McLaughlin and Gretchen Jordan of Sandia National Laboratories. They observed that the logic model approach has also been called "chains of reasoning," "theory of action," "performance framework," and "logical framework." [104] (See Figure 4.11.)

---

[103] Wholey, J.S. *EVALUATION AND EFFECTIVE PUBLIC MANAGEMENT*. Boston: Little, Brown, 1983.
[104] McLaughlin, J.A., and Jordan, G.B. Logic Models: A Tool for Telling Your Program's Performance Story, *Evaluation and Program Planning*, 22(1), 1999.

Strategy in the 21st Century, Second Edition

FIGURE 4.11: THE LOGIC MODEL FRAMEWORK

- **Input Measures >** Track items used in production or workflow processes.

- **Process Measures >** Monitor quality and efficiency of processes.

- **Output Measures >** Monitor what is produced.

- **Outcome Measures >** Monitor what is actually accomplished.

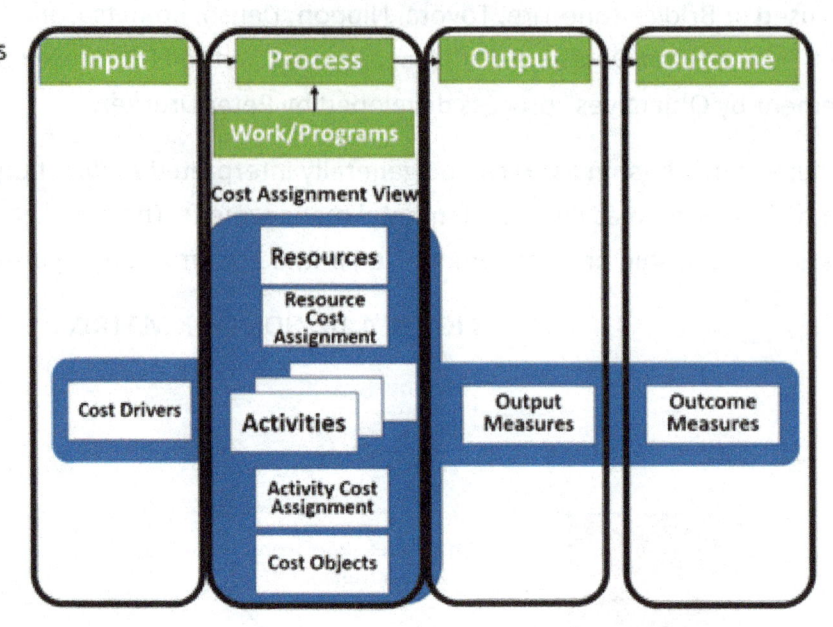

The Logic Model Framework is used by funders, managers, and evaluators of programs to evaluate the effectiveness of the program. It is a systematic and visual way to present shared relationships among the resources needed to operate a program, indicating the activities planned, and the changes or results the organization intends to achieve. Mapping the framework includes Planned Work: Resources/Inputs and Activities, along with Intended Results: Outputs, Outcomes, and Evaluation of Impact.

Identify Management Roles and Responsibilities Necessary to Align the Organization's Operating Model with the Strategy and Strategic Operating Plan

Once the strategic operating plan framework is defined, accountabilities must be assigned, communicated, understood, and agreed upon. We recommend individually assigning responsibility for each element of the "operating model" transformation plan (detailed in Phase V) and the strategic operating plan. This means assigning responsibilities to named individuals rather than departments or functions. Why? Unless someone, a person, is specifically assigned to be responsible for each strategy, objective, initiative, transformation, and measure, there will be no day-to-day leadership and management oversight in achieving plan outcomes. Put another way, "If everyone is assumed to be accountable...then no one will be accountable." It is an obligation of the organization and the people who work in it to account for their activities, accept responsibility for them, and disclose the results in a transparent manner.

The importance of identifying accountabilities cannot be overemphasized. A primary breakdown in strategy management is failure to recognize a fundamental requirement for effective execution, that is, establishing and accepting "accountability" for results. However, note that being responsible for the implementation of an aspect of the strategic operating plan does not mean that the responsible person is the one who does the work related to implementation. It means that the responsible person's role is to ensure that the work is done, whether he or she does it or someone else does it.

The senior leadership team needs to be transparent about which leader has *authority and responsibility* for each component of the strategy, operational transformations required and the strategic operating plan. Unless roles and responsibilities are clearly defined, implementation will falter and expected outcomes will not be achieved.

- At the *overarching goal level,* a single champion for the overarching goal ensures that top leadership is engaged with the entirety of the plan. Most frequently this Overarching Goal Champion will be the organization's most senior-level executive (CEO, Executive Director, Agency Director, President, etc.).
- At the *objective level,* a single individual should be identified as Objective Champion for the oversight of a particular strategic objective. This individual will likely be a member of the senior leadership team.
- At *initiative and operational transformation level,* a single individual should be identified for managing development and execution of a given transformation or high priority strategic initiative. This person will not necessarily be a member of the leadership team but will have the commitment level, skills, attitude, and resources to appropriately execute a particular project.

In Phase V, transformational roles and responsibilities will be described in detail.

Develop Implementation Plans for Strategic Objectives

Implementation of a strategic operating plan is improved when all levels of the leadership team work together to identify and define key performance indicators for each strategic objective. *A key performance indicator (KPI) is a measure for which the organization has data that helps quantify the achievement of a desired strategic objective.* Key performance indicators give an "indication" if a particular objective is being achieved *and* help to answer the question: "How would we know a result if we achieved it?"

2.2(1)

2.2(5)

People working in any organization must be able to translate the high-altitude expressions of the strategic plan into everyday talk – real people talk. Once the entire team equates the goals, strategies, and objectives of the plan with measurable KPIs containing specific targets, then the abstract notion of strategy is replaced with a clear understanding of deliverables and the challenge they provide.

Ultimately, a balanced set of key performance indicators provides feedback about the validity of the hypotheses that underlie the strategic plan. Responses predicted at the beginning of the strategy formulation process are continually checked for validity each time a performance measurement is conducted. When new learning based on performance occurs, this drives necessary changes at the strategic and operational levels of the organization.

An effective strategic operating plan requires development of performance indicators, targets for each indicator, and alignment of strategic initiatives/projects to accomplish the targeted performance level and therefore to achieve the objective. Follow these four tasks to guide this process:

Identify Observable Evidence of Improvement, and then Translate Into Candidate KPIs

Every leadership team would love to discover the "silver bullet" of performance measurement, a single miracle indicator that, closely monitored, would let the organization know they are on track to faster growth and unparalleled success. Unfortunately, this scenario is the stuff of fantasy. No one indicator can holistically predict future results for an organization.

Today's organizational environment demands a balanced approach to performance measurement, one that employs a blend of indicators focused on where the organization is now with where it wants to be in the future. Performance indicators should be established for dual tracking of *internal* performance, such as capacity-building, operations, training, financial results, and *external* performance focused in the areas of customer satisfaction, stakeholder satisfaction, and market share.

Organizations that use a balanced approach to performance measurement can influence their external and internal operating environments. Those that do not are destined to spend more time and energy reacting to unforeseen "events" – moving from one firefight to another.

An effective technique for developing acceptable indicators is to engage the broader involvement of team members in the development process. Questions to answer when evaluating a potential indicator are:

- Is the indicator *valid*?
    - Does it truly measure what it should, which is accomplishment of the objective?
- Is the indicator *valuable*?
    - Will it help the leadership team better understand what is truly happening?
    - Will it enable leadership to steer through the ups and downs of the business cycle that every organization experiences?
- Is the indicator *easy* to track?
    - Does the data already exist, or would it require a gargantuan or expensive effort to track the information?
- Does the indicator hold the team to an appropriate level of *accountability*?
- Does the indicator *communicate* a positive message to the team? For example, "system up-time" sends a positive message to the work force versus "system down-time" which sends a negative message.
- Is it *a leading or lagging* indicator?
    - Does it help predict a desired organizational outcome by providing some leading indication? Or does it lag behind, simply reporting on outcomes after the fact?

Phase IV: Strategic Planning

Ideally, a strategic management system is best served when it includes a balanced set of leading and lagging indicators (think "Balanced Scorecard" here). Note: If the cause-effect logic of a strategy map is valid, then ALL of the indicators are "leading" for any objectives "above" it on the strategy map...and ALL of the indicators are "lagging" for any objectives that are "below" it on the strategy map.

Table 4.10 illustrates a practical exercise a planning team can complete to effectively identify performance indicators.

- Identify what would be different from a sensory perspective, i.e., What would the team see, hear, or feel that would indicate positive change?
- Brainstorm/identify a targeted set of potential indicators for each strategic objective included in the strategic operating plan.
- Rank each indicator from 1 (Low) to 5 (High) for A–F.
- Calculate a final rank (average score for A–F) for comparison purposes of all potential indicators.
- Select those vital few indicators that best fit the situation.

TABLE 4.10 – PERFORMANCE MEASUREMENT EXERCISE

Sample HR Objective: Cultivate and retain a highly competent and motivated staff

Sensory Evidence	Potential Indicators	A Valid	B Value	C Ease	D Accountable	E Communicate	F Lead/Lag	Final Rank
Hear from Customers who observe deliveries are timely	On time delivery	4	4	2	4	4	Strong Lead	3
Hear/see from employees & CFO assignments completed on time	Employee Overtime	3	4	5	4	3	Lead	4
See in results of climate survey & customer feedback – Employees tell us this is a great place to work	Employee Satisfaction	5	5	3	5	5	Strong Lead	1
Feel/see as part of culture & HR records that increasing number of employees who stay with our company for a long time and are promoted from within	Employee Retention	4	4	4	5	5	Lead	2
See in behavior of business development team & sales records that our staff is more productive	Sales Lead to Close Ratio	3	4	4	3	4	Lag	5

Sensory Evidence	Potential Indicators	A Valid	B Value	C Ease	D Accountable	E Communicate	F Lead/Lag	Final Rank
We see employees who volunteer time in our community outreach events	Employee volunteer engagement score	3	3	3	3	5	Lead	7
We see employees increase their job knowledge, skills, and abilities	Job Task Competency Score	2	3	2	2	4	Lead	8
We see employees who attain professional certification and credentialing	Employee Development Score	3	3	2	2	4	Lead	9
We see a work force who look different and have diverse backgrounds, origins, and perspectives, with equal access to professional development and promotion opportunities	Diverse Voice Representation Score	4	3	3	3	3	Lead	6

Define and Establish a Target for Each Selected KPI

In collaboration with each objective champion, key performance indicators should be selected, and a performance measure should be constructed for each indicator. Information required to construct a performance measure includes the following:

- Formula for calculating the indicator.
- Source of variable level information. *A variable is a quantity that may take on any of a set of values, for example, total number of customers served in one year.*
- Baseline information on every variable included in the formula. *A baseline is the organization's actual performance for the most recent reporting period.*
- External benchmark information (if available). *A benchmark is an external comparison point, for example, an industry-wide statistic.*
- Reporting frequency.
- Data collection and reporting responsibility.
- Acceptable targets or target ranges for each indicator. *A target is the specific performance level the organization seeks for a particular indicator.*

Figure 4.11 provides a sample performance measure with targets.

TABLE 4.11 – SAMPLE SET OF KPIS WITH TARGETS

Goal: Protect and grow the core business.
 	
Financial Objective:
- Exceed top line revenues over expenses.
    - KPI = Profit per customer. **Target = 32%**
 	
Customer Objective:
- Deliver up-to-date, relevant, and effective standard offerings that meet customer expectations.
    - KPI = Percent repeat business. **Target = 40%**
 	
Internal Objective:
- Establish and maintain a customer-centric prospect to order, fulfillment, and customer service process.
    - KPI = Average cycle time from order to delivery. **Target = 72 hours**
 	
Learning & Growth Objective:
- Cultivate and retain a highly competent and motivated staff.
    - KPI = Percent staff retention. **Target = 85%**

Define Tactical Guidelines

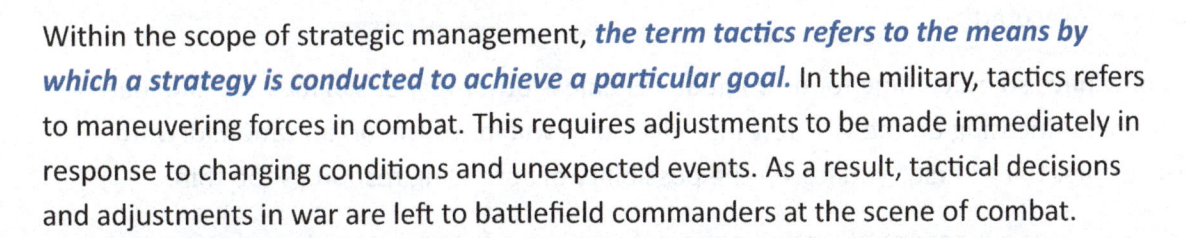

Within the scope of strategic management, *the term tactics refers to the means by which a strategy is conducted to achieve a particular goal.* In the military, tactics refers to maneuvering forces in combat. This requires adjustments to be made immediately in response to changing conditions and unexpected events. As a result, tactical decisions and adjustments in war are left to battlefield commanders at the scene of combat.

2.2(1)

2.2(2)

The concept of tactics also applies to organizations that have deployed a strategy into their core functions. The desired objectives must be coordinated in and among core functions. Tactics refer to how to use the means available to conduct a strategy. Yet, top management is usually more concerned with strategic outcomes, what needs to be accomplished. Thus, tactical guidelines are easily overlooked.

This does not mean tactics need to be fully detailed in the implementation plan; this is simply not practical. It does mean that tactical considerations must be accounted for while making plans to implement strategic objectives. Doing this helps to ensure achievement of the expected results.

The following considerations regarding tactics are useful:

- If the implementation of a strategic objective needs significant tactical decision making, ensure that the management team has the required experience or that more experienced management monitors and coaches the implementation team.

- While senior management should not be expected to intervene in the day-to-day implementation process, it can provide useful "tactical guidelines," that is, coaching advice, tips, and suggestions about how to complete a particular assignment based on their expertise and/or experience.
- Managers and/or staff from other areas may need to provide assistance because of their ability to operate in new and difficult situations.
- The more that lower levels of management are involved in all stages of the strategy management process, the less that tactical guidelines will be needed as lower-level managers acquire expertise and experience in using strategic management tools and techniques.

Define Tactics and Integrate Them into Strategic Initiatives and Projects to be Executed

For each objective, the responsible objective champion must work with the team to define *the tactics to be used to achieve a particular objective*, especially the strategic initiatives and projects to be launched. Fundamental to identifying, prioritizing, and time-phasing initiatives is recognizing that resources – employee time and capital that can be invested – are always limited.

2.2(1)
2.2(2)

A "Strategic Initiative" is *a collective endeavor with a defined beginning and endpoint to reduce performance gaps and help accomplish strategic objectives*. Typically, initiatives are enterprise-level projects that impact the organization's strategy and require a longer duration of time to be executed.

Most employees only have so much time for new initiatives unless other responsibilities are eliminated. We strongly recommend focusing on the vital few initiatives that will move the organization forward. When you prioritize "first things first," you lessen the possibility of spreading resources too thin.

Table 4.12, which continues our case study including sample initiative for each objective, demonstrates how high-level strategies are integrated into the Strategic Operating Plan.

Phase IV: Strategic Planning

TABLE 4.12 – SAMPLE STRATEGIC OPERATING PLAN WITH INITIATIVES

Goal: Protect and grow the core business.

Financial Objective:

- Exceed top line revenues over expenses.
  - KPI = Profit per customer   Target = 32%

    Initiative 1: Launch "Go deeper, Go faster" program.

    Initiative 2: Build a distribution network.

Customer Objective:

- Deliver up-to-date, relevant, and effective standard offerings that meet customer expectations.
  - KPI = Percent repeat business   Target = 40%

    Initiative 3: Design and execute a formal product management process.

Internal Objective:

- Establish and maintain a customer-centric prospect to order, fulfillment, and customer service process.
  - KPI = Average cycle time from order to delivery   Target = 72 hours

    Initiative 4: Define roles and responsibilities across functions.

    Initiative 5: Streamline the customer service process.

Learning & Growth Objective:

- Cultivate and retain a highly competent and motivated staff.
  - KPI = Percent staff   Target = 85%

    Initiative 6: Launch a formal internal mentoring program.

The process for developing and planning initiatives is straightforward. We recommend this process.

- *With your team, compile a list of candidate initiatives.* Generally, candidate strategic initiatives have already been discussed by the team in earlier parts of the strategic planning process. Our recommendation is to progressively capture these in a "parking lot" or "bike rack" as your team works through the earlier phases. Now, as the process of formally identifying potential initiatives unfolds, the team and objective owner will want to keep in mind three key questions.
  - Is the initiative consistent with the perceptions of the executive leadership team?
  - Does the initiative contribute significantly to the achievement of strategic objectives?
  - Does the initiative require significant "cross functional" support and therefore needs to be managed at the enterprise level?

- *Evaluate each candidate initiative.* The second step is to evaluate *each* candidate initiative to determine if it should be included in the strategic operating plan. The evaluation process becomes more explicit by asking and probing three more questions.

- o Is the initiative consistent with the market assessment? (See Phase II – Environmental Assessment)
- o Is the initiative financially feasible?
- o Is the initiative operationally feasible?
- *Prioritize initiatives.* A list of candidate initiatives can be prioritized in many ways. We recommend that teams use one of these three approaches. (See Figures 4.12, 4.13, and 4.14.)
    - o A **2x2 Prioritization Matrix** is a graphical tool that displays the strategic importance of a particular initiative and the expected Return on Investment (ROI).

FIGURE 4.12: 2X2 PRIORITIZATION MATRIX

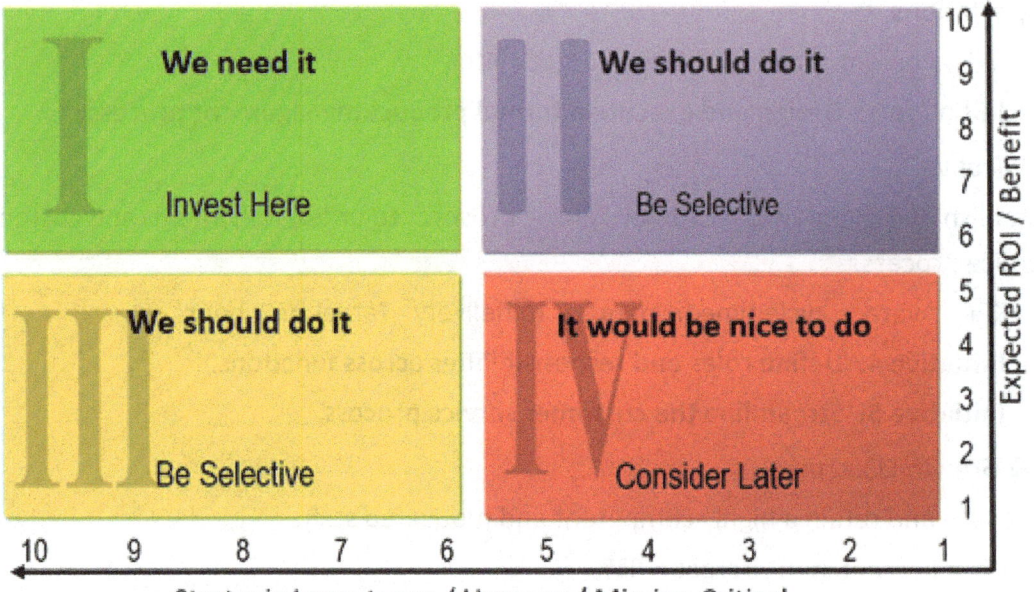

	I We need it — Invest Here	II We should do it — Be Selective
	III We should do it — Be Selective	IV It would be nice to do — Consider Later

X-axis: Strategic Importance / Urgency / Mission Critical (10 → 1)
Y-axis: Expected ROI / Benefit (1 → 10)

- o A **Weighted Scoring** method is a tool that provides a systematic process for selecting projects based on many criteria.

FIGURE 4.13: WEIGHTED CRITERIA SCORING

		Requirement Score		
Criteria	Weight	Initiative 1	Initiative 2	Initiative 3
Budget required	20%	40	80	20
Benefits to customers	40%	30	70	50
# of objectives covered	30%	40	60	70
Time needed	10%	50	60	80
Weighted Scores	100%	37	68	53

- o A **Paired Comparison** prioritizes a list of items where evaluation criteria are subjective, or where they are competing in importance.

Phase IV: Strategic Planning

FIGURE 4.14: PAIRED COMPARISON SCORING

Initiatives	A	B	C	D	Score	Priority
A		1	1	1	3	1
B			0	0	0	4
C				1	2	2
D					1	3

All three methods are useful, but we find that the 2x2 matrix most often stimulates the best team collaboration. Use of the matrix prompts team-based consideration of each strategic initiative separately to determine how they rank along two dimensions. On the horizontal axis, the team rates the strategic importance, urgency, and mission-critical nature of each potential initiative. On the vertical axis, the team considers the expected ROI or strategic benefit of the initiative.

Initiatives that rank highly among both dimensions should be considered first for investing. Initiatives that rank high along one dimension should be considered next. Initiatives that do not rank highly across either dimension should be considered last...if at all. (See Figure 4.15.)

FIGURE 4.15: EXAMPLE 2X2 PRIORITIZATION MATRIX

I. We need it — Expand & enhance therapy gym for Med-A rehab-to-home — Invest Here

II. We should do it — Provide outpatient therapy services — Be Selective

III. We should do it — Invest in AI Prescriptive-Care Technologies — Be Selective

IV. It would be nice to do — Refurbish kitchen & dining room — Consider Later

Expected ROI / Benefit

Strategic Importance / Urgency / Mission Critical

The example comes from a Skilled Nursing Facility (SNF). The overall mission of this SNF is to provide exceptional health care to senior adults. The leadership team is considering four potential initiatives: 1) Invest in AI predictive care technology, 2) Refurbish the kitchen and dining hall, 3) Offer outpatient therapy services to people from the community, and 4) Invest in expanding the current therapy gym and services to enhance services to senior adults.

- While investing in AI Predictive Technologies (such as "smart clothing") (Quadrant III) is mission-critical, the overall return on investment is relatively low because of the enormous expense to implement.
- Refurbish Kitchen and Dining Hall (Quadrant IV) – This initiative is not as mission-critical as other initiatives under consideration and has very little return on investment.
- Offer Outpatient Therapy (Quadrant II) – This initiative is tempting because it may quickly generate additional revenues. However, it is not central to the mission to provide therapy to people from the local community. Yet, quadrant two initiatives may be appealing because they may help fund more mission-critical endeavors.
- Expand Therapy Services to Seniors (Quadrant I) – This initiative is mission-critical to providing quality healthcare for seniors and has a very high financial return for the required investment.

o *Define roles and responsibilities* - Having roles and responsibilities clearly defined is important at the initiative level. Careful attention must be given to clarifying specific roles and responsibilities linked to execution of an initiative throughout the organization and incorporating them into job descriptions and expectations. A responsibility assignment matrix (i.e., RACI matrix) is a helpful tool which describes the participation of various roles in completing initiatives or deliverables for a strategic plan. RACI is an acronym derived from the four key responsibilities most typically used. (See Figure 4.16.)

FIGURE 4.16: SAMPLE RACI MATRIX

Initiatives	CEO	CFO	COO	S&M	CIO
Open Asian office	I	A	R	C	C
Train the workforce on the new CRM		I	A/R	I	C
Deliver on sales forecast	I	A	C	R	
Integrate new acquisitions operationally	A	C	R	I	I

RACI = Responsible, Approves, Consulted, Informed (BOK 2.0)
RAPID = Recommend, Agree, Perform, Input, Decide (BOK 3.0)

- **R** – Who has overall *responsibility* for the initiative? This individual will not necessarily be a member of the leadership team but will be someone who has the commitment level, skills set, and resources to appropriately organize and execute an initiative.
- **A** – Who *approves* the initiative for execution?
- **C** – Who must be *consulted* regarding the initiative?
- **I** – Who must be kept *informed* regarding the initiative as it is executed?

o *Consider contingencies* – This task requires the team to consider the need for contingencies. All strategic initiatives are not realized according to plan. In fact, strategic planning is often experimental because it deals with untried initiatives being deployed in new and uncertain circumstances. This potential for variance raises the need for contingency planning before a new initiative is deployed. Consider contingencies with respect to size, scope, cost, and duration of strategic initiatives. Ask questions such as:

- Can this initiative be reduced in size?
- Can it be changed with respect to its scope?
- Can the total cost of the project be reduced?
- Can the planned duration of the implementation process be lengthened or put on hold?

o *Time phase initiatives* - **Define a preliminary timeframe** for each strategic initiative in preparation for implementation of the strategic operating plan. (See Figure 4.17.)

FIGURE 4.17: SAMPLE GANTT CHART 2.2(1)

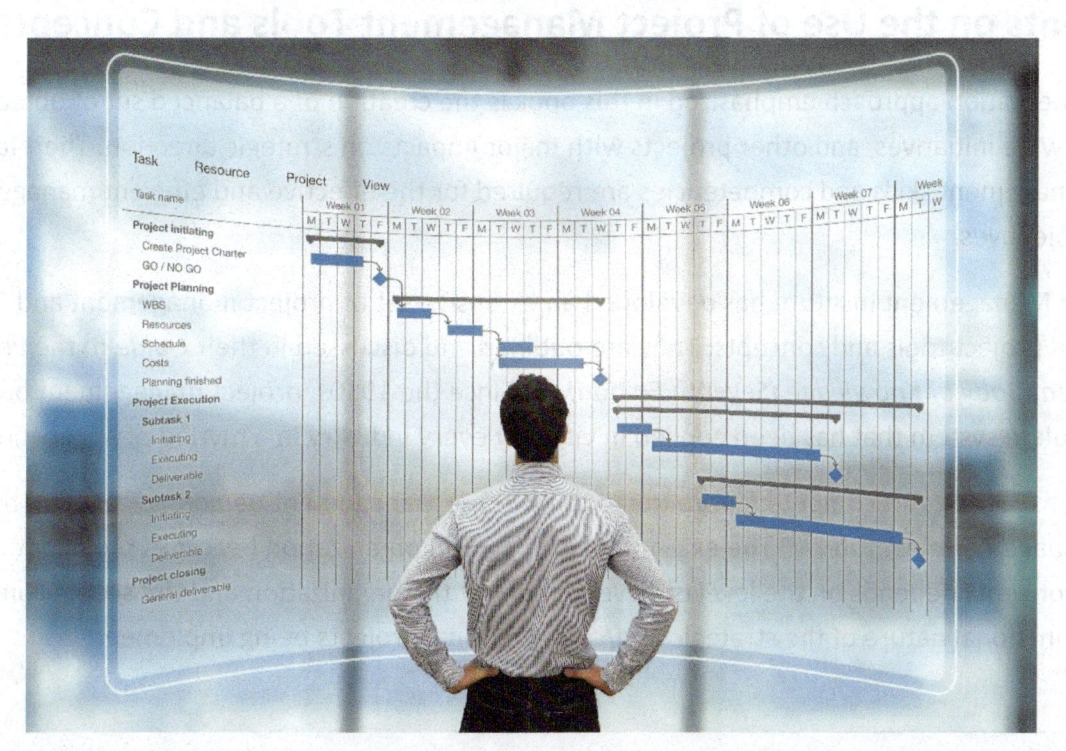

Gantt Charts are often used in time phasing initiatives, projects, and tasks. The Gantt Chart was devised by *Henry Gantt* in the early 20th century; it visualizes the schedule for an initiative or project. Gantt Charts illustrate the start and finish dates of the critical elements of an initiative or project.

Other benefits from using Gantt Charts include:

- Improving communication and team cohesion
- Avoiding resource overload
- Measuring the progress of initiatives
- Seeing overlapping activities and task dependencies
- Managing time better

o *Document initiative information* - The final step in initiative planning is to document relevant information, which is often called a "Scoping Document" or "Charter." Some key points to include in this document:

- Who is responsible for and involved in the work?
- When will the initiative begin and end?
- What investments (people, time, finances) will be needed to implement this initiative?
- What are the constraints the team will face in implementing this initiative?
- What new opportunities will the organization gain by implementing this initiative?
- What action steps need to be undertaken to achieve the deliverable?
- What are the anticipated measurable outcomes of this initiative?

Comments on the Use of Project Management Tools and Concepts

The implementation approach emphasized in this book is the creation of a balanced set of objectives, enterprise-wide initiatives, and other projects with major impacts on strategic direction. Therefore, project management skills and competencies are required for the effective and efficient management of strategic objectives.

The Project Management Institute has developed an extensive set of project management and agile/hybrid project tools and concepts. They are outlined and discussed in their *Guide to the Project Management Body of Knowledge (Seventh Edition)*. [105] Since the 1950s, project management has evolved into a complete system that has been applied in virtually every industry in a myriad of applications.

Organizations lacking this competency are urged to have key management personnel certified by the Project Management Institute. [106] The extent to which a given organization becomes proficient in these tools and concepts depends on the level of development of the organization and the scope, complexity, and multifunctional nature of the strategic and/or operational projects being implemented.

---

[105] https://www.pmi.org/pmbok-guide-standards/foundational/pmbok
[106] https://projectmanagementacademy.net/

Phase IV: Strategic Planning

Develop Implementation Plans for Strategic Objectives in Non-Project Formats

While new strategies are most often developed using the tools and concepts of project management, there are many strategies (or portions of strategies) that are best initiated in other organizational formats. Table 4.13 summarizes useful strategic implementation formats.

TABLE 4.13 – USEFUL STRATEGIC IMPLEMENTATION FORMATS
• ***Initiatives/Projects.*** In general, project management is most effective and efficient when outcomes include a degree of risk and uncertainty; the assignment is complex, multifunctional, multidisciplined, and long-run; and outcomes are new or unique. In this situation, the unprogrammed activities present challenges for the personnel involved.
• Project management should only be used for strategic initiatives when it can be justified. Too many organizations are now using project management for smaller-scale assignments. This is overkill when simpler organizational and management techniques are available that will address the need.
• ***Cross-functional coordination committees.*** Despite the many criticisms of traditional committees, they serve an important purpose by maintaining long-term surveillance over a wide variety of trends, concerns, and policies that need continuous monitoring, evaluation, interpretation, and feedback. In strategic management there are many activities of this nature, especially those that require long-term, incremental change.
The work of a cross-functional coordinating team is not easily translated into key performance indicators measured and tracked on a dashboard. A cross-functional coordinating team is a more subtle and important asset to the strategic thinking process, akin to what experienced strategic management professionals are doing continuously.
For example, an organization considering entering international markets might assign a cross-functional coordinating team to investigate the necessary policies, problems, and prospects of moving the organization in this direction. This may not be a move that can be accomplished in a given budget year. Nevertheless, if the organization is considering a move in this direction, a committee assignment could be the right strategic format and low-cost investment in a study that could lead to a major strategic initiative.
• ***Team assignments.*** These assignments are for activities that management has decided to initiate on an exploratory and limited basis before approving a full-scale project. This is an intermediate step to be used where the outcomes and/or means of achieving them are in the early stages of development, with benefits and competitive advantages accruing to early adopters that are seen as more than offsetting the risks. These are action-oriented activities, as opposed to deliberative and advisory committee assignments.

TABLE 4.13 – USEFUL STRATEGIC IMPLEMENTATION FORMATS
• ***External contracts.*** Securing external assistance from an experienced consultant may be the best course of action for undertaking assignments that are outside the organization's expertise and experience. Even when an organization has developed an advanced strategic management system and the competencies required to use it, management may still find it useful to get outside expertise, advice, and counsel.
• ***Individual assignments.*** At times, a strategy requires additional study, analysis, research, or simply more information before the leadership approves it and commits to its implementation. These assignments are usually low-cost and can be assigned to an individual within the organization without interfering with ongoing activities.

These formats facilitate the planning process by helping determine the most appropriate planning approach to be used. This way all strategies are not automatically organized as projects. Many strategies are not ready for immediate implementation in the next operating cycle. They require further analysis, study, deliberation, or consensus building before launching a full-blown effort.

Here are examples on the appropriate use of these alternate organizational formats:

Cross-functional committee assignments. With respect to strategic management, and especially strategic thinking, the key uses of a cross-functional committee are:

- Engaging in long-term deliberations on key issues and points of disagreement among members of the strategic management team.
- Monitoring and evaluating new strategies that management needs and offer recommendations to management.
- Making in-depth analysis and evaluations requiring shared opinions from several core functions.
- Analyzing selected costs and benefits that management wants to include in future strategic operating plans, but for which sufficient information is not available.

These are examples of situations where cross-functional committee assignments are likely to be the most effective:

- An organization is contemplating expanding its international operations and needs to identify their best options.
- An organization is considering a new product or program that has a narrow entry window in the very near future.
- An organization wants to invest in green technology and reduce its carbon footprint.
- An organization is considering the impact of facility closures and early retirement plans.
- An organization contemplating a strategic partnership needs additional information and policies on how to proceed.

Since committee organization, procedures, and reporting systems are well-developed in most organizations, these committee assignments are best made using the organization's established procedures and practices – so long as they:

- Clearly define the expected outcomes
- Appoint or have the committee appoint/elect a chairperson
- Specify committee membership
- Dissolve the committee as soon as management is satisfied with the outcome(s)
- Require meeting agendas and meeting notes
- Require reports on a regularly scheduled basis

Team assignments. A team-based approach is useful for assignments preceding the organization of a strategic project because teams can be:

- Easily created and terminated
- Highly focused on specific outcomes
- Either analytic or action-oriented
- Highly creative and, depending on the desired outcomes, innovative
- Very synergistic in developing and evaluating a concept or test approach

For example, the following situations call for a team-based approach:

- An organization wants to undertake a test market study for a new product or service before launching a full-scale operation.
- An organization wants a run focus groups to explore some aspects of a new strategy before committing to a full-scale project.
- An organization wants to evaluate a new approach to customer service with a few established customers before ramping up a new strategic approach for a given product line.
- An organization wants to interview several subject matter experts with diverse subject matter expertise.

External contracts. *Often organizations planning to embark on a course of action need critical expertise, a key piece of information, or input from experts* before committing to a significant effort. Outside resources should be employed in the following types of situations:

2.1(2)
2.1(4)

- Necessary experience and expertise do not exist inside the organization.
- The expertise included in the concept should include the judgment, opinion, and counsel of the experts identified in the plan of work.
- Outside expertise and opinion should be limited to specific strategic information for which the organization has a level of comprehension sufficient to evaluate the use of the information and/or advice being sought, otherwise seek an alternative resource.

Consider the following examples where outside resources should be engaged:

- An organization wants to enter the Eastern European market and needs information and advice on which of their products or services is most appropriate to incorporate in a market-entry project.
- An organization needs technical information and advice about several new IT systems—other than what they can learn from vendor personnel.
- An organization is considering its first acquisition of a smaller organization operating in a new (to the organization) market.

Individual assignments. Some assignments are most effectively and efficiently done by individuals who have the required combination of experience, expertise, and knowledge of the organization and its strengths and weaknesses. Individual assignments are appropriate in the following situations:

- The individual can produce the analysis more efficiently and economically than a team or committee.
- The assignment can be limited to one core function, management discipline, or knowledge area.
- The individual can complete the assignment with minimal supervision.
- The individual is allotted the necessary time and resources to complete the assignment in a timely manner while still meeting their other commitments.

Examples of situations where individual assignments are appropriate include:

- Gathering information on locations for offices in new markets.
- Gathering information about competitors' products, services, and markets.
- Conducting primary research through interviews, questionnaires, opinion surveys, and focus groups on topics that will ultimately be addressed through projects but for which vital preliminary information is needed.
- Conducting secondary research using relevant resources.

In summary, the primary advantage of these different strategic implementation formats – cross-functional committees, teams, outside experts, and individual assignments – is that they facilitate the strategic management process by organizing, tracking, and addressing the myriad of important details that require attention *before* initiating a full-scale project. Using these alternative formats will contribute greatly to making strategic thinking a continuous process –organized to reinforce and facilitate strategic planning.

Reconcile Implementation Requirements of the Strategic Operating Plan with Available Implementation Resources

While developing implementation plans for *each* strategy/objective, confirming that required personnel and other resources are available is customary. *This step is not sufficient to ensure implementation*. No matter how large or small, every organization has limited resources that must be carefully allocated.

Nothing is gained when resources are allocated "on paper" but, in reality, are spread too thin to be effective.

Determining available resources is an important set of calculations. The implementation requirements for a given strategy naturally compete with the resource expectations for other strategies and with present demands made by ongoing activities. These realities often cause greater competition for the use of resources.

Once the strategic management team has a realistic comparative estimate of committed versus available resources, whether currently available or new resources that must be secured, adjustments based on priorities, scheduling, scope, scale, and content modifications can be made. If these estimations are being made for the first time, there will inevitably be miscalculations. In such cases, it is advisable to err on the side of *overestimating* required resources (present demands) and *underestimating* available resources (future needs).

Write a Summary Implementation Budget

What now remains is to submit a detailed request for funding and staffing approval, which should be outlined in sufficient detail to permit management to authorize expenditures and the use of resources. Good governance requires leaders to anticipate, forecast, and manage the investment required. ***A strategic budget provides this guidance and basis for the orderly allocation of resources.*** Special emphasis should be placed on delineating the assumptions that underlie the plan.

2.2(3)

The bottom line is that leaders and managers must fully understand the "money side" to the decisions they are making. They need to know where the funds are going and the benefit that will be obtained from investing in specific initiatives. It is important to prepare and present a strategic budget that:

- Identifies any changes made in the strategic operating plan since the longer-term strategic plan was submitted.
- Provide a summary of required funding and other resources necessary, including staffing for each of the initiatives in the strategic operating plan.
- Articulate the major assumptions underpinning each strategic initiative.
- Identify any new non-capital expenses or any reallocation of existing resources.
- Identify any new capital expenses or investments that can be amortized over multiple years.
- Estimate new revenues (if any) to be generated or cost savings to be realized in the next few years.

Obtain Necessary Governance and Management Approval and Authorization for the Strategic Operating Plan

Once the strategic operating plan is constructed, the income and expenses associated with the plan must be budgeted and approved by the Board, owners, or relevant stakeholders.

As with the strategic plan, each organization will have its own approval process for management decision making. Since the operating plan contains a precise description of the actionable initiatives and operational projects to be undertaken, it requires top leadership approval, as well as approval at any intermediate levels required by the organization. This approval process needs to be formalized and followed to complete the strategic operating plan process.

In many organizations, the team charged with leading the strategic planning process is separate and potentially removed from the group designated to guide the budgeting and resource allocation process. The budget implementation process is typically focused on a fiscal year of operation while the goals, objectives, and initiatives require years of sustained effort to achieve. Hence, budgets commonly have financial measures that bear little connection to the longer-range focus of the strategic operating plan.

The integrated nature of the strategic operating plan demands the leadership team works with a balanced set of performance criteria, not just financial measures. This naturally forces the CFO or whomever is responsible for the organization's financial management and the management team to develop a "holistic" strategic focus in order to analyze, understand, and mitigate between present and future resource demands and effectively deploy them across the entire strategic operating plan.

By defining the *key drivers* of revenue and profit growth, the process of developing the strategic operating plan helps leaders become more comfortable committing to aggressive strategic goals. The process also reveals which current programs are successfully working toward the agreed-upon financial outcomes and which should be jettisoned. Budgetary and resource constraints will drive plan revisions and changes in authorized funding levels and priorities for their use. Consequently, any or all of the following changes in the strategic operating plan may be necessary:

- Reallocating funds to other strategic objectives *within* a given core function.
- Reallocating funds among the strategic objectives in *other* core functions.
- Expanding the resources available for implementing new organization-level strategies.
- Modifying the scope of the strategy and/or the strategic objective itself.
- Adjusting the rate of progress and duration of the new/revised strategies based on management, staff, and other resources available.
- Rescheduling strategic initiatives as necessary because of funds availability.

Distribute and Communicate the Strategic Operating Plan

Once the strategic operating plan and supporting budget are approved, a *staff/stakeholder-level communications plan* must be created and approved. For successful strategic operating plan implementation, the intent of the plan must be effectively communicated to all stakeholders but especially to the internal team.

Effective communications should never be confused with spin. When presenting the case for the plan and detailing any required changes in the organization's operating model, give the bad news along with the good, for example, on any planned work-force restructuring. The entire strategic management process

Phase IV: Strategic Planning

will be undermined by loss of trust if employees lose confidence in the accuracy and honesty of what they are told by senior leadership. Senior leaders should deliver messages personally in face-to-face meetings when possible. Written information should be presented so that it reaches all who will be impacted: That means that the specific needs of different groups of employees has to be considered.

Frequently, both strategic and operational planning begin with an intense burst of communication within the organization – then nothing! Clear and continuous communication is an important requirement for effective strategic and operational planning – from the top to the bottom of the organization and back up, creating a feedback loop within the organization's most important resource: the people that make it go.

Participation of the team in strategy development is a powerful plan internalization process, as employees start to buy into the plan because of their involvement in establishing its content. Ensuring that clear and comprehensive communications are shared and maintained will reinforce the team's commitment and energize them as the organization moves toward implementation.

The process to implement a strategic operating plan is often undervalued and or even neglected by the leadership team, especially compared to the team's focus on ongoing operations. As organizations move into a continuous-change mode of operating, implementation and change management skills become valued attributes of all managers. Leadership teams must fully embrace the developing body of knowledge around these skills to be successful in today's operating environment. This is the focus of Phase V "Strategy Execution."

Phase V – Strategy Execution

Once a strategic operating plan has been developed, the organization's leadership team is positioned to execute it to achieve the intended results. To ensure success in execution, work must be done to integrate the strategic operating plan with the ongoing processes of the organization.

Strategy development to this point has been a thought process. That is to say, the collective strategic thinking of participants has brought forward environmental and contextual analysis and evaluation, creation/evaluation/selection of alternative strategies, development of a strategic plan, and, finally, a corollary actionable strategic operating plan. All the good work done to this point (in theory) is developmental and no action has yet been initiated.

Too often, when a leadership team turns its attention to making strategy actionable, they launch the plan by assigning functional teams within business or program units to execute the chosen initiatives, consider their work done, and declare "mission accomplished." But that response is often too hasty and ignores important questions. Is the organization design ready for the change needed? Are the teams aligned behind the plan? At the team level, do those charged with implementation sufficiently understand the rationale and benefits of implementing the initiatives flowing from the strategy? These gaps invariably translate into confusion, frustration, unwanted costs, lost opportunities and, ultimately, failure to execute. When failure in execution occurs, the resulting lost value is significant regardless of sector.

Unfortunately, many strategies fail at execution because leaders and managers do not understand nor appreciate the importance of alignment of the strategy with the organization's operating model. The obvious corollary is that leaders and managers often lack the necessary strategy implementation (i.e., organizational transformation) knowledge, skills, and mindset) required to be effective. We refer to this dynamic as the "Strategy Execution Gap" (see Figure 5.1).

FIGURE 5.1: STRATEGY EXECUTION GAP

Strategy execution requires active listening, facilitating, and questioning:

- What are the implications of the new strategy on the way we currently work?
- *What will be required of each member of the leadership team to implement the changes required to successfully execute the new strategy?*
- Will our key stakeholders "buy into" and support the new strategy?
- How do we get everyone on the same page?
- Do we have the bandwidth to execute the strategic operating plan?
- What happens if we fail at execution?
- What can we do to mitigate the chances that failure will occur?

To be successful at strategy execution there are three primary tasks which must be prioritized and completed by the leadership team.

Task 1 – Design and Transform the Operating Model
Task 2 – Engage Stakeholders and Align Behind the Strategy
Task 3 – Implement the Strategic Operating Plan

Task 5.1 – Design and Transform the Operating model

For effective execution, a leadership team must be able to align the organization's operating model to the new strategy. An operating model is "how" the organization works to create value for its customers and build trust among its stakeholders. The model includes everything from how the organization sources its products and services to how it structures its business, program areas, departments, and teams. An

Phase V: Strategy Execution

operating model serves as a schematic for executing the organization's strategic operating plan.

Aligning an operating model, including processes, policies, unit roles, and individual roles, to an organization's new strategy is "Organizational Transformation." This alignment is a necessity for successful execution.[107] [108]

The new strategy, by definition, changes how work is completed and can produce a misalignment of the strategy with how the organization currently functions. To avoid this failure, the longer-term strategy and the nearer-term strategic operating plan often require significant changes in the organization's design, structures, roles, responsibilities, and processes. These changes occur through the transformation plan, which delineates and sequences the initiatives required to align the operating model to the organization's strategy (i.e., transform the organization). Failure to transform the organization's operating model so it aligns with the strategy is a major contributor to the strategy execution gap shown below.[109]

Transformation and then alignment require understanding how each business unit, department, team, and the individuals in these structures support the organization's strategy and the "Strategy-Operating Model Cycle" (see Figure 5.2).

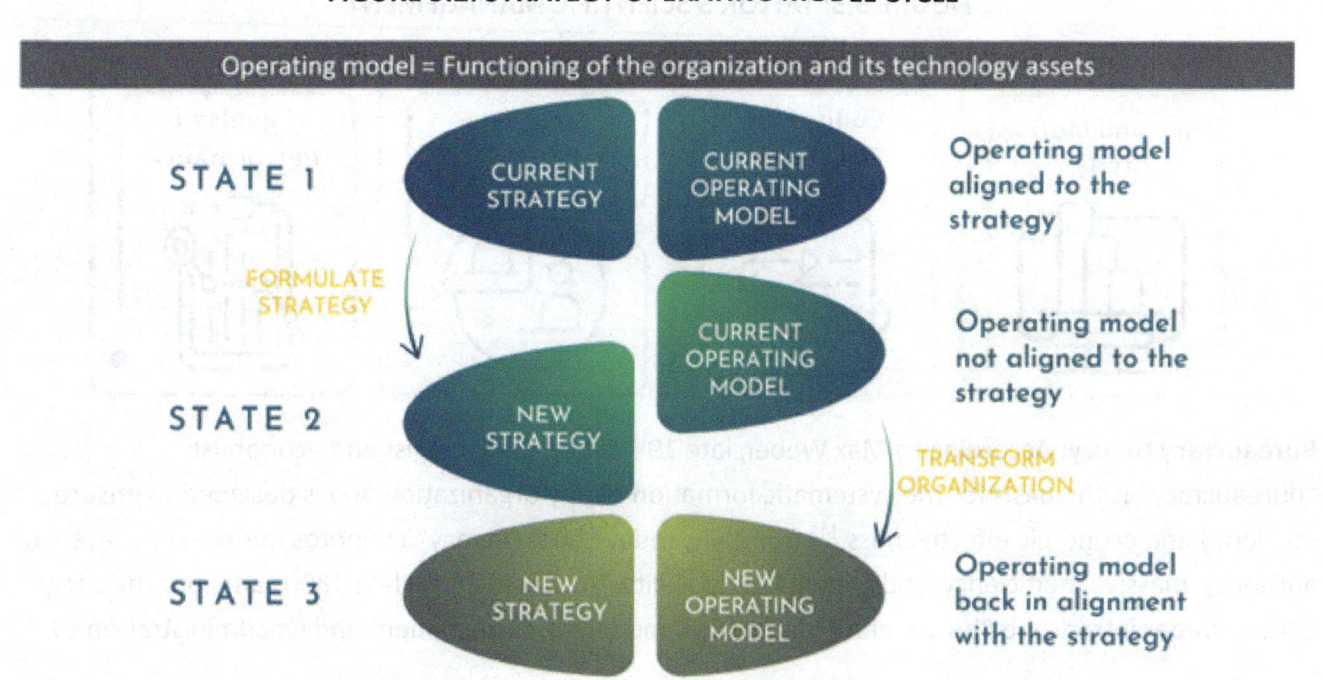

FIGURE 5.2: STRATEGY-OPERATING MODEL CYCLE[110]

Operating model = Functioning of the organization and its technology assets

State	Strategy	Operating Model	Alignment
STATE 1	CURRENT STRATEGY	CURRENT OPERATING MODEL	Operating model aligned to the strategy
	FORMULATE STRATEGY		
STATE 2	NEW STRATEGY	CURRENT OPERATING MODEL	Operating model not aligned to the strategy
		TRANSFORM ORGANIZATION	
STATE 3	NEW STRATEGY	NEW OPERATING MODEL	Operating model back in alignment with the strategy

---

[107] IASP BOK 3.0, p5
[108] Hadaya P., and Gagnon, B. Mapping an Agile Future. *Strategy Magazine,* 35 (May), p18-21, 2020.
[109] IASP BOK 3.0, p5.
[110] Hadaya, P. and Gagnon, B. Mapping an Agile Future, *Strategy Magazine* , 35 (May), p18-21, 2020.

Strategy in the 21st Century, Second Edition

The leadership team, strategic planning teams, business and functional management teams, and their staff must all work together to translate strategy and strategy execution processes into readily understood components including effective and efficient organizational design, an individual/shared accountability model, targeted employee job descriptions, and individual development plans. The process of transformation begins by selecting, communicating, educating, and applying a chosen framework for organizational design.

IASP defines organizational design as "the process of configuring an organization's operating model in an appropriate manner to better achieve the strategy. *In essence, organizational design is configuring the key components – that is, how to arrange to do the work necessary to achieve an organization purpose and strategy while delivering high-quality customer and employee experience effectively and efficiently.* As such, organizational design is a complementary area of professional practice to enterprise architecture as both practices aim to configure the organization's operating model." [111]

Baldrige Model

Evolution of Organization Design Approaches

Scientific management: In the early 1900's, the quest was to make organizations run like efficient, well-oiled machines. Frederick Taylor exemplified its application to work, using time-motion studies to optimize and codify tasks, train employees, and measure performance.[112] (See Figure 5.3.)

FIGURE 5.3: TAYLOR'S SCIENTIFIC MANAGEMENT

Time and Motion Study → Codify New Methods into Rules → Mutual Understanding → Levels of Performance

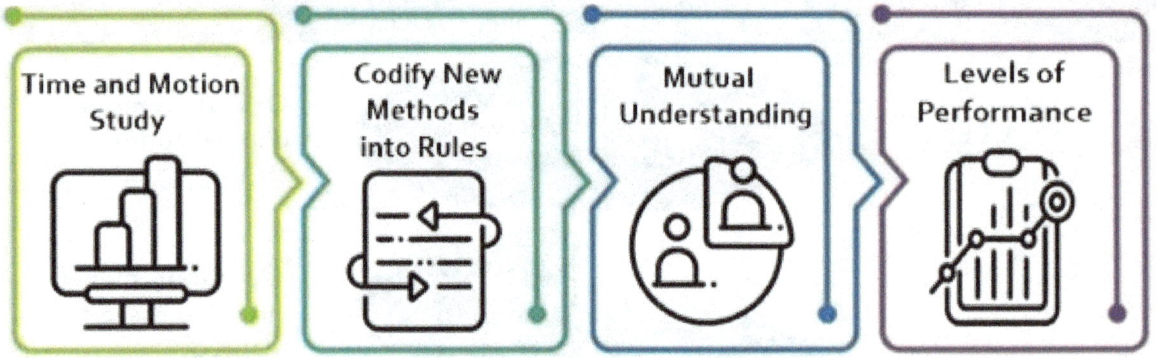

Bureaucracy theory: According to Max Weber, late 19th century sociologist and economist, "bureaucracy" is the basis for the systematic formation of any organization and is designed to ensure efficiency and economic effectiveness.[113] Ironically, today "bureaucracy" connotes unnecessary layers of authority, massive inefficiency, and overall lack of agility. However, in the late 1800s and into the early 1900s, Weber introduced "bureaucracy" as an ideal model for management and its administration to

---

[111] IASP, BOK 3.0, 3.1.4
[112] Taylor F. *The Principles of Scientific Management*, Harper & Brothers Publishers, 1919.
[113] Weber M. *Wirtschaft und Gesellschaft*. Mohr Siebeck Verlag, Tübingen, 1922.

Phase V: Strategy Execution

bring an organization's power structure into focus and ensure it drives performance. For years this formed the basis of management theory and organizational practice. (See Figure 5.4.)

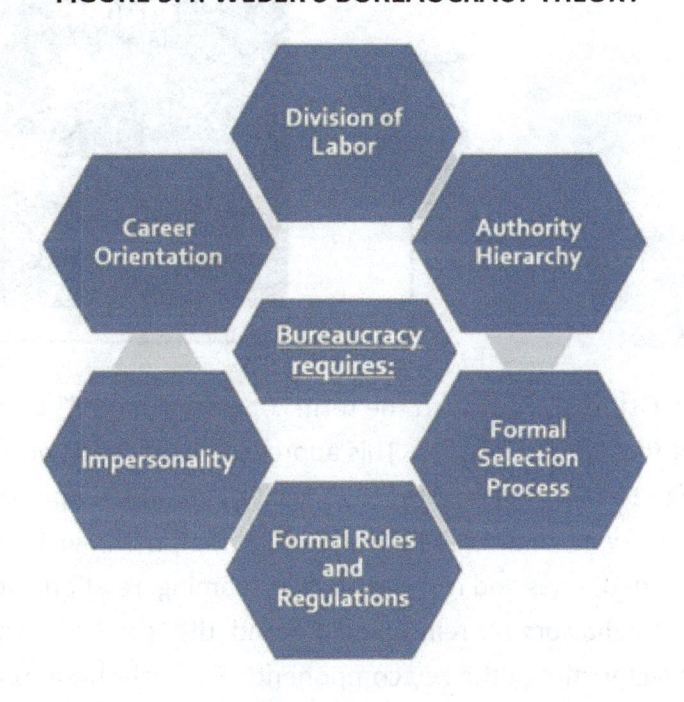

FIGURE 5.4: WEBER'S BUREAUCRACY THEORY

Organizations as systems: In the mid-1900's, thinking shifted towards viewing organizations as systems composed of distinct subsystems that work together to form the whole. This system's approach was used to understand organizational behavior, organizational change, and organizational development. Myriads of systems models exist, each focusing on somewhat different features. Two of the earliest, Galbraith's Star Model[114] and Nadler and Tushman's Congruence Model,[115] together illustrate the key aspects of this important advance. They provide simple, compelling graphics that help leaders and practitioners see beyond the linear hierarchy. They reveal the interdependencies among components: changing one affects all the others. The inputs, outputs, and activities show that organizations are information processing systems, embedded in larger systems. These models emphasize opportunities to reduce transaction inefficiencies and improve effectiveness in the process flows. (See Figures 5.5 and 5.6.)

---

[114] Galbraith J.R. Organization Design. In *Handbook of Organization Development* (Ed. Cummings T.G.), 2008.
[115] Nadler D. & Tushman M. *A Model for Diagnosing Organizational Behavior.* Organizational Dynamics v9, #2, 1980.

FIGURE 5.5: GALBRAITH'S STAR MODEL **FIGURE 5.6: NADLER-TUSHMAN CONGRUENCE MODEL**

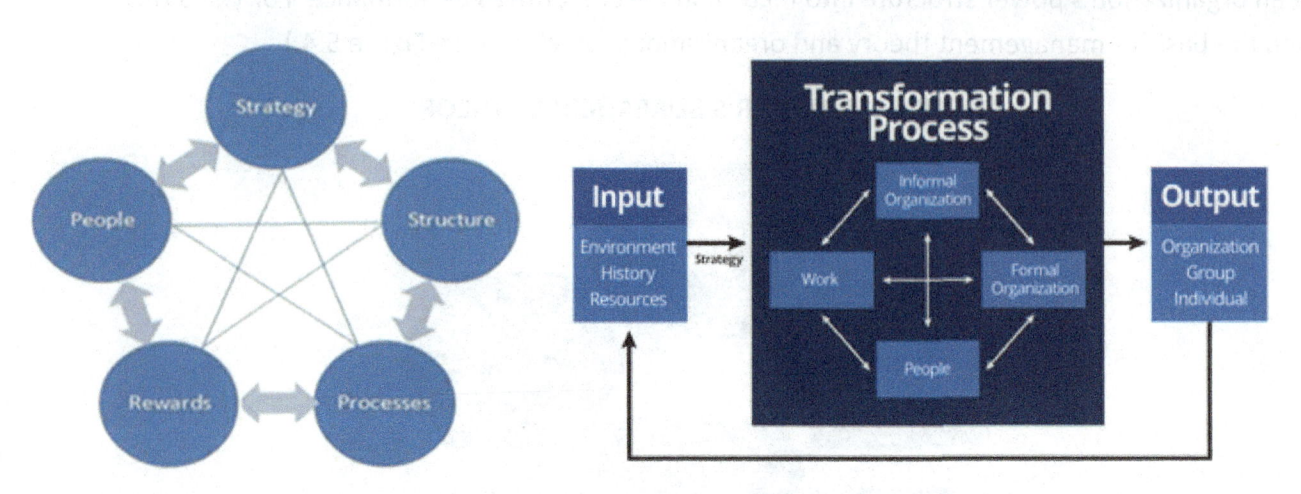

Operating models: In 2004, Osterwalder coined the term "operating model" to describe how a system's components work together to generate flow. [116] This approach introduced two key shifts in emphasis, both influenced heavily by the emerging importance of agility. First, the emphasis is on each of the components supporting delivery of value to the ultimate customer, which include how work is completed, technologies needed, roles and responsibilities, teaming, relationships, how leadership is distributed, and how desired behaviors are reinforced. Second, the "canvas" is the medium for groups to "paint on" to show the characteristics of the key components. Through this approach, focus shifts from leaders depending on experts for the right answers since these may change rapidly. Instead, engaging the wisdom and creativity of those who will be delivering the strategy accelerates execution. (See Figure 5.7.)

FIGURE 5.7: OSTERWALDER'S OPERATING MODEL CANVAS

Strategic alignment: Leadership teams expend considerable effort involving many resources and events to gain insights for their future, formulate a strategic plan, and assign business teams to execute the plan.

---

[116] Osterwalder A. and Pigneur Y. *Business Model Generation,* John Wiley & Sons, 2010.

Phase V: Strategy Execution

Then they are disappointed when this effort does not pay off. What usually goes wrong? In most cases, the organization is not capable of delivering and, as a result, incurs unwanted costs, lost opportunities, and lost value. Why? The root issue is almost always some aspect of alignment: The organization's operating model and its components are misaligned with what is required to deliver the new strategy.

The solution to misalignment has been to translate strategy into strategy execution by building a new operating model whose components mutually support and reinforce each other to deliver the strategy. "Transform," "align," and "design" the operating model are terms we use to describe what is needed. Designing, transforming, and aligning the operating model remains an essential aspect of strategy execution, but it is no longer adequate. This process needs to be dynamic and ongoing. In today's world, static, one-time, or even periodic alignment no longer suffices. Our world is changing too fast!

For an organizational operating model "framework" to enable achievement of desired strategic outcomes, it must focus on the organization's primary operational components (sometimes referred to as "building blocks"). The strategy professional's role is to facilitate the team's evaluation of the current organizational design model, assess and define the "to-be" state, and identify the gaps to guide transformation. To begin the transformation and organizational design process, a specific "systems focused" framework for identifying the organizational components to include in the transformation process is needed. In general, organizational design frameworks are built on the foundational elements of systems thinking. These components will vary depending on the organizational design framework being considered. [117] [118] [119]

Business ecosystems: This visualization of operating models fits well into the concepts of business ecosystems, adapted from research into ecosystems in the natural world. Moore[120] suggested that a business ecosystem is "an economic community supported by a foundation of interacting organizations and individuals — the organisms of the business world. In a business ecosystem, companies coevolve capabilities around an innovation: they work cooperatively and competitively to support new products, satisfy customer needs, and eventually incorporate the next round of innovations." (See Figure 5.8.)

---

[117] Stanford N. *Organization Design: The Practitioners Guide*. Routledge, London, (3rd ed) 2018.
[118] Thayer R., Carnino M., and Zybach W. *Syngineering: Building Agility into Any Organization*. United Kingdom: Changemakers Books, 2021.
[119] Haines, S.G. *The Complete Guide to Systems Thinking and Learning*. HRD Press, 2000.
[120] Moore J.F. *The Death of Competition: Leadership & Strategy in the Age of Business Ecosystems*. Harper Business, 1996.

FIGURE 5.8: OPERATING MODELS AND THEIR ECOSYSTEMS

Combining the concepts of operating model and ecosystem enables the organization to be seen as part of a larger business ecosystem within the natural ecosystem.

Further, operating models are high-level outlines of the organizational design. For the Organizational Design practitioner, a more detailed design will complete the picture. This is a helpful hierarchy for strategy execution: natural ecosystems, business ecosystems, operating models, and detailed design.

Emergence of Agile or Adaptive Design Methods

The need for agile or adaptive design is driven by three closely related technology-based trends: accelerating change, iterative strategies, and the application of "agile" concepts. Taken together they signal that alignment of the operating model with strategy must shift from a periodic linear process to one that is more organic and continuous. The organization itself must take on agile capabilities allowing it to sense and respond to changes in its environment and adapt its operating model accordingly.

Change is accelerating: We live in a dynamic world often characterized by the acronym VUCA: volatile, uncertain, complex, and ambiguous. Organizations and their ecosystems encounter constant change with little hope for equilibrium or even predictability. In ancient Greece, Heraclitus said, "Change is the only constant in life," to which Benjamin Franklin added two millennia later, "One's ability to adapt to those changes will determine your success in life." This is even more true today. Researchers have explored how the mathematics and physics of natural complexity and chaos can be transformed into useful models for making sense of this new world and its consequences for organizations. Snowden's Cynefin framework is one of many such efforts. [121]

---

[121] Snowden, D.J., Boone, M.E. *A Leader's Framework for Decision Making*, HBR, November 2007. https://www.youtube.com/watch?v=N7oz366X0-8

Phase V: Strategy Execution

Strategy more iterative: In today's changing world, business strategy is not static nor is strategy execution linear. Affirming mission and purpose, developing strategy, positioning the organization to execute, then *managing in a way that maintains focus on and commitment to the strategy* is a dynamic and iterative process. [122] Traditional operating models align the system to deliver on the strategy much like a machine. We use terms like balanced, aligned, or healthy to describe this aspect of implementation. In this new world we need more: *We must build on the essential capability to adapt as environments change.* Organizations are now viewed as organisms and we accordingly now use terms such as agile, living, or adaptive. Strategy comes to life when the traditional alignment of organization structures is complemented with dynamic capabilities adjusted in real time.

1.1(5)

2.2(7)

"Agile" concepts: *The Agile Manifesto*[123] appeared in 2001, addressing the massive increase in volatility. It integrated previously disparate approaches to facilitate rapid software development. Its 12 principles emphasize customer outcomes, iterative work, cross-functional self-managed teams, rigorous accountabilities, and decision making at appropriate levels. These principles greatly facilitated software development and soon were applied to organization design. [124] Figure 5.9,[125] developed by McKinsey & Co. consultants, shows some key shifts occurring when organizations begin to function with agility. The consultants stated that in 2018 around 85% of organizations globally were experimenting with "agile."

---

[122] Chugh J. *Bringing Agility to Strategy: Is Misalignment silently eroding your company's success?* Emergence, The Journal of Business Agility, Conference Special Edition, p33, 2022.
[123] Beck K., et al. *The Agile Manifesto*. Agile Alliance, 2021. http://agilemanifesto.org
[124] Worley C., Williams T., Lawler E. *The Agility Factor: Building Adaptable Organizations for Superior Performance,* Jossey-Bass Publishing, 2014.
[125] Wouter A. et al. *The five trademarks of agile organizations,* McKinsey & Co., 2018. https://www.mckinsey.com/capabilities/people-and-organizational-performance/our-insights/the-five-trademarks-of-agile-organizations

Strategy in the 21st Century, Second Edition

FIGURE 5.9 ORGANIZATIONS ARE BECOMING MORE AGILE

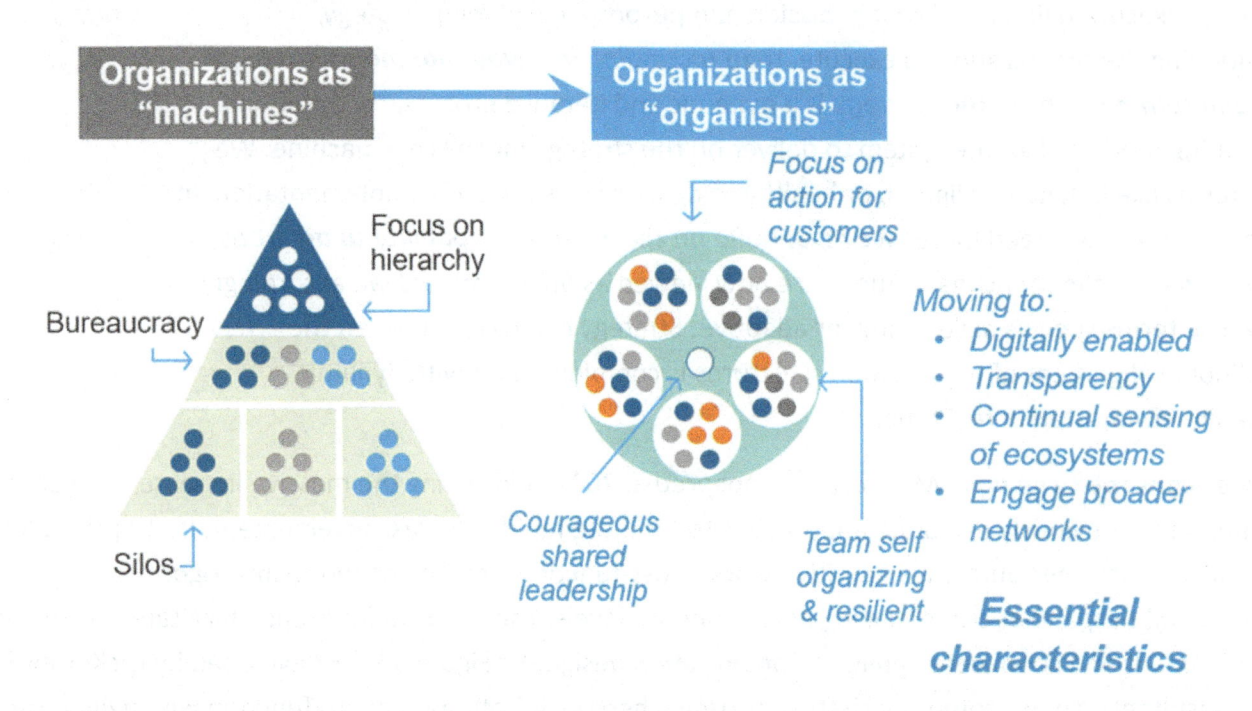

In a January 2018 article entitled "The five trademarks of agile organizations," McKinsey & Company research highlighted key shifts occurring when organizations begin to function with agility. McKinsey's team of Wouter Aghina, Karin Ahlback, Aaron De Smet, Gerald Lackey, Michael Lurie, Monica Murarka, and Christopher Handscomb stated that in 2018, around 85% of organizations globally were experimenting with "agile." They introduced their findings with the following:

"Our experience and research demonstrate that successful agile organizations consistently exhibit the five trademarks described in this article. The trademarks include a network of teams within a people-centered culture that operates in rapid learning and fast decision cycles which are enabled by technology, and a common purpose that co-creates value for all stakeholders." [126]

---

[126] https://www.mckinsey.com/capabilities/people-and-organizational-performance/our-insights/the-five-trademarks-of-agile-organizations

More than 40 variations of agile methods exist. Some are more fluid, emergent, and tightly aligned with agile principles. [127] [128] [129] Others, more structured, such as the Scaled Agile Framework (SAFe), are used to align large corporate hierarchies. A myriad of methods sit between the fluid and structured opposites, many with niche applications, all aiming *to build in capabilities to sense and respond to changing conditions.*[130]

2.2(7)

The range of agile/adaptive methods: The emergence of agile methods dovetailed with the evolution of other organization design approaches. Those mentioned earlier emphasized *seeing the organization as a system and using leadership power to build structures that could control the work and drive out inefficiencies*. Adaptive methods instead focus on who will have power and who will have a voice in controlling the work. These methods were emerging earlier than the 1950s.

Systems Perspective
Core Values

Pioneering work by F.E. Emery and E.L. Trist exploring human dynamics to counterbalance the mechanical mindsets, so prevalent in work at the time, led to the creation of self-managing teams. [131] Subsequent developments focused on broadening employee involvement in ways including Emery's Search Conference and open systems,[132] Harrison Owen's Open Space method,[133] and the Emily Axelrod's conference model for engagement and organization design. [134]

Parallel efforts, stretching back even further, introduced participatory decision making and distributed leadership as an organization's core governance. The original formulation was described as Sociocracy by Gerard Endenburg.[135] This concept was updated as Holacracy by Brian Robertson.[136]

Socio-technical organization design was closely related to and built on Emery and Trist's work, with procedures for integrating more "technical" work process and reporting structures with inclusion of policies and human systems. Examples were Stu Winby's Work Information Network and Decision Accelerator, perfected at Hewlett-Packard's innovation labs, and Jay Galbraith, Susan Mohrman, and Edward Lawler's methods at the Center for Organizational Excellence.[137] These practitioners embraced the need for building technology into organizations, under the rubric of "digital design."

---

[127] Kesler, G. and Kates, A. (2010) *Leading Organization Design: How to Make Organization Design Decisions to Drive the Results You Want.* Jossey-Bass Publishing, 2010.

[128] Robertson, B. *Holacracy: The New Management System for a Rapidly Changing World.* Henry Holt & Co.

[129] Thayer R., Carnino M., and Zybach W. *Syngineering: Building Agility into Any Organization.* United Kingdom: Changemakers Books, 2021.

[130] Willeke E. Fit-for-Purpose Agility: There Is No "One True Agile". *Cutter Business Technology J.*, v33, #4, 2020.

[131] Emery F. & Trist E. The Causal Texture of Organizational Environments. *Human Relations* v. 18, pp 21-32, 1965.

[132] Emery M. *The Current Version of Emery's Open Systems Theory,* Springer Publishing, 2000.

[133] Owen H. *Open Space Technology: A User's Guide (3rd ed.).* Berrett-Koehler Publishing, 2008.

[134] Axelrod R. Getting Everyone Involved: How One Organization Involved its Employees, Supervisors, and Managers in Redesigning the Organization, *The Journal of Applied Behavioral Science,* v. 28, #4, 1992.

[135] Endenburg, G. *Sociocratie: Een Redelijk Ideal [Sociocracy: A Reasonable Ideal].* Zaandijk, Woudt, 1975.

[136] Robertson, B. *Holacracy: The New Management System for a Rapidly Changing World.* Henry Holt & Co., 2015.

[137] Pasmore W. A., Winby S., Mohrman S. A., and Vanasse R, Sociotechnical Systems design: A reflection and look ahead. *Journal of Change Management,* in press.

A leadership team's ability to evolve an organization's operational model so it can respond to conditions as they arise has never been more important. Each adaptive method offers that potential, but experience suggests that each works in some circumstances, but not others. How does one choose? What are the criteria? Two groups of practitioners offer quite different yet complementary solutions to this dilemma.

Our colleagues at Syngineering Solutions have synthesized a framework that accommodates the methods described above, and outlines ways to choose among them. The framework is introduced in the book *Syngineering: Building Agility into Every Organization*, and we have incorporated an updated version as part of our Mastering Agile Organizational Design Certification Program.[138] The principles and concepts that underly their framework are described in the section below.

Dr. Pierre Hadaya, Professor, School of Management, Universite du Quebec, IASP Director at Large, Canada, with coauthor Bernard Gagnon, have proposed a different approach, the *Business Capability Framework*. This approach articulates a business architecture (i.e., how the organization currently functions) from an enterprise perspective based on a shared business vocabulary. This helps organizations design their target or aspired operating model and define key value streams. From here, the organization can incorporate refinements, additions, and cross-mappings opportunistically as dictated by business priorities. Shifting to agile and enterprise-focused operations is a natural follow-on. This Business Architecture approach [139] is detailed in IASP's BOK 3.0 [140] and outlined more fully in the section after the next one.

Agile Organization Design Framework

The agile or adaptive framework described by Syngineering builds on socio-technical and agile principles and brings in two important additional perspectives. The first is from Sally Parker and Lori Heffelfinger,[141] [142] who see organizations as living systems, capable of flourishing just as they are: the potential is there, it simply needs to be freed.

The natural world is an inspirational model of how to free the lifeforce inside our human organizations and can help us see the will, skill, and passions that may currently be trapped and remove barriers to the flow of essential resources: energy, material, ideas, nutrients. (See Figure 5.10.)

The second additional perspective comes from the Syngineering book mentioned earlier. The authors matured their ideas within an extended network of organization design practitioners. As they explored the myriad of adaptive methods that had been developed by these practitioners, they noticed patterns in

---

[138] https://www.lblstrategies.com/training-and-certification/mastering-adaptive-organizational-design-certification/

[139] Hadaya, P. and Gagnon, B. *Business Architecture: The Missing Link in Strategy Formulation, Implementation and Execution.* ASATE Publishing, Montreal, 2017.

[140] IASP, BOK 3.0, 3.1.3 – 3.2.3.

[141] Heffelfinger, L. & Parker, S. *Transformation Through Adaptive Leadership*, in *The Secret Sauce of Leading Transformational Change* by Ziskin I., Routledge Publishing, 2022.

[142] Parker, S. *Designing Living Organizations: Tapping and Unleashing Implementation and Execution.* ASATE Publishing, Montreal, 2023.

which methods tended to work in specific circumstances. From this they synthesized tools to allow leaders and practitioners to map their ecosystems and choose the appropriate methods.

By combining living systems and methods mapping with agile values and socio-technical approaches, they produced five key principles for designing adaptive organizations, ones that can be translated or adapted to the unique context of any organization.

PRINCIPLE 1: A NORTH STAR PROVIDES IDENTITY

Any discussion of strategy execution must start here. *An organization's North Star supplies a clear identity that defines what the organization is and what it is not.* It enables members at all levels to constantly rethink how to deliver unique value. *An organization's identity includes its strategic direction: mission, vision, values, and goals.* This is the lens through which all levels of the organization sense and respond to changes - both internal and external. The North Star is both enduring and fluid as the ever-changing world requires organizations to think of strategic direction and strategy in shorter time frames.

1.1(1)

For an organization's design to be agile, there must be ample opportunity for individual, interpersonal, small-group, and large-group collective sensemaking and storytelling that crosses siloes, incorporates diversity of thinking and demographics, and creates a psychologically safe environment for honesty, challenge, non-conformity, and experimentation. A North Star based on clear identification of customer needs is a primary agile organizational design tenet aimed at constantly shaping the organization to deliver on those needs. The Dalai Lama advocated: "In order to carry a positive action, we must develop here a positive vision."

PRINCIPLE 2: ORGANIZATIONS ARE INTEGRATED SYSTEMS

Agile organizational design builds on and extends the systems concept. It recognizes that organizations, and their ecosystems are simply people working to achieve their respective or shared goals. The diagram below is adapted from the Operating Model Canvas, which makes clear *how resources flow from suppliers through internal and partner's activities and produce and distribute products that convert to revenues*. Each ecosystem is defined by the interdependent elements and their relationships, both with each other and their external environments. (See Figure 5.10.)

P.1(b)3

Strategy in the 21st Century, Second Edition

FIGURE 5.10: INTEGRATED ORGANIZATIONAL SYSTEMS

- Interconnected and interdependent elements
- Design, maintain, and renew themselves
- Integral part of larger ecosystems

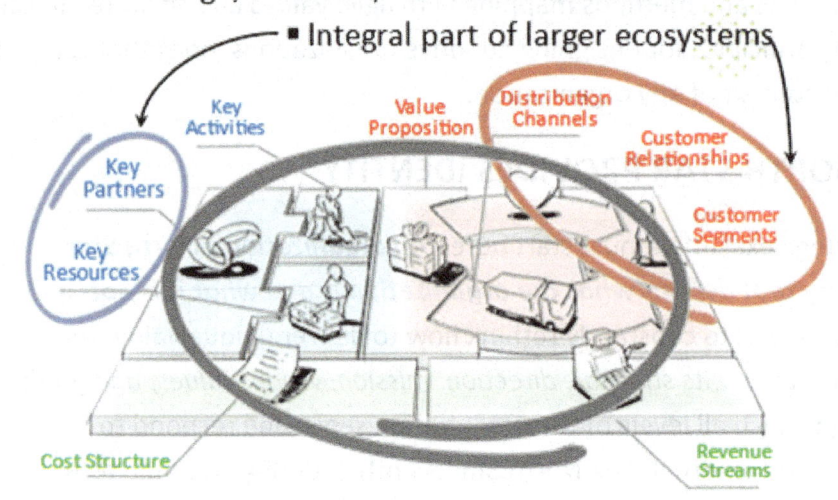

The components of the diagram shown below are adapted from Galbraith's star, updated to better reflect the nature of agile design. The blue portions are internal to the organization. To realize sustainable customer and stakeholder value, each 7 P component must be defined, understood, appreciated, nurtured, and integrated and aligned with the day-to-day operating environment (see Figure 5.11).

FIGURE 5.11: COMPONENTS OF AN INTEGRATED SYSTEM

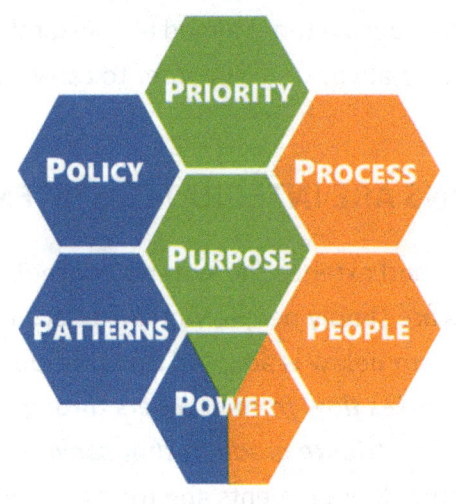

Traditional organizational design models, covered earlier in this phase also focus on aligning these components, but using leadership and hierarchical structures as the vehicles for work to be defined, completed, and controlled. In adaptive or agile methods, organizational design is not about creating a new organization chart. Instead, *the focus is on the nature of the relationships between critical operating components, especially mission, priorities, process, and the resources required.* In this view of organizations, leadership control shifts to shared power, and rigid structure shifts to

Baldrige Model

Integration

208

flexible patterns of relationships, all within an integrated system of interconnected and interdependent components.

PRINCIPLE 3: CO-CREATION ACTIVATES DORMANT POTENTIAL

A primary advantage of an adaptive or agile design is the positive impact "co-creation" has on the culture of the organization. Co-creation accesses the inherent wisdom in an organizational system, which helps unleash its lifeforce. It supports an essential shift in our relationship to power: from power-via-control to power-in-flow. *An essential ingredient for effective co-creation is the inclusion of diverse thinking perspectives and work-life experience.* A diverse set of employees and other key stakeholders coming together to co-create an organization's operating model and detailed organizational design activates untapped energy and potential across the enterprise.

5.2(7)

This co-creation organizational design approach is based on human-centered collaboration built on purpose, relationship, authenticity, and foundational trust. Co-creation requires deep human interactions, consistent teamwork, prompt collaboration, and mutual trust built on a solid foundation of psychological safety. Trust grows when team members feel safe to take chances and be vulnerable in front of their team. [143]

Three important guideposts in the co-creation process are:

- Each team must understand the key organizational components and how they connect into the larger system.
- Each team needs to internalize the strategic thinking behind the design choices being considered and the actions to be taken.
- The teams working together should bring design thinking to life in an adaptive and collaborative design process.

When the organization, in and of itself, participates in the act of sensing, making meaning, and strategizing, then the organization is better positioned to activate strategic direction. Engaging the 'whole' of the system fosters pull (i.e., buy-in) and builds strategic capabilities.

PRINCIPLE 4: USE AGILE DESIGN THINKING TO EMBED ADAPTIVE CAPABILITIES

As organizations and teams come together to design their operational model, they benefit by adopting an agile design thinking approach.[144] Agile design thinking enables adaptive organizational design. Businesses like Google, Amazon, and Netflix have validated the success of agile design thinking.

---

[143] Miller, S., Kirkpatrick, S. *The Government Leader's Field Guide to Organizational Agility: How to Navigate Complex and Turbulent Times*, 2021.
[144] https://www.youtube.com/watch?v=-ySx-S5FcCl

Strategy in the 21st Century, Second Edition

Agile design thinking seeks to solve complex problems by *approaching the challenge from the user's perspective and turning the insights and innovations that follow into products and services as soon as possible.* It deploys non-linear human-centered methods which integrate emotional intelligence into structured experimentation, to rapidly release innovation and creativity, and deliver unexpected solutions to previously unsolvable challenges. The diagram below shows the five generic steps involved, with the caveat that the entire activity is quite interactive: for example, participants in the midst of prototyping can jump back when they discover uncompleted portions of Define (see Figure 5.12):

3.1(4)

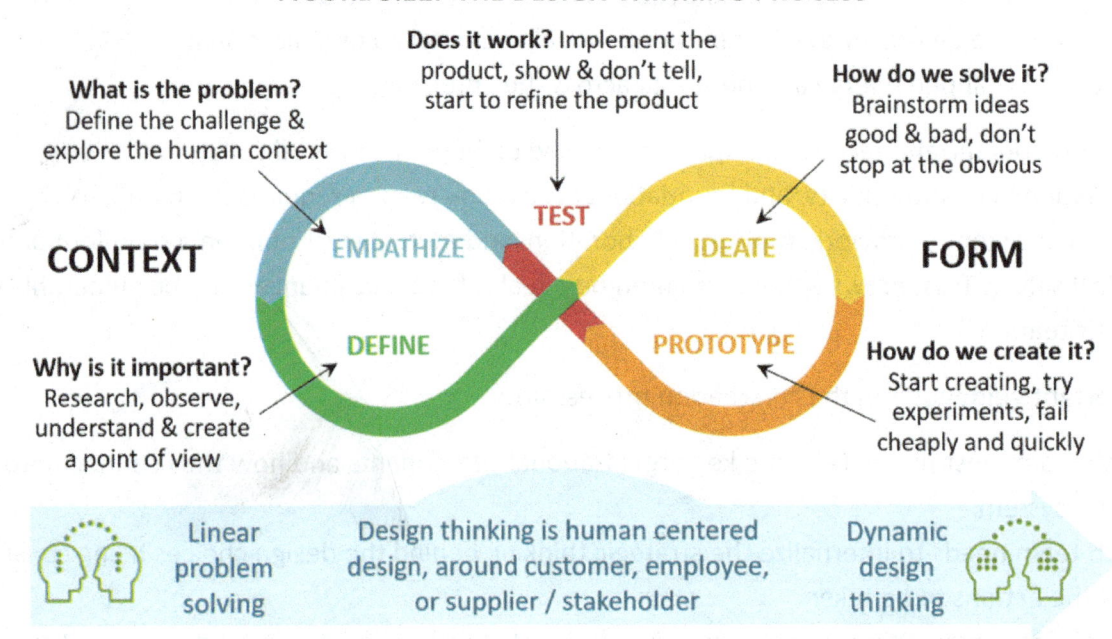

FIGURE 5:12: THE DESIGN THINKING PROCESS

Moving to an agile design thinking-based operating model is not easy, especially for established organizations with distinct hierarchies and functional models. It requires recognizing and balancing new and old mindsets and finding the right balance between a rigid static structure and total chaos. To be successful, leaders must shift their thinking process from an "organization as machine" to a "living system" model which is dynamic and flexible.

Another important shift in thinking must occur when facing complex organizational design issues. Managing these issues as polarities is a key to achieving sustainable and agile solutions. Thinking in terms of polarities is about "both-and" thinking and discourages "either-or" decision making and action.[145] For example, in many organizations, inappropriate design questions are posed, such as, "Do we centralize authority or distribute authority?" or "Should we be moving away from our hierarchical structure to a matrix structure or to a self-organizing structure?" In fact, there may be a need for each depending on the circumstances and for both present and emerging customer needs.

---

[145] https://www.harvardbusiness.org/navigating-complexity-managing-polarities/

These polarities occur at all levels in the organization, so the skills to manage them must be embedded at all levels. This is yet another example of how an "agile organization" functions. Below are some additional examples of common polarities to be managed. (See Table 5.1.)

TABLE 5.1 – ORGANIZATIONAL POLARITIES

Internal Focus		Customer Collaboration
Control & Predict		Sensing & Responding
Analysis & Thinking	AND	Intuition & Feeling
Right Answers		Right Questions
Structure		Flexibility
Centralized		Distributed

PRINCIPLE 5: TAILOR THE APPROACH TO THE CONTEXT

A number of important considerations in achieving an effective organizational design exist, but none are more important than having a clear and shared understanding of the interrelated set of conditions that exist inside the organization and across its ecosystem.

To gain this understanding, strategy professionals must help their team understand their organization's unique context, i.e., where are we positioned in the ecosystem and how do we assess our culture? Armed with this information, the team's challenge is to adapt their system's components to achieve the desired future state. Given the complexity and volatility involved, ecosystem maps have emerged as a helpful tool to support the design process.

Three key dimensions are involved in developing ecosystem maps.

First, look at where the organization is in its lifecycle. Living systems evolve through continuous cycles of change and adaptation, with each cycle having four phases of development: inventing or renewal, birthing and growing, maturing, and releasing. This is true for individuals, teams, departments, entire organizations, and even for business ecosystems. Each phase has a predominant focus and builds the capability to manage increased complexity and support growth. Entities can get stuck in one phase or another by trying to move too fast or by failing to adapt to changing environmental conditions.

Trying to move too quickly leads to inadequate development. Failing to adapt leads to poor response to change, risk, and becoming irrelevant. Both of these situations signal a failure to evolve. Those that cannot evolve, die. (See Figure 5.13.)

Strategy in the 21st Century, Second Edition

FIGURE 5.13 ORGANIZATIONAL LIFE CYCLE

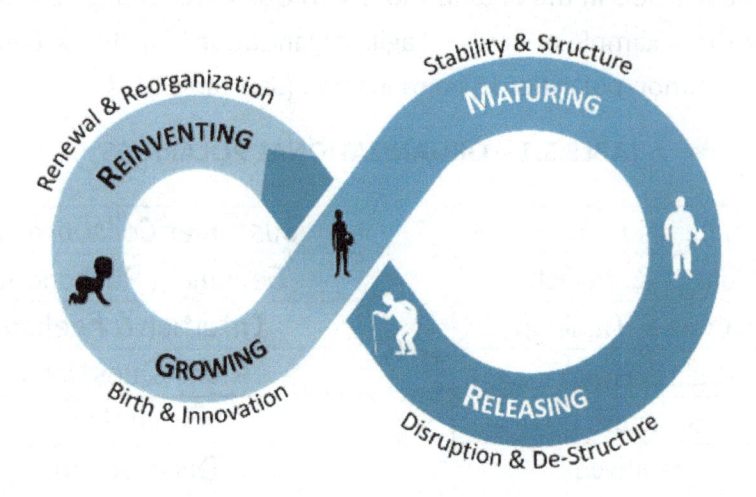

Second, where in the business ecosystem does the organization exist? To envision this, ascertain how complex the organization, industry, and its products and services might be and contrast that with how quickly these are changing. The soft drink bottling business, despite a myriad of technological advances, is still relatively simple and stable: mix drinks and move to market. The online fashion business is also simple, but with massive volatility in customer tastes. Might universities with their academic disciplines be complex yet stable? Is the telecommunications industry a good example of complex and volatile? (See Figure 5.14.)

FIGURE 5.14: GENERIC BUSINESS ECOSYSTEMS

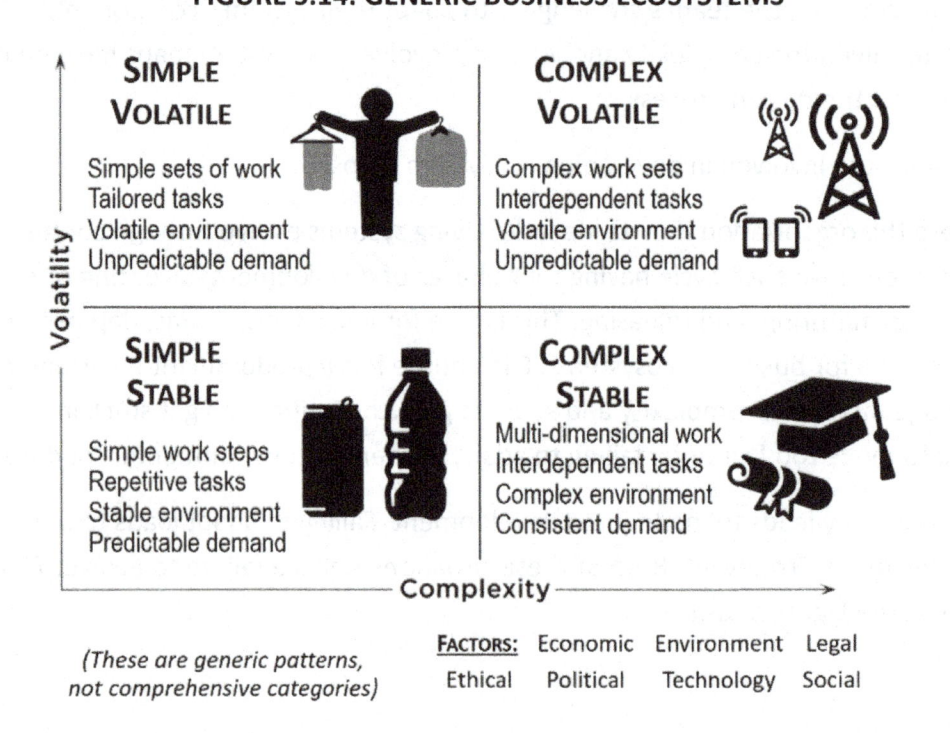

SIMPLE VOLATILE
- Simple sets of work
- Tailored tasks
- Volatile environment
- Unpredictable demand

COMPLEX VOLATILE
- Complex work sets
- Interdependent tasks
- Volatile environment
- Unpredictable demand

SIMPLE STABLE
- Simple work steps
- Repetitive tasks
- Stable environment
- Predictable demand

COMPLEX STABLE
- Multi-dimensional work
- Interdependent tasks
- Complex environment
- Consistent demand

Volatility ↑ / Complexity →

(These are generic patterns, not comprehensive categories)

FACTORS: Economic, Environment, Legal, Ethical, Political, Technology, Social

Third, how would you describe the organization's operating culture? This is the set of norms, expectations, and unwritten rules that govern how people behave. Specific business ecosystems naturally favor certain types of cultures. In simple and stable ecosystems, directive cultures with careful planning

Phase V: Strategy Execution

and standard processes tend to emerge. Increasing complexity drives a need for more involvement. Increased volatility requires cultures with more flexible and speedy decision-making. Of course, models are simplifications. Culture itself is multi-dimensional and shows up differently in different departments and functions. These diagrams are intended not as solutions, but to provide lenses through which the organization can see itself in ways it perhaps never has before. (See Figure 5.15.)

FIGURE 5.15: GENERIC BUSINESS CULTURES

Flexible Culture
- Multi-tasking workers
- Flexible mindsets
- Enabling leadership
- Consultative decisions

Adaptive Culture
- Multi-skilled labor
- Linked networks
- Clear accountabilities
- Distributed decisions

Directive Culture
- Unskilled labor
- Standard processes
- Careful planning
- Hierarchical control

Participative Culture
- Expert specialists
- Collaborative work
- Matrix management
- Shared decisions

(Y-axis: Flexibility; X-axis: Involvement)

Helping the organization understand these three dimensions can yield insights into what it needs and how to attain this. Is the organization approaching old age and in need of a natural rebirth? Has the business ecosystem become dramatically more complex and/or volatile, yet the organizational culture has lagged behind? Remarkably, transformation softens hearts when an organization creates these diagrams and sees for itself the realities of its circumstance.

THE AGILE ORGANIZATION DESIGN CYCLE

The five principles noted above are generic for most change project efforts but look quite different in each specific culture. To understand these differences, discuss how activities are sequenced in a change effort. Organizations initiate activities, mobilize resources, develop high-level designs, complete detailed designs, and incorporate these into their operations. The Syngineering Solutions design cycle mirrors these steps and is based on the Gestalt cycle of experience that describes the natural response of any living organism to stimuli.

Stage 1 Sense: Scan for changes and decide whether to act. In more heirarchical cultures, introduce adaptive design concepts and practices. Expand stakeholder involvement beyond strategic planning groups to broaden buy-in and begin co-creation.

Stage 2 Mobilize: Charter the effort, mobilize the needed resources, validate the direction and strategy, and diagnose the shortfalls to delivering on strategy. As much as possible, enlist groups

Strategy in the 21st Century, Second Edition

to do this and proceed in interactive steps.

Stage 3 Frame: Develop the high-level operating model and its component designs. This is the heart of agile design: components that are not only aligned but also have capabilities for sensing and responding built into their DNA.

Stage 4 Customize: Deploy the operating model to units for detailed design. Make plans to best involve every unit. In parallel support functions, design the supporting talent and performance management systems to best facilitate the operating model.

Stage 5 Sustain: Implementation is well underway with Customize. Sustain makes course corrections for alignment and agile capabilities and, as soon as possible, transitions to a sustainable state of sensing and responding.

The stages are often depicted as a chain of arrows that loop back on themselves. This symbolizes an organization pausing its normal operations just long enough to use design thinking in revising how it works. The sustain arrow is intentionally canted upwards, signaling a new and improved trajectory. (See Figure 5.16.)

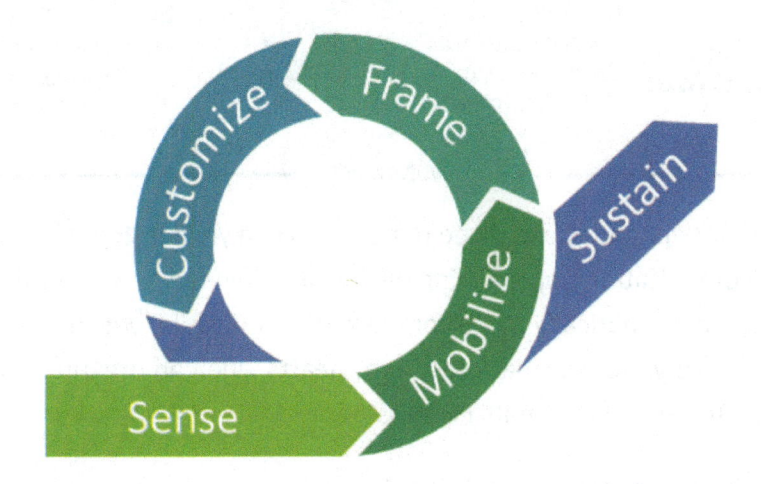

FIGURE 5.16: SYNGINEERING SOLUTIONS DESIGN CYCLE

Choosing effective methods: Organizational context is often the first activity in Sense. At this point, the organization can realistically consider what specific design methods would work in its particular culture. The methods we mentioned earlier – Sociocracy, self-managed work teams, conference design, Holacracy, agile design, digital design, and many more – each have their pluses. The diagram below shows where some of these methods fit. Design projects might work best in a Directive organization used to such projects. Stages become project phases, with steering reviews to pass from phase to phase. Design conferences might best help Participative organizations generate the deliverables for each stage. Flexible cultures speed up the process with prototyping design workshops and rapidly operationalizing the outcomes. Adaptive cultures have these capabilities built in. Change happens naturally. (See Figure 5.17.)

Phase V: Strategy Execution

FIGURE 5.17: GENERIC METHODS

What about culture change? A challenge arises for leaders and practitioners when context dimensions suggest that culture itself is part of the problem and must change. This situation is common and addressing it is often critical for an organization's survival. A reason many change efforts fail is that they cannot address this shift. Either the change effort is so rooted in the new culture that it is rejected by the current one or the leaders and practitioners are using tried and true, familiar methods that fail to make a dent in changing the culture. (See Figure 5.18.)

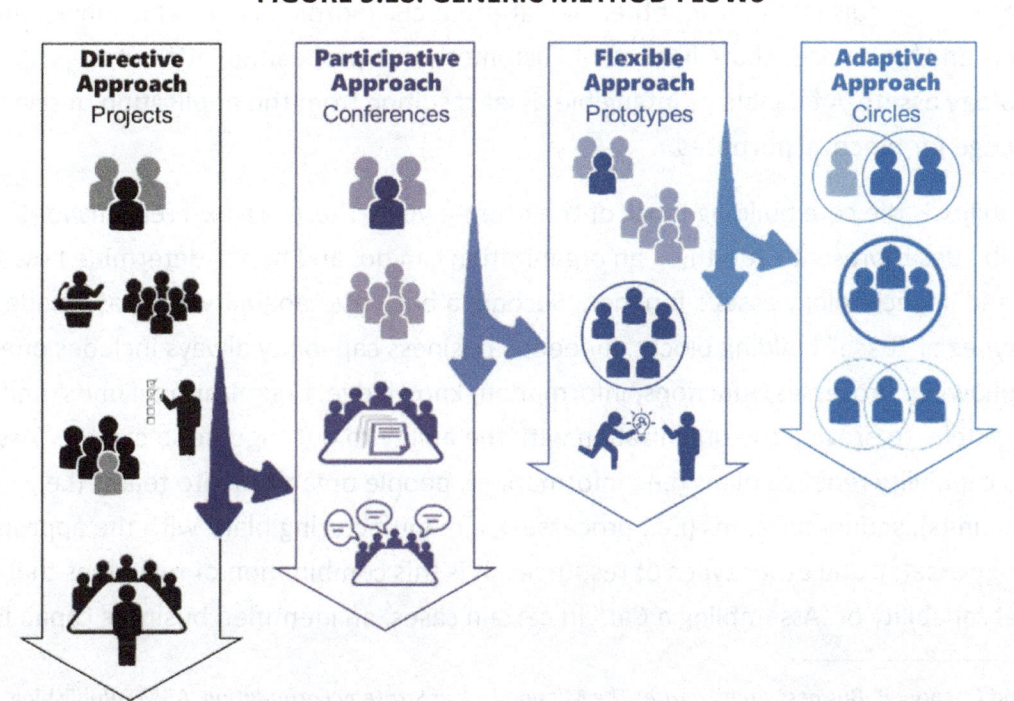

FIGURE 5.18: GENERIC METHOD FLOWS

215

The previous diagram suggests the way out of this conundrum. It shows four common generic approaches, with time flowing down the page. Each situation is addressed with hybrid methods, starting with a method the organization is familiar with, and smoothly shifts mid-stream to one more suited to the culture that fits the ecosystem. The key is co-creation: The organization and its leadership must diagnose and agree to the changes needed. While difficult, this requires the very versatility and experimentation that agile design fosters. Today's organizations deserve nothing less.

Business Capability Framework

Alternatively, consider Dr. Pierre Hadaya, and coauthor Bernard Gagnon's *Business Capability Framework*. It comprises the following eight complementary types of resources, components, or building blocks that must be aligned with strategy:[146]

1. **Business capability.** An integrated set of resources designed to work together to attain a specific result.
2. **Function.** A type of work performed by the organization (e.g., accounting, marketing)
3. **Process.** An ensemble of activities that transforms a set of inputs into a set of products and/or services.
4. **Organizational unit.** A permanent or temporary team of people with a common set of goals and whose management is entrusted to one or more of its members.
5. **Information.** "Facts provided or learned about something or someone" (*New Oxford American Dictionary*) that the organization possesses. Data become information when a pattern is detected.
6. **Knowledge.** Skills and expertise held by the organization, its members, and its resources (e.g., AI algorithm).
7. **Brand.** A name, term, design, symbol and/or logo associated with a number of products and/or services to distinguish them from other similar products and/or services and convey that these products and/or services share important customer value proposition attributes.
8. **Technology assets.** A tangible or intangible asset resulting from the application of scientific knowledge for practical purposes.

Business capability is the core building block of their framework. There are two reasons for this. First, business capabilities represent everything an organization can do, and hence determine how the organization and its technology asset's function. Second, a business capability is always made up of the other seven types of "base" building blocks. Indeed, a business capability always includes one or more of each of the following: processes, functions, information, knowledge, organizational units, and technology assets. For example, to provide the organization with the ability to put together a car, the "Assembling a Car" business capability requires plans (i.e., information), people organized into teams (i.e., organizational units), sequential steps (i.e., processes), a manufacturing plant with the appropriate tools (i.e., technology assets), and other types of resources. It is this combination of resources that yields the organizational capability of "Assembling a Car." In certain cases, an identified business capability can also

---

[146] Hadaya, P. and Gagnon, B. *Business Architecture: The Missing Link in Strategy Formulation*, ASATE Publishing, 2017.

be made up of a brand. For example, the Coca Cola Company's "selling capability" could not manage to sell 1.9 billion servings a day in more than 200 countries were it not for the power of its brands.

The *Business Capability Framework* is at the heart of the enterprise architecture approach Hadaya and Gagnon (2021) have devised to help organization integrate the five strategy groups of activities outlined in BOK 3.0, as well as obtain the maximum benefits from their strategic endeavors.[147][148] This novel approach encompasses three complementary components: (1) the target enterprise architecture (TEA); (2) the transformation plan; and (3) the enterprise architecture team.[149]

The TEA describes how the organization, and its assets will need to function as a whole to support the execution of the new strategy. TEA is thus synonymous with target operating model. Designing the TEA is the first activity of the Transform Organization group of activities. As mentioned above, this plan is designed using the eight types of building blocks above.

The TEA can be subdivided into three facets.

- The first is the *target business architecture* that focuses on business capabilities, functions, processes, organizational units, knowledge, information, and brands.
- The second facet concentrates on the *information technology (IT) assets* (e.g., software applications and technology infrastructure) at the heart of the operating model. This facet is further divided into four domains: data, applications, technologies, and security.

The third facet addresses *non-IT technology assets* (e.g., manufacturing plants, warehouses, distribution centers, planes) that are important to the operating model. For example, the TEA of a parcel delivery company such as FedEx needs to include a target parcel delivery technology architecture that defines how its sorting centers, the sorting technologies in these centers, and its transport technologies (e.g., airplanes, trucks) need to be used in the future to efficiently pick up parcels from its customers and deliver them to their final destination. (See Figure 5.19.)

---

[147] Hadaya, P. and Gagnon, B. Mapping an Agile Future, *Strategy Magazine*, 35(May), 18-21, 2020
[148] Hadaya, P. and Gagnon, B. Making the Promise of Strategy a Reality with the Enterprise Architecture Approach, *Strategy Magazine*, 36(May), 26-29, 2021.

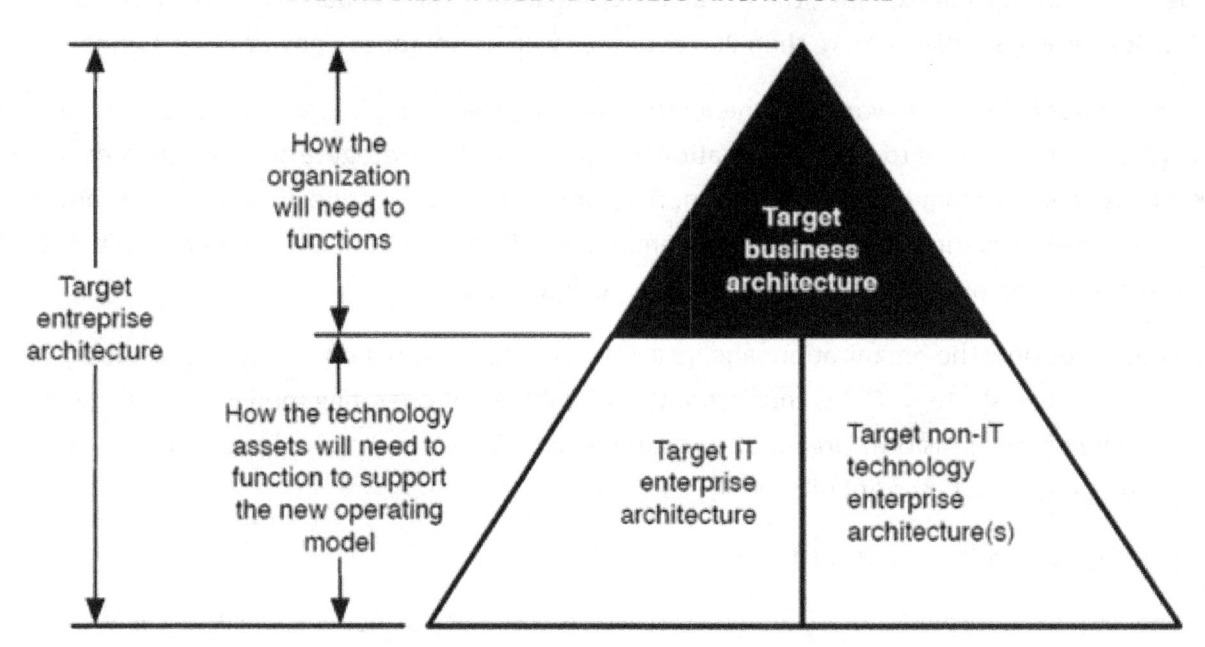

FIGURE 5.19: TARGET BUSINESS ARCHITECTURE [150]

The transformation plan *"regroups all the building block transformations to be made to the operating model into projects and orders the timing sequence of their execution so that the benefits the transformation projects will collectively generate are maximized" (BOK 3.0)*. This plan originates from the strategic initiatives identified during strategy formulation. The *transformation plan* is based on a comparison between the current enterprise architecture and TEA to identify the transformations that must be executed to improve the organization's ability to execute its new strategy. Recognize that every organization has an enterprise architecture even if it was not purposefully designed or if it Is not documented.

The enterprise architecture team is responsible for creating the TEA and the transformation plan as well as to align the work of all stakeholders (e.g., program managers, solution architects, project managers, and process experts) throughout the transform organization group of activity.[151] In addition, it must support strategists during strategy formulation as well engage stakeholders (e.g., to establish a sense of urgency, communicate about the strategic plan and its execution) and govern (e.g., manage architecture reviews, detect architecture problems tied to several projects and help find solutions). (See Figure 5.20.)

---

[150] Hadaya, P. and Gagnon, B. *Business Architecture: The Missing Link in Strategy Formulation.* ASATE Publishing, pp 6-8, 2017.

[151] Hadaya, P. and Gagnon, B. Making the Promise of Strategy a Reality with the Enterprise Architecture Approach, *Strategy Magazine*, 36(May), 26-29, 2021.

Phase V: Strategy Execution

FIGURE 5.20: RESPONSIBILITIES OF THE ENTERPRISE ARCHITECTURE TEAM [152]

Jim Stockmal, former IASP Board President and co-lead author of the BOK 3.0, provides these thoughts on building organizational capabilities for strategy execution success. Jim leads our *Mastering Agile Organizational Design Certification Program.* [153] [154]

> *I had the opportunity to listen in on a panel discussion around 'designing for speed.' The panel was made up of luminaries in the field of organizational design and change, including Dick Axelrod, Sue Mohrman, and Stu Winby. Invariably, the discussion came around digital disruption and how organizations are being challenged on several fronts, including handling perpetual feedback from customers, decision making, and handling the speed of change. Many organizations were designed for efficiency – that is, repeatably delivering value to customers in a cost effective and efficient manner. Those organizations that become digitally disrupted, whether at the infrastructure level, the operating level, or at the business model level, are finding it difficult to change rapidly, mainly due to the cultural artifacts associated with an efficient design.*
>
> *Others have found it difficult even using agile methods and collaborative, empowered teams. To these experts, agile is not enough if you do not address all the component elements – people, systems, policies, processes, systems, and data – that are still needed to deliver goods and services. These organizational design experts understand the dilemma facing leaders wanting faster change but know it does not happen overnight. These experts are trying to figure out how to do this correctly. One key to success is getting teams to be productive working on these issues more quickly. Leveraging the underpinnings of organizational development theory and practice such as participatory design and ethical design principles, they believe agile, collaborative, and flexible team capacity-building will help address the dilemma by taking on one design component at a time.*

---

[152] Adapted in IASP BOK 3.0 from Hadaya, P. and Gagnon, B. *Business Architecture: The Missing Link in Strategy Formulation.* ASATE Publishing, pp 9-12, 2017.
[153] https://www.lblstrategies.com/training-and-certification/mastering-agile-organizational-design-certification/
[154] IASP, BOK 2.1, Supplemental Readings, Domain 3 - Preparation for Strategy Transformation, p165.

Strategy in the 21st Century, Second Edition

Then I read an article by Jeanne Ross from MIT [155] who addressed the issue of strategy execution from the lens of a business architect. Executing a digital strategy can be a challenge because so many different elements must be synchronized to deliver an integrated solution. She posits that architecting for 'efficiency is no longer sufficient.' Business architecture must also focus on agility. She reaches a similar conclusion to the organization design (OD) experts, "...designing rapid reuse of individual business components **and** empowered teams."

In her article, Jeanne Ross gives an example of a 'continual release' concept in action, reliant on empowered, cross-functional collaborative teams and management acting as "coaches." Unlike the OD experts and Zachman, she calls for clear mission (at the enterprise and team level), reuse of common business and technical components, and great knowledge sharing. These three "must haves" are key to building the capacity of the organization to execute, "...a great strategy is valuable only if a company is capable of executing that strategy." As strategists, we owe it to our organizations to consider either a business architecture approach or an OD approach, because the elements discussed here are critical for organizational success in the age of disruption.

Task 5.2 - Engage Stakeholders and Align the Team Behind the Strategy

In the previous task, *Design and Transform the Operating Model*, the operating model is redesigned. While this work is very important, it is not sufficient to ensure effective implementation of the strategic operating plan.

In this task, *Engage Stakeholders and Align Behind the Strategic Operating Plan*, the goal is to achieve both deep and broad understanding, acceptance, internalization, and support for two codependent elements central to execution, i.e., making the necessary changes to the operating model and successfully implementing the initiatives in the strategic operating plan. [156]

To lay the groundwork for implementation of the strategic operating plan, the next task requires considering and addressing several important sets of activities.

Engage, Involve, Communicate, and Roll Out the Strategy and Strategic Operating Plan

Throughout this book, we emphasize the importance of engaging and involving key stakeholders in the development and execution of strategy. As noted at the end of Phase IV, common sense tells us that a basic requisite for *aligning an entire team behind the*

2.2(2)

---

[155] Ross, Jeanne, MIT expert recaps 30-plus years of enterprise architecture, *MIT Management*, August 10, 2020
[156] It is highly recommended that all IASP exam takers carefully review the IASP BOK 3.0, Chapter 5: Engage Stakeholders

strategic operating plan is to effectively communicate the intent and desired benefit of the plan. The communications effort should "win hearts and minds" and ultimately change behaviors.

All leaders must communicate, communicate, and communicate. Aligning the team begins with leaders and managers communicating their understanding, commitment, and long-term view to others in the organization. In this process, leaders will identify potential "change agents" who can help to tell the entire workforce the proposed effort is an enterprise-wide priority.

Communication requires careful preparation. Effectively communicating the organization's strategy requires integration of five closely related components:

- Messages must be presented clearly, in detail, and exude integrity and authenticity.
- The messenger must be appropriate for the message.
- The recipient of the message must choose to listen, request clarity, and trust the sender of the message.
- The way the message is sent and delivered must suit the circumstances and the needs of both the sender and the receiver.
- The substance of the message must resonate and connect, on some level, with the values of the receiver.

Senior leaders and managers at all levels must deliver messages personally whenever possible. Written information should be presented so that it reaches all those who are impacted by the strategy: That means considering the specific needs of different groups of employees.

1.1(3)

When presenting the case for the plan and detailing any required changes in the operating model, bad news should be communicated along with the good, e.g., work force restructuring. The strategic management process will be undermined by loss of trust if employees do not have confidence in the accuracy and honesty of what they are told by senior leadership.

Communication must flow from the top to the bottom of the organization and then back up, creating a feedback loop involving the organization's most important resource, its people. Often, both strategic and operational planning involves an intense burst of initial communication within the organization—then nothing! A key requirement for effective execution is clear and continuous communication throughout the entire strategic management journey. (See Figure 5.21.)

FIGURE 5.21: CONTINUOUS COMMUNICATIONS THROUGHOUT THE JOURNEY

Don't wait to communicate until you finish the strategic planning journey!

- Is the organization ready to execute this plan?
- Does the organization align behind "how we get there"?
- Do all stakeholders embrace our desired future state?
- Does the organization agree with prioritized SWOT? Anything missing?
- Who's on the team and what does the "journey" look like?

Early in the process, communicate who is on the planning team and what the journey will entail. Once the environmental assessment, SWOT analysis, and other foresight activities are completed, it is time to communicate the results and request input. As the strategic direction is developed, maintain good communication to ensure all stakeholders embrace the desired future state. And, finally, as the team prepares to implement the plan, maintain constant communications to ensure successful execution.

A critical milestone in this journey is rolling out the new operating model and strategic operating plan. Ensuring that clear and comprehensive communications occur when the plans are unveiled will reinforce the team's commitment and energize the team for implementation. (See Figure 5.22.)

FIGURE 5.22: SAMPLE PLAN ROLLOUT AGENDA

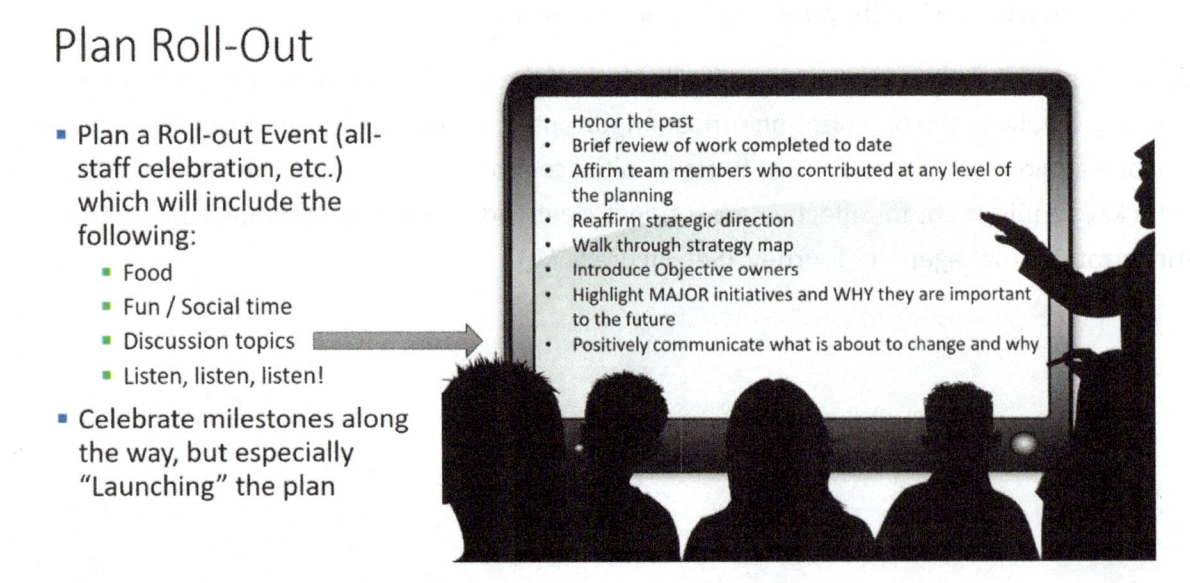

Plan Roll-Out

- Plan a Roll-out Event (all-staff celebration, etc.) which will include the following:
    - Food
    - Fun / Social time
    - Discussion topics
    - Listen, listen, listen!
- Celebrate milestones along the way, but especially "Launching" the plan

- Honor the past
- Brief review of work completed to date
- Affirm team members who contributed at any level of the planning
- Reaffirm strategic direction
- Walk through strategy map
- Introduce Objective owners
- Highlight MAJOR initiatives and WHY they are important to the future
- Positively communicate what is about to change and why

Phase V: Strategy Execution

Create a Performance Culture

A requisite for effective execution is to create a culture centered on performance. This level of strategic maturity requires a systematic, agile, and empowering approach to managing the organization at all levels. An organization's culture permeates leaders, managers, and staff, influencing how they think, feel, and act. When a "performance culture" becomes ingrained within an organization, individual and collective actions rise to a new level and deliver dramatically improved results. Critical elements in creating a performance culture include:

1.1(5)

- **Establish and maintain expectations**. A fundamental requirement for effective execution is to establish and manage expectations to create buy-in and help maintain an *organizational culture that values transparency and accountability*. Unless performance expectations are understood, valued, and met, neither transparency nor accountability can be maintained. Regardless of an organization's situation, the process begins with leaders and managers frequently communicating to the organization their personal understanding, commitment to, and long-term view of the strategy and execution plan.

  1.2(1)

- **Restructure the operating model, as necessary**. In each of the transformation frameworks, the goal is the same: improving decision-making, completing assignments, ensuring follow through, providing timely feedback, and promoting further improvements. When implemented correctly, changes to the organization's operating model will support a culture centered on performance.

- **Be clear and transparent on accountabilities**. Central to creating a performance culture is establishing accountabilities. Any accountability framework must clearly define roles and responsibilities for each strategic element. The senior leadership team must be transparent about authority and responsibility for each strategic component and the strategic operating plan. Without clear roles and responsibilities, implementation will falter and expected outcomes will not be achieved.

- **Invest in Professional Development**. Professional development is another essential element in executing the strategic operating plan and creating a culture centered on performance. Strengthening the capacities of employees is a must in today's rapidly changing environment. Professional development involves investing in the education, training, coaching, and certifications that employees need to achieve individual performance objectives. Even though employee performance objectives are often operational, strategic intent is preserved by aligning professional development investments with the capacities needed to effectively execute the plan.

- **Incentivize desired behavior**. Incentivizing employees and teams for accomplishing the strategy is closely linked with investments in professional development. While recognition and rewards are both effective incentives, the approach used should be an appropriate fit for the individual or team. Leaders should always think through the notion of "value" from the perspective of the individual employee. Additionally, leaders must ensure that recognition and rewards are timely, sincere, meaningful, and tied to desired results. People want to know that their ideas and work is valued, and they are valued. Money is appreciated as an incentive, and depending on the sector, can motivate team members toward desired outcomes. However, leadership needs to ensure that shorter-term bonuses align with, rather than distract from, the longer-term strategy.

Ensure Line of Sight to Strategy

On May 25, 1961, President Kennedy gave a highly memorable speech focused on putting a man on the moon and returning him safely to earth. Several months after that speech was given, a group of reporters allegedly visited NASA to interview administrators to learn about progress being made toward achieving President Kennedy's goal. As the reporters were leaving NASA, one noticed a man in a white suit and mask standing in the middle of an empty room vacuuming the floor. The reporter was curious and opened the door, walked in, and asked the worker "What are you doing?" The worker immediately looked up and responded, "I'm putting a man on the moon and bringing him home safely." The worker knew that if dust or debris were to get in the electronics, it could jeopardize the entire mission.

Alignment from top leadership down through the organization was emphatically demonstrated in that front-line moment. Consider, if someone were to ask each of your employees, "What are you doing?" Would they be able to express how their day-to-day work contributes to the higher-level strategy of the organization? If yes, there is a clear line of sight to strategy.

In the broadest sense, organizational alignment is the process of building individual and collective accountability throughout the organization for strategy implementation. Success increases when everyone across the organization understands how they fit into the bigger picture and what is expected of them to help the organization succeed. Collective accountability requires inclusiveness, a common language, and transparent decision-making.

Integration

In aligned organizations with clear line of sight to strategy, a shared vision connects to:

- *Strategic initiatives that are actionable and understood across the organization.*   2.2 (2)
- *A resource allocation and budget formulation process that is informed by strategy and their operational requirements,* each of which are updated as needed in response to changes in circumstances.   2.2 (3), 2.2 (4)
- *Customer-focused processes that are efficient and effective.*
- Day-to-day work aligned with business and support unit objectives and efforts.   6.1
- Key stakeholders working in a collaborative fashion.
- *Effective, efficient performance measurement occurring* on a scheduled basis.   4.1(1)
- Employee job descriptions describing how strategy is made actionable.   5.2(4)
- *Employee development plans focused on improving knowledge, skills, and abilities* in place and implemented.   5.2(5)

Phase V: Strategy Execution

The strategy practitioner's role is to help integrate strategy, people, processes, technology, and operations by aligning the strategic operating plan horizontally across and vertically down through the organization.

To ensure alignment, the senior leadership team, along with unit level leadership, must be clear on what alignment means for *each* function or unit. This requires leaders to assess the impact of the strategic operating plan, including what resources will be required and what skill sets each unit must possess.

Further, it requires leaders to think through how best to integrate the strategic operating plan within the ongoing processes of the organization and to adjust the processes as needed to align with the strategy. What must each unit stop doing to free up resources to better execute the plan? What impacts will result from shifts in resource allocation for other key departments and stakeholders? Ultimately, alignment occurs when organizational level objectives are "cascaded" to align department level objectives and the work employees do day-to-day.

From a process perspective, understanding how to cascade from the beginning is important. Cascading starts by "translating" the organization-wide strategic plan (referred as *Tier 1*) down to business units, support units or departments (*Tier 2*). [157] In 2016, the Balanced Scorecard Institute (BSI) team articulated leading practices for cascading.[158] They highlighted three ground rules to facilitate the Tier 1 to Tier 2 cascading process. Each ground rule is illustrated below using a balanced scorecard strategy map model.

- *Ground Rule 1*: This is not a top-down or a bottom-up process, but a two-way process. Leadership must work closely and consistently with managers to understand what units must accomplish to drive performance at the organization-wide level. (See Figure 5.23.)

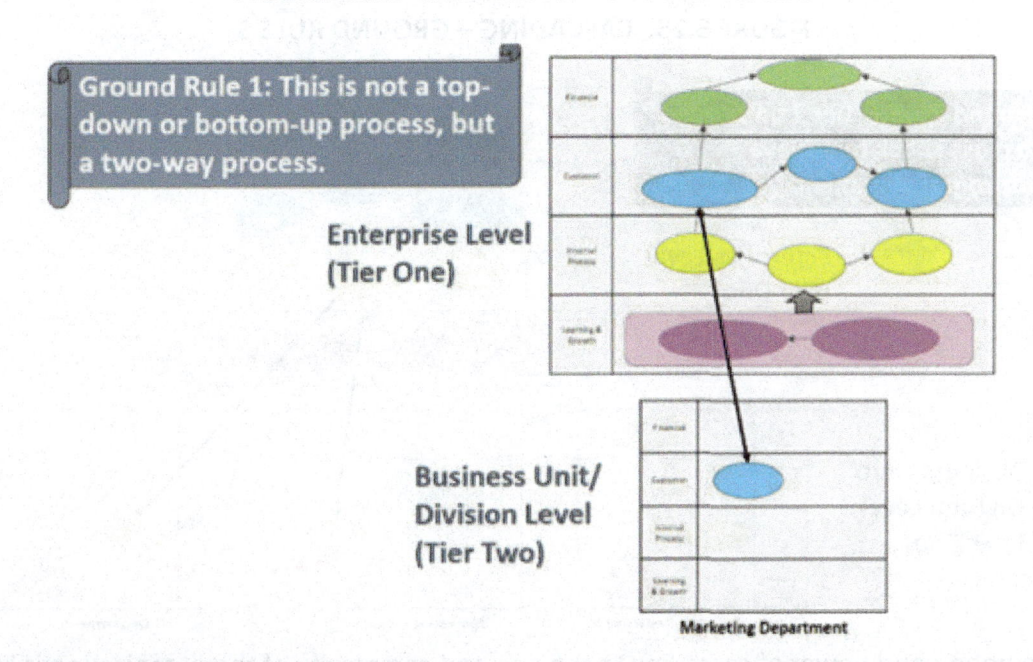

FIGURE 5.23: CASCADING – GROUND RULE 1

___

[157] IASP BOK 3.0, Chapter 6, 6.3.1
[158] Rohm, H., Wilsey, D., Perry, G.S., and Montgomery D. *The Institute Way*, pp. 243-250, 2016.

Strategy in the 21st Century, Second Edition

- *Ground Rule 2:* Not all objectives at Tier 1 level are cascaded to each Tier 2 unit. Some organization-wide objectives align with specific functions and departments. Only those Tier 1 objectives that are relevant to Tier 2 should be cascaded. (See Figure 5.24.)

FIGURE 5.24: CASCADING – GROUND RULE 2

- *Ground Rule 3:* Tier 2 units need to cross check to achieve horizontal alignment. Often a Tier 1 objective will be relevant to more than one Tier 2 unit or function. In such cases, careful attention must be placed on communication and coordination across Tier 2 units to avoid unnecessary duplication of efforts. (See Figure 5.25.)

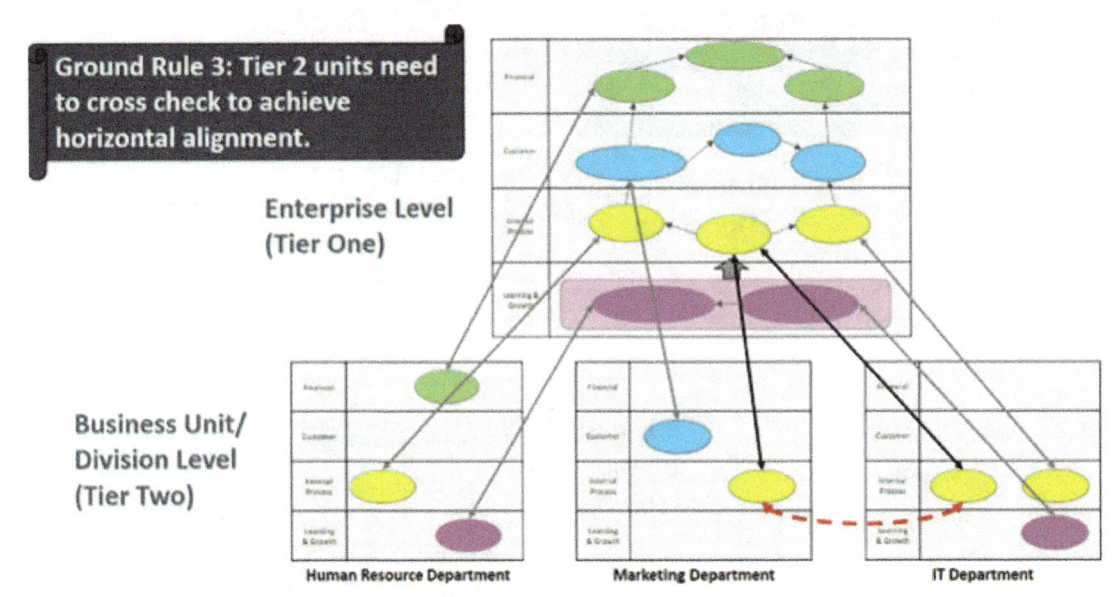

FIGURE 5.25: CASCADING – GROUND RULE 3

Adapting the notion and power of cascading to the size and complexity of the organization is important. (See Figure 5.26.)

226

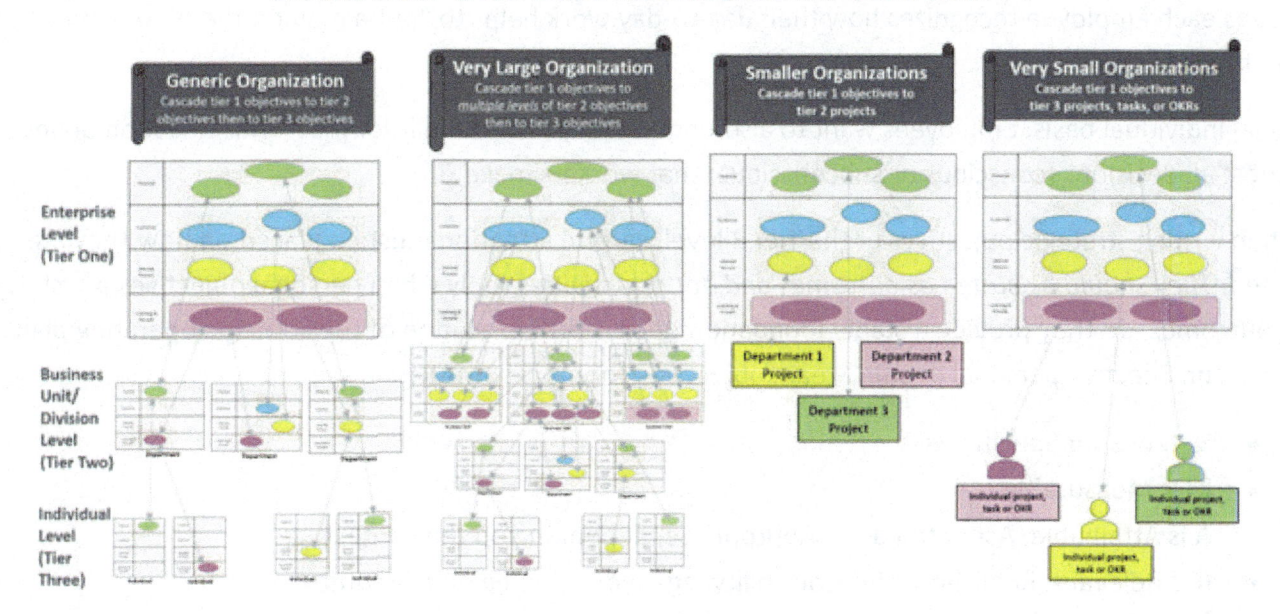

FIGURE 5.26: CASCADING ACROSS SIZE AND COMPLEXITY

Some objectives may be mandatory for all business, program, and support units. Others can be cascaded by asking each unit how they can contribute to attaining the objective for the next one to three years. Still others may be managed through discretionary alignment. (Mandatory objectives are often found in franchise organizations, while discretionary objectives are more often found in portfolio organizations.)

Align Individual Roles

Aligning individual roles to strategy is a final determinant of successful alignment with the strategic operating plan. It requires understanding how each employee's or small team's work fits into the organization's strategy. Strategy practitioners coordinate with the HR department to translate strategy, strategy execution processes, and language into job descriptions and individual development plans.

Individual alignment means each employee's or small team's work is aligned to their unit's Tier 2 objectives. Alignment at this level is considered Tier 3 alignment. (See Figure 5.27.)

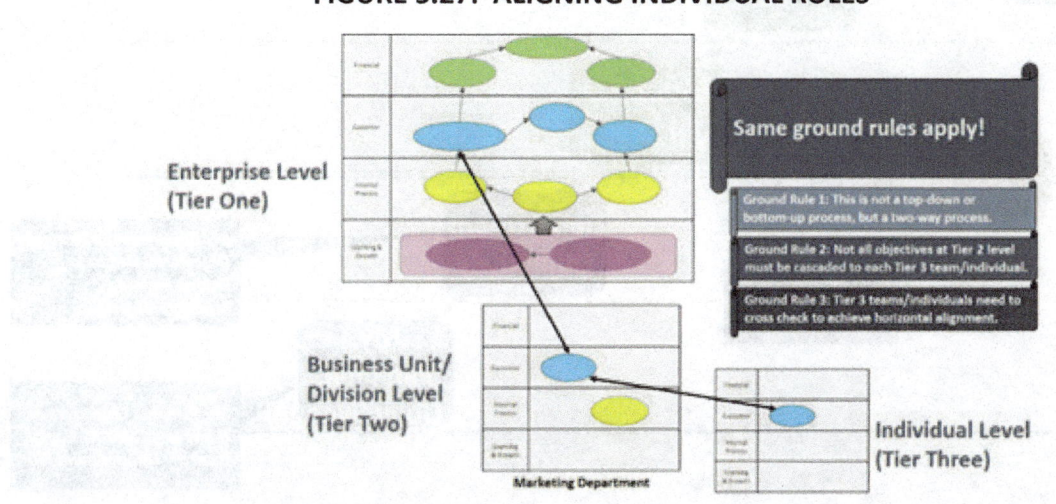

FIGURE 5.27: ALIGNING INDIVIDUAL ROLES

Strategy in the 21st Century, Second Edition

Alignment at this level can only be maintained when strategy is understood as everyone's job. To do so means each employee recognizes how their day-to-day work helps to "put a man on the moon and bring him home safely."

On an individual basis, employees want to also understand, "What's in it for me?" This question drives almost all decisions (conscious or subconscious) that workers make,

When writing strategic objectives at the Tier 3 level, careful attention must be placed on how they are stated. *They should be stated as outcomes and not as activities.* Only when personal objectives are stated as outcomes, do they provide a stable foundation upon which execution of the strategic operating plan can occur. Effective personal or small-team objectives should be **SMART:**

- **S** stands for Specific
- **M** is Measurable
- **A** is Attainable, Aspirational, or Appropriate, depending on the context
- **R** is Relevant, Realistic, or Responsibility, again developing on the context
- **T** means Time frame for achievement or Timely

INCREASE AGILITY OF ALIGNMENT

The goal of strategic alignment is to maintain "line of sight" linkages to the strategic objectives at all levels of the organization. In an aligned organization, individual-level objectives support unit- or departmental-level objectives, which in turn support enterprise-level objectives, goals, and vision. (See Figure 5.28.)

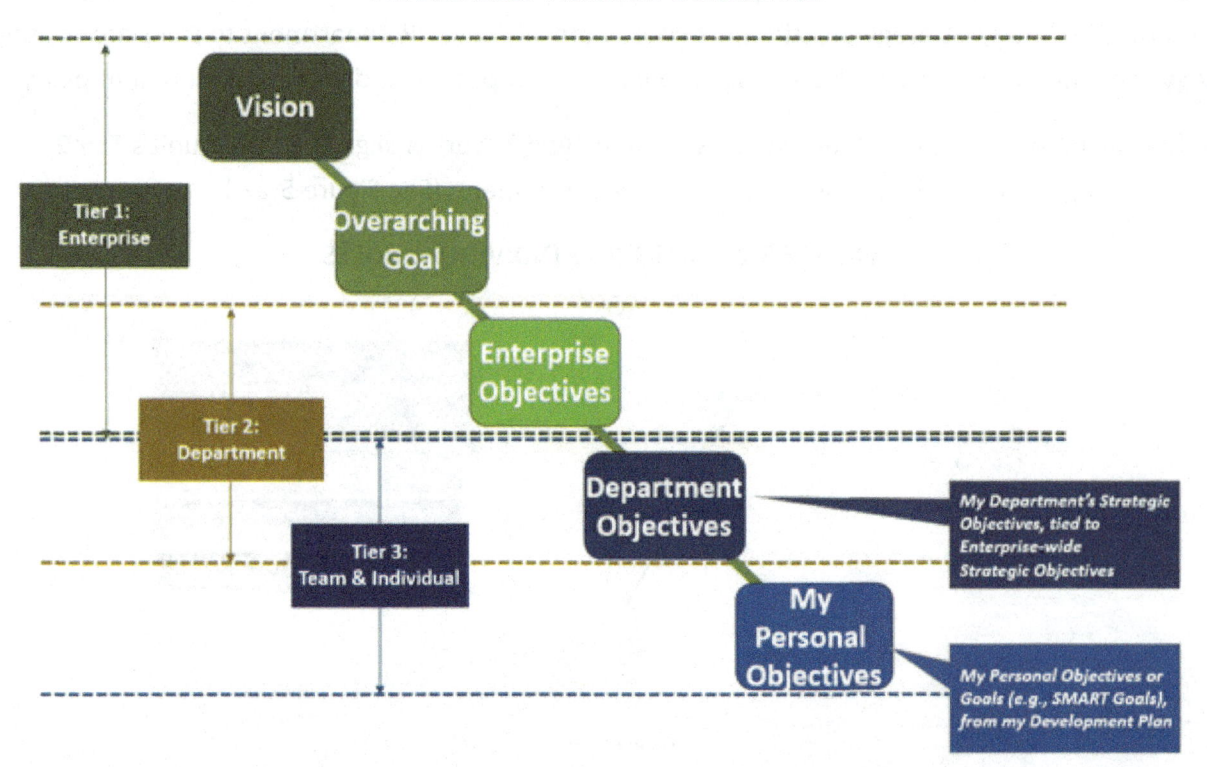

FIGURE 5.28: ALIGNED OBJECTIVES

Phase V: Strategy Execution

In traditional cascading, each element of the hierarchy is defined and together summarizes the path forward over the next year. Take a moment to review a simple example of alignment for Amy's Ice Cream Palace (see Figure 5.29):

FIGURE 5.29: SIMPLE EXAMPLE OF ALIGNMENT

- **Tier 1: Enterprise**
  - Vision: Making the world a better place one scoop at a time!
  - Overarching Goal: Increase market share by 35% in 5 years
  - Enterprise Objectives: Objective – Increase Brand Awareness
- **Tier 2: Department**
  - Department Objectives: IT Objective – Improve social media presence and access
- **Tier 3: Team & Individual**
  - My Personal Objectives: Webmaster Objective – Increase social media KSAs

In situations where increased agility is required, the cascading looks somewhat different as unit-level and individual objectives cover shorter time periods, often a quarter of a year at a time. (See Figure 5.30.)

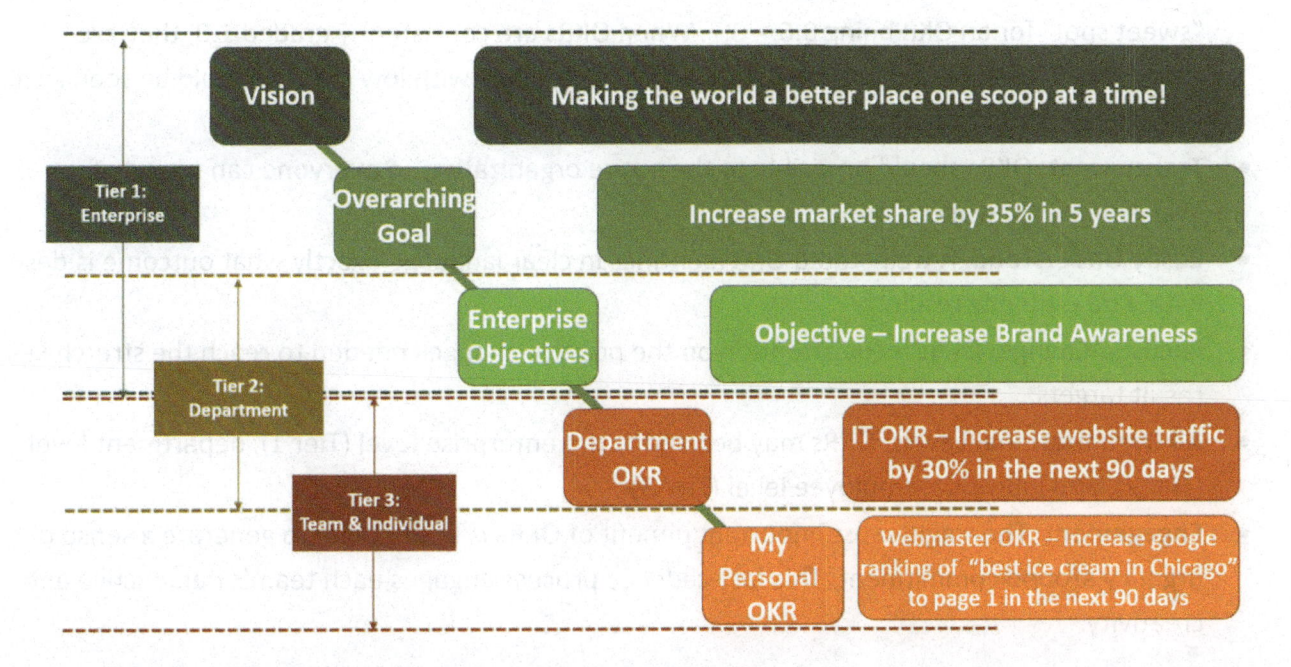

FIGURE 5.30: AGILE EXAMPLE OF ALIGNMENT

- **Tier 1: Enterprise**
  - Vision: Making the world a better place one scoop at a time!
  - Overarching Goal: Increase market share by 35% in 5 years
  - Enterprise Objectives: Objective – Increase Brand Awareness
- **Tier 2: Department**
  - Department OKR: IT OKR – Increase website traffic by 30% in the next 90 days
- **Tier 3: Team & Individual**
  - My Personal OKR: Webmaster OKR – Increase google ranking of "best ice cream in Chicago" to page 1 in the next 90 days

For Agility, Manage With OKRs

As noted earlier, one emerging management technique to facilitate agile objective setting and management is the use of Objectives and *Key Results* (OKRs). (See Table 4.9)

"**Objectives**" refers to where the organization wants to go – specific outcomes for a set period. "**Key Results**" refers to how far the organization has progressed in pursuit of these objectives.

The purpose of OKRs is to connect organizational, department level, and individual (or small team) objectives to measurable results while having all team members and leaders work together in one unified direction.

A key element of OKRs is that they assure that everyone in the organization knows what is expected of them and they are aware of what others are working on. OKRs are visible to everyone as the organization moves towards the same overarching goal(s) and enterprise objective(s). OKRs are typically part of a quarterly planning cadence.

Key features of OKRs include:

- **Agile**: OKRs have become increasingly popular for organizations seeking to build in more agility into their strategic management and performance system.
- **Ambitious**: Objectives should require the organization to "stretch" and feel somewhat uncomfortable. The expectation should be that not all OKRs will be met each quarter. The guidance is to seek that sweet spot between aspirational and very realistic.
- **Measurable**: Each OKR should be measurable and easy to grade with a number. For example, Google uses a 0–1.0 scale to grade each key result at the end of a quarter, with the performance "sweet spot" for an OKR being 0.6 - 0.7. When OKRs are consistently graded 1.0, they are considered to be not ambitious enough. Conversely, OKRs with low grades should be seen as data to help refine the next quarter's OKRs.
- **Transparent**: OKRs should be visible to the entire organization so everyone can see what everyone else is working on.
- **Easily Understood**: A well-stated OKR identifies in clear language exactly what outcome is desired with a quantifiable result.
- **Focused Change**: OKRs focus attention on the positive changes needed to reach the stretch key result targets.
- **All Organizational Levels**: OKRs may be used at the enterprise level (Tier 1), department level (Tier 2), and individual employee level (Tier 3).
- **Engagement**: The single-most important benefit of OKRs is their ability to generate a sense of urgency around commitment. This fast-cadence process engages each team's perspective and creativity.

Task 5.3 – Implement the Strategic Operating Plan

The strategic operating *plan implementation process* is often undervalued and neglected compared to the efforts dedicated to planning, managing, and controlling ongoing operations. Managers and top executives commonly think that their responsibility for strategic management ends when the plan is completed. In fact, their work has just begun. Management processes for strategy implementation require ongoing engagement, leadership, thoughtful governance, and management's careful attention to delegate responsibilities and provide oversight to ensure the work gets done.

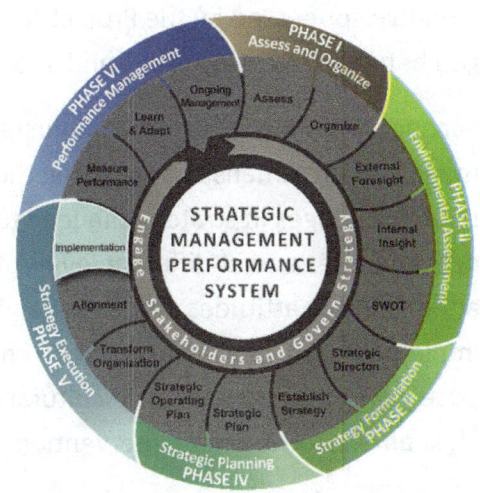

Note: Many of these points are emphasized in a recent white paper, "Future of Strategy Implementation," sponsored by the Strategy Implementation Institute, and coauthored by Antonio Nieto-Rodriguez, Robin Speculand, Randall Rollinson, Ricardo Sastre, Joe DeCarlo, Gurpreet Rehal, and Michele Manocchi. [159]

Implementing a newly developed or refined strategy and strategic operating plan differs from simply implementing operational changes. Changes in the components of strategy – that is, vision, mission, values, policies, goals, strategies, objectives, initiative, and measures of the organization's success or failure – reverberate through the organization and its operations. In contrast, planned changes originating at an operations level are usually conducted *within* the framework of a current strategic direction, strategic plan, and strategic operating plan. Organizations that routinely implement large-scale changes in operations can be highly challenged in executing even the smallest strategic initiative that requires a fundamental change in organizational culture or shared values. How this added dimension is managed is a primary key to successful strategy implementation.

To address this challenge, leaders must focus on *proven practices* for successfully implementing the strategic operating plan as a plan of action. From the outset, the leadership team must decide who and how to involve other key stakeholders before implementation begins. The new strategy's scope will provide clues. Each of the organization's units must have representation in the planning, coordination, and delivery of the subsequent actions.

At this point, effort by the leadership team and staff is at its highest to make the plan operational and integrate it in the existing organization. Over time, the level of attention to sustaining interest and enthusiasm for the new strategy often diminishes. Implementation falters. This occurs for two reasons.

---

[159] http://www.bridgesconsultancy.com/wp-content/uploads/2016/10/The-Future-of-Strategy-Implementation-White-Paper-final.pdf

First, leaders often do not know how to implement strategy because implementation is not well developed and clearly understood as a process requiring their oversight. In recent years there has been increasing private sector focus on improving execution of the strategic plan. An example is the Brightline Initiative sponsored by the Project Management Institute, dedicated to helping organizations bridge the gap between strategy design and strategy delivery. [160]

Second, many leaders do not understand that implementation proceeds simultaneously along several management dimensions requiring their diligent attention throughout the journey. For example, even modest changes in strategy can lead to managerial, operational, cultural, and technical changes at differing rates and at different levels of resistance, These require distinctive levels of response and adjustment in attitudes and behavior. Strategies that emphasize changes at the technical level pose fewer implementation challenges than do changes at the managerial and organizational level. These, in turn, pose fewer problems than do cultural changes, which are the most complex dimension of change and the least amenable to direct intervention.

The Vital Role of Leaders

Too often leaders do not understand or appreciate the important role they play to ensure that strategic level execution occurs within day-to-day operations. Robin Speculand, strategy implementation expert, offers several insights into this dynamic. [161]

- "This current generation of leaders has been taught how to create a plan but not how to execute it."
- "Many leaders are guilty of delegating the execution and not paying adequate attention to it."
- "If leaders regard strategy execution as a standalone project, it will fail."
- "When leaders create the right conditions for execution and guide people through the journey, it demonstrates their authentic commitment and sincerity."
- "A significant shift in strategy requires a significant change in a leader's day-to-day activities across the organization."
- "When leaders execute a long-term strategy, but are measured and rewarded for short-term performance, this creates a tense juxtaposition that many organizations fail to address."

So, what must leaders do to ensure implementation's success? A common set of implementation capabilities and competencies (including leadership excellence) are now being codified by the Strategy Implementation Institute. [162] (See Figure 5.31.)

---

[160] https://www.brightline.org/
[161] Speculand, R. *Excellence in Execution: How to Implement Your Strategy,* pp 20-27, 2017.
[162] https://www.strategyimplementationinstitute.org/strategy-implementation-body-of-knowledge-sibok/

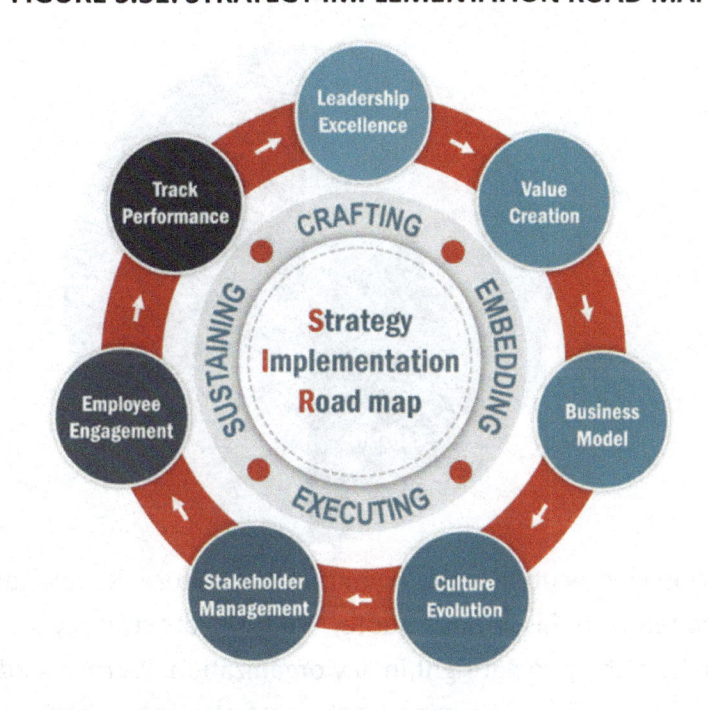

FIGURE 5.31: STRATEGY IMPLEMENTATION ROAD MAP

The figure summarizes the challenges a leadership team may face. In addition, consider the following leadership capabilities that are essential for implementing strategy:

- Evaluate the organization's strategy as a hypothesis to be tested and refined as the future unfolds.
- Inspire your team to do what *you* want done because *they* want to do it.
- Stay involved by providing high-level oversight of the implementation process.
- Refine the key managerial roles, responsibilities, and capabilities required to implement a strategic operating plan.
- Marshal resources by ramping up investment in capabilities that matter most while seeking to reduce investment in everything else.
- Consistently measure and control implementation performance.
- Adapt, change, modify, and revise the implementation process as required.

Each of these capabilities are maximized by leadership that communicates the strategic operating plan's implementation requirements. This is no small challenge: It requires significant investment of time and effort.

Key Contextual Factors that Impact Implementation Processes

Beyond the role of leadership, an organization's current circumstances and situational factors fundamentally impact implementation. A primary role of strategy management professionals is to help leaders understand the contextual and situational challenges they may encounter as they implement the plan. Even modest changes in an organization's strategy can lead to managerial, operational, cultural, and technical changes causing internal resistance requiring appropriately measured response and adjustment in attitudes and behavior. (See Figure 5.32.)

FIGURE 5.32: KEY CONTEXTUAL FACTORS

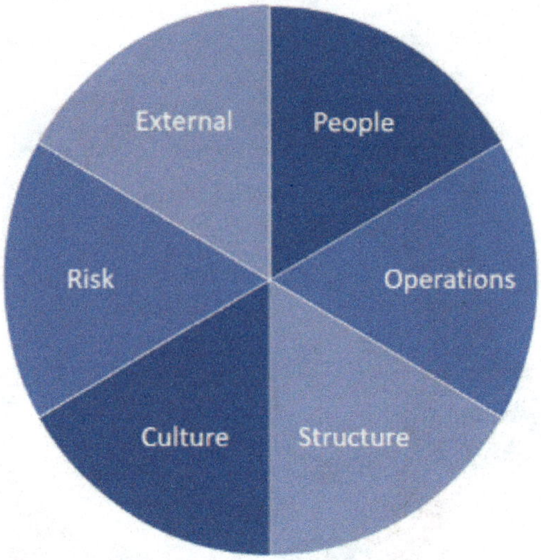

[Pie chart with six segments: External, People, Operations, Structure, Culture, Risk]

Residing at the heart of strategy execution is the organization's culture. Renowned management theorist Peter Drucker is often credited with this famous quote, "Culture eats strategy for breakfast." Organizational culture is a hard thing to get right in any organization. It grows and evolves over time and is often the result of action, inaction, and reaction on the part of an organization's leadership. Culture can be thought of as the lasting effect of every event or personal interaction that has taken place in the history of the organization. As such, culture has a dramatic impact on every individual and their willingness to support change.

The business classic *Good to Great* by Jim Collins delivers wisdom when it comes to overcoming difficulties leaders face during implementation. Placing the right people in the right jobs helps to ensure an organization will operate efficiently and effectively. Collins notes that: *"People are not your most important asset. The right people are. Get the right people on the bus, the wrong people off the bus, and the right people in the right seats."* Put simply, implementation success depends in large measure on having the right people doing the right jobs. [163]

Leaders and strategy professionals must carefully consider key situational and contextual factors when trying to anticipate and communicate the nature and scope of organizational change required. In all cases leaders should focus on "the why" as they position and leverage strategy to shape culture. The work of Robin Speculand and Antonio Nieto Rodriguez at the *Strategy Implementation Institute* highlights a rapidly advancing, digital transformation reality, which requires that "strategy eat culture for breakfast" or risk certain failure.

---

[163] Collins, J. *Good to Great*, p 13, 2001.

Phase V: Strategy Execution

Implementation Best Practices

Every organization must determine how they will implement their strategic operating plan. In this section we cover six key actions to guide the implementation process.

- **Determine your strategy cadence**. Determine the speed at which you intend to implement the plan. The answer always depends on the context, as execution happens at a different pace for different organizations and for different industries. Leaders must use the strategy's intent and the urgency surrounding it to dictate the pace or rate by which execution should happen. [164]

    Some organizations and industries move deliberately with implementation...as in moving at a snail's pace. Other organizations, aware of impending threats or timely opportunities, are compelled to implement strategy faster say...at a rabbit's pace. And then there are the cheetahs, those organizations feeling a sense of urgency in the face of immediate disruption that drives their "ACT NOW!" pace of change.

- **Conduct a readiness assessment.** Optimizing the implementation of strategy requires varying levels of internal change, or improvement, on the part of people and processes linked to strategy execution. These changes occur within several different dimensions. Change will vary in degree and begins by conducting a readiness assessment to identify and improve the weakest dimensions first. The results of an implementation readiness assessment will point leaders to where their organization is weakest and where implementation should initially focus.

    Based on 20 years of research, Robin Speculand has identified eight competency sets that are key to strategy implementation and should be included in a readiness assessment: [165]

    - Engaging the **People**
    - Sharing the **Business Case**
    - Constantly **Communicating**
    - Putting in place the right **Measures**
    - Aligning execution and **Culture**
    - Change and innovate **Processes**
    - **Reinforcing** the right actions
    - **Reviewing** and monitoring the execution

    The above elements were created for the private sector. To guide readiness assessment in the public sector, there are nine competency sets. A description of these competencies and LBL's thinking around strategy execution in the public sector is included in Appendix 10.

- **Cut before you add**. In most cases, start by trimming back current programs, products, services, or processes so the team can focus on what is most important in terms of executing the strategic operating plan. No matter how large or small, every organization has limited time, human, and

---

[164] Speculand, R., *Excellence In Strategy Execution*, 2017, 42-44.
[165] Speculand, R., *Excellence in Execution: How to Implement Your Strategy*, 2017, 50-52.

financial resources. It is harmful to roll out a new set of strategic initiatives to a workforce that is already stretched too thin. Err on the side of overestimating required resources to execute your strategy while underestimating available resources. Simultaneously, carefully review the value of the current projects against the proposed new strategic objectives. (See Figure 5.33.)

FIGURE 5.33: CUT BEFORE YOU ADD

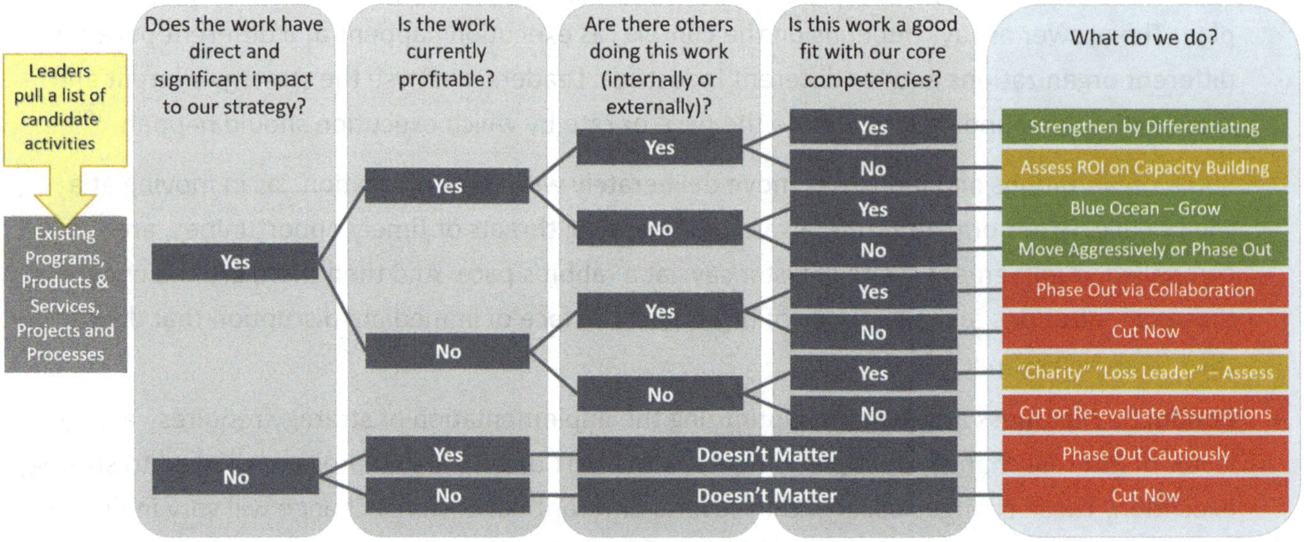

To facilitate this process, list the candidate activities to evaluate for continuation. Then use a decision tree tool modified from the MacMillian Matrix [166] to identify four major criteria to use to evaluate a specific business activity and what to do with it once the evaluation is complete:

- Does the work have a *direct and significant impact on our strategy*?
- Is the work *currently profitable*?
- Are there many *others doing this work*?
- Is this work *a good fit* with our core competencies?

As you move from left to right, the tree leads you to a decision about how to treat the priority, project, process, product, or program in question. This tool is designed to generate team collaboration and decision-making around what should be cut BEFORE adding new initiatives.

Note: For organizations in public and nonprofit sectors, we recommend modifying the profitability criterion to focus on the ease of attracting program support and funding.

- **Create 90-day windows**. Plans that break up strategic initiatives and project execution into quarterly segments make it easier to understand what is necessary to achieve the organization's strategy. Here are five guidelines to facilitate the process:

---

[166] Modified from this article: https://trinaisakson.com/wp-content/uploads/2014/04/27-Shift-MacMillan-Matrix-as-Decision-Tree.pdf

Phase V: Strategy Execution

- o *Create an effective action plan* by *prioritizing the most important work to be done* in the next 90 days.
- o Make sure the *outcome is specific* so it can be tied back to your organization's strategic objective.

2.2(1)

- o Set the *completion date* for each task within 90 days. This approach contributes to effective quarterly planning sessions and weekly leadership team meetings.
- o Assign *one person* to be responsible for each action.
- o Lastly, make actions *fun*!

- **Emphasize the role of middle level managers**. Middle level managers play a central role by providing oversight and support to implementation of initiatives and actions. Executive leaders and managers must work together to ensure strategic learning is taking place throughout the organization to guide the execution journey. Middle managers must be empowered and supported by leadership as the linchpins of execution.

Middle managers role includes the following: [167]

- o Absorbing information from above and below.
- o Bridging potential communication gaps by understanding and clearly communicating the strategic priorities of execution.
- o Ensuring that the right actions are being taken while providing corrective feedback.
- o Clarifying individual responsibilities and expected outcomes.
- o Coaching by sharing best practices, learning from mistakes, removing roadblocks, and providing feedback.

- **Take action**. To provoke your thinking on when to implement strategy, consider these questions:
  - o Is it better to postpone your strategy launch until you have an execution plan 100% finalized? Or is it better to get going before every detail of the execution plan is in place?
  - o Is it more important for your organization's success to start acting sooner or wait for the fully completed plan?
  - o What are the benefits of generating meaningful traction sooner than later?

When a strategic operating plan is substantially but not fully complete is a good time to get things going. Waiting until the operating plan is 100% complete creates unnecessary delays. Getting the operating plan in motion sooner rather than later results in action. Mistakes may be made, but the organization can learn from those mistakes and can make course corrections.

To summarize, executive leaders and managers (including project managers) have distinct responsibilities for strategy execution. *At the highest levels, leaders must create psychologically safe conditions and stay continuously involved in the execution journey.* Similarly, mid-level and project managers must be empowered to

1.1(4)
1.1(5)

---

[167] Speculand, R. *Excellence in Execution: How to Implement Your Strategy,* pp 50-52, 2017.

act on behalf of the organization. Central to both levels of engagement are more specific responsibilities. Leaders must:
- Prioritize and have the necessary resources in place before execution begins.
- Create the conditions for managers, teams, and individuals to develop clear roles, responsibilities, and accountabilities that reflect their capabilities.
- Engage with employees throughout the journey, while managers principally guide them to take the right actions along the way.

Balance short-term versus long-term thinking, while managers must take small steps in the beginning and progressively go faster as implementation picks up momentum.

Phase VI – Performance Management

Once the operating model is aligned with strategy, the plan is cascaded down into the organization, and the strategic operating plan is being implemented, the leadership team needs to manage performance.

According to IASP, *"Performance Management is the process of achieving desired organizational outcomes. It includes all organizational activities aimed at ensuring that the organization's strategic goal(s) and objectives are met in an effective and efficient manner."*[168]

Glossary

This set of processes unfolds dynamically, often requiring mid-course correction in execution or even in strategy. The leadership team now centers on implementing the strategic operating plan and realizing intended results. The three primary tasks in managing the performance of any organization are:

Task 6.1 – Measure Performance
Task 6.2 – Learn and Adapt
Task 6.3 – Engage Stakeholders and Govern Strategy as an Ongoing Process

Task 6.1 – Measure Performance

A measure is a quantifiable value used to track and manage operations or assess strategic performance.

Measures & Indicators

Peter Drucker's sage advice, "What gets measured, gets managed," emphasizes the need for timely performance feedback. This is especially true for the discipline of strategic management.

Improvement in organizational performance cannot occur unless leadership intentionally measures and manages strategic performance.

---

[168] IASP BOK 2.0.

Strategy in the 21st Century, Second Edition

Performance measurement *is the process of collecting, analyzing, and reporting information specific to performance of a component of the strategic operating plan.*

Performance management *is* broader in scope and includes budgeting and financial reporting, market management, customer intelligence gathering, and business and other management processes, including the management of people and nurturing the development of a positive organizational culture. (See Figure 6.1.)

FIGURE 6.1: FROM MEASUREMENT TO MANAGEMENT

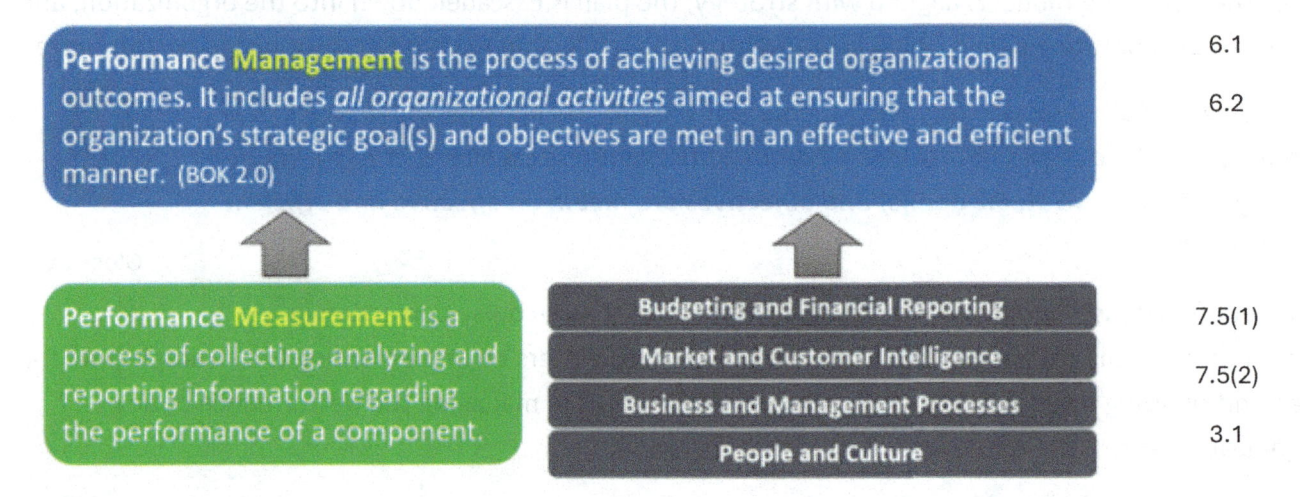

Performance Management is the process of achieving desired organizational outcomes. It includes *all organizational activities* aimed at ensuring that the organization's strategic goal(s) and objectives are met in an effective and efficient manner. (BOK 2.0)

Performance Measurement is a process of collecting, analyzing and reporting information regarding the performance of a component.

- Budgeting and Financial Reporting
- Market and Customer Intelligence
- Business and Management Processes
- People and Culture

As discussed in Phase IV, a key to improved performance is *establishing Key Performance Indicators (KPIs) and targets* at the objective level prior to defining initiatives and initiative measures. Both levels of performance measurement and management are important, but the work begins by assigning performance measures at the strategic objective level. Strategy practitioners must work closely with the leadership team in selecting appropriate performance indicators and setting realistic targets for each.

Much of the information on performance management centers on monitoring pre-established "measures" of success from across the value-creation process. (See Figure 6.2.)

FIGURE 6.2: PERFORMANCE MEASUREMENT CATEGORIES

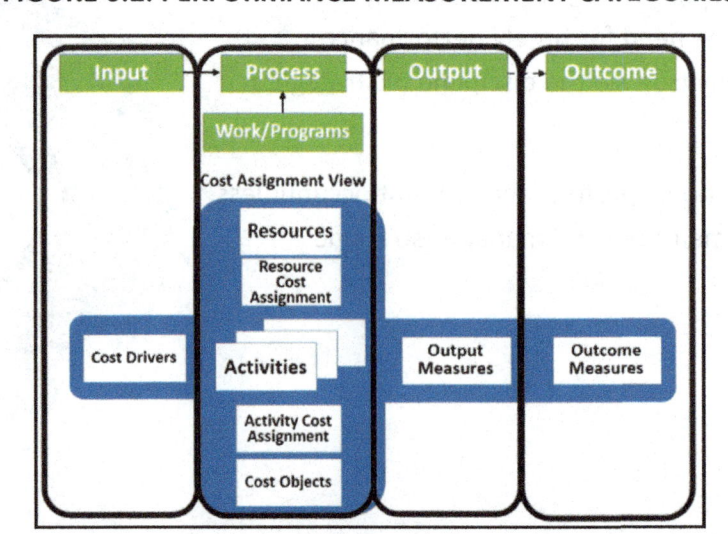

Phase VI: Performance Management

In general, performance measures can be developed within four major logically related categories.

1. **Input measures** to track items that are used in production or workflow processes.
2. **Process measures to monitor quality and efficiency of processes.**
3. **Output measures to monitor what is produced.**
4. **Outcome measures** to monitor what is accomplished.

7.1(2)
7.1(1)

When measuring strategic performance, first focus on the **outcome measures**.

There are three levels of strategic outcomes or performance measures (see Figure 6.3):

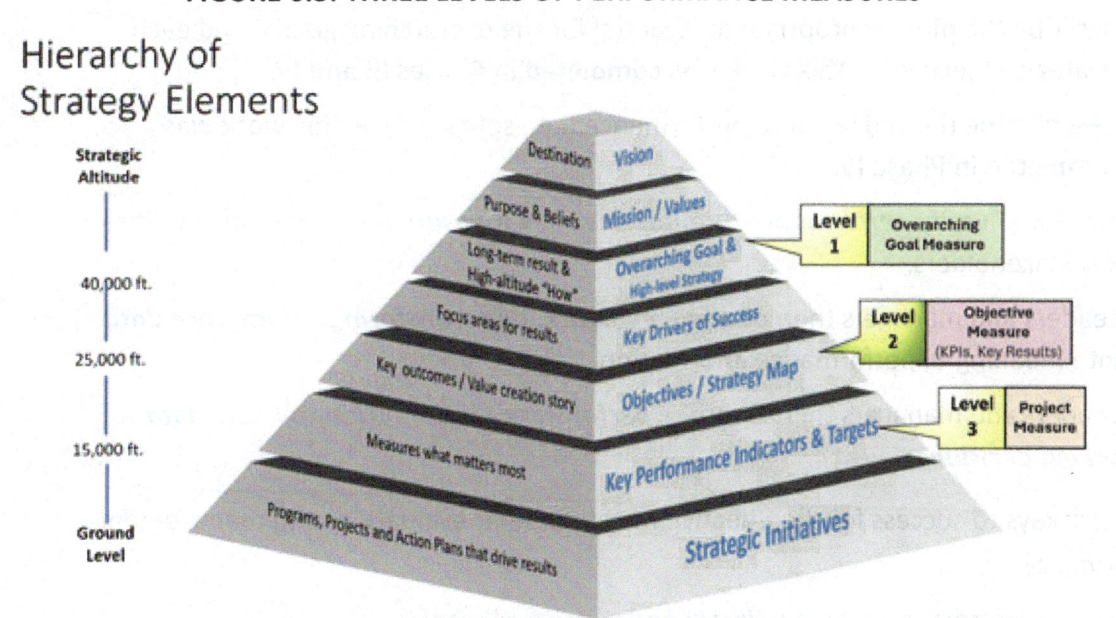

FIGURE 6.3: THREE LEVELS OF PERFORMANCE MEASURES

Level 1 strategic performance measures, which are linked to the over-arching goal or goals, reside at strategy's highest altitude, and are expected to be achieved with a "targeted end result."

Level 2 measures apply to Strategic Objectives that reside at mid-altitude. We most frequently refer to these measures as Key Performance Indicators (KPIs).

Level 3 measures are more tactical in nature. They cover lower-altitude strategic initiatives, programs, projects, and their associated outputs and outcomes of performance.

Across all three levels, the most important point of emphasis is selecting indicators that will effectively monitor progress in achieving desired outcomes.

For example, a leading state-level commodity organization in the U.S. soybean industry had a goal of "achieving maximum profitability and global competitive positioning for soybean producers." A measure of this goal was to have 600 million bushels of their states' soybeans being "utilized" annually by the year 2020. Measuring this overarching goal was the focus for Level 1 performance measurement.

Strategy in the 21st Century, Second Edition

To accomplish this overarching goal, the organization identified "increase yield" as a strategic objective. Assessing if the objective was being achieved required leaders to measure, over time, the increased profitability of soybean farmers on a per acre basis. This KPI was the focus for Level 2 performance measurement.

An initiative to achieve increasing yield per acre was the Profitability and Production Matters Program. A desired outcome of the initiative was to increase farmers' adoption of production best practices. Measuring adoption of leading production practices became the focus for Level 3 performance measurement.

A typical performance measurement process includes five distinct components:

- Describe the most appropriate measure(s) for the overarching goal(s) and each strategic objective. – **This work was completed in Phases III and IV.**
- Describe the desired result of performance (i.e., set target). – **This work was completed in Phase IV.**
- *Track and verify performance data for each key measure and communicate it* to key stakeholders.   4.1(1)
- Leaders and managers then *analyze, evaluate, and transform performance data* into meaningful performance information.   4.1(3)
- Leaders and managers then *leverage performance information to make data-driven decisions.*   4.1(4)

Here are six keys to success for the effective measurement, evaluation, and management of performance:

1. Track performance data in a *timely and consistent* manner.   4.2(2)
2. Verify the *validity* of data – The importance of data governance is critical. The distilled wisdom of Dr. Peter Aiken [169] underscores this point.   4.1(1)

    "Bad Data + Anything Awesome [will always yield] Bad Results"

3. *Compare actual performance data/results to desired results* (Figure 6.4).   4.1(3)
4. *Visualize performance data* using different types of charts (Figure 6.5).
5. Adopt a Percent to Target mindset for effective communications (Figure 6.6).
6. Apply performance ranges and color indications (Figure 6.7).
7. Beginning with #3, performance management compares an organization's *actual results to its desired results.* Any discrepancy, where *actual* is less than *desired*, constitutes (by definition) a performance improvement zone requiring attention. (See Figure 6.4).   4.1(4)

---

[169] Peter Aiken, an acknowledged Data Management (DM) authority, is an Associate Professor at Virginia Commonwealth University, past President DAMA International, and Associate Director of the MIT International Society of Chief Data Officers. His latest venture is http://anythingawesome.com/.

Phase VI: Performance Management

FIGURE 6.4: EXAMPLE OF COMPARING ACTUAL RESULTS TO DESIRED RESULTS

The right data, communicated clearly, is very powerful, especially when leaders understand how current performance compares to desired performance. Consider a pilot flying an airplane. The pilot cannot efficiently make critical navigation decisions if presented with a mass of data in a spreadsheet. Pilots need a dashboard showing visuals of the essential indicators to monitor to safely fly the plane. Just as for pilots, executive leadership needs essential data presented in a logical, easy-to-understand way.

Data visualization is an important consideration in managing performance. In most cases when trying to understand trends and statistics, the human brain processes charts and graphs better than text and numbers. There are many ways to visualize data. (See Figure 6.5.)

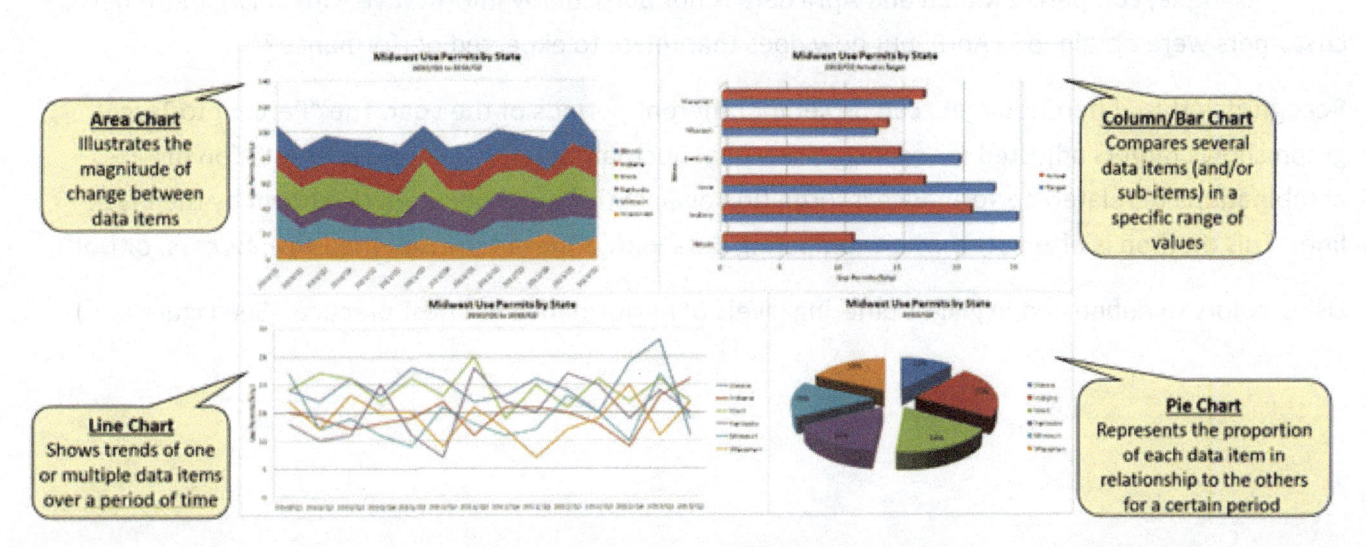

FIGURE 6.5: VISUALIZE USING DIFFERENT TYPES OF CHARTS

243

Strategy in the 21st Century, Second Edition

We suggest adopting a *"percent to target" mindset to help* **effectively communicate performance data** because raw data, however valuable, does not always effectively communicate strategic performance results. Comparing raw data with a target provides more useful information because it is then tied to organizational expectations. (See Figure 6.6.)

1.1(3)

FIGURE 6.6: ADOPT A "PERCENT TO TARGET" MINDSET FOR EFFECTIVE COMMUNICATION

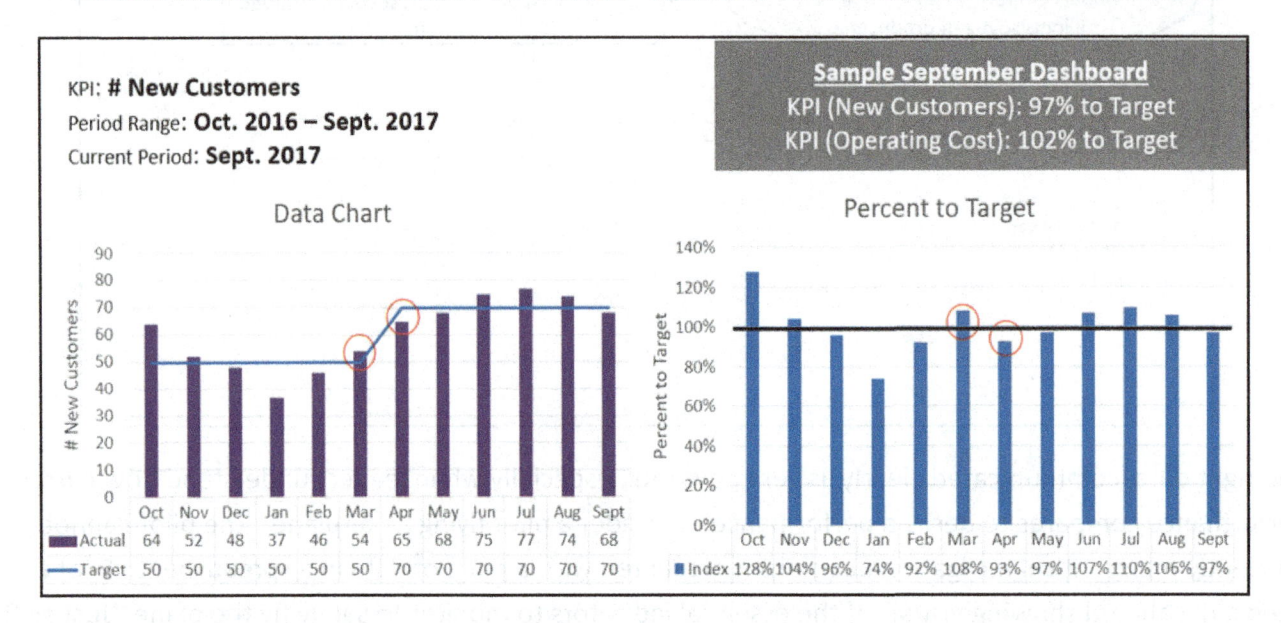

KPI: **# New Customers**
Period Range: **Oct. 2016 – Sept. 2017**
Current Period: **Sept. 2017**

Sample September Dashboard
KPI (New Customers): 97% to Target
KPI (Operating Cost): 102% to Target

Data Chart

	Oct	Nov	Dec	Jan	Feb	Mar	Apr	May	Jun	Jul	Aug	Sept
Actual	64	52	48	37	46	54	65	68	75	77	74	68
Target	50	50	50	50	50	50	70	70	70	70	70	70

Percent to Target

	Oct	Nov	Dec	Jan	Feb	Mar	Apr	May	Jun	Jul	Aug	Sept
Index	128%	104%	96%	74%	92%	108%	93%	97%	107%	110%	106%	97%

For example, the "Data Chart" graph (above left) plots raw data points for the KPI "Number of New Customers" reported monthly over a one-year period of time. To better understand the performance being achieved, positive or negative, the actual data is compared to a set target which, in this case, is demarcated with a blue line. In this example, the new customer numbers appear to be impacted by seasonal factors that create fluctuations in securing new customers.

In this example, comparing March and April data is not particularly informative. Obviously, more new customers were obtained in April, but how does that relate to expected performance?

Recognizing this, different targets can be set for different periods of the year. The "Percent to Target" graph shows targets adjusted for expected seasonal fluctuations. This enables presentation of combinations of related performance information against the same benchmark (shown by the black line). This method is often used when comparing data with different units of measure, targets, or both.

Using colors to define and highlight differing levels of performance is a best practice. (See Figure 6.7.)

Phase VI: Performance Management

FIGURE 6.7: APPLY PERFORMANCE RANGES AND COLOR INDICATION

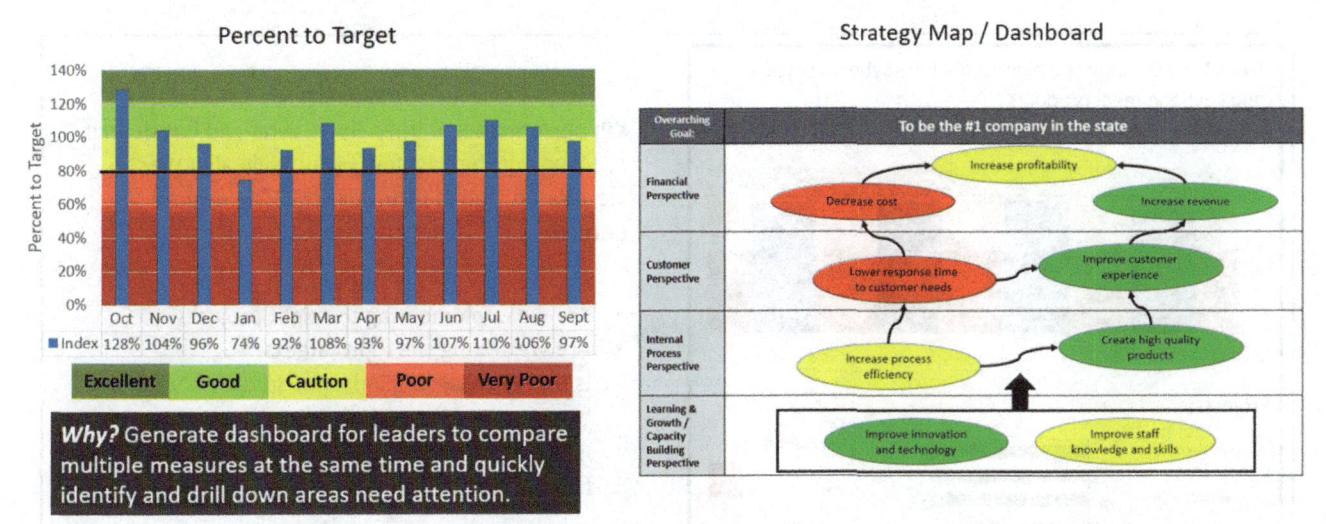

Each color band on the Percent to Target vertical axis ranks monthly performance as Excellent, Good, Caution, Poor, and Very Poor. The color-coded strategy map shows performance for each objective.

Once a *percentage to target* is set and communicated through color coding, leadership should analyze, evaluate, and transform *performance data* into meaningful *performance information* to support decision making. There are three keys to success in this transformation process.

First, ask critical probing questions such as:

- What happened?
- Why did it happen?
- If a KPI did not meet the desired target, the entire leadership team should be asking "Why not?"
- Now what should we do?
- Are there seeming correlations and cause-and-effect relationships among data elements?

Returning to our case study, here is a sample performance review summary (see Figure 6.8):

245

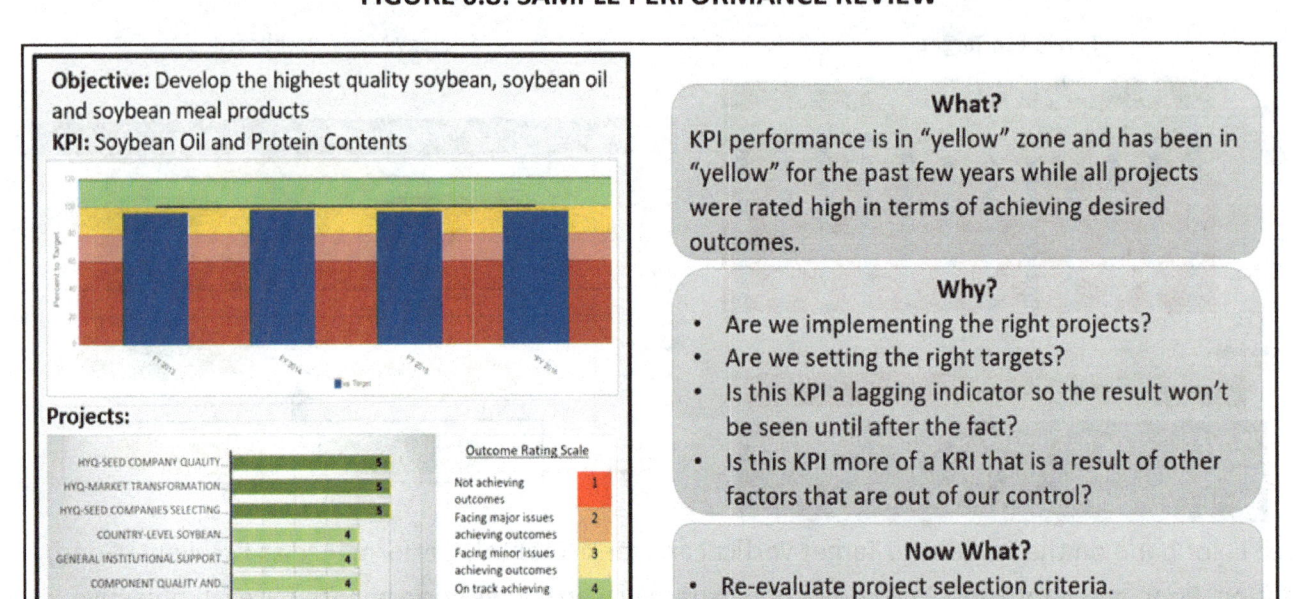

FIGURE 6.8: SAMPLE PERFORMANCE REVIEW

Objective: Develop the highest quality soybean, soybean oil and soybean meal products
KPI: Soybean Oil and Protein Contents

Projects:
- HYQ-SEED COMPANY QUALITY... 5
- HYQ-MARKET TRANSFORMATION... 5
- HYQ-SEED COMPANIES SELECTING... 5
- COUNTRY-LEVEL SOYBEAN... 4
- GENERAL INSTITUTIONAL SUPPORT... 4
- COMPONENT QUALITY AND... 4
- UI VARIETY TRIALS ANALYSIS FOR... 4
- ISB SOYBEAN QUALITY TECHNICAL... 5

Outcome Rating Scale:
1. Not achieving outcomes
2. Facing major issues achieving outcomes
3. Facing minor issues achieving outcomes
4. On track achieving outcomes
5. Exceed performance achieving Outcomes

What?
KPI performance is in "yellow" zone and has been in "yellow" for the past few years while all projects were rated high in terms of achieving desired outcomes.

Why?
- Are we implementing the right projects?
- Are we setting the right targets?
- Is this KPI a lagging indicator so the result won't be seen until after the fact?
- Is this KPI more of a KRI that is a result of other factors that are out of our control?

Now What?
- Re-evaluate project selection criteria.
- Develop leading indicators.

Note that KPI performance indicated above is in the yellow zone and has been in yellow for the past few years, while all other projects are rated high in terms of achieving desired outcomes. The organization's Board wants to know "Why is this the case?" They begin by asking a series of hard questions.

- Are we implementing the right projects?
- Are we setting the right targets?
- Is this KPI a lagging indicator so the result will not be seen until after the fact?
- Is this KPI a broader outcome measure whose performance is the result of a more complex set of factors outside of our control? (For example, a soybean farmer might be tempted to use "basis"[170] as a KPI to evaluate profitability, without seeing that many other factors including transportation costs, storage costs, supply and demand, and local conditions contribute to establishing basis.)

Eventually the board leadership agreed to re-evaluate project selection criteria and develop some new *leading indicators* of success.

As in the case study, eventually *data-driven decisions must be made to improve performance. To make effective decisions on the question of "what to do?"* the team needs to listen and learn as it explores alternative courses of action, makes choices, and acts to execute them.

4.1(1)
4.1(3)
4.1(4)

The real benefit of informed decision-making is knowing that data-driven decisions are on a better footing than decisions based on instinct alone.

---

[170] **Basis is the** difference between the current local cash price for corn or soybeans and the futures price of the contract with the closest delivery month. https://www.extension.iastate.edu/agdm/crops/html/a2-40.html

Phase VI: Performance Management

Data-based decision making applies to the private sector, government, and nonprofits. In the private sector, better decision making leads to better financial performance. In government, programmatic decisions based on outcomes and costs will result in more cost-effective use of taxpayer dollars. And in the nonprofit sector, resource allocation decisions are better informed by analysis producing better stewardship of limited resources. In all sectors, a result will likely be higher customer-satisfaction scores.

Data-based decision making should be tempered by other inputs to the decision process – political judgments, impact on customers and stakeholders, governance issues, and environmental issues, among others. These other inputs may be difficult to quantify but remain important in the process of making choices. For instance, political judgments play a strong role in government program decisions while donor considerations impact nonprofit and association decision making.

Intelligent Risk Taking & Balancing Value

Also, recognize that when executive-level attention is placed on a specific metric, *Campbell's Law* may come into play.[171] The pitfall that Donald Campbell identified in the social sciences world is that the more a metric was emphasized and used for social decision making, the more susceptible it was to distortion and corruption.

Campbell used the crime rate as an example. He pointed out that a decrease in a city's crime rate may not demonstrate a true reduction in the number of crimes that have been committed but may simply reflect how the police force has changed procedures to lower the number. The police may have decided, for example, to change which police encounters need to be formally recorded. They may also have downgraded some crimes to less serious classifications.

In the era of *big data*, Campbell's Law is often cited as a warning about the dangers of making *data-driven decisions* based on a single key performance indicator. For example, a sales manager who requests monthly reports on the number of calls each sales representative makes may inadvertently cause problems if this metric is an important criterion for bonuses. According to Campbell's Law, once the salespeople know they are being evaluated on this metric alone, they may put more effort toward making sales calls and spend less time on other important tasks, such as trying to close sales.

Examples of Campbell's Law at work abound. Here are a few:

- A manufacturing company gave all employees a financial reward for eliminating workplace injuries: This produced underreporting, perversely incentivizing a LESS SAFE work environment.
- A major public-school district whose funding was based on higher test scores held "test parties" where teachers and administrators fraudulently changed standardized test answers to increase the school district's funding.
- Employees at a multinational financial services company, incentivized for opening accounts, were caught opening new accounts for unsuspecting customers without their permission.

---

[171] Campbell, Donald T. Assessing the impact of planned social change, *Evaluation and Program Planning*. 2 (1): 67–90, 1979.

To avoid efforts to "game the system," one possible solution is to *identify two or more metrics that will combine to serve as guard rails, preventing emphasis on a single metric.* Adding "guard rail metrics" will help avoid unintended consequences that can result from overemphasizing just one metric. (See Figure 6.9.)

FIGURE 6.9: EXAMPLE OF GUARD RAILS

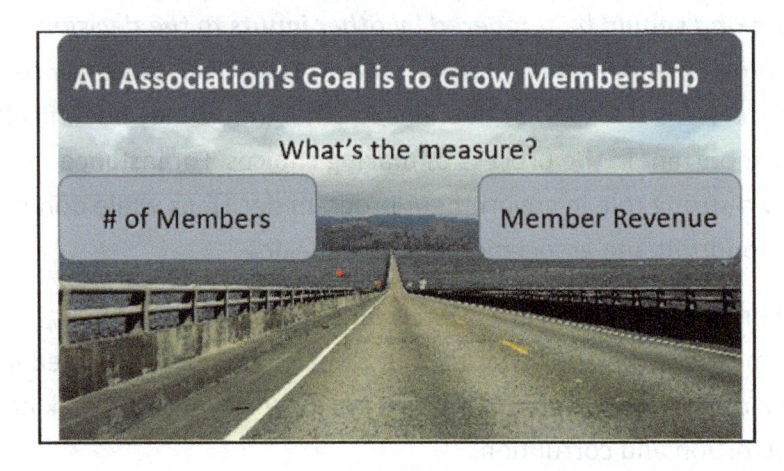

For example, many membership associations have "tiered pricing" for members. Small businesses may enter a low-price tier, whereas large corporations may desire the benefits from a higher-priced tier. An association that only places emphasis on the *number* of new members can benefit by adding a guard-rail metric on overall membership *revenue*. This will counter the temptation to just recruit new members to the cheapest membership tier. Adding in the revenue measure emphasizes the importance of recruiting new members across all membership levels.

Task 6.2 – Learn and Adapt

For organizational learning and agile adaptation, a reliable stream of performance information must be available on a timely basis to assess the effectiveness of the strategy and strategic operating plan.

Strategy practitioners must collaborate closely with their team to understand that performance measurement and management are integrated processes, not an event.

Collecting, reporting, and visualizing performance information is the easy part. Learning from performance information to adapt to changing circumstances and continuously improve processes and systems is the hard part. Strategy practitioners have a leading role to play in this regard.

An immutable fact in strategy management is that strategies and tactics are always subject to change, depending on circumstances. Robert Kaplan and David Norton put it this way: "Even the most well-

Phase VI: Performance Management

conceived, most-likely-to-succeed strategy needs real-world monitoring. Things change; the environment in which the strategy was developed may no longer be operative." [172]

Important to remember is that feedback on strategy obtained by measuring performance must be used to drive *organizational learning* and appropriate adaptation for successful strategy execution. Without learning and adapting, organizations and individuals will simply repeat old practices. Henry Ford's quote is instructive: "If you always do what you've always done, you'll always get what you've always got."

Strategic learning occurs when organizations integrate valid data and evaluative thinking into their work and, in doing so, adapt their strategies and tactics in response to what they learn. Strategic learning makes intelligence gathering and evaluation a part of a strategy's development and implementation – embedding "lessons learned" so they can positively influence the process.

2.1(2)

Baldrige Core

Here are three definitions of *organizational learning* (see Figure 6.10):

FIGURE 6.10: ORGANIZATIONAL LEARNING DEFINITIONS

"*Organizational learning* is a process of detecting and correcting error."
(Chris Argyris, Double Loop Learning in Organizations," HBR, September-October 1977)

"A *learning organization* is an organization skilled at creating, acquiring, and transferring knowledge, and at modifying its behavior to reflect new knowledge and insights...."
(David Garvin, Building a Learning Organization," HBR, July-August 1993)

"*Strategic learning* is the use of data and insights from a variety of information-gathering approaches—including evaluation—to inform decision-making about strategy. Strategic learning makes intelligence gathering and evaluation a part of a strategy's development and implementation."
(Julia Coffman and Tanya Beer, Strategic evaluation to support learning: principles and practices, Center for Evaluation Innovation, June 2011)

In 1977, Chris Argyris (the late Professor Emeritus at Harvard Business School and expert in organizational learning) described this process as *double-loop learning*.[173] Double-loop learning changes people's assumptions and, therefore, their responses. (See Figure 6.11.)

FIGURE 6.11: DOUBLE-LOOP LEARNING

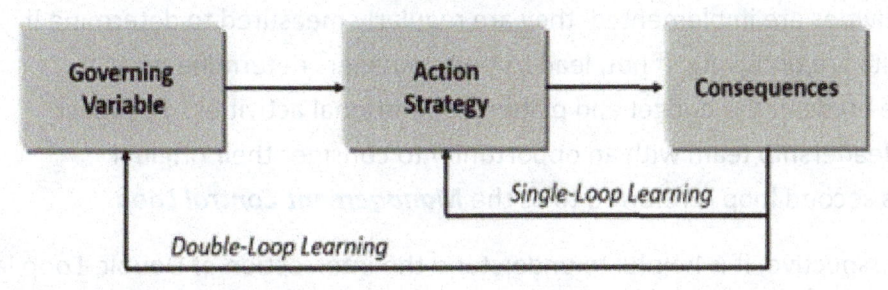

Governing Variable → Action Strategy → Consequences

Single-Loop Learning

Double-Loop Learning

---

[172] Kaplan, R., Norton. D. *The Office of Strategy Management*, HBR Magazine, October 2009.
[173] Argyris, Chris. *Knowledge for Action: A Guide to Overcoming Barriers to Organizational Change*, 1993.

Strategy in the 21st Century, Second Edition

In double-loop learning, feedback from management consequences can cycle back into the action-strategy development process, including the governing variables and assumptions used to develop the strategies in the first place.

In Robert Kaplan and David Norton's 2000 article, "Double-Loop Management: Making Strategy a Continuous Process," they applied Argyris' double-loop learning concept to strategic management. [174] Two feedback loops were introduced to allow organizations to monitor and evaluate their strategy, update their plan, and, in turn, adapt their strategies to a changing environment. (See Figure 6.12.)

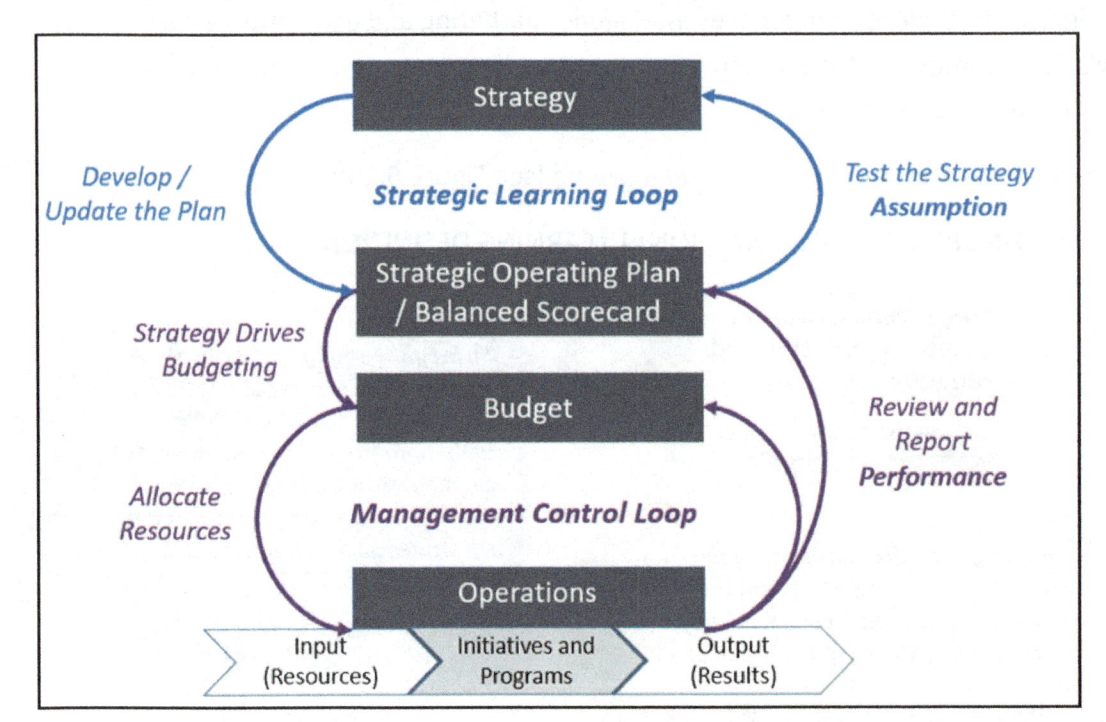

FIGURE 6.12: DOUBLE-LOOP LEARNING – TWO FEEDBACK LOOPS

In the first loop, the overall strategic operating plan is monitored and tracked by using performance data to evaluate the original assumptions underlying the plan. If necessary, the plan and its budget are updated to reflect what has been learned. This loop is referred to as the *Strategic Learning Loop*.

2.1(1

In the second loop, resources are allocated to initiatives and programs to execute the plan. As these activities are implemented, they are regularly measured to determine if the intended results are occurring. If not, leaders and managers determine what changes should be made in the budget and planned operational activities. Feedback also provides the leadership team with an opportunity to consider their original assumptions. This second loop is referred to as the *Management Control Loop*.

2.2(7)

From a systems perspective, it is helpful to understand the intersection of Double-Loop learning and the three levels of performance measurement discussed earlier. (See Figure 6.13.)

---

[174] Kaplan, R., Norton David. *Double-Loop Management System*, HBR, 1/19/2011.

Phase VI: Performance Management

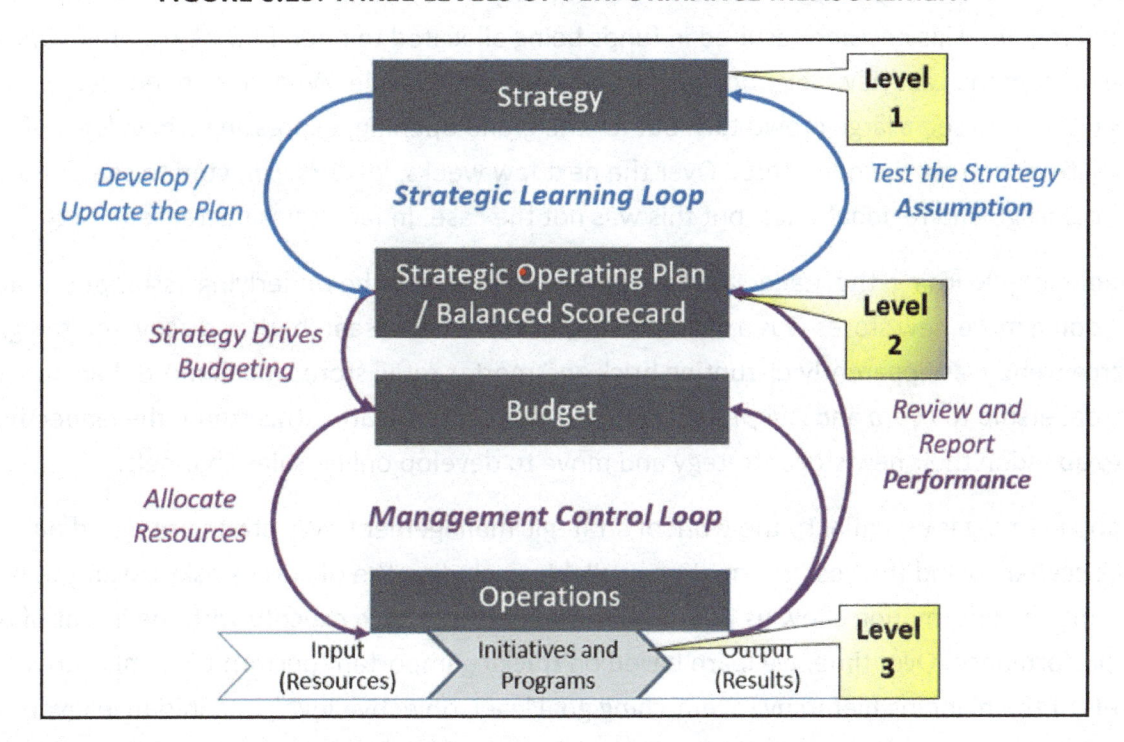

FIGURE 6.13: THREE LEVELS OF PERFORMANCE MEASUREMENT

Level 1 addresses the *Overarching Goal* level, a component of the organization's longer-term strategic direction and strategic learning loop. **Level 2** addresses the *Strategic Objective* level, components of the organization's strategic operating plan and strategic learning loop. **Level 3** addresses the *Initiative* level, which, over time, integrates into operations as part of the management-control loop.

We use this double-loop learning example from the Windy City Shoes case study in our Mastering Strategy course.[175] (See Figure 6.14.)

FIGURE 6.14: DOUBLE-LOOP LEARNING - EXAMPLE

---

[175] IASP, BOK 3.0, Chapter 6, 6.3.6 (p140)

As presented in the figure above, the owners of Windy City Shoes decided to add stores in the Chicagoland region. This decision resulted in funds being allocated to open four new stores. One of the stores was built in the Lakeview neighborhood on Chicago's north side. When it opened, everyone on the team was pleased to see a large crowd turn out for the grand opening, expressing a high level of customer satisfaction for the new store. Over the next few weeks, leaders expected to see a substantial increase in Chicagoland regional sales, but this was not the case. In fact, sales decreased.

Using double-loop learning, the leadership team began to question the underlying assumptions and whether adding more new stores was a valid strategy. On further research, they discovered the growing e-commerce trend was apparently disrupting brick and mortar retail stores much more than anticipated, requiring leadership to *Learn* and *Adapt* its strategy. After contemplating this trend, the leadership team decided to abandon their new store strategy and move to develop online sales channels.

Double-loop learning is essential to the work of strategic management. We strategize based on alternative scenarios and the best information available, including the oft-times risky assumptions these scenarios and the information allow us to make about the future. We execute with the intent of driving strategic performance. Over time, we learn based on tracking important performance measures at all three levels of the planning hierarchy (overarching goal level, objective level, and initiative level).

Organizations that apply double-loop learning will gain key advantages, such as:

- Growing capability to monitor performance against the strategy.
- Improved ability to work as a team to interpret data and gain strategic insights.
- A practical way to update the measures included in the strategic operating plan.
- Maturing ability to adapt overall strategy to the changing environment.
- A framework for making strategy management a continuous process.

For an organization to take advantage of double-loop learning, three vital attributes must be in place.

- *The ability for all employees, departments, and groups within an organization to collaborate effectively.*

    Baldrige Core Value

- *The ability for all employees to network with others outside the organization,* gaining new sources of useful information and helpful perspectives in the process. This includes networking with customers, external industry experts, and even with competitors or rivals.

- *The ability for all employees to feel safe, innovate, and experiment without fear of reprisal or marginalization.* **Organizations whose culture promotes rewarding those who think innovatively see the greatest success in adapting and solving the pressing issues the organization faces.**

    Valuing People

Phase VI: Performance Management

To enable an organization-wide adaptive mindset, three primary practices are recommended by Steven Kenney and the American Management Association (AMA).[176]

- *Create Self-Directed Teams.* According to the AMA, "The foundation of any bottom-up transformation starts with the empowerment of self-motivated, self-directed teams. An abundance of structure and rule-setting tends to inhibit creativity and adaptiveness, particularly when the structure is hierarchical, the default organizational form for many prior to today's knowledge era."

- *Bridge the Stove Pipes Through Employee Engagement.* The AMA suggests "… breaking down the siloes between departments, divisions, and units within an organization. An organization cannot adapt to new circumstances if vital information is hoarded by any group. Only an unfettered exchange of insights and ideas among all the groups and sub-groups within the organization can build a comprehensive understanding of the environment and generate the right adaptations and solutions."

- *Create Venues Where Employees Can Practice Adaptive Thinking.* "Leadership must create space and time for innovation. Often the 'safe place to innovate' is established within the organization but outside the normal organizational forms—for example, 'tiger teams.' Just as importantly as creating the space and time, the upper echelons of the organization (as well as supervisors at all levels) must demonstrate a genuine commitment to listening to the ideas from up, down, and across the organization, reinforcing positive behaviors when people use their safe venues to raise new ideas about how to adapt to what's changing in the environment."

Task 6.3 – Engage Stakeholders and Govern Strategy as an Ongoing Process

To be effective at performance management, stakeholder engagement and strategic governance must be a continuous and integrated process.

Stakeholder Engagement – "To do all that is necessary to get the various stakeholder groups, particularly employees, to commit themselves to make the new strategy work." [177]

Strategic Governance – The role of the Board of Directors and management team. Their charge is "to oversee the (entire) strategic management process. It

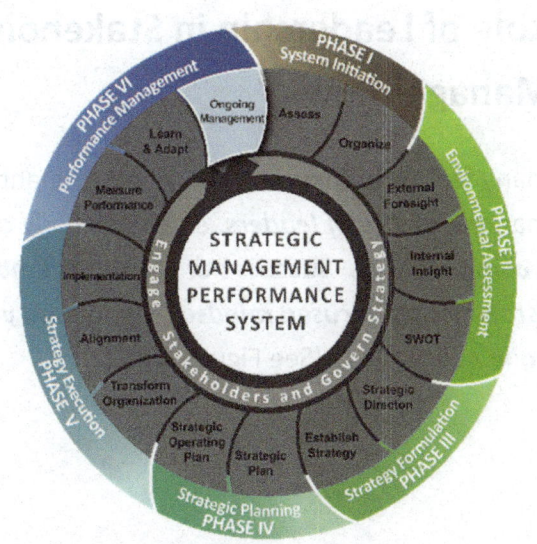

---

[176] Steven Kenney. *Creating Adaptive Organizations*, American Management Association, Summer 2019. http://www.amanet.org/training/articles/creating-adaptive-organizations.aspx
[177] IASP BOK 3.0, Chapter 5

entails, amongst other things, monitoring the external environment, setting group and individual performance objectives, tracking and evaluating deliverables and results throughout the organization, as well as learning from these activities and adapting whenever needed." [178]

Long after the annual operating cycle has been completed, the actions dedicated to strategy execution continue. *Members of the organization and other key stakeholders* make decisions and adjust to the emerging changes in the environment that ripple through the organization, including the operating model. Failure to effectively engage key stakeholders and govern this ongoing process accounts for many of the difficulties encountered in organizations who fall into the *Strategy Execution Gap*.

P.1b(2)

P.1b(3)

To overcome this dynamic, stakeholder engagement and proactive strategic governance must be at work in all phases and tasks of the Strategic Management Performance System (SMPS) Framework. This is particularly true when it comes to Phase VI: Performance Management.

The performance management process is dynamic and constantly in need of improvement. **This is a central point**. It is not a linear process. Key stakeholder engagement and strategic governance will always be particularly important at varied times in the process, especially when it comes to managing strategy execution.

An effective way to cultivate engagement and mitigate the disruptive forces pressing on the organization is to adopt a continuous improvement mindset and build a governing capability requiring key stakeholders' appropriate participation throughout the process. By doing so, the Board or governing body (to a lesser extent) and management (to a much larger extent) mitigate the challenges of winning over and motivating the workforce to embrace the strategy and strategic operating plan, both of which are subject to change at any time.

Role of Leadership in Stakeholder Engagement and Performance Management [179]

Many factors influence strategic performance. Certainly, no factor Is more important than *the ability of leaders, either formally or informally, to influence others to achieve a common goal.* Success here requires *emotionally intelligent leaders to embrace a "stakeholder-focused mindset" expressed via active listening, continuous learning, and agile navigating*. (See Figure 6.15.)

1.1(5)

---

[178] IASP BOK 3.0, Chapter 6
[179] Summarized, quoted, and adapted based on IASP BOK 3.0, Chapter 5, 5.1, Key Concepts and Definitions

Phase VI: Performance Management

FIGURE 6.15: STAKEHOLDER FOCUSED MINDSET ILLUSTRATION

(Diagram: Stakeholder Focused Mindset with Active Listening, Continuous Learning, Agile Navigation — Emotionally Intelligent Leader)

These five tenants of this logical argument, expressed in IASP BOK 3.0, are filled with powerful insights on leadership's role in closing the strategy execution gap and enabling performance management:

1. There are four stakeholder engagement roles Board and executive-level leaders must deliver in the performance management process.
    - Be direction setters
    - Be change agents
    - Be chief advocates for the vision
    - Be coaches

2. These roles require leaders to engage in a wide range of activities.
    - Challenging the process by searching for opportunity, experimentation, and taking risks.
    - *Inspiring a shared vision by enlisting others.* — 1.1(1)
    - Enabling others to engage in the process by fostering collaboration.
    - *Modeling the way forward, leading by example, and planning small wins.* — 1.1(2)
    - Encouraging the heart by recognizing contributions and celebrating achievements. — 1.1(3)

3. While leaders are certainly different in their individual characteristics, successful leaders share several leadership enabling characteristics.
    - A guiding vision of what they want to do and the strength to persist in its pursuit. Leaders create their own destiny.
    - Passion for a vocation, a profession, or a course of action. Leaders who communicate with passion give hope and inspiration to others.
    - Integrity, doing the right thing even when no one is looking, creates trust between leaders and followers.

- Curiosity with a desire to learn, take risks, experiment, and try new things.
- Daring, which includes learning from adversity.

4. These leadership characteristics underpin a *stakeholder-focused mindset* aimed at achieving three primary outcomes.
    - A shared, permeating, enduring, and implicit *culture* focused on accountability and agility.
    - Mutual *trust* and confidence across the organization in contractual performance, honest communications, expected competence, and a capacity for unguarded interaction.
    - A *psychologically safe* Boardroom and workplace where anyone can and is encouraged to speak up, at any time, without fear of reprisal.

5. Effective leaders are skilled at unlocking the power of performance management. Specific leadership skills and abilities required for this include:
    - Establishing and maintaining a sense of urgency to navigate stakeholder resistance to change. A sense of urgency helps remove or mitigate sources of complacency.

        This requires:
        o Taking risks
        o Managing crises
        o *Bringing in outside consultants to stimulate discussion and action*   2.1(4)
        o Communicating the need for urgency
        o Delegating authority, particularly to those responsible for strategic results

    - *Building and implementing an Engagement Operating Model*, led by the leadership team, results in the capability, structure, role definition, and activities required to manage performance strategically.   5.2(3)

        This requires:
        o A guiding coalition
        o Roles and organizational units in place to engage employees throughout the organization
        o Incentives, including a reward-and-recognition program
        o Activities, processes, methods, and techniques required to support all facets of stakeholder engagement

    - *Developing communication, stakeholder engagement*, and management plans unleashes understanding and buy-in to the strategy and the corresponding changes required in the operating model. *This point has been emphasized throughout and is highlighted here again.*   1.1(3)

        This requires: (for *communications*)   P.1b(2-3)
        o Key messages
        o Target audiences
        o Targeted engagement methods
        o Communications calendar
        o On-going communications and engagement activities

Phase VI: Performance Management

This requires: (for *engagement*)
- o Identification of stakeholders
- o Stakeholder analysis
- o Stakeholder mapping
- o Stakeholder planning
- o Plan implementation
- o Progress reviews

This requires (*for management*)
- o Systematic identification, analysis, planning, and implementation of actions designed to engage stakeholders

- *Engaging stakeholders and continuously improving* based on the communications, stakeholder engagement, and management plans. This capability empowers leadership and the guiding coalition to succeed in the near term and long term.

This requires:
- o Agility
- o Foresight
- o Incentives
- o Teamwork and collaboration
- o Group and virtual facilitation

Role of Governance in Performance Management [180]

Effectively navigating an ever-changing environment to achieve a vision requires *good governance within a system* by which an organization's strategy is developed, directed, and controlled. Quoting from IASP BOK 3.0, 6.1.1, "While governance includes oversight it is a broader concept including the structures, systems and practices an organization puts in place for:

1.2(1)

- Defining ground rules and assigning decision rights for decision-making
- Aligning strategy setting with relevant regulations, policies, and guidelines
- Overseeing delivery of service, including matters related to Diversity, Equity, and Inclusion (DEI)
- Reporting on performance, often by committee."

Again, quoting from IASP BOK 3.0, 6.1.1, "Although the board of directors is the guardian of organizational governance, for alignment and consistency, governance should occur at every level of an organization with decision-making authority delegated to the appropriate layer of management." (See Figure 6.16 – Nonprofit Organization Illustration.)

---

[180] Summarized, quoted, and adapted based on IASP BOK 3.0, Chapter 6, 6.1, Key Concepts and Definitions

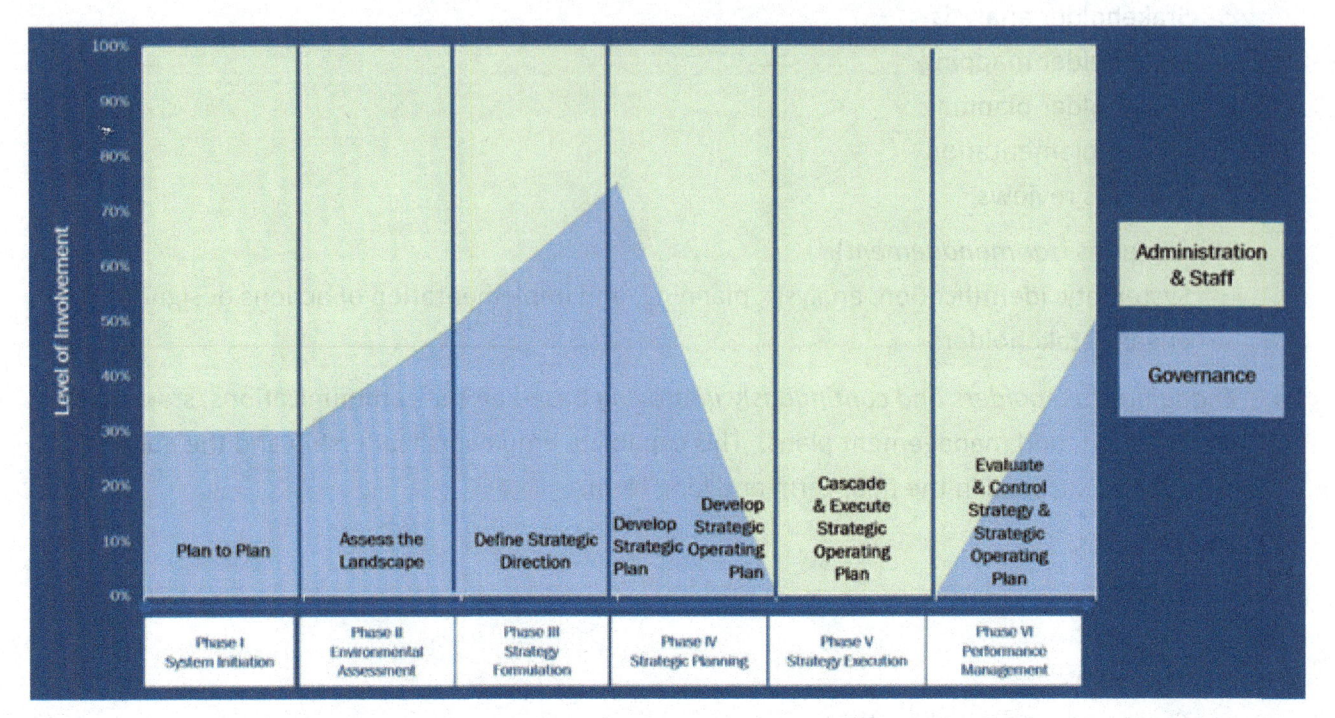

FIGURE 6.16: STRATEGIC MANAGEMENT ROLES AND RESPONSIBILITIES - NONPROFIT ORGANIZATION ILLUSTATION

Depicted on the horizontal axis are the six essential phases of the strategic management process. The vertical axis depicts an estimation of the appropriate degree of involvement by the nonprofit Board, shaded blue, and senior management, shaded green, at different points in the process. *The bottom Line*: The Board's governance role is more intense in the beginning of the strategic management process and diminishes as the management team gets closer to executing the approved strategy, and then again becomes more intense as the monitoring, evaluation, feedback, and action-taking processes unfold.

As noted earlier, governance of strategy is to oversee (and guide) each of the primary strategy activity groups as defined by IASP's Body of Knowledge Framework. It includes the structures, systems and practices required for oversight to occur. (See Figure 0.1.)

Phase VI: Performance Management

FIGURE 0.1: BOK 3.0 FRAMEWORK [181]

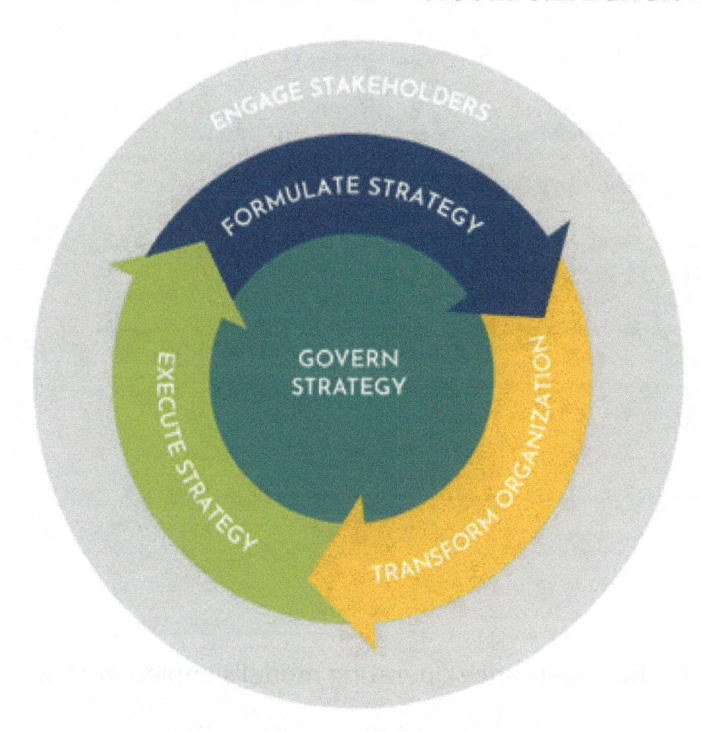

IASP Body of Knowledge (BOK 3.0):
The 5 Domains of Strategy
...an iterative process

FORMULATE STRATEGY
to devise the what the new strategy will be

TRANSFORM ORGANIZATION
to transform the organization to align its operating model with its new strategy

EXECUTE STRATEGY
to deliver value to the organization's stakeholders, as defined by the strategy

ENGAGE STAKEHOLDERS
to do all that is necessary to get all stakeholders to commit themselves to make the new strategy work

GOVERN STRATEGY
to oversee the previous four activity groups

Governance of strategy requires creation and adoption of a governance operating model, including:

- Monitoring the external environment.
- Setting group and individual performance objectives.
- Tracking, evaluating, and forecasting financial performance, risk, deliverables, and results.
- Learning from these activities and making adaptive decisions whenever required with clear role delineation.

These governing activities may be performed by a Board of Directors, Corporate Board, Board of Regents, Board of Trustees, an executive committee, a transformation leadership team, program and project sponsors, or other governance bodies, each tasked with a clearly defined governing role.

In each case, we agree with Dr. Pierre Hadaya: It is important to delineate the appropriate activities and responsibilities of the **Board of Directors** vs. **Management** for each key strategy component including resource development and allocation (financial and human), risk, and the various stakeholder value propositions, i.e., owners, customers, partners, and employees. Together, these activities and responsibilities form the organization's governance and engagement operating model (See Figure 6.17.)

---

[181] Hadaya, P. *Govern Your Strategy to Success*. ASP 2021 Annual Conference, and adapted for IASP BOK 3.0, 1.4 Strategy System Activity Groups, 2021.

Strategy in the 21st Century, Second Edition

FIGURE 6.17: GOVERNANCE AND ENGAGEMENT OPERATING MODEL [182]

			KEY STRATEGY COMPONENTS					
			FINANCE	ENTERPRISE RISKS	SOCIAL RESPONSIBILITY	CUSTOMER STRATEGY	PARTNER STRATEGY	EMPLOYEE STRATEGY
STRATEGY ACTIVITY GROUPS	FORMULATE STRATEGY	Board	• Oversee Strategy, Long-term Financial Plan and Enterprise Risks					
		Management	• Recommend Strategy, Long-Term Financial Plan and Enterprise Risk Appetite					
	TRANSFORM ORGANIZATION	Board	• Oversee Organizational Transformation (includes transformation budget utilization, enterprise risk management and stakeholder engagement)					
		Management	• Recommend and Report on the Organizational Transformation • Manage the Organizational Transformation Execution					
	EXECUTE STRATEGY	Board	• Oversee Strategy Execution (includes operation budget utilization, enterprise risk management and stakeholder engagement)					
		Management	• Recommend and Report on Strategy Execution • Manage Strategy Execution					

Additional activities are critical and closely related to the governance operating model's implementation.

The Board of Directors:

- Provides adequate resources.
- Engages a Chief Executive Officer with the necessary skills and experience to manage operations.
- Ensures policies, procedures, governing documents, and structure are coordinated with the organization's work so they move the organization forward towards its vision rather than create unnecessary obstacles.

Management determines, among other things:

- The design and reporting structure of the organization.
- The operational teams' and committees' structure and charters.
- Allocation of resources, financial and human.
- Building a management team and its accountability and authority.
- Performance management and incentives.
- The policies and procedures that assure effective operation.

To successfully govern strategy and manage performance, both the Board of Directors and management must work together. This requires a strong working relationship between the Board and management leadership, built on mutual trust and respect, working together while not overstepping roles and responsibilities.

---

[182] Hadaya, P. (2021) *Govern Your Strategy to Success*. ASP 2021 Annual Conference.

Phase VI: Performance Management

It is not enough to have the correct Board-level and operating-level structures established to govern strategy and manage performance: Their effectiveness depends on having the right people in place. In today's fast changing world, diverse voices with diverse skills, experiences, and knowledge need to be around the Boardroom table and occupy the organization's offices. And these individuals need to be strategic and critical thinkers with a passion for the organization's vision and mission.

Strategy Management Calendar

The key to maintaining alignment and achieving continuous improvement is integrating strategic planning, operational planning, budgeting, and other key business processes. A common way to do this is by creating a Strategy Management Calendar (see Figure 6.18).

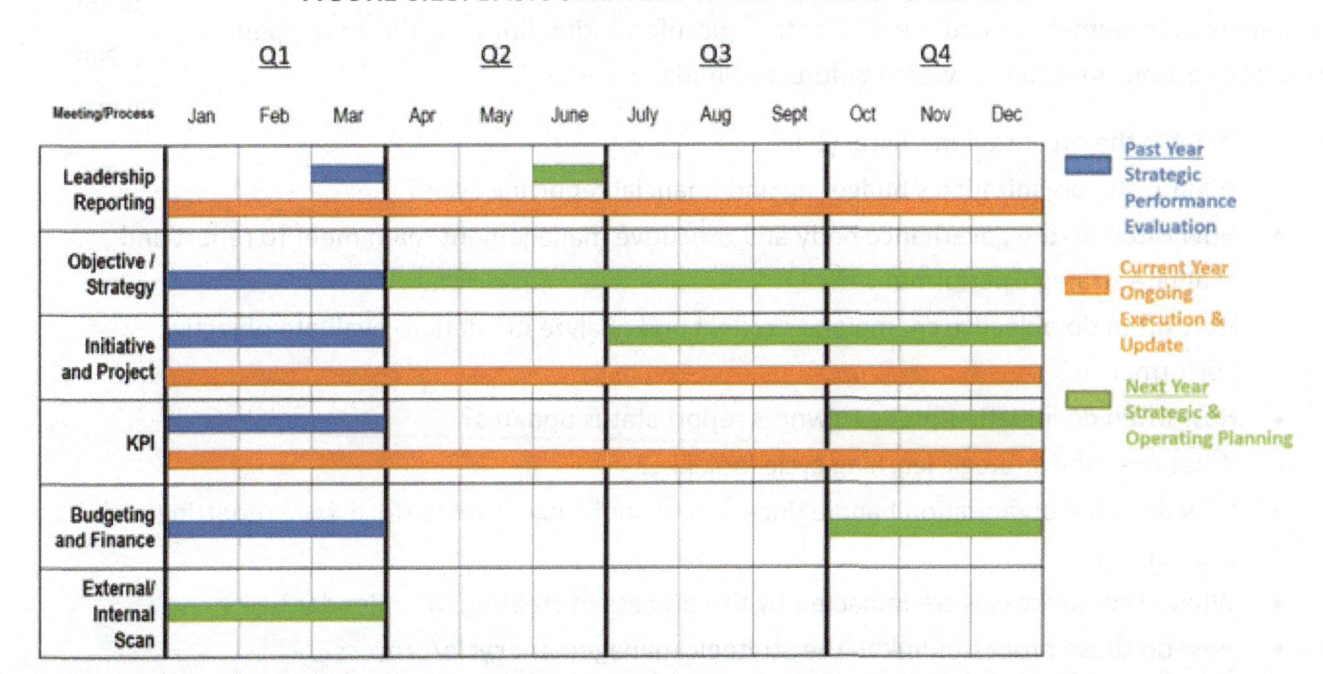

FIGURE 6.18: BASIC STRATEGY MANAGEMENT CALENDAR

Note: A more robust strategy management calendar is included in the appendices. (See Appendix 11.)

For larger organizations, a Strategy Management Office or a Chief Strategy Officer may be required to establish, manage, and coordinate the strategic management process. Someone must provide high-level oversight, or the process will be abandoned or, at a minimum, deemphasized. This is not to say every organization must have a Chief Strategy Officer, Chief Execution Officer, or Chief Transformation Officer. Rather, someone at the senior staff level must have the requisite skills, motivation, and availability to take on this responsibility. [183]

Organizations that utilize a strategy management calendar leverage it to:

- Facilitate an ongoing strategic planning and management process

---

[183] https://www.brightline.org/resources/thinkers50-cso-playbook/

- **Build an integrated process** for coordinating, aligning, and prioritizing key plans, decisions, and results
- Provide for *resource allocation*
- Close the strategy execution gap by *aligning strategy with "everyday work"* as well as closely monitoring strategic execution
- ***Improve accountability, communication, and transparency*** across the organization
- Ensure ongoing communication and engagement with external and internal stakeholders
- Facilitate *quality performance management* of the organization (double-loop learning)

ADLI Evaluation Dimensions

2.2(3)
2.2(4)
2.2(2)
1.1(3)
2.2(5)
2.2(6)
2.2(7)

A strategy management calendar enables strategic information flow. For this to happen, several questions must be answered before a calendar is created.

- What is the organization's fiscal year?
- What is the organization's budgeting and financial reporting cycle?
- How often do the governance body and executive management team meet to report and evaluate strategic performance?
- How often do objective champions s collect and analyze KPI data to evaluate objective performance?
- How often do initiative/project owners report status updates?
- What does the strategic learning cycle look like?
- How does the organization handle department/individual level performance reporting and evaluation?
- What other processes are impacted by the process of creating the calendar?
- How do those processes link to the strategic management cycle/process?

As noted earlier, the speed at which an organization implements the strategic operating plan is central to managing strategic performance. The answer always depends on the context, as execution occurs at different paces for different organizations and within different industries. Leaders must factor in both strategic intent and urgency to dictate the cadence at which their execution and performance management will take place.

A performance management cycle and strategic management calendar should be designed to reflect the organization's chosen strategy cadence and be adaptive to the changes needed in performance management in response to disruptions. Some organizations and industries move quite deliberately with implementation occurring over an annual cycle. Other organizations, aware of impending threats or timely opportunities, are compelled to implement strategy on a quarterly basis. And then there are those who feel such a sense of urgency in the face of immediate disruption that drive an "ACT NOW!" pace of change. For these organizations, a monthly performance management cycle is recommended.

Phase VI: Performance Management

Research by Kaplan and Norton on leading practices of successful Balanced Scorecard users has identified nine cross-functional processes that should be managed or integrated by an Office of Strategy Management (see Figure 6.19).

FIGURE 6.19: ROLES AND RESPONSIBILITIES OF THE STRATEGY MANAGEMENT OFFICE

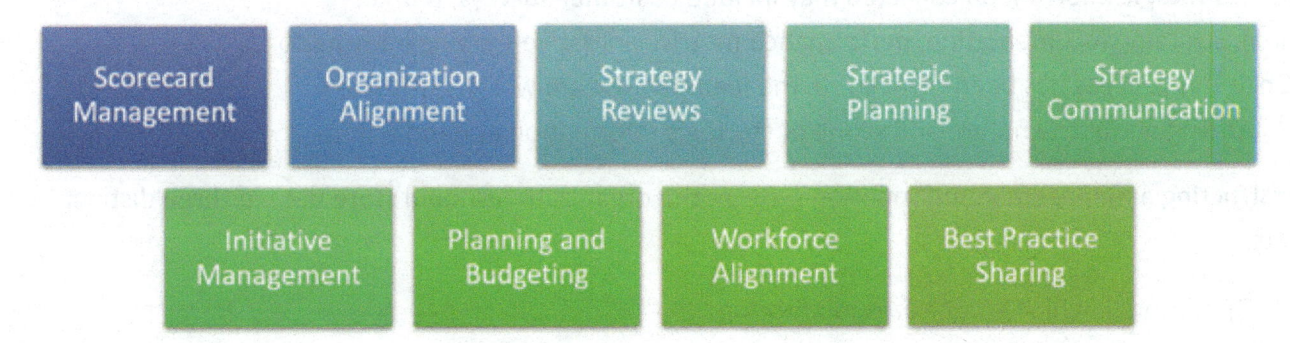

- Scorecard Management
- Organization Alignment
- Strategy Reviews
- Strategic Planning
- Strategy Communication
- Initiative Management
- Planning and Budgeting
- Workforce Alignment
- Best Practice Sharing

Three of these processes – scorecard management, organization alignment, and strategy reviews – are naturally the responsibility of the Office of Strategy Management. Three other critical processes – strategic planning, communications, and initiative management – can be performed by other organizational units and therefore must be carefully coordinated to assure integrated efforts. [184]

Kaplan and Norton believe (as do we) that "each of these processes should eventually be incorporated into a central organization with strategic focus. The three remaining processes – planning and budgeting, workforce alignment, and best practice sharing – are in the natural domain and responsibility of other functions. In these cases, the Office of Strategy Management plays a coordinating role, ensuring that the processes are tightly integrated with the enterprise strategy. By having the Office of Strategy Management either lead or coordinate the nine strategy execution processes, as shown above, previously disparate, unaligned, or missing management processes are performed in an integrated manner to deliver tangible results."

Strategy Management Office

In larger organizations, someone must lead the Office of Strategy Management, lest the opportunity to become and remain strategy-focused is not achieved. In some cases, this will be the Chief Strategy Officer's responsibility. In other cases, it will be delegated to someone who currently has management responsibilities in areas other than strategy management.

For more information on the roles and responsibilities of the Chief Strategy Officer, see the Brightline Initiative website, *The Chief Strategy Officer Playbook – How to transform strategies into great results.* [185]

---

[184] Robert Kaplan and David Norton. *Creating the Office of Strategy Management* http://www.hbs.edu/faculty/Publication%20Files/05-071.pdf
[185] Brightline, *The Chief Strategy Officer Playbook*,
https://thinkers50.com/wp-content/uploads/T50_BL_CSOPlaybook_ONLINE.pdf?x51045&x72597

Strategy in the 21st Century, Second Edition

Strategy Management Information System

Leadership teams should begin by *collecting strategic information and then consolidate it* as a "first generation" snapshot of the organization's strategic environment. For example, strategic information collected may include customer surveys, market research, strategy documentation, performance metrics, initiative scoping information, etc. Once this process has been completed, the leadership team will gain a shared understanding about the nature and scope of strategic information at hand.

2.1(2)

In constructing a management information system, the organization should store data in three distinct buckets:

- Operational, which emphasizes monitoring.
- Tactical, which emphasizes analysis.
- Strategic, which emphasizes management.

Building on this understanding, the team can then maintain a repository to use in both current and future cycles of the strategic management process. The key is to choose the right metrics to store in each of these areas, metrics that will allow management and the Board to ensure progress to continue toward achieving desired outcomes.

From the very beginning of the planning process, strategy practitioners must ensure that a functional, efficient, and timely reporting system is established. The organization needs timely information to manage execution of the strategy and, when necessary, make adjustments in an agile manner. There are many ways to store and report strategic information. Our point here is not to recommend one approach or another. Each solution has its place. The important point is to adopt a system that works for the team.

While an investment is required to build such a system, benefits include increasing transparency, creating a shared understanding, facilitating alignment, optimizing resources, and reducing risk. This enhances collaboration, *efficiency,* improved decision-making, and ultimately, better organizational performance.

We conclude this journey with the SMPS cyclical framework graphic as an affirmation to the reader that while this textbook has presented the SMPS in a linear fashion through six phases, there is a dynamic relationship between all phases and tasks.

Phase VI: Performance Management

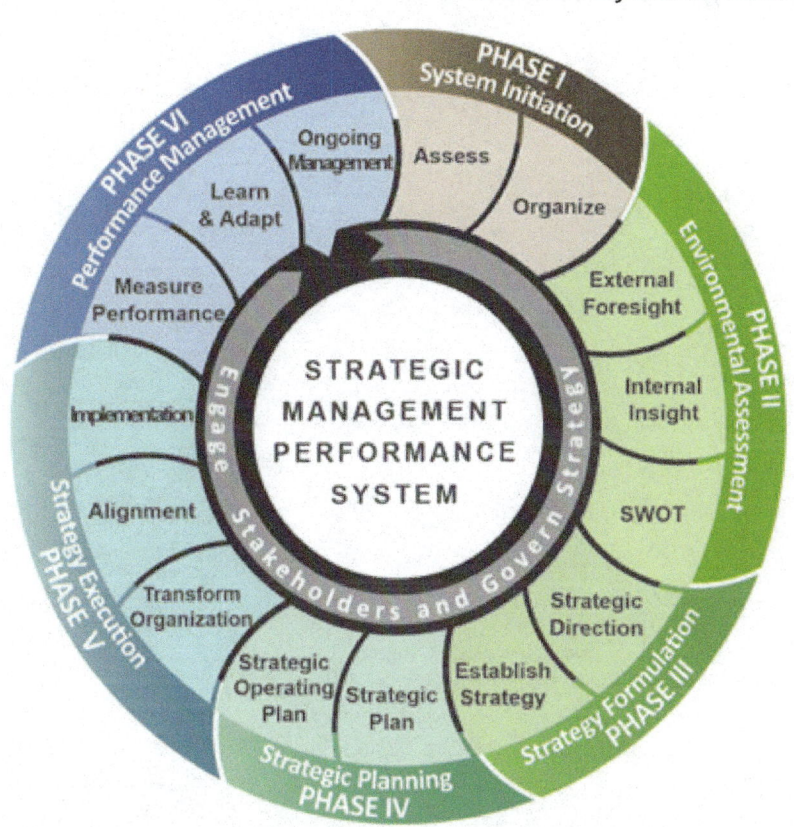

Strategic planning and management is not a project to be conducted every few years. Rather, it is an ongoing process and commitment to improving the impact and performance of the organization. In the words of a great general:

> *"Strategy is the great work of the organization… it is a unifying theme that gives coherence and direction to the actions and direction of an organization."*
> – Sun Tzu, The Art of War

At a time when change is faster and fiercer in virtually every area of life, a key to future success is having a robust, well-integrated approach to strategy setting, planning, measuring, and management.

We love the statement, "You don't need to know everything; you just need to know where to go to get the information." We hope this book will be a key resource and reference as you lead and manage strategy in the 21st Century.

As a parting note, thank you for your commitment to the study and practice of strategic management. We wish you success on your strategy management journey and consider you to be a professional colleague in this discipline.

The LBL Strategies' team welcomes your comments and feedback (contact@lblstrategies.com) and we would be honored to get to know you and your organization better. If the need arises, please do consider our complete set of strategic management-related training programs and our facilitation offering (www.lblstrategies.com).

Thank you.

Epilogue

The Strategic Management Performance System Framework, when fully implemented and managed, helps leadership teams align day-to-day operations with the organization's strategic focus.

As mentioned in Phase III, we believe that a disciplined team will generally outperform a single all-knowing leader. Keep this in mind as you incorporate strategic management discipline into your organization. The current operating environment is too complex for one person or a small group to fully understand. It requires the inclusion and diverse viewpoints of many to align behind a chosen strategy.

One key aspect of our approach to strategic management is its team-based nature, involving leadership, management, and key stakeholders at all levels. Our approach differs from the common belief that strategy is solely the responsibility of a select few. Over the past 40 years, we have emphasized a continuous, inclusive, and seamless team-based approach to strategy. This philosophy guides us in every aspect of our work.

In addition to our team-based approach, we continuously build on our knowledge since the first edition of this book. Going forward, our focus will include:

1. Gaining new insights on how and when to integrate AI into strategy management processes.
2. Expanding our knowledge and understanding of the intersection between strategic management and the Baldrige Performance Excellence Framework.
3. Broadening our knowledge and practice of strategic foresight in formulating and executing strategy.
4. Creating opportunities for active duty and retiring military strategists to transition into strategy roles in the private sector.
5. Enhancing our understanding of how culture impacts strategic management in developing countries, particularly Africa.
6. Developing tools and techniques for agile organizational design and transformation, resulting in effective execution.

Ultimately, our goal is to make a lasting impact. In the words of my dear friend and coauthor, Earl Young, we will "stay the course" and keep sharing our insights and educating our customers about the discipline and practice of strategic management as the path ahead for any organization who shares our goal.

Respectfully,

Randall Rollinson
rrollinson@lblstrategies.com

Appendix 1.1 – Crosswalk Strategic Management Tasks to 2023-24 Baldrige Builder & Results

	SMPS Task	Org. Profile	Leadership	Strategy	Customers	Measurement, Analysis & KM	Workforce	Operations	Results
PHASE I System Initiation	1. Assess Current Strategic Direction and Organizational Capabilities	P.1a P.1b P.2a P.2b	1.1(1) 1.1(3)	2.1(3) 2.1(6)			5.1(1)		
PHASE II Environmental Assessment	2. Design and Organize a Program Based on These Assessments	P.2b		2.1(1)					
	3. Practice Foresight when Conducting External Strategic Analyses	P.1b2		2.1(2)	3.1(1) 3.1(3)				7.1(1) 7.2
	4. Gain Insight by Conducting Internal Strategic Analyses	P.1a2 P.1a3	1.2(2)	2.1(4)		4.1	5.1 5.2	6.1 6.2	7.3(2)
PHASE III Strategy Formulation	5. Evaluate Results of Strategic Analysis via SWOT/OTSW	P.2a,b		2.1(2) 2.1(3)		4.1(4) 4.2(6)			
	6. Define the Strategic Direction of the Organization		1.1(1) 1.1(5)	2.1(5)					7.4(1)
	7. Establish High-Level Strategy	P.1b2	1.1(4)	2.1(2) 2.1(6) 2.2(4) 2.2(7)					7.2
PHASE IV Strategic Planning	8. Develop Strategic Plan			2.1(1) 2.1(3) 2.1(5) 2.1(6) 2.2(1) 2.2(2)					7.5(3)
	9. Develop Strategic Operating Plan			2.2(3) 2.2(5) 2.2(6)	3.2(5)		5.1(3) 5.1(4)		7.5(3)
PHASE V Strategy Execution	10. Design and Transform the Operating Model								
	11. Align Behind the Strategy		1.1(3) 1.1(4) 1.1(5)	2.2(3) 2.2(4) 2.2(5)		4.1(1)			7.4(1) 7.5(3)
	12. Implement the Strategic Operating Plan		1.2(1)	2.2					7.4(1) 7.5(3)
PHASE VI Performance Management	13. Measure Performance			2.2(5)	3.2	4.1 4.1(4)	5.2	6.1(5)	7.2 7.5(3)
	14. Learn and Adapt			2.2(7)		4.1(1) 4.1(4)			
	15. Engage Stakeholders and Govern Strategy as an Ongoing Process	P.2c				4.1(1) 4.1(3)		6.1(3) 6.1(6)	

Appendix 1.2 – Crosswalk Strategic Management Tasks to 2023-24 Baldrige Criteria & Results

	SMPS Task	Org. Profile	Leadership	Strategy	Customers	Measurement, Analysis & KM	Workforce	Operations	Results
PHASE I System Initiation	1. Assess Current Strategic Direction and Organizational Capabilities	P.1a P.1b P.2a P.2b	1.1a(1) 1.1b	2.1a(3) 2.1b(2)			5.1a(1)		
PHASE II Environmental Assessment	2. Design and Organize a Program Based on These Assessments	P.2b		2.1a(1)					
	3. Practice Foresight when Conducting External Strategic Analyses	P.1b2		2.1a(2)	3.1a(1) 3.1b(1)				7.1a 7.2a
	4. Gain Insight by Conducting Internal Strategic Analyses	P.1a2 P.1a3	1.2a(2)	2.1a(4)		4.1		6.1 6.2	7.3a(2)
	5. Evaluate Results of Strategic Analysis via SWOT/OTSW	P.2a P.2b		2.1a(2) 2.1a(3)		4.1b(2) 4.2c			7.4a(1)
PHASE III Strategy Formulation	6. Define the Strategic Direction of the Organization		1.1a(1) 1.1c(2)	2.1b(1)					
	7. Establish High-Level Strategy	P.1b2	1.1c(1)	2.1a(3) 2.1b(2) 2.2a(4) 2.2b			5.1 5.2 5.2c(2) 5.2c(3)		7.2
PHASE IV Strategic Planning	8. Develop Strategic Plan			2.1a(1) 2.1a(3) 2.1b(1) 2.1b(2) 2.2a(1) 2.2a(2)					7.5b
	9. Develop Strategic Operating Plan			2.2a(3) 2.2a(5) 2.2a(6)	3.2b		5.1a(3) 5.1a(4)		7.5b
PHASE V Strategy Execution	10. Design and Transform the Operating Model								
	11. Align Behind the Strategy		1.1b 1.1c(1) 1.1c(2)	2.2a(3) 2.2a(5) 2.2a(6) 2.2a(4)		4.1a(1)			7.4a(1) 7.5b
	12. Implement the Strategic Operating Plan		1.2a(1)	2.2a 2.2b					7.4a(1) 7.5b
PHASE VI Performance Management	13. Measure Performance			2.2a(5)	3.2	4.1	5.2	6.1b(1)	7.2 7.5b
	14. Learn and Adapt			2.2b		4.1a(1) 4.1b(2)			
	15. Engage Stakeholders and Govern Strategy as an Ongoing Process	P.2c				4.1a(1) 4.1b(1)		6.1a(3) 6.1b(2)	

Appendix 2 – 2023-24 - Baldrige Excellence Builder

Strategy in the 21st Century, Second Edition

BALDRIGE EXCELLENCE BUILDER®

Key questions for improving your organization's performance

business
nonprofit
government
education
health care

LEADERSHIP

STRATEGY

CUSTOMERS

MEASUREMENT, ANALYSIS, AND KNOWLEDGE MANAGEMENT

WORKFORCE

OPERATIONS

RESULTS

2023
2024

www.nist.gov/baldrige

Appendix 2

Contents

2   About the Baldrige Excellence Builder
The *Baldrige Excellence Builder* represents proven leadership and management practices for high performance.

4   Core Values and Concepts
These beliefs and behaviors found in high-performing organizations are the basis of the *Baldrige Excellence Builder*.

5   Baldrige Excellence Builder
Answer these questions about the most important features of organizational performance excellence.

15   Assessing Your Responses
Assess your answers to the *Baldrige Excellence Builder* questions.

17   Glossary of Key Terms
Learn the definitions of key terms in the *Baldrige Excellence Builder*.

I have always envisioned Stellar to be a company that is built to last. ... And if you ask how we can ensure that we are built to last, I would say the answer is Baldrige. ... Unlike many other certifications or performance excellence measures, it is not prescriptive—it is adaptable to any organization, at any point on its journey to excellence.

—Celeste Ford, Founder, Baldrige Award recipient
Stellar Solutions

1

275

Strategy in the 21st Century, Second Edition

About the Baldrige Excellence Builder

Is your organization doing as well as it needs to? How do you know? What and how should your organization improve or change?

Whether your organization is new, is growing, or has existed for many years, it faces daily and long-term challenges. It also has strengths that have served you well so far. The *Baldrige Excellence Builder* helps you assess your organization's strengths and opportunities for improvement. By completing and acting on this assessment, you will be better positioned to accomplish your mission, improve your results, and become more competitive.

The *Baldrige Excellence Builder* is based on the more detailed *Baldrige Excellence Framework* and its Criteria for Performance Excellence. For more than 32 years, Baldrige has been globally recognized as the leading edge of validated leadership and performance practice. Baldrige is a nonprescriptive framework that empowers your organization to reach its goals, improve results, and become more competitive. The Core Values and Concepts (see page 4), a set of beliefs and behaviors found in high-performing organizations, are the foundation of this framework.

A Focus on Improvement

The *Baldrige Excellence Builder* helps you understand how well you are achieving your goals and objectives:

- Are your processes consistently effective?
- Do your approaches address your organization's needs?
- How good are your results?
- Is your organization learning, innovating, and improving?

As you answer the *Baldrige Excellence Builder* questions and assess your responses, you will identify strengths and opportunities for improvement. Then, as you build on your strengths and address your opportunities, you create cycles of improvement within your organization.

A Systems Perspective

A systems perspective means managing all the components of your organization as a unified whole to achieve your mission, ongoing success, and performance excellence. It means ensuring that your plans, processes, measures, and actions are consistent. And it means ensuring that the individual parts of your organization's management system work together in a fully interconnected, unified, and mutually beneficial manner.

Appendix 2

How to Use the Baldrige Excellence Builder

Answer the Organizational Profile questions. The *Baldrige Excellence Builder* does not prescribe how you should structure your organization or its operations, or what its mission and goals should be. In the Organizational Profile (pages 5–6), you define what is most relevant and important to your organization's mission and performance.

The Organizational Profile sets the context for your answers to the rest of the questions. It can also serve as your first Baldrige self-assessment: if you identify topics for which you have conflicting, little, or no information, you can use those topics for action planning.

Answer the questions in categories 1–7 (pages 7–14). Your answers to these questions are an assessment against the most important features of organizational excellence. The categories represent seven critical aspects of managing and performing as an organization: (1) Leadership; (2) Strategy; (3) Customers; (4) Measurement, Analysis, and Knowledge Management; (5) Workforce; (6) Operations; and (7) Results.

Categories 1–6 (pages 7–12) each consist of two items (e.g., 1.1, 1.2), with many of the questions beginning with "how." In answering these questions, give information on your key processes:

- *Approach:* How do you accomplish your organization's work? How systematic and effective are your key approaches?
- *Deployment:* How consistently are your key approaches used in relevant parts of your organization?
- *Learning:* How well have you evaluated and improved your key approaches? Have improvements been shared within your organization? Has new knowledge led to innovation?
- *Integration:* How well do your approaches reflect your current and future organizational needs?

For the five items in category 7 (pages 13–14), report on the results that are the most important to your organization's success:

- *Levels:* What is your current performance?
- *Trends:* Are the results improving, staying the same, or getting worse?
- *Comparisons:* How does your performance compare with that of other organizations and competitors, or with benchmarks or industry leaders?
- *Integration:* Are you tracking results that are important to your organization? Are you using the results in decision making?

Assess your answers: process and results. Use the rubric on pages 15–16 to assess your answers to the questions in each item. Identify your strengths. Then look at the next higher level to see what you might improve.

Prioritize your actions. Celebrate your strengths and build on them to improve the things you do well. Sharing the things you do well with the rest of your organization can speed improvement. Also prioritize your opportunities for improvement; you cannot do everything at once. Think about what is most important for your organization at this time, and decide what to work on first. Develop an action plan, implement it, and measure your progress.

After you use the *Baldrige Excellence Builder*, please email us at baldrige@nist.gov to tell us about your experience.

Core Values and Concepts

The Baldrige Excellence Framework *and* Baldrige Excellence Builder *are based on these core values and concepts found in high-performing organizations.*

Systems perspective. A systems perspective means managing all the parts of your organization as a unified whole to achieve your mission and strive toward your vision.

Visionary leadership. Your organization's senior leaders set a vision for the organization, create a customer focus, demonstrate clear and visible organizational values and ethics, and set high expectations for the workforce.

Customer-focused excellence. Your organization must consider all product and/or service features and characteristics, all modes of customer access and support, and all organizational values and behaviors that contribute to value for your customers.

Valuing people. An organization's success depends on an engaged workforce that benefits from meaningful work, clear organizational direction, the opportunity to learn, and accountability for performance. The successful organization has a culture of equity and inclusion that capitalizes on the diverse backgrounds and characteristics, knowledge, skills, creativity, and motivation of its workforce, partners, and collaborators.

Agility and resilience. Agility requires a capacity for rapid change and for flexibility in operations. Organizational resilience is the ability to anticipate, prepare for, and recover from disasters, emergencies, and other disruptions, and—when disruptions occur—to protect and enhance workforce and customer engagement, supply-network and financial performance, organizational productivity, and community well-being.

Organizational learning. Organizational learning includes both continuous improvement of existing approaches and significant change or innovation, leading to new goals, approaches, products and/or services, and markets.

Focus on success and innovation. Ensuring your organization's success now and in the future requires understanding of the short- and longer-term factors that affect your organization and its environment. It also requires the ability to drive organizational innovation.

Management by fact. Management by fact requires you to measure and analyze your organization's performance, both inside the organization and in your competitive environment.

Societal contributions. Your organization's leaders should stress contributions to the public and the consideration of societal well-being and benefit. Your leaders should be role models for your organization and its workforce in the protection of public health, safety, and the environment.

Ethics and transparency. Your organization should stress ethical behavior in all stakeholder transactions and interactions. Senior leaders should be role models of ethical behavior and make their expectations of the workforce very clear.

Delivering value and results. Your organization should choose and analyze results that help you deliver and balance value for your key stakeholders. Thus, results need to include not just financial results, but also product and/or service and process results; customer and workforce satisfaction and engagement results; and leadership, strategy, and societal performance.

Appendix 2

Baldrige Excellence Builder

The Baldrige Excellence Builder includes questions on the most important features of organizational excellence, starting with a full Organizational Profile. For a more comprehensive set of questions, see the Baldrige Excellence Framework booklet *(business/nonprofit, education, or health care).*

P Organizational Profile

P.1 Organizational Description: What are your key organizational characteristics?

a. Organizational Environment

(1) **Product and/or Service Offerings** What are your main products and/or services? What is the relative importance (including percentage of revenue/budget) of each product or service to your success? What are the delivery methods for these products and/or services?

(2) **Mission, Vision, Values, and Culture** What are your MISSION, VISION, and VALUES? What are the defining characteristics of your organizational CULTURE? What are your organization's CORE COMPETENCIES, and what is their relationship to your MISSION and VISION?

(3) **Workforce Profile** What is your WORKFORCE profile? What are your WORKFORCE or employee groups and SEGMENTS and the KEY engagement drivers for each? What KEY changes are you experiencing in your WORKFORCE CAPABILITY, CAPACITY, and composition?

(4) **Assets** What are your major assets, such as facilities, equipment, technologies, and intellectual property?

(5) **Regulatory Environment** What are your KEY applicable regulations, and accreditation, certification, or registration requirements?

b. Organizational Relationships

(1) **Organizational Structure** What are your organizational leadership and GOVERNANCE structures? What are the KEY components of your organization's LEADERSHIP SYSTEM? What are the reporting relationships among your GOVERNANCE SYSTEM, SENIOR LEADERS, and parent organization, as appropriate?

(Continued on the next page)

(2) **Customers* and Stakeholders** What are your KEY market SEGMENTS, CUSTOMER groups, and STAKEHOLDER groups, as appropriate? What are their KEY requirements and expectations for your products and/or services, CUSTOMER support services, and operations, including any differences among the groups?

(3) **Suppliers, Partners, and Collaborators** What are your KEY types of suppliers, PARTNERS, and COLLABORATORS? What role do they play in producing and delivering your KEY products and/or services and CUSTOMER support services? What role do they play in contributing and implementing INNOVATIONS in your organization? What are your KEY supply-network requirements?

P.2 Organizational Situation: What is your organization's strategic situation?

a. **Competitive Environment**

(1) **Competitive Position** What are your size, share, and growth in your industry or the markets you serve? How many and what types of competitors do you have? What differentiates you from them?

(2) **Competitiveness Changes** What KEY changes, if any, are affecting your competitive situation, including changes that create opportunities for collaboration and INNOVATION, as appropriate?

(3) **Comparative Data** What KEY sources of comparative and competitive data are available from within your industry? What KEY sources of comparative data are available from outside your industry? What limitations, if any, affect your ability to obtain or use these data?

b. **Strategic Context**

What are your KEY STRATEGIC CHALLENGES, threats, ADVANTAGES, and opportunities?

c. **Performance Improvement System**

What is your overall SYSTEM for PERFORMANCE improvement? What KEY tools and methods are used as part of this SYSTEM?

Terms in SMALL CAPS are defined in the Glossary of Key Terms (pages 17–19).

* For health care organizations, "customers" are the direct recipients of the health care services you provide (e.g., patients and families).

For education organizations, "customers" are the users of your educational programs and services (e.g., students and parents).

See www.nist.gov/baldrige/publications for Baldrige frameworks tailored to the health care and education sectors.

Appendix 2

1 Leadership

1.1 Senior Leadership: How do your senior leaders lead the organization?

(1) How do SENIOR LEADERS set and DEPLOY your organization's MISSION, VISION, and VALUES?

(2) How do SENIOR LEADERS' personal actions demonstrate their commitment to legal and ETHICAL BEHAVIOR?

(3) How do SENIOR LEADERS communicate with and engage the entire WORKFORCE, KEY PARTNERS, and KEY CUSTOMERS?

(4) How do SENIOR LEADERS create an environment for success now and in the future?

(5) How do SENIOR LEADERS create a focus on action to achieve the organization's MISSION and VISION?

1.2 Governance and Societal Contributions: How do you govern your organization and make societal contributions?

(1) How does your organization ensure responsible GOVERNANCE?

(2) How do you evaluate the PERFORMANCE of your SENIOR LEADERS and your GOVERNANCE SYSTEM?

(3) How does your GOVERNANCE SYSTEM review the organization's PERFORMANCE?

(4) How do you address current and anticipated future legal, regulatory, and community concerns with your products and/or services, and operations?

(5) How do you require and foster ETHICAL BEHAVIOR in all interactions?

(6) How do you incorporate societal well-being and benefit into your strategy and daily operations?

(7) How do you actively support and strengthen your KEY communities?

Terms in SMALL CAPS are defined in the Glossary of Key Terms (pages 17–19).

Strategy in the 21st Century, Second Edition

2 Strategy

2.1 Strategy Development: How do you develop your strategy?

(1) How do you conduct your strategic planning?

(2) How do you collect and analyze relevant data and develop information for use in your strategic planning PROCESS?

(3) How do you identify strategic opportunities and stimulate INNOVATION?

(4) How do you decide which KEY PROCESSES will be accomplished by your WORKFORCE and which by external suppliers, PARTNERS, and COLLABORATORS?

(5) What are your organization's KEY STRATEGIC OBJECTIVES and their most important related GOALS?

(6) How do your STRATEGIC OBJECTIVES achieve balance among varying and competing organizational needs?

2.2 Strategy Implementation: How do you implement your strategy?

(1) How do you develop your ACTION PLANS?

(2) How do you DEPLOY your ACTION PLANS?

(3) How do you ensure that financial and other resources are available to support the achievement of your ACTION PLANS while you meet current obligations?

(4) What are your KEY WORKFORCE plans to support your STRATEGIC OBJECTIVES and ACTION PLANS?

(5) What KEY PERFORMANCE MEASURES OR INDICATORS do you use to track the achievement and EFFECTIVENESS of your ACTION PLANS?

(6) For these KEY PERFORMANCE MEASURES OR INDICATORS, what are your PERFORMANCE PROJECTIONS for your short- and longer-term planning horizons?

(7) How do you recognize and respond when circumstances require a shift in ACTION PLANS and rapid execution of new plans?

Terms in SMALL CAPS are defined in the Glossary of Key Terms (pages 17–19).

Appendix 2

3 Customers

3.1 Customer Expectations: How do you listen to your customers and determine products and/or services to meet their needs?

(1) How do you listen to, interact with, and observe CUSTOMERS* to obtain actionable information?
(2) How do you listen to potential CUSTOMERS to obtain actionable data and information?
(3) How do you determine your CUSTOMER groups and market SEGMENTS?
(4) How do you determine product and/or service offerings?

3.2 Customer Engagement: How do you build relationships and enhance the customer experience?

(1) How do you acquire and retain CUSTOMERS by building and managing relationships?
(2) How do you enable CUSTOMERS to do business with you, seek information, and obtain support?
(3) How do you manage CUSTOMER complaints?
(4) How do your CUSTOMER experience PROCESSES promote and ensure fair treatment for different CUSTOMERS, CUSTOMER groups, and market SEGMENTS?
(5) How do you determine CUSTOMER satisfaction, dissatisfaction, and ENGAGEMENT?

Terms in SMALL CAPS are defined in the Glossary of Key Terms (pages 17–19).

* For health care organizations, "customers" are the direct recipients of the health care services you provide (e.g., patients and families).

For education organizations, "customers" are the users of your educational programs and services (e.g., students and parents).

Strategy in the 21st Century, Second Edition

4 Measurement, Analysis, and Knowledge Management

4.1 Measurement, Analysis, Review, and Improvement of Organizational Performance: How do you measure, analyze, review, and improve organizational performance?

(1) How do you track data and information on daily operations and overall organizational PERFORMANCE?

(2) How do you select comparative data and information to support fact-based decision making?

(3) How do you analyze and review your organization's PERFORMANCE and capabilities?

(4) How do you use the findings from your PERFORMANCE reviews to develop priorities for continuous improvement and opportunities for INNOVATION?

4.2 Information and Knowledge Management: How do you manage your information and your organizational knowledge assets?

(1) How do you verify and ensure the quality of organizational data and information?

(2) How do you ensure the availability of organizational data and information?

(3) How do you secure sensitive or privileged data and information, information technology assets, and Internet-enabled SYSTEMS?

(4) How do you build and manage organizational knowledge?

(5) How do you identify and share best practices in your organization?

(6) How do you determine which opportunities for INNOVATION to pursue?

Terms in SMALL CAPS are defined in the Glossary of Key Terms (pages 17–19).

Appendix 2

5 Workforce

5.1 Workforce Environment: How do you build an effective and supportive workforce environment?

(1) How do you assess your WORKFORCE CAPABILITY and CAPACITY needs?

(2) How do you recruit, hire, and onboard new WORKFORCE members?

(3) How do you prepare your WORKFORCE for changing CAPABILITY and CAPACITY needs?

(4) How do you organize and manage your WORKFORCE?

(5) How do you address workplace health and accessibility for the WORKFORCE?

(6) How do you support your WORKFORCE via compensation and benefits?

5.2 Workforce Engagement: How do you engage your workforce for retention and high performance?

(1) How do you determine the KEY drivers of WORKFORCE ENGAGEMENT?

(2) How do you assess WORKFORCE ENGAGEMENT?

(3) How do you foster an organizational CULTURE that is characterized by open communication, HIGH PERFORMANCE, and an engaged WORKFORCE?

(4) How does your WORKFORCE PERFORMANCE management SYSTEM support HIGH PERFORMANCE?

(5) How does your LEARNING and development SYSTEM support the personal development of WORKFORCE members and your organization's needs?

(6) How do you manage career development for your WORKFORCE and your future leaders?

(7) How do you ensure that your PERFORMANCE management, PERFORMANCE development, and career development PROCESSES promote equity and inclusion for a diverse WORKFORCE and different WORKFORCE groups and SEGMENTS?

Terms in SMALL CAPS are defined in the Glossary of Key Terms (pages 17–19).

Strategy in the 21st Century, Second Edition

6 Operations

6.1 Work Processes: How do you design, manage, and improve your key products and/or services and work processes?

(1) How do you determine your KEY product and/or service requirements?

(2) How do you design your products and/or services to meet these KEY requirements?

(3) How do you determine your KEY WORK PROCESS and support PROCESS requirements?

(4) How do you design your KEY WORK PROCESSES and support PROCESSES to meet your KEY requirements?

(5) How does your day-to-day operation of your KEY WORK PROCESSES and support PROCESSES ensure that they meet your KEY PROCESS requirements?

(6) How do you improve your KEY WORK PROCESSES and support PROCESSES to improve product and/or service and PROCESS PERFORMANCE?

6.2 Operational Effectiveness: How do you ensure effective management of your operations?

(1) How do you manage the cost, efficiency, and EFFECTIVENESS of your operations?

(2) How do you manage your supply network?

(3) How do you provide a safe operating environment for your WORKFORCE and other people in your workplace?

(4) How do you ensure that your organization can anticipate, prepare for, and recover from disasters, emergencies, and other disruptions?

(5) What is your organization's overall APPROACH to risk management?

Terms in SMALL CAPS are defined in the Glossary of Key Terms (pages 17–19).

Appendix 2

7 Results

7.1 Product and Process Results: What are your product and/or service and process performance results?

(1) What are your RESULTS for your products and/or services?

(2) What are your PROCESS EFFECTIVENESS and efficiency RESULTS?

(3) What are your safety and emergency preparedness RESULTS?

(4) What are your supply-network management RESULTS?

7.2 Customer Results: What are your customer-focused performance results?

(1) What are your CUSTOMER satisfaction and dissatisfaction RESULTS?

(2) What are your CUSTOMER ENGAGEMENT RESULTS?

7.3 Workforce Results: What are your workforce-focused performance results?

(1) What are your WORKFORCE CAPABILITY and CAPACITY RESULTS?

(2) What are your RESULTS for workplace health and for WORKFORCE compensation and benefits?

(3) What are your WORKFORCE ENGAGEMENT RESULTS?

(4) What are your WORKFORCE and leader development RESULTS?

(Continued on the next page)

Strategy in the 21st Century, Second Edition

7.4 Leadership and Governance Results: What are your senior leadership and governance results?

(1) What are your RESULTS for SENIOR LEADERS' communication and engagement with the WORKFORCE, PARTNERS, and CUSTOMERS?

(2) What are your RESULTS for GOVERNANCE accountability?

(3) What are your legal and regulatory RESULTS?

(4) What are your RESULTS for ETHICAL BEHAVIOR?

(5) What are your RESULTS for societal well-being and support of your KEY communities?

7.5 Financial, Marketplace, and Strategy Results: What are your results for financial and marketplace performance and strategy implementation?

(1) What are your financial PERFORMANCE RESULTS?

(2) What are your marketplace PERFORMANCE RESULTS?

(3) What are your RESULTS for the achievement of your organizational strategy?

Terms in SMALL CAPS are defined in the Glossary of Key Terms (pages 17–19).

Appendix 2

Assessing Your Responses

For scoring guidelines, see the Baldrige Excellence Framework *booklet (business/nonprofit, education, or health care).*

Assessing Processes

Processes are the methods your organization uses and improves to do its work. The four factors used to evaluate processes are approach, deployment, learning, and integration (see page 3).

For process items (those in categories 1–6), read the process scoring rubric on page 16. For each item, assign one of the descriptors (reactive, early, mature, or role model) based on a holistic assessment of your processes.

Assessing Results

Results are the outputs and outcomes your organization achieves. The four factors used to evaluate results are levels, trends, comparisons, and integration (see page 3).

For results items (7.1–7.5), read the results scoring rubric on page 16. For each item, assign one of the descriptors based on a holistic assessment of your overall performance.

DESCRIPTOR	PROCESS	RESULTS
Reactive	• Operations are characterized by activities rather than by processes, and they are largely responsive to immediate needs or problems. Goals are poorly defined.	• Results that are important to the organization's ongoing success are missing, not used, or randomly reported.
Early	• The organization is beginning to carry out operations with repeatable processes, evaluation, and improvement, and there is some early coordination among organizational units. Strategy and quantitative goals are being defend.	• Results that are important to the organization's ongoing success are reported, tracked over time, and improving.
Mature	• Operations are characterized by repeatable processes that are regularly evaluated for improvement. Learnings are shared, and there is coordination among organizational units. Processes address key strategies and goals.	• Results that are important to the organization's ongoing success are trending in the right direction and doing well relative to competitors or other relevant organizations.
Role Model	• Operations are characterized by repeatable processes that are regularly evaluated for change and improvement in collaboration with other affected units. The organization seeks and achieves efficiencies across units through analysis, innovation, and the sharing of information and knowledge. Processes and measures track progress on key strategic and operational goals.	• The full array of results that are important to the organization's ongoing success are reported and trended over time, indicating top performance relative to other organizations.

Appendix 2

Glossary of Key Terms

The terms below are those in SMALL CAPS in the Baldrige Excellence Builder, *as well as terms relating to the scoring rubric. For additional definitions and examples, see the* Baldrige Excellence Framework *booklet (business/nonprofit, education, or health care).*

ACTION PLANS. Specific actions that your organization takes to reach its strategic objectives. These plans specify the resources committed to and the time horizons for accomplishing the plans.

See also STRATEGIC OBJECTIVES.

ALIGNMENT. A state of consistency among plans, processes, information, resource decisions, workforce capability and capacity, actions, results, and analyses that support key organization-wide goals.

See also INTEGRATION.

AGILITY. A capacity for rapid change and flexibility in operations.

APPROACH. The methods your organization uses to carry out its processes.

COLLABORATORS. Organizations or individuals who cooperate with your organization to support a particular activity or event or who cooperate intermittently when their short-term goals are aligned with or are the same as yours.

See also PARTNERS.

CORE COMPETENCIES. Your organization's areas of greatest expertise; those strategically important, possibly specialized capabilities that are central to fulfilling your mission or that provide an advantage in your marketplace or service environment.

CULTURE. The shared beliefs, norms, and values that characterize your workforce and are demonstrated within your organization.

See also ETHICAL BEHAVIOR and VALUES.

CUSTOMER. An actual or potential user of your organization's products, programs, or services.

See also STAKEHOLDERS.

CUSTOMER ENGAGEMENT. Your customers' investment in or commitment to your brand and product and/or service offerings.

DEPLOYMENT. The extent to which your organization applies an approach in relevant work units throughout your organization.

EFFECTIVE. How well a process or a measure addresses its intended purpose.

ETHICAL BEHAVIOR. The actions your organization takes to ensure that all its decisions, actions, and stakeholder interactions conform to its moral and professional principles of conduct. These principles should support all applicable laws and regulations and are the foundation for your organization's culture and values.

GOALS. Future conditions or performance levels that your organization intends or desires to attain.

See also PERFORMANCE PROJECTIONS.

GOVERNANCE. The system of management and controls exercised in the stewardship of your organization.

HIGH PERFORMANCE. Ever-higher levels of overall organizational and individual performance, including quality, productivity, innovation rate, and cycle time.

HOW. The systems and processes that your organization uses to achieve its mission requirements.

INNOVATION. Making meaningful change to improve products, services, processes, the organization, or societal well-being, and create new value for stakeholders. The outcome of innovation is a discontinuous or breakthrough change.

INTEGRATION. The harmonization of plans, processes, information, resource decisions, workforce capability and capacity, actions, results, and analyses to support key organization-wide goals.

See also ALIGNMENT.

KEY. Major or most important; critical to achieving your intended outcome.

KNOWLEDGE ASSETS. Your organization's accumulated intellectual resources; the knowledge possessed by your organization and its workforce in the form of information, ideas, learning, understanding, memory, insights, cognitive and technical skills, and capabilities.

LEADERSHIP SYSTEM. The way leadership is exercised, formally and informally, throughout your organization; the basis for key decisions and the way they are made, communicated, and carried out.

LEARNING. New knowledge or skills acquired through evaluation, study, experience, and innovation.

LEVELS. Numerical information that places or positions your organization's results and performance on a meaningful measurement scale.

MEASURES AND INDICATORS. Numerical information that quantifies the input, output, and performance dimensions of processes, products, programs, projects, services, and the overall organization (outcomes).

MISSION. Your organization's overall function.

PARTNERS. Key organizations or individuals who are working in concert with your organization to achieve a common goal or improve performance. Typically, partnerships are formal arrangements.

See also COLLABORATORS.

PERFORMANCE. Outputs and their outcomes obtained from processes, products, services, and customers that permit you to evaluate and compare your organization's results to performance projections, standards, past results, goals, and other organizations' results.

PERFORMANCE EXCELLENCE. An integrated approach to organizational performance management that results in (1) delivery of ever-improving value to customers and stakeholders, contributing to ongoing organizational success; (2) improvement of your organization's overall effectiveness and capabilities; and (3) learning for the organization and for people in the workforce.

PERFORMANCE PROJECTIONS. Estimates of your organization's future performance.

See also GOALS.

PROCESS. Linked activities with the purpose of producing a product or service for a customer (user) within or outside your organization.

RESILIENCE. An organization's ability to anticipate, prepare for, and recover from disasters, emergencies, and other disruptions, and when disruptions occur, to protect and enhance workforce and customer engagement, supply-network and financial performance, organizational productivity, and community well-being.

RESULTS. Outputs and outcomes achieved by your organization.

SEGMENT. One part of your organization's customer, market, product and/or service offering, or workforce base.

SENIOR LEADERS. Your organization's senior management group or team.

STAKEHOLDERS. All groups that are or might be affected by your organization's actions and success.

STRATEGIC ADVANTAGES. Those marketplace benefits that exert a decisive influence on your organization's likelihood of future success. These advantages are frequently sources of current and future competitive success relative to other providers of similar products and/or services.

STRATEGIC CHALLENGES. Those pressures that exert a decisive influence on your organization's likelihood of future success. These challenges are frequently driven by your organization's anticipated competitive position in the future relative to other providers of similar products and/or services.

STRATEGIC OBJECTIVES. The aims or responses that your organization articulates to address major change or improvement, competitiveness or social issues, and business advantages.

See also ACTION PLANS.

SYSTEM. A set of interrelated leadership and management elements of an organization used to integrate approaches, establish policies and objectives, and manage processes to achieve those objectives.

SYSTEMATIC. Well-ordered, repeatable, and exhibiting the use of data and information so that learning is possible.

TRENDS. Numerical information that shows the direction and rate of change of your organization's results or the consistency of its performance over time.

VALUES. The guiding principles and behaviors that embody how your organization and its people are expected to operate.

VISION. Your organization's desired future state.

VOICE OF THE CUSTOMER. Your process for capturing customer-related information.

WORK PROCESSES. Your organization's most important internal value-creation processes.

WORKFORCE. All people actively supervised by your organization and involved in accomplishing your organization's work, including paid employees (e.g., permanent, part-time, temporary, on-site, and remote employees, as well as contract employees supervised by your organization) and volunteers, as appropriate.

WORKFORCE CAPABILITY. Your organization's ability to accomplish its work processes through its people's knowledge, skills, abilities, and competencies.

WORKFORCE CAPACITY. Your organization's ability to ensure sufficient staffing levels to accomplish its work processes and deliver your products and/or services to customers, including the ability to meet seasonal or varying demand levels.

WORKFORCE ENGAGEMENT. The extent of workforce members' emotional and intellectual commitment to accomplishing your organization's work, mission, and vision.

BALDRIGE EXCELLENCE FRAMEWORK®, BALDRIGE CRITERIA FOR PERFORMANCE EXCELLENCE®, CRITERIA FOR PERFORMANCE EXCELLENCE®, BALDRIGE COLLABORATIVE ASSESSMENT®, BALDRIGE EXAMINER®, BALDRIGE EXCELLENCE BUILDER®, BALDRIGE EXECUTIVE FELLOWS PROGRAM®, (IM)PROVE YOUR PERFORMANCE®, PERFORMANCE EXCELLENCE®, THE QUEST FOR EXCELLENCE®, MALCOLM BALDRIGE NATIONAL QUALITY AWARD®, BALDRIGE PERFORMANCE EXCELLENCE PROGRAM®, and the Malcolm Baldrige National Quality Award medal and depictions or representations thereof are federally registered trademarks and service marks of the U.S. Department of Commerce, National Institute of Standards and Technology. The unauthorized use of these trademarks and service marks is prohibited.

Appendix 2

You've used the Baldrige Excellence Builder® to assess your organization. What's next?

Purchase the Baldrige Framework Booklet
The Baldrige Excellence Framework® (business/nonprofit, education, or health care) is a more comprehensive guide to organizational performance excellence.

Attend the Quest for Excellence® Conference
At Quest and other Baldrige conferences, you will learn best performance management practices from Baldrige Award recipients.

Attend the Baldrige Examiner Training Experience
Within the Baldrige Examiner Training course, you will work with experienced Baldrige examiners and learn how to use the Criteria for Performance Excellence®.

Apply for the Baldrige Executive Fellows Program
This one-year, leadership development experience prepares rising senior executives for impactful leadership and for achieving performance excellence in their own organizations.

Try the Baldrige Cybersecurity Excellence Builder
This voluntary self-assessment tool will help you better understand and improve the effectiveness of your organization's cybersecurity risk management efforts.

Explore Local Baldrige-Based Offerings
The Alliance for Performance Excellence, the consortium of state, local, and sector-specific Baldrige-based programs, offers resources and services to help your organization get better, faster.

Contact the Baldrige Program
We'll answer your questions about these and other Baldrige products and services.

---

a powerful set of mechanisms

Jim Collins, author of *Good to Great: Why Some Companies Make the Leap ... and Others Don't*

I see the Baldrige process as a powerful set of mechanisms for disciplined people engaged in disciplined thought and taking disciplined action to create great organizations that produce exceptional results.

Baldrige Excellence Framework®

Purchase your copy today.

Printed format: $30
Electronic format: $12
Volume discounts and
enterprise licenses available

Contents

About the Baldrige Excellence Framework®
How to Use the Baldrige Excellence Framework®
Criteria for Performance Excellence®
Scoring System
How to Respond to the Criteria
Core Values and Concepts
Changes from the 2021–2022 Baldrige Excellence Framework®
Glossary of Key Terms

Contact

For more information on the Baldrige Excellence Framework® or other products and services:
www.nist.gov/baldrige | 301.975.2036 | baldrige@nist.gov

CONNECT WITH BALDRIGE
@BaldrigeProgram #Baldrige

NIST
National Institute of
Standards and Technology
U.S. Department of Commerce

02/2023

T1668

Photo credits: ©Ribah/Shutterstock, ©Rostizna/Shutterstock

Appendix 3 – SMP/SPP Competencies Included in Each Domain and Subdomain

	SMP Content Outline		SPP Content Outline
DOMAIN 1 ENGAGEMENT			
1A CULTURE OF STRATEGIC MANAGEMENT AND AGILITY			
1A1	Coach organizational leadership working from a shared vision toward organizational performance-driven alignment and accountability to a strategic plan.	1A1	Drive tactical and project planning within a business unit in alignment with the overall strategic plan.
1A2	Design processes and drive a culture of strategic management and agility enterprise-wide and at all levels of the organization using a whole system approach.	1A2	Support a culture of strategic management, agility, and accountability.
1A3	Provide leadership and facilitate organizational capacity-building.	1A3	Facilitate the creation of unit planning at all levels.
1A4	Establish and manage a strategic management function to guide the strategic thinking, planning, and implementation processes.	1A4	Support unit personnel through cycles of change.
1A5	Facilitate processes that encourage innovation and identify and agree upon strategic options.	1A5	Facilitate processes to identify and agree upon strategic option
1A6	Model and guide effective sourcing, application, and sharing of knowledge and learning enterprise-wide.	1A6	Facilitate strategic planning reviews to continuously improve the business and department planning processes.
1A7	Build necessary relationships across country cultures, languages and geography with awareness and sensitivity.	1A7	Design and deliver enterprise-wide training to support the strategic direction.
		1A8	Design strategy evaluation and improvement to be a continuous rather than periodic process.
1B PLANNING TEAM EXPECTATIONS			
1B1	Establish a top management planning team process led by the chief executive that involves key internal and external stakeholders.	1B1	Direct a corporate planning team to ensure that the knowledge, timing, outcomes, processes, and infrastructures of planning and strategic management achieve organization-wide integration.
1B2	Orient assembled top management planning team to planning process.	1B2	Orient assembled planning team to the planning process.
1B3	Tailor the planning process to the needs of the organization.	1B3	Provide actionable feedback to support planning team members so team members perform optimally individually and as a unit
1B4	Support executive sponsorship efforts among senior management and key stakeholders to gain their advocacy for strategic change.	1B4	Advise leaders on how to involve and communicate the value of change to staff to minimize resistance.
1B5	Mentor and coach executive sponsors on strategic planning and management processes.		
1B6	Advise leaders on how to involve and communicate the value of change to staff to minimize resistance.		
DOMAIN 2 STRATEGY FORMULATION			
2A INTERNAL AND EXTERNAL ENVIRONMENTAL SCAN			
2A1	Organize systematic trend-spotting in sectors external to the organization and throughout the organization.	2A1	Collect and disseminate information about the organization's resources to assist with the development of the strategy plan.
2A2	Gather, analyze, and interpret environmental trends.	2A2	Facilitate analysis of internal processes for efficiency and effectiveness.
2A3	Monitor and assess early indicators of external trends in change drivers that could lead to disruption of the organization.	2A3	Monitor and assess the current internal and external environments.
2A4	Identify the key environmental indicators at play.	2A4	Identify relevant customer segmentation attributes.
2A5	Synthesize internal and external environmental data as appropriate to the context of the organization.	2A5	Contribute to plans for how the key environmental indicators are communicated.
2A6	Identify future customers/clients and the likely alignment with currently relevant products and services.	2A6	Provide benchmarking and best practice research
2A7	Analyze both the current and the future environment and create a range of scenarios which are the most likely and relevant.	2A7	Gather customer satisfaction data and intelligence regarding wants, needs, loyalty and retention.
2A8	Evaluate readiness or capacity for change and ensure recommended changes are informed by findings.	2A8	Evaluate readiness or capacity for change and ensure recommended changes are informed by findings.
2A9	Communicate data, both written and orally, to create actionable understanding.	2A9	Communicate data, both written and orally, to create actionable understanding.
2B STRATEGY DESIGN AND FORMULATION			
2B1	Create alternative strategic directions that create value for stakeholders and a competitive differentiation for the organization.	2B1	Support creation of and articulate the organization's distinctive core competencies and value proposition that result in a competitive differentiation.

3A5	Promote ethical consideration and communicate with employees on the minimum nonnegotiable behaviors through the organization code of conduct.	3A5	Enable employee engagement and attunement of their hearts and minds in support of the strategic direction.
3A6	Analyze the current and required corporate cultural components and identify the core values that support or hinder the strategy execution.	3A6	Assess the impact of organization design to corporate culture and recommend mitigation for gaps.
3A7	Assemble change leadership team(s) to monitor and assure movement in strategy development and execution		
3B ALIGNMENT OF OPERATIONS WITH STRATEGY			
3B1	Assess internal organizational cross-functional capabilities to close the gap between the current and desired state.	3B1	Facilitate the alignment of enterprise-wide operational plans with the organization strategy.
3B2	Facilitate analysis of the organization's functional components to identify impacts of and risks to implementation of the strategic plan.	3B2	Assess internal operational processes to identify actions necessary to close the gap between the current state and desired state.
3B3	Identify and sequence the transformation projects that must be executed to improve the organization's ability to execute its strategy.	3B3	Assess what capital resources, technology or capabilities are needed to implement the strategy.
3B4	Create transformation plan(s).	3B4	Promote the value of organizational changes that support strategy development and execution.
3C OPERATIONAL PLANNING FOR IMPLEMENTATION			
3C1	Facilitate the development of an implementation plan that supports the organization's strategies.	3C1	Assist the management team in developing a clear strategic change agenda, common framework, and language.
3C2	Identify specific activities and resources needed to realize the organization's strategies.	3C2	Facilitate the development of an actionable plan from the organization's strategies.
3C3	Determine and assist senior management in assigning and allocating resources, finances, timelines, and desired outcomes for each activity.	3C3	Identify specific activities and resources needed to realize the organization's strategies.
3C4	Foster senior management ownership of a viable operational plan for change.	3C4	Build and create management ownership of a viable operational plan for change.
2B2	Articulate to senior management the importance of the organization's distinctive core competencies and the strategies that result in competitive differentiation.	2B2	Assist in the formulation of the vision and mission statements to be clear in defining the organization's purpose.
2B3	Facilitate the crafting of vision and mission statements that clearly articulate the organization's purpose.	2B3	Support comprehensive economic and portfolio analysis of tentative/alternative strategic directions to ensure their viability, growth, and sustainability.
2B4	Assist senior management with the identification of business models that drive value for stakeholders and achieve the expected performance outcomes.	2B4	Assist with industry and organizational structural analysis.
2B5	Facilitate leadership in the identification and selection of the organization's objectives, core strategies, and key results.	2B5	Advise on options to grow top line revenue and lower costs to improve cash flow and increase profit margins.
2B6	Anticipate changes that can impact or support the successful execution of the strategy.	2B6	Assist in the development of appropriate feedback loops to validate strategy options
2B7	Assess the potential impact of competitor activities, macro changes and regulatory policies on strategic direction.		
2B8	Assess and advise on options to enhance value proposition and to improve return on investment.		
2B9	Develop appropriate feedback loops to validate strategy options.		
DOMAIN 3 PREPARATION FOR STRATEGY INTEGRATION			
3A ALIGNMENT OF THE ORGANIZATION DESIGN WITH STRATEGY			
3A1	Educate senior management on organization design/ redesign principles and its relationship to the success of strategy execution and management.	3A1	Educate middle management on organization design/ redesign principles and its relationship to the success of strategy execution and management.
3A2	Select the organization design framework in consultation with management and organization design professionals.	3A2	Identify organization structures affected by the proposed strategy.
3A3	Design plan for implementation, including how organization structure should be modified enterprise-wide.	3A3	Support organization design professionals and middle management to redesign the organization and align it with the new strategy.
3A4	Advocate for and coach senior management on change management plan for organizational design effort.	3A4	Plan and sequence changes transpired from organizational redesign.

Appendix 3

3C5	Use specific frameworks and structures to build and evaluate the multi-year business plan and the links between the corporate strategic plan.	3C5	Determine and allocate resources, finances and timelines for each activity.
3C6	Monitor the selection, and execution of strategic plan initiatives and projects, communicating issues and risks to senior management.	3C6	Integrate, communicate, and cascade all the strategic planning components into an annual planning and budgeting process across and down the entire organization.
3C7	Develop an enterprise-wide communication plan to disseminate information about strategy and implementation.	3C7	Leverage, align, and cascade the business strategy into multi-year business plans for departments and major functional areas.
		3C8	Identify desired outcomes for each activity.

DOMAIN 4 STRATEGY EXECUTION AND EVALUATION
4A STRATEGY EXECUTION AND TRANSFORMATION

4A1	Facilitate the development of annual and project plans that align with the strategy.	4A1	Facilitate the development of annual and project plans that align with the strategy.
4A2	Educate and coach senior leadership on change management.	4A2	Engage with critical internal and external stakeholders in the strategy execution process.
4A3	Cultivate executive sponsorship of senior management to lead and support the strategic change.	4A3	Guide development of strategic and transition planning activities throughout the organization.
4A4	Collaborate on executive communications that facilitate a high-performance culture.	4A4	Assist in the development and implementation of a change management program that informs and engages stakeholders.
4A5	Lead the strategy management function to execute the strategy implementation process.	4A5	Recommend a portfolio management system to support the process by which strategic plan initiatives are selected, executed, and monitored.
4A6	Serve as the trusted advisor to senior management as the strategy is executed.	4A6	Serve as the trusted advisor to project teams and change management teams as they implement the strategic initiatives.
4A7	Facilitate development of performance-based systems that motivate and incentivize people to change.	4A7	Assist management in developing and executing an annual implementation and review process that drives continuous improvement.
		4A8	Teach and coach teamwork, change management, and project management skills to support strategy implementation.
		4A9	Anticipate changes that can impact or support the successful execution of the strategy.

4B GOVERNANCE AND DECISION MAKING

4B1	Identify with senior management the strategy evaluation criteria, steps, and procedures for decision-making.	4B1	Support creation of a governance plan.
4B2	Create a governance plan for decision-making regarding strategic plan execution.	4B2	Guide management to adhere to the established governing structure and decision hierarchy for modifications in their plans.
4B3	Communicate the governance structure and decision hierarchy modifications in their plans.		
4B4	Assess performance of current governance structures and decision hierarchy.		

4C STRATEGIC PERFORMANCE MANAGEMENT

4C1	Facilitate senior management in identifying the performance metrics and targets for strategic objectives.	4C1	Facilitate management in identifying the performance metrics and targets for strategic initiatives.
4C2	Oversee the operation of a monitoring and accountability process to track implementation of the change.	4C2	Design and report strategy performance dashboards and identify information sources.
4C3	Recommend corrective action based on opportunities, issues, risks and lessons learned affecting strategy implementation and execution.	4C3	Facilitate strategy review meetings.
4C4	Measure and monitor organizational health and take corrective actions.	4C4	Support communications to managers and employees about progress being made towards achieving the strategy.
		4C5	Evaluate the KPI data and trends to determine if strategies are on track and identify improvements
		4C6	Evaluate the change management effectiveness.

Appendix 4 – SPP Content Outline and Knowledge Needed for Competent Performance

SPP Content Outline and Knowledge Needed for Competent Performance		
Domain 1 ENGAGEMENT		**Knowledge Needed for Domain 1 Competence**

1A	**CULTURE OF STRATEGIC MANAGEMENT AND AGILITY**	**Knowledge Needed for Domain 1 Competence**
		• Knowledge and application of **Strategic Management Philosophy**
		  • Elements of a strategic management function
		  • How to think with a systems perspective
		  • How to design agile planning and strategy management processes
		  • How to cascade strategy and goals throughout the organization
		  • How to assure alignment to the strategy through synthesis of top down and bottom up planning
		  • How to apply change management principles that best fits the organization
		  • How to implement change structures, processes and culture needed to transform an organization
		  • How to leverage the role and importance of executive sponsorship
		
		• Knowledge and application of **organizational performance models and how to choose the best fit model**
		  • How to assess strategic options in relation to desired outcomes
		  • How to design processes that garner buy-in for strategic change
		  • How to create a culture of accountability and learning
		
		• Knowledge and application of **communication methods to share knowledge and learning**
		  • How to communicate complex ideas at middle management level
		    • How to select communication strategies and methods to align strategy across the organization
		    • How to communicate the design of the process at various stages and to the various levels of the organization
		    • How to teach and coach middle managers to enhance communication skills
		    How to assess and use fact-based data to drive decisions
		  • How to engage internal and external stakeholders to assure buy-in and stay-in to the planning process
		    • How to motivate people to share information and knowledge (actionable understanding) in cross-functional teams
		    • How to draw out lessons learned into actionable understanding
		
		• Knowledge and application of **interpersonal and group process facilitation skills**
		  • How to demonstrate executive presence and emotional intelligence
		    • How to create credibility at the middle management level
		    • How to build relationships at the middle management level
		  • How to coach the middle manager
		    • How to affirm people while delivering a range of feedback, i.e. corrective, constructive feedback.
		  • How to facilitate group processes
		    • How to facilitate focused planning sessions

1A1	Drive tactical and project planning within a business unit in alignment with the overall strategic plan.	
1A2	Support a culture of strategic management, agility, and accountability.	
1A3	Facilitate the creation of unit planning at all levels.	
1A4	Support unit personnel through cycles of change.	
1A5	Facilitate processes to identify and agree upon strategic option	
1A6	Facilitate strategic planning reviews to continuously improve the business and department planning processes.	
1A7	Design and deliver enterprise-wide training to support the strategic direction.	
1A8	Design strategy evaluation and improvement to be a continuous rather than periodic process.	
1B	**PLANNING TEAM EXPECTATIONS**	
1B1	Direct a corporate planning team to ensure that the knowledge, timing, outcomes, processes, and infrastructures of planning and strategic management achieve organization-wide integration.	
1B2	Orient assembled planning team to the planning process.	
1B3	Provide actionable feedback to support planning team members so team members perform optimally individually and as a unit.	
1B4	Advise leaders on how to involve and communicate the value of change to staff to minimize resistance.	

Strategy in the 21st Century, Second Edition

		• How to listen and synthesize input into the process design
		• How to bring a conversation to resolution
		• How to inject innovative thought into solution-seeking
		• When and how to resolve conflicts among middle management
		• How to provide meaningful, constructive feedback to planning groups
		    • How to apply various motivational theories to keep advancing plan development and execution
		        • How to motivate middle managers toward planning activities
		        • How to engage staff at various levels to minimize resistance
		
		• Knowledge and application of **multi-cultural inclusion**
		    • How to be effective in a multi-cultural environment
		    • How to be cross-culturally competent
		    • How to select the members for an effective planning team

Domain 2 STRATEGY FORMULATION		**Knowledge Needed for Domain 2 Competence**

2A	**INTERNAL AND EXTERNAL ENVIRONMENTAL SCAN**	• Knowledge and application of **various approaches to external and internal environmental scanning**
		    • How to apply appropriate categorizations for change drivers (e.g., PESTEL, STEEP)
		    • How to use scenario planning to assess strategic options
		    • How to identify the core competencies of a business unit
		    • How to apply various approaches to SWOT analysis and select the appropriate approach for the organization
		        • How to conduct an effective SWOT analysis of organization-wide processes, structures and culture in light of the new strategies **and** to close gaps between current and desired future state
		
		• Knowledge and application of **various theories around strategy design** (e.g., scenario planning, Porter's Five Forces, etc.) and how to select the most appropriate for the organization
		    • How to communicate the differences between mission, vision and purpose
		    • How to segment a customer base
		    • How to create a compelling value proposition for the customers of the organization
		    • How to leverage creativity and innovation to enhance customer value
		
		• Knowledge and application of **data collection and analysis processes and tools**
		    • How to conduct data analysis
		        • How to interpret and make sense of SWOT data to select the most relevant aspects to achieve optimal performance How to identify, gather and assess usefulness of data from internal sources
		    • How to leverage strengths and assets to achieve desired performance.
		    • How to identify barriers and risks to strategy implementation
		    • How to make sense of data to project its likely impact to customers and on the organization itself

2A1	Collect and disseminate information about the organization's resources to assist with the development of the strategy plan.	
2A2	Facilitate analysis of internal processes for efficiency and effectiveness.	
2A3	Monitor and assess the current internal and external environments.	
2A4	Identify relevant customer segmentation attributes.	
2A5	Contribute to plans for how the key environmental indicators are communicated.	
2A6	Provide benchmarking and best practice research	
2A7	Gather customer satisfaction data and intelligence regarding wants, needs, loyalty and retention.	
2A8	Evaluate readiness or capacity for change and ensure recommended changes are informed by findings.	
2A9	Communicate data, both written and orally, to create actionable understanding.	
2B	**STRATEGY DESIGN AND FORMULATION**	

Appendix 4

2B1	Support creation of and articulate the organization's distinctive core competencies and value proposition that result in a competitive differentiation.	• How to convert research findings into actionable understanding • How to use a variety of approaches assess customer satisfaction • How to construct surveys to collect objective, unbiased data understanding • How to construct survey items that would effectively assess customer intelligence that can be leveraged in scenarios and product decisions in alignment with the strategic plan. • How to recognize relevant benchmarks
2B2	Assist in the formulation of the vision and mission statements to be clear in defining the organization's purpose.	

2B3	Support comprehensive economic and portfolio analysis of tentative/alternative strategic directions to ensure their viability, growth, and sustainability.	• Knowledge and application of **communication tools and skills**
		    • How to get buy-in organization-wide
		        • How to select and implement different types of feedback loops (e.g., experiential data)
		        • How to use available communication tools, select and use the appropriate tool
		    • How to organize, synthesize and disseminate information in written and oral communication.
		    • How to create a business case for strategic alternatives
		        • How to present rationale for relevant options
		        • How to present strategies that result in competitive differentiation effectively and confidently to middle management while facilitating discussion and decision-making

2B4	Assist with industry and organizational structural analysis.	
2B5	Advise on options to grow top line revenue and lower costs to improve cash flow and increase profit margins.	

2B6	Assist in the development of appropriate feedback loops to validate strategy options	• Knowledge and application of **interpersonal and group facilitation skills**
		    • How to identify and appropriately attune to key audiences (e.g., their dynamics, culture, etc.)
		    • How to identify and appropriately attune key audiences (e.g., their dynamics, culture, etc.) to the strategy
		How to engage others in creating options

Domain 3 PREPARATION FOR STRATEGY INTEGRATION		**Knowledge Needed for Domain 3 Competence**

3A	**ALIGNMENT OF THE ORGANIZATION DESIGN WITH STRATEGY**	• Knowledge and application of **different approaches to organizational design** (e.g., human centered design, LEAN thinking, etc.)
		    • How to apply relevant organization design frameworks available
		    • How to apply form follows function to redesign the structure of the organization to accommodate the strategies chosen

3A1	Educate middle management on organization design/ redesign principles and its relationship to the success of strategy execution and management.	

3A2	Identify organization structures affected by the proposed strategy.	• Knowledge and application of **various modes of external and internal environmental scanning**
		    • How to assess internal resources in service to the strategic plan
		        • How to identify critical internal and external stakeholders to engage in the strategy execution process
		        • How to engage finance and IT personnel to gather information to inform the resource plan for implementation

3A3	Support organization design professionals and middle management to redesign the organization and align it with the new strategy.	
3A4	Plan and sequence changes transpired from organizational redesign.	

3A5	Enable employee engagement and attunement of their hearts and minds in support of the strategic direction.	• How to identify and quantify the capital resources, technology and capabilities required to execute the activities and tasks required to move from current to future state
3A6	Assess the impact of organization design to corporate culture and recommend mitigation for gaps.	• How to assess gaps in training needs • How to engage HR professionals to design and use effective, learner-focused training through a variety of settings, i.e. virtual, webinar, face to face • How to analyze and identify gaps presented in the current culture and the current operational processes towards the desired state • How to identify the activities and tasks required to move from current to future state • How to map the shift from the current organization chart and corporate cultural components and what it needs to be
3B	**ALIGNMENT OF OPERATIONS WITH STRATEGY**	• Knowledge and application of **different functional levels of planning**
3B1	Facilitate the alignment of enterprise-wide operational plans with the organization strategy.	• How to identify the interdependencies of the transformation projects and how to properly sequence them
3B2	Assess internal operational processes to identify actions necessary to close the gap between the current state and desired state.	• How to facilitate development of the strategic change agenda, common framework and language across various levels of the organization • How to construct SMART objectives
3B3	Assess what capital resources, technology or capabilities are needed to implement the strategy.	• How to create a tactical plan for implementation and execution • How to connect tactics and actions with strategies. • How to facilitate transition planning
3B4	Promote the value of organizational changes that support strategy development and execution.	• How to create a transition plan • How to sequence transition planning activities • How to plan a robust performance monitoring system
3C	**OPERATIONAL PLANNING FOR IMPLEMENTATION**	• How to select an integrated portfolio management system that coordinates with product management and financial systems.
3C1	Assist the management team in developing a clear strategic change agenda, common framework, and language.	• How to communicate to programmers on how to customize portfolio system features to align with enterprise needs
3C2	Facilitate the development of an actionable plan from the organization's strategies.	• How to collaborate with appropriate departments to create a training plan and a communications plan enterprise-wide to support teamwork in pursuit of the strategy plan.
3C3	Identify specific activities and resources needed to realize the organization's strategies.	• How to create multi-year departmental business plans
3C4	Build and create management ownership of a viable operational plan for change.	• How to link elements of the strategic plan to the multi-year business plans • How to collaborate with appropriate department and functional managers to cascade the business strategy into multi-year business plans
3C5	Determine and allocate resources, finances and timelines for each activity.	
3C6	Integrate, communicate, and cascade all the strategic planning components into an annual planning and budgeting process across and down the entire organization.	• Knowledge and application of **change management principles** • How to develop and implement a change management program • How to apply principles of change management and integrate them into the design plan
3C7	Leverage, align, and cascade the business strategy into multi-year business plans for departments and major functional areas.	• How to educate middle managers to understand change management and assist them in intervening at various stages in response to change
3C8	Identify desired outcomes for each activity.	• Knowledge and application of **project management principles** • How to apply project management principles, techniques, and tools

Appendix 4

		<ul><li>How to identify the resources and competencies required for each project (e.g., staff, IT, etc.)</li><li>How to facilitate sequencing the priorities</li></ul><ul><li>Knowledge, skills and strategies to **facilitate engagement and buy-in**<ul><li>How to engage finance and IT personnel to prioritize the strategy resource plan</li><li>How to engage appropriate organization design professionals</li><li>How to engage stakeholders toward execution of the strategy plan<ul><li>How to effectively educate and coach middle management in both implementation and execution<ul><li>How to engage middle management in the operational planning and strategy execution to assure buy-in, stay-in for organizational redesign</li><li>How to use different models to facilitate prioritization in a group setting (e.g. Delphi)</li></ul></li></ul></li><li>How to facilitate development of a team and teamwork<ul><li>How to influence project and change management teams</li><li>How to facilitate cross-functional teams to enhance organizational capabilities<ul><li>How to facilitate cross-functional team discussion around portfolio information needs among business units.</li></ul></li></ul></li></ul></li><li>Knowledge and application of **communication tools and strategies**<ul><li>How to develop and select communication strategies and methods to engage employees to understand and embrace the strategic direction</li><li>How to assist middle managers to use relevant communication tools and techniques to communicate plans throughout their business unit.</li></ul></li></ul>
Domain 4 STRATEGY EXECUTION AND EVALUATION		**Knowledge Needed for Domain 4 Competence**
4A	STRATEGY EXECUTION AND TRANSFORMATION	<ul><li>Knowledge and application of how to **govern the execution of the plan and process**<ul><li>How to create a governance plan</li><li>How to design and implement the hierarchical structure for decision-making related to the plan</li><li>How to develop appropriate policies to support the hierarchical structure</li><li>How to train and communicate to middle management to assure consistent procedures are followed</li><li>How to monitor, identify gaps and report on the consistency of decision-making to appropriate parties and recommend corrective action</li></ul></li><li>Knowledge and application of how to **deconstruct the strategic plan into annual plans of work**</li><li>How to identify strategic planning components to integrate into annual planning and budgeting processes</li></ul>
4A1	Facilitate the development of annual and project plans that align with the strategy.	
4A2	Engage with critical internal and external stakeholders in the strategy execution process.	
4A3	Guide development of strategic and transition planning activities throughout the organization.	
4A4	Assist in the development and implementation of a change management program that informs and engages stakeholders.	
4A5	Recommend a portfolio management system to support the process by which strategic plan initiatives are selected, executed, and monitored.	

305

4A6	Serve as the trusted advisor to project teams and change management teams as they implement the strategic initiatives.	• Knowledge and strategies to **create a performance culture**
		  • How to select and apply relevant performance management systems (i.e. Balanced Scorecard)
		  • How to select and apply a variety of models of success metrics (e.g., SMART, OKR, KSMs)
		  • How to identify relevant metrics and measures of success for the strategic plan
		    • How to develop measurable performance metrics and targets tied to the desired outcomes
		  • How to design and use a monitoring function consistent with the level of organizational and business plan complexity
		    • How to assure the strategy plan impacts work at all levels of the organization
		  • How to design performance reporting systems (e.g., dashboard)
		  • How to collect and assess feedback on the strategy implementation and execution
		    • How to capture and assess feedback that could lead to changes to the plans
		    • How to apply lessons learned from the change management evaluation
		    • How to collaborate with appropriate personnel to identify and implement changes required to performance-based systems
		  • How to facilitate a strategy review meeting using performance data
		    • How to prioritize the interventions for corrective action
		      • How to intervene appropriately and course correct to realize performance outcomes
		
		• Knowledge, strategies and tools to **monitor and respond to performance results**
		  • How to analyze performance drivers
		  • How to collect and assess key performance data and trends that reflect on strategy execution relative to the future state and established performance projections
		  • How to forecast the impact to strategy execution based on performance
		  • How to use performance metrics and feedback loops to assess risks to strategy execution
		  • How to conduct regular reviews and validations of strategic decisions and change management process (e.g., double loop learning)
		  • How to design, implement and deploy strategy performance dashboards
		  • How to develop mitigation strategies and tactics for identified gaps
		  • How to apply appropriate interventions given a specific stage in the cycle of change
		
		• Knowledge, strategies and skills to **facilitate group engagement**
		  • How to engage appropriate middle management and gain commitment to the plan
		    • How to facilitate development of performance projections
		  • How to facilitate implementation of an annual review process that drives continuous improvement
		  • How to facilitate solution-seeking to recalibrate processes for improved performance.
		
		• Knowledge of and application of **interpersonal communication skills and use of communication tools**
		  • How to cultivate and sustain a trust relationship

4A7	Assist management in developing and executing an annual implementation and review process that drives continuous improvement.	
4A8	Teach and coach teamwork, change management, and project management skills to support strategy implementation.	
4A9	Anticipate changes that can impact or support the successful execution of the strategy.	
4B	**GOVERNANCE AND DECISION MAKING**	
4B1	Support creation of a governance plan.	
4B2	Guide management to adhere to the established governing structure and decision hierarchy for modifications in their plans.	
4C	**STRATEGIC PERFORMANCE MANAGEMENT**	
4C1	Facilitate management in identifying the performance metrics and targets for strategic initiatives.	
4C2	Design and report strategy performance dashboards and identify information sources.	
4C3	Facilitate strategy review meetings.	
4C4	Support communications to managers and employees about progress being made towards achieving the strategy.	
4C5	Evaluate the KPI data and trends to determine if strategies are on track and identify improvements	
4C6	Evaluate the change management effectiveness.	
		• How to apply relevant communication tools and techniques for various audiences • How to collaborate with appropriate internal personnel, including change agents, to roll out communications enterprise-wide • How to create reporting and communication processes about decisions made regarding the plan and changes to t • How to capture and communicate lessons learned

Appendix 5 – SMP Content Outline and Knowledge Needed for Competent Performance

Domain 1 ENGAGEMENT		
1A	**CULTURE OF STRATEGIC MANAGEMENT AND AGILITY**	**Knowledge Needed for Domain 1 Competence**

1A1	Coach organizational leadership working from a shared vision toward organizational performance-driven alignment and accountability to a strategic plan.	• Knowledge and application of **Strategic Management Philosophy**
		  • Elements of a strategic management function
		  • How to think with a systems perspective
		  • How to apply change management principles that best fits the organization
		  • How to design agile planning and strategy management processes
		  • How to define organizational policy to align strategy across the organization
		  • How to cascade strategy and goals throughout the organization
		  • How to assess organizational capacity and leverage the ecosystem to build that capacity
		  • How to design change structures, processes and culture needed to transform an organization
		  • How to facilitate the role and leverage the importance of executive sponsorship
		  • How to facilitate the role and leverage the importance of internal and external stakeholders
		
		• Knowledge and application of **organizational performance models and how to choose the best fit model**
		  • How to design processes that garner buy-in for strategic change
		  • Planning approaches and options for consideration by the planning team
		  • How to create a culture of accountability and learning
		  • How to assess gaps in leadership capacity
		  • How to assess strategic options in relation to desired outcomes
		
		• Knowledge and application of **communication methods to share knowledge and learning**
		  • How to communicate complex ideas at executive level
		  • How to select communication strategies and methods to align strategy across the organization
		  • How to teach and coach leaders to enhance communication skills
		  • How to document and deliver rationale for strategies assessed, proposed and selected
		  • How to communicate the design of the process at various stages and to the various levels of the organization
		  • How to assess and use fact-based data to drive decisions
		  • How to reinforce executive sponsorship for strategic change among senior management and key stakeholders (e.g., communications, incentive plans)
		
		• Knowledge and application of **interpersonal and group process facilitation skills**
		  • How to demonstrate executive presence and emotional intelligence

1A2	Design processes and drive a culture of strategic management and agility enterprise-wide and at all levels of the organization using a whole system approach.	
1A3	Provide leadership and facilitate organizational capacity-building.	
1A4	Establish and manage a strategic management function to guide the strategic thinking, planning, and implementation processes.	
1A5	Facilitate processes that encourage innovation and identify and agree upon strategic options.	
1A6	Model and guide effective sourcing, application, and sharing of knowledge and learning enterprise-wide.	
1A7	Build necessary relationships across country cultures, languages and geography with awareness and sensitivity.	
1B	**PLANNING TEAM EXPECTATIONS**	
1B1	Establish a top management planning team process led by the chief executive that involves key internal and external stakeholders.	
1B2	Orient assembled top management planning team to planning process.	
1B3	Tailor the planning process to the needs of the organization.	
1B4	Support executive sponsorship efforts among senior management and key stakeholders to gain their advocacy for strategic change.	
1B5	Mentor and coach executive sponsors on strategic planning and management processes.	

1B6	Advise leaders on how to involve and communicate the value of change to staff to minimize resistance.	• How to create credibility at executive level
		• How to build relationships at executive level
		• How to coach executives
		• How to facilitate group process
		• How to listen and synthesize input into the process design
		• How to bring a conversation to resolution
		• How to inject innovative thought into solution-seeking
		• How to engage staff at various levels to minimize resistance
		• When and how to resolve conflicts among top management
		
		• Knowledge and application of **multi-cultural inclusion**
		  • How to be effective in a multi-cultural environment
		  • How to be cross-culturally competent
		  • How to design changes in process required by inclusion of multi-cultural representation
		  • How to value and blend multi-cultural input into a final result
		  • How to select the members for an effective planning team

Domain 2	**STRATEGY FORMULATION**	
2A SCAN	**INTERNAL & EXTERNAL ENVIRONMENTAL**	**Knowledge Needed for Domain 2 Competence**

2A1	Organize systematic trend-spotting in sectors external to the organization and throughout the organization.	• Knowledge and application of **various approaches to external and internal environmental scanning**
		  • How to design consistent trend-spotting processes
		  • How to apply appropriate categorizations for change drivers (e.g., PESTEL, STEEP)
		  • How to identify potential synergistic impacts in environmental developments
		  • How to develop and implement an effective monitoring process for strategic issues (e.g., external risk threats and enterprise opportunities)
		  • How to recognize patterns and interdependencies in environmental developments
		  • How to recognize and assess future trends in change drivers and evaluate relevance to the organizational strategy
		  • How to make sense of the environmental data and its impact on the organization
		  • How to identify opportunities and assess value of customer segments and elements of the product portfolio
		  • How to use tools such as personas to inform strategic direction
		  • How to match customers with product portfolio
		  • How to use scenario planning to assess strategic options
		  • How to assess organizational capacity for change
		  • How to identify the core competencies of the organization
		  • How to apply various approaches to SWOT analysis
		  • How to select and implement the appropriate SWOT approach for the organization
		  • How to conduct a SWOT analysis of organization-wide processes, structures and culture in light of the new strategies

2A2	Gather, analyze, and interpret environmental trends.	
2A3	Monitor and assess early indicators of external trends in change drivers that could lead to disruption of the organization.	
2A4	Identify the key environmental indicators at play.	
2A5	Synthesize internal and external environmental data as appropriate to the context of the organization.	
2A6	Identify future customers/clients and the likely alignment with currently relevant products and services.	
2A7	Analyze both the current and the future environment and create a range of scenarios which are the most likely and relevant.	
2A8	Evaluate readiness or capacity for change and ensure recommended changes are informed by findings.	

Appendix 5

2A9	Communicate data, both written and orally, to create actionable understanding.	• Knowledge and application of **various theories around strategy design** (e.g., scenario planning, Porter's Five Forces, etc.) and how to select the most appropriate for the organization
		   • How to craft clear and concise mission and vision statements
		   • How to communicate the differences between mission, vision and purpose
		   • How to identify relevant business model options and how to select the appropriate one for the organization
		   • How to create compelling value proposition for the customers of the organization
		   • How to create strategic positioning and competitive advantage
		   • How to leverage creativity and innovation to enhance customer value
		
		• Knowledge and application of **communication tools and skills**
		   • How to identify and appropriately attune to key audiences (e.g., their dynamics, culture, etc.)
		   • How to identify and appropriately attune key audiences (e.g., their dynamics, culture, etc.) to the strategy
		   • How to present the strategies that result in competitive differentiation effectively and confidently to senior management while facilitating discussion and decision-making
		   • How to get buy-in organization-wide
		   • How to design different types of feedback loops (e.g., experiential data) and how to determine which to use
		   • How to conduct regular reviews and validations of strategic decisions (e.g., double loop learning)
		   • How to use communication tools available, select and use the appropriate tool
		   • How to present data effectively and persuasively to various audiences using various formats (e.g., virtual, face to face and written reports)
		
		• Knowledge and application of **group facilitation skills**
		   • How to facilitate identification and selection of desired outcomes
		   • How to facilitate identification and selection of core strategies and key results
		   • How to engage others in creating options
		   • How to facilitate identification and selection of performance metrics (e.g., key success measures and organization key results)
		   • When and how to apply conflict resolution to reach consensus

2B	**STRATEGY DESIGN AND FORMULATION**	
2B1	Create alternative strategic directions that create value for stakeholders and a competitive differentiation for the organization.	
2B2	Articulate to senior management the importance of the organization's distinctive core competencies and the strategies that result in competitive differentiation.	
2B3	Facilitate the crafting of vision and mission statements that clearly articulate the organization's purpose.	
2B4	Assist senior management with the identification of business models that drive value for stakeholders and achieve the expected performance outcomes.	
2B5	Facilitate leadership in the identification and selection of the organization's objectives, core strategies, and key results.	
2B6	Anticipate changes that can impact or support the successful execution of the strategy.	
2B7	Assess the potential impact of competitor activities, macro changes and regulatory policies on strategic direction.	
2B8	Assess and advise on options to enhance value proposition and to improve return on investment.	
2B9	Develop appropriate feedback loops to validate strategy options.	
Domain 3 PREPARATION FOR STRATEGY INTEGRATION		**Knowledge Needed for Domain 3 Competence**
3A	**ALIGNMENT OF THE ORGANIZATION DESIGN WITH STRATEGY**	• Knowledge and application of **different approaches to organizational design** (e.g., human centered design, LEAN thinking, etc.)

Strategy in the 21st Century, Second Edition

3A1	Educate senior management on organization design/ redesign principles and its relationship to the success of strategy execution and management.	
3A2	Select the organization design framework in consultation with management and organization design professionals.	
3A3	Design plan for implementation, including how organization structure should be modified enterprise-wide.	
3A4	Advocate for and coach senior management on change management plan for organizational design effort.	
3A5	Promote ethical consideration and communicate with employees on the minimum nonnegotiable behaviors through the organization code of conduct.	
3A6	Analyze the current and required corporate cultural components and identify the core values that support or hinder the strategy execution.	
3A7	Assemble change leadership team(s) to monitor and assure movement in strategy development and execution	
3B	**ALIGNMENT OF OPERATIONS WITH STRATEGY**	
3B1	Assess internal organizational cross-functional capabilities to close the gap between the current and desired state.	
3B2	Facilitate analysis of the organization's functional components to identify impacts of and risks to implementation of the strategic plan.	
3B3	Identify and sequence the transformation projects that must be executed to improve the organization's ability to execute its strategy.	
3B4	Create transformation plan(s).	
3C	**OPERATIONAL PLANNING FOR IMPLEMENTATION**	

- How to identify relevant organization design frameworks available and how to select the appropriate one for the organization
- How to apply form follows function to redesign the structure of the organization to accommodate the strategies chosen
- How to align the overall work environment to support performance
- How to document the framework
- Knowledge and application of **various modes of external and internal environmental scanning**
  - How to use various SWOT analysis approaches and select those appropriate for the organization
  - How to facilitate a SWOT analysis of functional components in light of the new strategies
  - How to develop thresholds of risk appetite and tolerance
  - How to analyze the values of the current culture and assess gaps towards the desired state
  - How to identify the activities and tasks required to move from current to future state
  - How to map the shift from the current organization chart and corporate cultural components and what it needs to be
- Knowledge and application of **different functional levels of planning**
  - Why and how to create a business plan
    - How to link elements of the strategic plan and the sequenced priorities into financial planning
    - How to select the appropriate frameworks and structure for the business plan
  - How to identify the interdependencies of the transformation projects and how to properly sequence them
  - How to integrate interdependencies with organizational capacity to change
  - How to create a tactical plan for implementation and execution
    - How to synthesize and document tactical plans into a coordinated transformation plan that addresses change processes, structure and culture
    - How to facilitate development of the strategic change agenda, common framework and language across various levels of the organization
  - How to create a communications plan to support the development of the desired culture throughout the organization
    - How to develop a monitoring function consistent with the level of organizational and business plan complexity
    - How to develop appropriate communication and reporting mechanisms to ensure consistent behavior organization-wide
    - How to identify relevant communication strategies that recognize predictable responses to change and select those appropriate for the organization

Appendix 5

3C1	Facilitate the development of an implementation plan that supports the organization's strategies.	• Knowledge and application of **change management principles**
		  • How to apply principles of change management and integrate them into the design plan
		  • How to help senior management to understand change management and assist them in intervening at various stages in response to change

3C2	Identify specific activities and resources needed to realize the organization's strategies.	

3C3	Determine and assist senior management in assigning and allocating resources, finances, timelines, and desired outcomes for each activity.	• Knowledge and application of **project management principles**
		  • How to utilize project management principles, techniques, and tools
		  • How to allocate resources
		  • How to create a budget to support the organization's strategy
		  • How to identify the resources and competencies required (e.g., staff, IT, etc.)
		  • How to facilitate sequencing the priorities

3C4	Foster senior management ownership of a viable operational plan for change.	
3C5	Use specific frameworks and structures to build and evaluate the multi-year business plan and the links between the corporate strategic plan.	

3C6	Monitor the selection, and execution of strategic plan initiatives and projects, communicating issues and risks to senior management.	• **Facilitating Group Engagement and Buy-In**
		  • How to effectively educate and coach senior management in both implementation and execution
		  • How to facilitate senior management to establish core values
		  • How to engage senior management in the operational planning and strategy execution to assure buy-in, stay-in and change leadership
		  • How to engage appropriate organization design professionals
		  • How to create and facilitate cross-functional teams to enhance organizational capabilities
		  • How to create, communicate expectations, facilitate the initial meetings of and support a change leadership team

3C7	Develop an enterprise-wide communication plan to disseminate information about strategy and implementation.	
	Domain 4 STRATEGY EXECUTION AND EVALUATION	**Knowledge Needed for Domain 4 Competence**

4A	**STRATEGY EXECUTION AND TRANSFORMATION**	• Knowledge and application of how to **govern the execution of the plan and process**
		  • How to create a governance plan
		  • How to design and implement the hierarchical structure for decision-making related to the plan
		  • How to assign roles for decision-making within the structure
		  • How to develop appropriate policies to support the hierarchical structure
		  • How to train and communicate to assure consistent procedures are followed
		  • How to develop an appropriate enforcement process for ethical decision-making
		  • How to enforce the consistency of decision-making

4A1	Facilitate the development of annual and project plans that align with the strategy.	
4A2	Educate and coach senior leadership on change management.	
4A3	Cultivate executive sponsorship of senior management to lead and support the strategic change.	
4A4	Collaborate on executive communications that facilitate a high-performance culture.	• How to deconstruct the strategic plan into annual plans of work
4A5	Lead the strategy management function to execute the strategy implementation process.	• Knowledge and Strategies to **create a Performance Culture**

4A6	Serve as the trusted advisor to senior management as the strategy is executed.	<ul><li>How to identify and use relevant performance management systems (i.e. Balanced Scorecard)</li><li>How to apply a variety of models of success metrics (e.g., SMART, OKR, KSMs)</li><li>How to select strategic values to drive a culture of high performance</li><li>How to collaborate and communicate to define a culture of high performance</li><li>How to define measures of success for the strategic plan<ul><li>How to develop measurable performance metrics and targets tied to the desired outcomes</li></ul></li><li>How to design performance reporting systems (e.g., dashboard)<ul><li>How to design and use a monitoring function consistent with the level of organizational and business plan complexity</li><li>How to collect and assess feedback on the strategy implementation and execution</li></ul></li><li>How to work the strategy plan at all levels of the organization</li><li>How to assess efficiency and effectiveness in systems, processes and human performance<ul><li>How to evaluate effectiveness of change leadership team and decision-making hierarchy</li></ul></li><li>How to facilitate the development of strategy evaluation criteria<ul><li>How to capture and assess feedback that could lead to changes to the plans</li></ul></li><li>How to collaborate with appropriate personnel to identify and implement changes required to performance-based systems<ul><li>How to link incentives to desired strategic outcomes and values</li><li>How to identify and enforce incentives and consequences of non-compliance with the defined values</li></ul></li><li>How to measure organizational health<ul><li>How to collect and assess information on organizational health to identify required corrective action</li></ul></li><li>How to prioritize the interventions for corrective action<ul><li>How to intervene appropriately to realize performance outcomes</li><li>How to intervene and course correct</li></ul></li></ul><ul><li>**Facilitating Group Engagement**<ul><li>How to engage appropriate senior management and gain commitment to the plan</li><li>How to facilitate consensus among senior management</li><li>How to persuade senior management to take appropriate action</li></ul></li><li>Knowledge of and Application of **Communication Skills and Use of Communication Tools**<ul><li>How to cultivate and sustain a trust relationship</li><li>How to apply relevant communication tools and techniques for various audiences<ul><li>How to use appropriate tools to map and communicate transformation projects</li><li>How to create reporting and communication processes about decisions made regarding the plan and changes to it</li></ul></li></ul></li></ul>
4A7	Facilitate development of performance-based systems that motivate and incentivize people to change.	
4B	**GOVERNANCE AND DECISION MAKING**	
4B1	Identify with senior management the strategy evaluation criteria, steps, and procedures for decision-making.	
4B2	Create a governance plan for decision-making regarding strategic plan execution.	
4B3	Communicate the governance structure and decision hierarchy modifications in their plans.	
4B4	Assess performance of current governance structures and decision hierarchy.	
4C	**STRATEGIC PERFORMANCE MANAGEMENT**	
4C1	Facilitate senior management in identifying the performance metrics and targets for strategic objectives.	
4C2	Oversee the operation of a monitoring and accountability process to track implementation of the change.	
4C3	Recommend corrective action based on opportunities, issues, risks and lessons learned affecting strategy implementation and execution.	
4C4	Measure and monitor organizational health and take corrective actions.	
		<ul><li>How to collect and assess feedback on the governance structure</li><li>How to capture and communicate lessons learned</li><li>How to educate on the differentiation between implementation planning and execution</li><li>How to create a communication plan to focus management on plan progress and challenges<ul><li>How to communicate bad news to senior management</li><li>How to communicate plan progress to senior management</li><li>How to communicate plan progress enterprise-wide</li></ul></li><li>How to collaborate with appropriate internal personnel, including change agents, to roll out communications enterprise-wide</li></ul>

Appendix 6 – Detailed Outline of IASP BOK 3.0

CHAPTER 1 INTRODUCTION
- 1.1. Objective of the ASP Body of Knowledge 3.0
- 1.2. Design Principles
- 1.3. Defining Strategy and Strategy Management
- 1.4. The Strategy System Activity Groups
- 1.5. Structure of the BOK
- 1.6. Chapter References

CHAPTER 2 FORMULATE STRATEGY
- 2.1. Key Concepts and Definitions
  - 2.1.1. Mission
  - 2.1.2. Vision
  - 2.1.3. Values
  - 2.1.4. Stakeholder Value Propositions
  - 2.1.5. Regulations/Policies/Guidelines
  - 2.1.6. Goal
  - 2.1.7. Strategic Objective
  - 2.1.8. Target
  - 2.1.9. Measure
  - 2.1.10. Key Performance Indicator
  - 2.1.11. Key Drivers of Success
  - 2.1.12. Strategic Initiative
  - 2.1.13. Strategic Planning
- 2.2. Key Activities
  - 2.2.1. Conduct External Environmental Scan
  - 2.2.2. Conduct Internal Environmental Scan
  - 2.2.3. Develop Shared Vision
  - 2.2.4. Develop Strategy Alternatives
  - 2.2.5. Select Strategy
  - 2.2.6. Complete Strategic Plan
- 2.3. Tools
  - 2.3.1. Scenario Planning
  - 2.3.2. Strategic foresight)
  - 2.3.3. Futures Research
  - 2.3.4. PESTEL/STEEPLE
  - 2.3.5. Porter's Five Forces
  - 2.3.6. Porter's Generic Strategies
  - 2.3.7. Industry Mapping
  - 2.3.8. Zoom-Out/Zoom-In
  - 2.3.9. Market Assessment
  - 2.3.10. Customer Assessment – Current and Potential
  - 2.3.11. Surveys
  - 2.3.12. SWOT
  - 2.3.13. Seven S
  - 2.3.14. Benchmarking
  - 2.3.15. AT Kearney's Consolidation-Endgame Curve
  - 2.3.16. McKinsey's Nine-Box Matrix

2.3.17. Malcolm Baldridge Quality Program
2.3.18. Key Drivers Analysis
2.3.19. Interviews
2.3.20. Focus Groups
2.3.21. Blue Ocean Strategy
2.3.22. Collins' Hedgehog Concept
2.3.23. Heat Mapping
2.3.24. Value Chain Analysis
2.3.25. Core Competency Analysis
2.3.26. Work Environment Analysis
2.3.27. Core Operating Analysis
2.3.28. Location and Resource Analysis
2.3.29. Valuable Rare Inimitable and Non-Substituable
2.3.30. Boston Consulting Group's Growth Share Matrix
2.3.31. Portfolio Analysis
2.3.32. Programs and Services Assessment
2.3.33. Customer Experience Curve
2.3.34. Dynamic Capabilities
2.3.35. Product Lifecycle Assessment
2.3.36. Customer Adoption Curve
2.3.37. Marketing Mix
2.3.38. Nominal Group Technique
2.3.39. Voting
2.3.40. DeBono's Six Thinking Hats
2.3.41. Organic Growth Versus Acquisition Growth
2.3.42. Boston Consulting Group Business Innovation Model
2.3.43. Business Model Canvas
2.3.44. Strategy Canvas
2.3.45. Ansoff's Grid
2.3.46. Miles and Snow's Typology
2.3.47. Prioritization
2.3.48. Balance Scorecard and Strategy Maps
2.3.49. Strategic Gap Analysis
2.3.50. Objectives and Key Results
2.3.51. Time-Phased Strategies

CHAPTER 3 TRANSFORM ORGANIZATION
3.1. Key Concepts and Definitions
    3.1.1. Strategic Alignment and Accountability
    3.1.2. Organizational Transformation
    3.1.3. Organizational Design and Development
    3.1.4. Capabilities Development
3.2. Key Activities
    3.2.1. Design the Target Enterprise Architecture
    3.2.2. Develop the Transformation Plan
    3.2.3. Plan and Execute Transformation Projects
3.3. Tools
    3.3.1. Workforce Planning
    3.3.2. Prioritization
    3.3.3. Contingency Planning

Appendix 6

      3.3.4. Execution Capability Profile
      3.3.5. Gantt Chart
      3.3.6. Critical Path Method
      3.3.7. Program Evaluation and Review Technique
      3.3.8. Readiness Assessment
      3.3.9. Strategic Operating Plan
      3.3.10. Design Thinking
      3.3.11. Agile

CHAPTER 4 EXECUTE STRATEGY
  4.1. Key Concepts and Definitions
      4.1.1. Execution Challenges
      4.1.2. Operations/Value Chain Activities
      4.1.3. Operational Excellence and Continuous Improvement
  4.2. Key Activities
  4.3. Tools
      4.3.1. Business Process Management
      4.3.2. Lean
      4.3.3. Six Sigma
      4.3.4. Quality Management
      4.3.5. Kaizen
      4.3.6. Kanban
      4.3.7. Theory of Constraint
      4.3.8. Business Intelligence
      4.3.9. Data Analytics
      4.3.10. Artificial Intelligence
      4.3.11. Machine Learning
      4.3.12. Geospatial Analysis

CHAPTER 5 ENGAGE STAKEHOLDERS
  5.1. Key Concepts and Definitions
      5.1.1. Leadership
      5.1.2. Change Management
      5.1.3. Stakeholder Management
      5.1.4. Communication
      5.1.5. Rewards and Recognition
      5.1.6. Culture
      5.1.7. Facilitation
      5.1.8. Psychological Safety
      5.1.9. Teamwork/Collaboration
  5.2. Key Activities
      5.2.1. Secure Senior Leadership Support
      5.2.2. Organize Strategy Management Teams
      5.2.3. Develop Communication and Stakeholder Engagement Plans
      5.2.4. Engage Stakeholders
  5.3. Tools
      5.3.1. Kurt Lewin's Unfreeze/Change/Re-Freeze
      5.3.2. Emotional Cycle of Change
      5.3.3. Kubler-Ross Model
      5.3.4. Change Acceptance Curve

        5.3.5. Hersey-Blanchard Situational Leadership Model
        5.3.6. Management by Wandering Around
        5.3.7. McKinsey's Influence Model
        5.3.8. Kotter's 8-Step Change Model
        5.3.9. Prosci's ADKAR Model
        5.3.10. Stakeholder Mapping
        5.3.11. Communications Planning
        5.3.12. Cultural Assessment
        5.3.13. Collaboration Technologies

CHAPTER 6 GOVERN STRATEGY
    6.1. Key Concepts and Definitions
        6.1.1. Decision Making
        6.1.2. Governance
        6.1.3. Capital Planning
        6.1.4. Budgeting
        6.1.5. Performance Management
        6.1.6. Reporting
        6.1.7. Diversity, Equity, and Inclusion
        6.1.8. Committees
    6.2. Key Activities
        6.2.1. Govern the Formulation of the Strategy
        6.2.2. Govern the Organizational Transformation
        6.2.3. Govern the Execution of the Strategy
        6.2.4. Design, Implement and Update the Governance Operating Model
    6.3. Tools
        6.3.1. Cascading Objectives
        6.3.2. Strategy Management Calendar
        6.3.3. Balanced Scorecard

Appendix 7 – The Art of War, by Sun Tzu (Translated by Lionel Giles)

Around 2,300 years ago, Sun Tzu is credited for having written *The Art of War*, a compilation of essays that remains, to this day, profound wisdom on the conduct of war. In summary, there are several important themes developed by Sun Tzu we can effectively apply to strategy challenges in business and organizational life today.

Environmental Scan:

1. **Strategic Planning and Rational Analysis**
   - Planning based on rational analysis of the best quality information available.
2. **Importance of Information and Related Processing Capability**
   - Secure the best information available. Protect the sources and processing capabilities from compromise.
3. **Importance of Knowledge, Wisdom and Understanding**
   - A theme that is imbedded in virtually every other theme, especially in regard to knowing self and opposition.
4. **Study the Past and Analyze Current Conditions to Create an "Edge"**
   - Leads to knowledge, which, if properly focused, can lead to success.
   - Strive to become the superior force in more than mere numbers. This is achieved through focused knowledge and experience, which, in turn, is gained by studying and observing situations, conditions, people, and events; remembering what was observed; comparing the observations to one another as well as to contemporary circumstances; and by disciplined application of the results of the observations in the pursuit of strategic objectives.
   - Know yourself, your opposition, and the environment within which interaction will occur.

Strategy:

5. **Staying Focused on Strategic Objectives**
   - Keep attention to all resources and related action focused on achieving strategic objectives as promptly as possible. Avoid becoming distracted by the nuances and intricacies of implementing complex strategies and tactics.
6. **Suitability of Strategies and Tactics to Situation**
   - Match the suitability of strategies and tactics to the market's phase, section, pattern, and volatility.
7. **Inherent Advantages and Disadvantages**
   - Understand and guard against the inherent disadvantage in every advantageous situation. Likewise, remain alert and capitalize on advantages that arise in distressed situations.
8. **Opportunistic Flexibility in Adapting Strategies and Tactics to Situation**
   - Capitalize on emerging opportunities created by changing market conditions. Employ a well thought out trading plan and remain flexible in adapting tactics to ever-changing market conditions within the context of each pre-determined strategy.

Self:

9. **Ethical Conduct**
   - Be moral and ethical; let it guide your thinking, decision-making and actions.
10. **Rely on Your Own Preparation**
    - Rely on your own preparations. Do not hope for success based on the opposition not preparing.
11. **Competent Management**
    - Develop a balanced management skill set to enable prudent resource utilization.
12. **Disciplined Emotions**
    - Minimize emotional influences (hope, fear, greed).

Organization / Management:

13. **Disciplined Organization and Financial Management**
    - Discipline, efficient, and effective organization, and utilization of all resources (people, plans, tools, capital), in the capacity to which they are best suited, in all situations, is critical to success.
    - Ensure appropriate financing and provisioning of all activities (prior to and during).
14. **Clear Communication**
    - Ensure clear communication in all aspects of the development, testing, and implementation of strategies and tactics.
15. **Deception and "Shaping"**
    - Practice deception in plans, strategy, and tactics (and its corollary) when facing adversaries.

Warnings:

16. **Avoidance of Being Deceived and "Shaped"**
    - Take precautionary steps to avoid being deceived by the opposition.
17. **Reward, Replenish and Invest in Support Structure**
    - Be sure to allocate appropriate parts of the profits of successful strategies to all resources employed in the portfolio management and risk management activity.
18. **Patience, Positioning, and Timing**
    - Develop patience and discipline in positioning and timing the use of all resources in adapting to ever-changing circumstances.
19. **Avoidance of Catastrophic Loss**
    - Avoid catastrophic mistakes by promptly adapting strategies and tactics to current circumstances, thereby keeping the consequences of mistakes small and manageable.
20. **Preservation and Protection of Resources**
    - At all times seek to keep all resources in profitable and advantageous positions. Likewise, quickly liquidate unprofitable positions and minimize exposure to situations with inordinate risk to uncertain market movements.

Appendix 8 – Nominal Group Technique

Phase II: Environmental Assessment
The Nominal Group Technique

How to use this template

Why use it? – To consolidate, clarify and prioritize the Opportunities, Threats, Strengths and Weaknesses.

When to use it? – Anytime there is a need to prioritize Opportunities, Threats, Strengths and Weaknesses.

Instructions: This is highly structured process involves full participation by all team members. It is a non-threatening four step process that provides anonymity for individuals while ensuring broad based collection of opinion and analysis of opportunities, threats, strengths and weaknesses. Follow the four steps described below to complete a paper and pencil SWOT ranking process. *If anonymity is of high value to a team, modify the process so that team members provide their input via online (or some other confidential method).* Meet as a leadership team to review the findings, discuss the implications and draw preliminary conclusions.

STEP 1: SILENT GENERATION OF IDEAS

Each person silently thinks about the Opportunities, Threats, Strengths and Weaknesses and writes his/her thoughts on a blank sheet of paper. These are usually short written phrases. Each area (such as Strengths) is done separately. Everyone works alone silently during this step. (Another option is to have the team members fill out the worksheets prior to the meeting and then bring the sheets with them to the meeting.)

STEP 2: ROUND ROBIN REPORTING OF IDEAS

Next begin the round robin reporting of ideas using individuals' notes made in Step 1. Start with a volunteer, ask for <u>one</u> Opportunity from the individual's list and record it on the flip chart. Ask the next person for <u>one</u> Opportunity from his/her list and add it to the flip chart.

Continue with this process by asking each person to contribute <u>one</u> Opportunity until everyone has made a contribution. A person can choose to pass if they want to in this first round but eventually everyone is encouraged to make some contribution.

The round robin process of collecting Opportunities and recording them on the flip chart continues as long as people have new Opportunities to contribute. No critical discussion of the Opportunities is done during this step. When all of the Opportunities are recorded label each one with a number or a letter...this will help in Step 4. Repeat the same round robin process for Threats, Strengths and Weaknesses.

STEP 3: DISCUSSION: LOOKING FOR CLARIFICATION AND DUPLICATION

Now open up the discussion for the purpose of clarifying any of the ideas that were contributed. Team members are encouraged to ask each other the meaning of words and phrases that were recorded on the flip chart. Also, at this point combine any ideas that are basically duplicates on any given list, and categorize the remaining items as necessary.

The purpose of this step is to provide individuals the opportunity to give fuller explanations of their ideas. And secondly to combine any duplicate ideas so as not to split the ranking points. Make sure that ideas are not evaluated and do not allow arguments to develop.

Strategy in the 21st Century, Second Edition

Phase II: Environmental Assessment
The Nominal Group Technique

STEP 4: RANKING OF OPPORTUNITIES, THREATS, STRENGTHS AND WEAKNESSES

Give each team member a set of OTSW priority sheets - one for Opportunities, one for Threats, one for Strengths and one for Weaknesses. Each person is to write on the appropriate sheet the number (or letter) of the Opportunities, Threats, Strengths and Weaknesses he/she believes most important or highest priority.

For example: On the Opportunity priority sheet each person will write the number (or letter) of the Opportunity he/she feels is of highest priority in the "1st priority" box, the second highest in the "2nd priority" box, the third highest in the "3rd priority box", etc. down to the fifth priority.

Collect all of the priority sheets and tally the rankings on a master sheet. Add up the score for each item. The items with the highest scores can be considered *preliminarily*, the highest priority. There are usually 5-6 items that float to the top as the highest priorities for each of the four areas – Opportunities, Threats, Strengths and Weaknesses. Write the number or letter of the highest priorities at the bottom of each tally sheet.

Note: As you can see in the instructions above, we recommend altering the traditional order of "SWOT" analysis to be an "OTSW" analysis (e.g. Opportunities, Threats, Strengths, and Weaknesses).

Implications:

Conclusions:

Appendix 8

Phase II: Environmental Assessment
The Nominal Group Technique

OPPORTUNITIES Review list of <u>opportunities</u> and select 5 opportunities that you feel are highest priority. Write the number of each one in the appropriate box. Example: The most important opportunity goes in the 1st priority box; second most important goes in 2nd priority box; etc. Identify each opportunity by the number or letter listed on the flip chart.	**1st priority** **5 points** Opportunity
2nd priority **4 points** Opportunity	**3rd priority** **3 points** Opportunity
4th priority **2 points** Opportunity	**5th priority** **1 point** Opportunity

Strategy in the 21st Century, Second Edition

Phase II: Environmental Assessment
The Nominal Group Technique

THREATS Review list of <u>threats</u> and select 5 threats that you feel are highest priority. Write the number of each one in the appropriate box. Example: The most important threat goes in the 1st priority box; second most important goes in 2nd priority box; etc. Identify each threat by the number listed on the flip chart.	**1st priority** **5 points** Threats
2nd priority **4 points** Threats	**3rd priority** **3 points** Threats
4th priority **2 points** Threats	**5th priority** **1 point** Threats

Appendix 8

Phase II: Environmental Assessment
The Nominal Group Technique

STRENGTHS Review list of <u>strengths</u> and select 5 strengths that you feel are highest priority. Write the number or letter of each one in the appropriate box. Example: The most important strength goes in the 1st priority box; second most important goes in 2nd priority box; etc. Identify each strength by the number or letter listed on the flip chart.	**1st priority** **5 points** Strength
2nd priority **4 points** Strength	**3rd priority** **3 points** Strength
4th priority **2 points** Strength	**5th priority** **1 point** Strength

Strategy in the 21st Century, Second Edition

Phase II: Environmental Assessment
The Nominal Group Technique

WEAKNESSES Review list of <u>weaknesses</u> and select 5 weaknesses that you feel are highest priority. Write the number of each one in the appropriate box. Example: The most important weakness goes in the 1st priority box; second most important goes in 2nd priority box; etc. Identify each weakness by the number or letter listed on the flip chart.	**1st priority**　　　　**5 points** Weakness
2nd priority　　　　**4 points** Weakness	**3rd priority**　　　　**3 points** Weakness
4th priority　　　　**2 points** Weakness	**5th priority**　　　　**1 point** Weakness

Appendix 8

Phase II: Environmental Assessment
The Nominal Group Technique

Opportunities [Priorities]

1.	16.
2.	17.
3.	18.
4.	19.
5.	20.
6.	21.
7.	22.
8.	23.
9.	24.
10.	25.
11.	26.
12.	27.
13.	28.
14.	29.
15.	30.
1st 2nd 3rd 4th 5th	

Phase II: Environmental Assessment
The Nominal Group Technique

Threats [Priorities]

1.	16.
2.	17.
3.	18.
4.	19.
5.	20.
6.	21.
7.	22.
8.	23.
9.	24.
10.	25.
11.	26.
12.	27.
13.	28.
14.	29.
15.	30.

1st   2nd   3rd   4th   5th

Appendix 8

Phase II: Environmental Assessment
The Nominal Group Technique

Strengths [Priorities]

1.	16.
2.	17.
3.	18.
4.	19.
5.	20.
6.	21.
7.	22.
8.	23.
9.	24.
10.	25.
11.	26.
12.	27.
13.	28.
14.	29.
15.	30.

1st   **2**nd   **3**rd   **4**th   **5**th

Strategy in the 21st Century, Second Edition

Phase II: Environmental Assessment
The Nominal Group Technique

Weaknesses [Priorities]

1.	16.
2.	17.
3.	18.
4.	19.
5.	20.
6.	21.
7.	22.
8.	23.
9.	24.
10.	25.
11.	26.
12.	27.
13.	28.
14.	29.
15.	30.
1st **2nd** **3rd** **4th** **5th**	

Phase II: Environmental Assessment
The Nominal Group Technique

Appendix 8

OTSW PRIORITIES

<u>Five</u> top ranked priorities: Opportunities, Threats, Strengths and Weaknesses

OPPORTUNITIES	THREATS
1ST	1ST
2ND	2ND
3RD	3RD
4TH	4TH
5TH	5TH

STRENGTHS	WEAKNESSES
1ST	1ST
2ND	2ND
3RD	3RD
4TH	4TH
5TH	5TH

Appendix 9 – Differentiating Your Customer Value Proposition

Strategy in the 21st Century, Second Edition

STRATEGICALLY ESSENTIAL BUT FRUSTRATINGLY ELUSIVE

Differentiating your customer value proposition

CREDERA

CREDERA.COM

Appendix 9

Contents

Introduction	2
PART 1: The importance of CVP and CPP	3
PART 2: Credera's approach to CVP and CPP	4
PART 3: Understanding the threat of disruption	10
PART 4: A real world case study: Stripe	11
The path to CVP and CPP success	13

Introduction

As disruptive forces rapidly transform today's business landscape, organizations face the daunting task of crafting and refining robust strategies for growth, transformation, and competitive advantage.

The backbone of any such strategy is a clear understanding of one's customer value proposition (CVP) and competitive positioning profile (CPP)—critical elements that define how a business leverages its capabilities to connect with its customers and differentiate from its competition. And yet, too few organizations dedicate the requisite time and effort to defining their CVP, using it to shape their strategy, and aligning their enterprise to it.

Credera's proprietary approach to CVP and CPP is informed by strategy consulting engagements with companies ranging in size from regional trailblazers to S&P 100 global leaders.

Read on and explore our approach to helping businesses navigate these foundational aspects of strategic planning.

Strategy in the 21st Century, Second Edition

PART 1

The importance of CVP and CPP

Most of Credera's strategy engagements focus on revenue growth through some combination of transformation, alignment, and execution. No matter the weightings among these factors, an analysis of customers, competitors, and capabilities always plays a central role. Failing to strategize with these three Cs in mind risks misalignment, misdirection, suboptimal outcomes, and exhausted teams.

This whitepaper will address how building strategy around an informed CVP and thoughtful CPP contributes to a clear North Star that supports enterprise capability alignment, enables effective execution, and leads to sustainable growth and competitive advantage.

> " Building strategy around an informed CVP and thoughtful CPP contributes to a clear North Star…

Appendix 9

Credera's approach to CVP and CPP

We understand that each company is unique, so we meet our clients where they are and help them move forward incrementally to define or refine their CVP and incorporate it into their strategic planning, the resulting strategic initiatives, and organizational design. Our CVP engagements are informed by external analyses such as market trends, competitor analysis, and customer insights (what do customers need and want, and what is the customer's perception of the company's current value proposition?).

It is important to note that whether intentional or not, every company presents a CVP to customers via each decision it makes around its products and services, its customer experience, and its brand promise. We help clients be intentional and aligned around these critical strategic decisions.

We work with clients in this three step approach to defining their CVP.

1. Start with positioning

Leveraging analysis, we begin by engaging senior leadership teams in workshops to elicit their diverse and knowledgeable perspectives as they purposefully define their CVP and decide how to position their company and its products and services compared to its competitors and their products and services.

Strategy in the 21st Century, Second Edition

> ❝ Each company is unique, so we meet our clients where they are and help them define or refine their CVP.

We create visuals of the insights and outcomes of these sometimes-difficult conversations, and we've found the exercise helpful in navigating complex desicion-making and agreement.

Some companies will define a universal CVP that can then be expanded upon for each line of business, regional market, or specific product or service lines. More often, companies approach CVP by customer segment—a customer group based on differing characteristics—such that a unique CVP will be needed to address each segment. In our experience, the number of customer segments used for marketing (in which messaging and channels are much more specific and targeted) is a good starting place for CVP segmentation, but the segments can often be broken into smaller groupings where CVP elements apply equally to more than one segment.

As an illustrative example of CVP by customer segment, consider the types of customers a fast-food restaurant desires to serve and the potential segmentation of those customers based on their differing needs and expectations. Example segments might include families with young children, teenagers, business customers (lunch break, commuters), and travelers.

Appendix 9

We consider the value perspective of a customer segment across the elements of product/service (function, quality, relevance, price), relationship (customer experience), and brand (image). In other words, how does the customer in the segment perceive value across each element, and what value does the company intend and desire to present to the market?

We further guide the analysis and discussion by determining what is basic (i.e., table stakes) that any customer would expect from a similar product/service versus what would truly differentiate this offering from competitors. We challenge the team further by ideating on attributes that inspire or emotionally engage the customer segment and generate loyalty. The intent is not to fill out every box in the model but to make intentional choices.

2. Explore enterprise capabilities and execution

Once senior leaders have aligned around the most important CVP attributes for a customer segment, we turn our attention to the enterprise capabilities and execution, assessing each attribute to determine if any are at risk, if any merit investment consideration, or if any should be considered as aspirational for future focus. This framework provides a Now/Next/Future approach for prioritization.

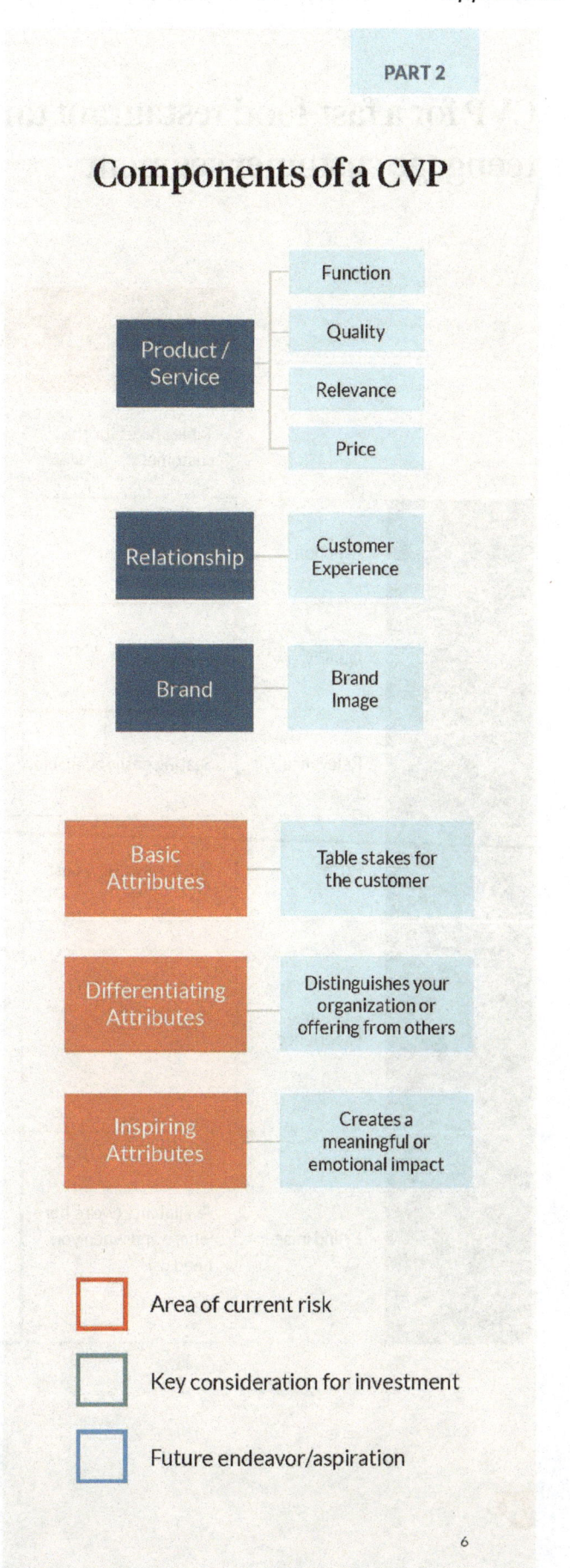

PART 2

Components of a CVP

- **Product / Service**
  - Function
  - Quality
  - Relevance
  - Price
- **Relationship**
  - Customer Experience
- **Brand**
  - Brand Image

- **Basic Attributes** — Table stakes for the customer
- **Differentiating Attributes** — Distinguishes your organization or offering from others
- **Inspiring Attributes** — Creates a meaningful or emotional impact

☐ Area of current risk
☐ Key consideration for investment
☐ Future endeavor/aspiration

Strategy in the 21st Century, Second Edition

PART 2

CVP for a fast-food restaurant targeting teengage customer segment

		Basic Attributes	Differentiating Attributes	Inspiring Attributes
		Table stakes for the customer	Distinguishes your organization/offering from others	Creates a meaningful or emotional impact
Product / Service	Function	Tasty food Good WiFi		
Product / Service	Quality	Fresh		
Product / Service	Relevance	Seating easily available	Teen friendly	
Product / Service	Price	Full meals at low cost	Loyalty discounts	
Relationship	Customer experience		Loyalty app	Sponsorship and engagement with local schools, teams, and events
Brand	Brand image	Availability (we're here where and when you need us)	Partnerships with "influencers" to build exposure among teens	

LEGEND
- Area of current risk
- Key consideration for investment
- Future endeavor/aspiration

© 2023 Credera All Rights Reserved

3 Dive into CPP

Defining the CVP for each customer segment provides the foundation for visualizing CPP and making strategic decisions. The first step in CPP is defining competitor segments to group competitors with similar attributes. Since each customer segment has different needs and expectations, competitor segments may vary for different customer segments.

To continue the fast-food example, the teen segment not only values a good meal but also needs a place to meet up with others. This means competitors may be further afield than simply looking at other restaurants. Another competitor segment is entertainment venues (such as movie theaters) that provide full food service.

We look at the various permutations of customer segments as juxtaposed with competitor segments and build a CPP to visualize and test the CVP in the context of competing for a specific customer segment against specific competitor segments. The visualization technique of a CPP is highly effective in guiding the decision-making process. We start with the key CVP attributes defined for a customer segment and then score the current-state emphasis for each attribute.

The second step is to overlay the perceived current-state emphasis of the various competitor segments. At this point, current-state CPP becomes easy to see. Visualizing a comparative view of the company vs. competition helps the client determine if their CVP is differentiated enough from competitors. It highlights strategic questions such as whether and where investments or divestments should be made to alter the future-state CPP.

CPP for a fast-food restaurant targeting teengage customer segment

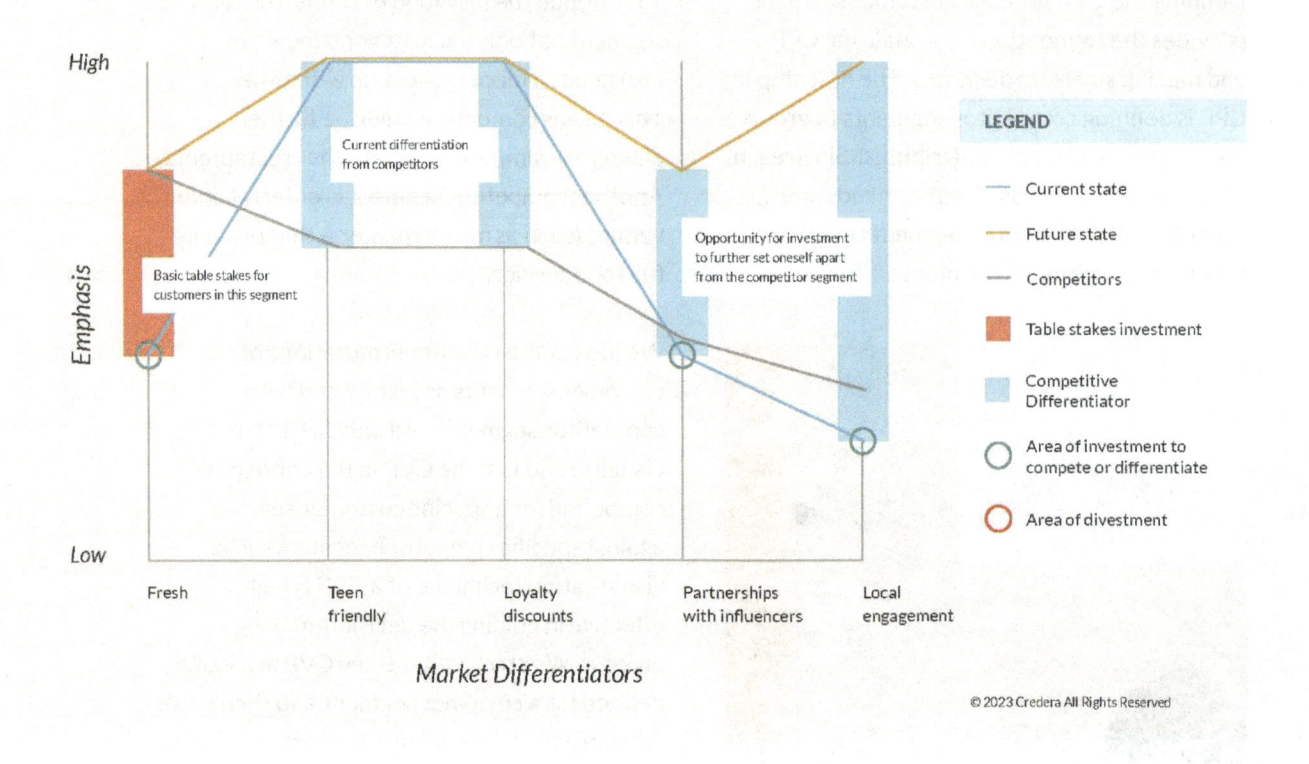

(Chart: Emphasis [Low to High] vs. Market Differentiators: Fresh, Teen friendly, Loyalty discounts, Partnerships with influencers, Local engagement)

Legend:
- Current state
- Future state
- Competitors
- Table stakes investment
- Competitive Differentiator
- Area of investment to compete or differentiate
- Area of divestment

Annotations on chart:
- Basic table stakes for customers in this segment
- Current differentiation from competitors
- Opportunity for investment to further set oneself apart from the competitor segment

© 2023 Credera All Rights Reserved

The CPP example above makes clear the company's CPP for the teen customer segment as compared to similar restaurants. The company's next step is to make decisions. For instance, if there isn't a viable and affordable way to differentiate from competitors, or if there is a table stakes item that isn't worth the investment to appeal to this segment, the company could abandon focus on the teen segment and focus on other customer segments.

In this example, the market has shifted such that fresh food is now a basic expectation with the teen segment, and an investment will need to be made to at least match the competition in this aspect. The CVPs for the other three customer segments (families with young children, business customers, and travelers) likely also share this "fresh food" attribute, making the investment more attractive.

The CPP also confirms that the differentiated elements of "teen-friendly" and "loyalty discounts" are distinguished from the competitors in this segment, and it validates that investments in "partnerships with influencers" and "local sponsorship/ engagements" provide alternative paths to further differentiation from competitors.

Appendix 9

PART 3

Understanding the threat of disruption

CVP and CPP are not "set it and forget it" strategy elements. While some industries evolve faster than others, fast-paced and disruptive advances in technology are realities in today's economy. For example, though many types of artificial intelligence (AI) have been used for decades, the recent step change in the accuracy of generative AI (such as ChatGPT) has opened eyes and imaginations to the potential applications of AI. It is sparking a wave of competitive disruption.

However, a technology-first approach to AI can be a recipe for disaster. This is the proverbial "hammer looking for a nail." Any AI initiative should begin with a robust AI strategy, which aligns with a vision and purpose and requires a clear understanding of one's underlying data and technology foundation, which will impact the feasibility of one's ideas.

One approach to ideating AI use cases is to consider current CVP and CPP by asking key questions, like:

1

How can we further differentiate our CVP?

AI solutions should complement or improve one's existing CVP. Improving features or experiences that aren't important to your customers won't help you gain or preserve market share. Remember, the CVP is not about outperforming your competitors in all categories but only in those most important to your own target customers.

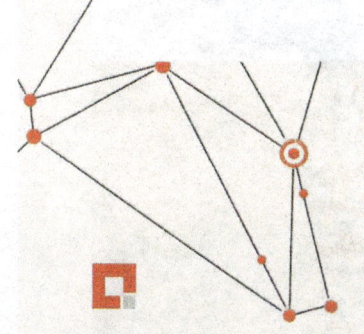

2

Does research back our CVP?

Your CVP should be backed and validated by research and insights into your customers. Valuable insights into what your customers want can come from many sources, both inside and outside your organization. To understand what your customers want, start by listening to what they say and, more importantly, pay attention to what they do. A potential use case for AI is to use your existing data to gain insights into your customers.

3

Does our CVP need to change?

Technologies like AI offer opportunities to deliver value to customers that previously may not have been possible. If your current CVP isn't clearly tied to customer needs, or your product isn't gaining market share or share of wallet, reconsidering your CVP with AI in mind could be a path to new product opportunities.

Conversely, new technologies can threaten once successful CVPs, turning yesterday's advantages into today's table stakes or worse, rendering them obsolete. Any new technology with this significance should be cause for consideration.

341

Strategy in the 21st Century, Second Edition

A real world case study: Stripe

A thoughtful and deliberate customer value proposition can dislodge or disrupt established, powerful competitors offering similar products and services. The payments processing company Stripe is an excellent example of using an intentional CVP and CPP to win in a highly competitive market.

Before Stripe entered the market in 2011, merchants had two options for accepting customer payments online: either set up a merchant account on their own in-house or use a payment service like PayPal. Merchant account setup was slow and costly. PayPal simplified the account setup process but passed along the complicated fee structure to customers.

To compete in the payments space, Stripe targeted small online businesses (74% of their customer base is less than $50 million in annual revenue) and built their CVP on convenience, customer experience, and price. Merchants could set up an account in minutes, and Stripe's API allowed for a customizable, fully integrated checkout experience instead of opening a third-party page. Stripe also eliminated complicated and variable pricing in favor of a simple, per-transaction fee. See the next page for an illustrative example of this CVP.

A winning CPP usually requires investment tradeoffs, such as choosing not to invest in features and benefits offered by competitors in favor of alternatives more important to your target customer segment.

For example, the benefits of convenience, customer experience, and price came at the cost of longer fund transfer times and more developer support to integrate checkout into merchant websites. Customers willingly traded the status quo for greater flexibility, more straightforward pricing, and shorter cash cycle times. The resultant CPP (see next page) ultimately worked in Stripe's favor, growing it from a startup to a unicorn with a valuation of over $1 billion in three years.

Appendix 9

PART 4

Stripe's CVP and CPP

Stripe's CVP

		Basic Attributes	Differentiating Attributes	Inspiring Attributes
Product / Service	Function	Payment processing	Ecommerce and online payments, multitude of currencies, out of the box reporting options	
	Quality	Secure transactions, accurate transactions	Customizable CX	
	Relevance		Quick setup	
	Price	Fair pricing	Predictable costs	
Relationship	Customer experience	Live chat and knowledge base	24/7 phone support	
Brand	Brand image		To increase the GDP of the internet	

LEGEND
- ☐ Area of current risk
- ☐ Key consideration for investment
- ☐ Future endeavor/aspiration

Stripe's CPP

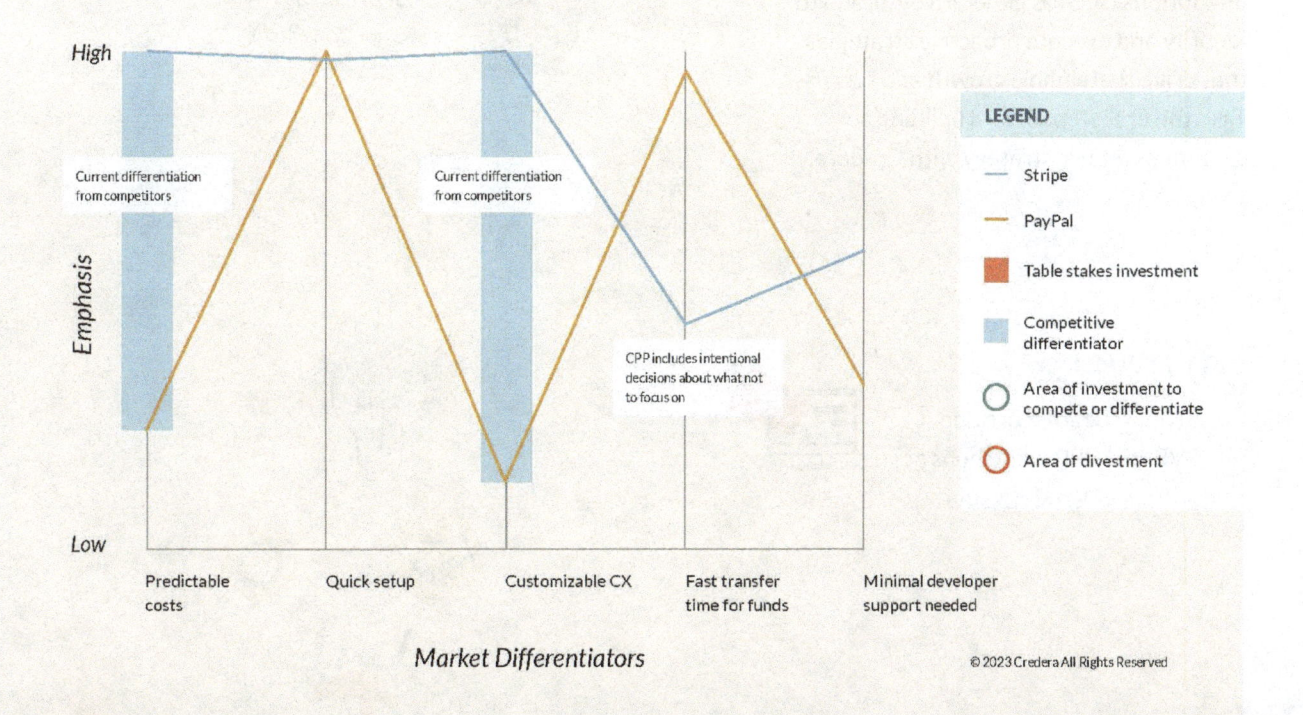

Chart: Emphasis (High to Low) vs Market Differentiators

Market Differentiators (x-axis): Predictable costs, Quick setup, Customizable CX, Fast transfer time for funds, Minimal developer support needed

Annotations:
- Current differentiation from competitors (at Predictable costs)
- Current differentiation from competitors (at Customizable CX)
- CPP includes intentional decisions about what not to focus on

LEGEND
- — Stripe
- — PayPal
- ▬ Table stakes investment
- ▬ Competitive differentiator
- ○ Area of investment to compete or differentiate
- ○ Area of divestment

© 2023 Credera All Rights Reserved

Strategy in the 21st Century, Second Edition

The path to CVP and CPP success

Businesses that succeed in today's competitive landscape place the customer at the heart of their strategy. They know their target customers and understand their customer's needs. They are intentional about their CVP and CPP and align their capabilities to these elements. With the right approach and guidance, they navigate ever-changing market dynamics to evolve a strategy that drives sustainable growth and market success.

Credera thrives in guiding businesses through this process. Our customer-centric approach and innovative CVP and CPP frameworks empower companies to better understand their customers and competition, to be intentional in their strategic investment decisions, to assess and react to potential disruptions (such as generative AI), and to identify and execute proactive strategies that drive sustainable growth and success. Take the first step toward building a customer-centric strategy with Credera.

AUTHOR TEAM

Gail Stout Perry
Partner

Jim Nadalini
Principal

Bobby Pennington
Principal

Grant Dow
Senior Consultant

GET IN TOUCH

Reach out to learn more about our CVP and CPP workshops at findoutmore@credera.com

Appendix 9

CREDERA

CREDERA.COM

Appendix 10 – Strategy Execution in the Public Sector

The challenge we face.

Strategy execution in the public sector can be most challenging. All too often large-scale initiatives fail at execution for reasons unique to government and non-governmental agencies. For example, governmental organizations incur higher levels of risk due to the large financial investment required, public scrutiny and most importantly, not delivering on their core mission for which they are legally accountable to deliver to the public.

1. Another contributing factor is the complex nature of strategy execution in governmental agencies, e.g., a mission-focused strategy to improve the quality and cost effectiveness of healthcare or improve national security. In situations like these, agencies are faced with executing multiple strategies that can be difficult to roll up to the overall agency strategy, or to a major program strategy, like an agency's IT modernization or cyber security strategy.

2. To be sure the public sector is very different from the private sector in many important ways. This includes the impact of political influences, frequent leadership turnover, extensive stakeholder oversight, and leaders with enormous responsibility and limited authority due to the legislative processes and legal authorities in place.

3. Over the past 15 years or so there has been an increasing focus on improving strategy execution in the private sector. And while great work has been done regarding corporate America, (Insert references) little research or program development work has taken place to address this same concern in the public sector. To be sure we should certainly take advantage of what can be learned from the private sector, as we put our primary focus on identifying specific solutions unique to the realities of the public sector.

Our hypothesis and relevant research for addressing this challenge.

Government officials, agency directors, and managers have important moral and legal obligations to deliver on their mission via implementation of strategic initiatives, programs, and priorities that deliver positive results for citizens, taxpayers and partners. To meet this obligation, agencies first define their vision and goals for the future, then develop strategic plans to achieve those ends, and ultimately implement efforts to engage all of their respective stakeholders in strategies and tactics to achieve the desired outcomes.

Unfortunately, as with the private sector, governmental agencies and programs often fail at strategy execution because their leaders and their workforce to a large extent lack understanding of, and appreciation for, the multi-dimensional nature and foundational requirements for effective and efficient strategy execution. The obvious corollary to this hypothesis is leaders often lack necessary strategy execution knowledge, skills, abilities, and attitudes to be effective. We refer to this dynamic as the "Strategy Execution Gap."

For example, when leaders fail to embrace execution as their primary job, an execution gap and/or attitude gap likely exists. When a strategic plan is deployed for implementation without the requisite technical skills required, poorly defined roles, accountabilities, and objectives, the strategy execution gap grows wider.

Strategy in the 21st Century, Second Edition

When ineffective communication or one-way communications patterns exist, plainly exhibited at the top of the organization, then repeated down through mid-level leaders, alignment of the organization's strategy with its people, structure, culture, and technology seem insurmountable, if not impossible.

Our hypothesis was validated in 2019 when LBL Strategies and George Washington University, Center for Excellence in Public leadership, along with the Association for Strategic Planning, Government Community of Practice, and the Illinois Government Finance Officers Association surveyed five thousand managers in the public sector regarding factors influencing strategy execution. [186]

One clear validator of our hypothesis was the perceived differences of respondents in terms of assessing their agencies effectiveness in crafting versus implementing strategy.

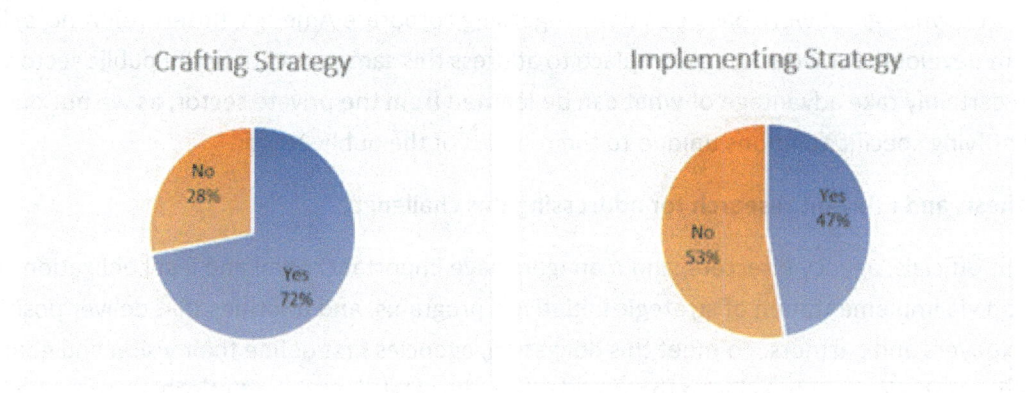

Another survey question pointed to the reality of the strategy execution gap when respondents were asked about how successful their organization had been over time in implementation of strategy.

---

[186] https://www.lblstrategies.com/wp-content/uploads/2020/07/LBL-CS-SEPS_Survey-03.pdf

Appendix 10

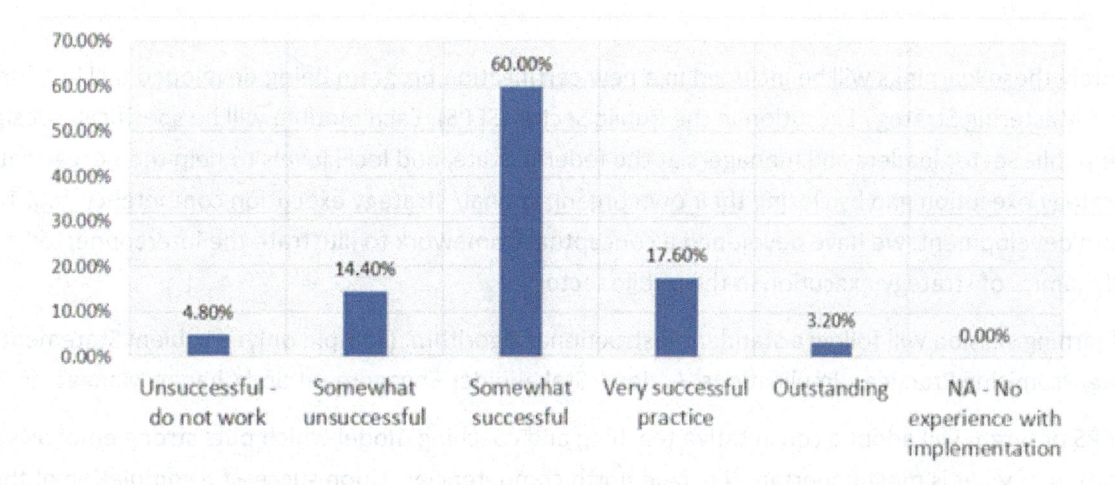

Category	Percentage
Unsuccessful - do not work	4.80%
Somewhat unsuccessful	14.40%
Somewhat successful	60.00%
Very successful practice	17.60%
Outstanding	3.20%
NA - No experience with implementation	0.00%

Our perceptions were largely confirmed when we calculated the most frequently chosen reasons for implementation failure.

Reasons for implementation failure (approximate percentages from bar chart):
- Lack of leadership (~21%)
- Poor communication (~17%)
- Everyone is already too busy (~15%)
- Insufficient resources (~14%)
- Don't understand the reason for change (~6%)
- Lack of sufficient training and development (~6%)
- Poor alignment with the culture (~5%)
- Stakeholder interference (~5%)
- Poor synchronization of the strategic planning... (~5%)
- No follow up or reviews (~4%)
- Poor recognition and reinforcement (~3%)
- Lack of investment e.g. new technology (~2%)
- The wrong measures are being used (~2%)

After discussing the findings with an experienced set of MITRE execution professionals (list names), including Marie Muscella, Chief of Strategy and Planning, Center for Government Effectiveness and Modernization (CGEM), and her outreach to the Human and Organizational Systems research team at MITRE, a growing collaboration emerged.

The scope and purpose of the collaboration.
Rather than attempting to validate our original work via a second survey with a larger sample size, a decision was made to focus on identifying practical strategy execution solutions of value to government agencies, officials, leaders, and managers. The approach chosen was to leverage the existing knowledge and insights of seasoned public sector execution consultants and practitioners. Our goal for this collaboration is to identify and share leading strategy execution behaviors and practices.

The purpose of this white paper is to summarize what we currently know in terms of leading/promising practices senior MITRE and LBL Strategies consultants have witnessed/used to positively influence effective and efficient strategy execution in the public sector.

Strategy in the 21st Century, Second Edition

Ultimately these learnings will be included in a new certification program being developed by LBL Strategies entitled Mastering Strategy Execution in the Public Sector (SEPS). Each module will be specifically designed to enable public sector leaders and managers at the federal, state, and local levels to help their organizations <u>close the strategy execution gap by closing their own organizational/ strategy execution competency gap</u>. To guide program development, we have developed a conceptual framework to illustrate the interconnected and "vortex-like" dynamics of strategy execution in the public sector.

Each learning session will follow a standard instructional algorithm. (Sample only: Problem Statement, Leading/Promising Practices, Implications, Actions, Stakeholder Engagement and Change Management)

The SEPS program will adopt a consultative teaching and coaching model which puts strong emphasis on actual application of what is most important, i.e. <u>true north competencies</u>. Upon successful completion of the program, participants will obtain a university-based certification in strategy execution in the public sector.

Strategy Execution in the Public Sector Framework

The *Strategy Execution in the Public Sector Framework* (which will be animated to demonstrate its vortex nature) is <u>both static and dynamic</u> and depicts the starting point to understand, then execute various aspects of strategy execution.

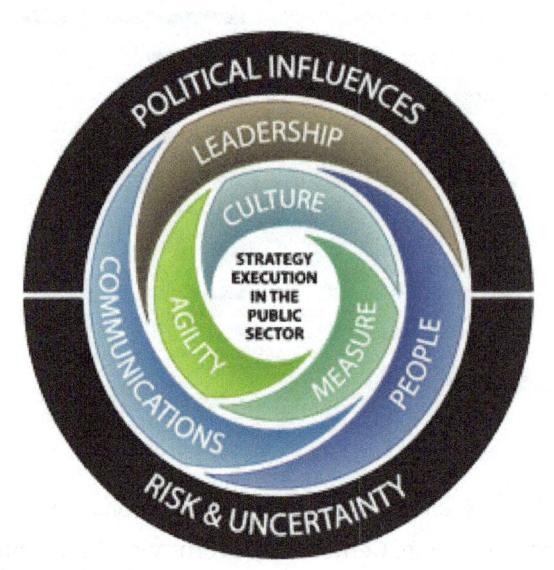

Our depiction of the eight key drivers of strategy execution success is designed to portray the fluid nature of strategy execution. As the execution process unfolds the eight key drivers merge at different times and different levels of concentration as the execution process transitions. The eight key drivers are continual and influence strategy execution throughout the process.

Strategy execution competencies

To organize leading/promising practices we have categorized them by key driver or "competency" in the proposed SEPS framework. There are eight sets of interrelated competencies represented in the model via Outer, Middle and Inner Rings. While all eight competencies are central to execution, it will require knowledge, skills, abilities, and attitudes in one, more than another, at different times in the overall execution process. Even though the rings depict the most critical competencies in that ring, all competencies are present in each ring.

Appendix 10

- *The Outer Ring* - This ring reflects the impact of Political Influences and Risk & Uncertainty on strategy execution. While these dynamics are present throughout the strategy management process, it is essential to address them in greater detail during the transition from strategy development to execution of the strategic plan. For example, understanding the informational needs and engagement styles of the political stakeholders are important as an organization develops their execution plan.

- *The Middle Ring* - This ring reflects the impact of Leadership, Communications, and People on execution. These three capability sets are in the middle for a reason. Intentional and focused interaction of these competencies is essential for execution to be effective. In this ring ideas that originated in the strategy development process and defined as objectives start transitioning into execution. This process requires effective and penetrating communication, reflecting the culture of the organization to inspire contributors to the effort to define, adopt and sustain the changes the organization intends to achieve.

- *The Inner Ring* - This ring reflects the confluence of Culture, Agility and Measurement. These competencies are the primary motivators essential for the execution effort and for the performance measurement that allows the organization to respond with agility to execution and make "course corrections" indicated by the performance measurement/feedback processes.

Strategy execution capability sets described.

Below is a high-level description of each key driver, and an associated set of competencies required in either static and/or dynamic conditions.

1. Political Influences - In the Outer Ring, defining, understanding, and prioritizing political influences is essential. A careful and thoughtful stakeholder analysis will highlight what is important for the stakeholder to know as well as what they need to act on. Stakeholder engagement is a process that is on-going and will shift as new influences emerge or as the political environment shifts. The public sector must consider competing demands on limited resources, allocated by policies and processes controlled by multiple stakeholders, which are also potential sources of both political influence and risk.

   For large scale program plans, in which strategy execution teams are dedicated to ensuring that implementation is not only planned and delivered, but also to ensure that outcomes are achieved, they must be able to operate effectively disseminating accurate stakeholder analysis findings, and recommended tactics. One of the responsibilities of leadership, where it coincides with political influences, is to balance the demand, organizational capacity, and removal of barriers. This includes preventing the addition of non-essential activities, something that is challenging but critical to overall success.

   As noted earlier, the public sector is incredibly complex, e.g., servicing a multitude of customers as well as engaging with a variety of partners and stakeholders, often with conflicting agendas. In the Outer Ring closest to the line between strategy development and the execution of the strategic plan, the effect of political influences is the strongest. Even though these influences will play a part in each of the execution rings, the effect of it on the entire process is usually the greatest at the beginning. At this stage, an organization's leadership will have to focus their attention up the hierarchy and, sometimes, externally, as policies are defined and processes are developed, since most of the influence will originate from policy makers and senior government officials outside the organization.

Often political influences are mostly a concern of senior leadership. These same considerations will trickle down internal political influences on all levels of the organization to varying degrees as they relate to the organization itself. Management at all levels must take notice of these influences as they relate to employee buy-in and adjust organizational messaging accordingly via a robust and disciplined communications and stakeholder engagement effort.

2. Risk & Uncertainty – In many cases these political influences can create very substantial organizational risk and uncertainty that must be considered at the start of the execution process. In addition, due to the nature of public sector organizations, the execution effort is susceptible to risk & uncertainty that originates from outside the organization. Leadership plays a critical role in reducing risk & uncertainty by ensuring cross functional teams are aligned for effective execution, and that their budgets are based on the requirements of the execution process to ensure that the required resources are available. Every agency leadership team and execution team must be aware and understand how best to navigate these influences.

    In addition, organizational risk & uncertainty in various government organizations can be affected by various "outside risks," such as global pandemics, natural disasters, severe economic downturns, or acts of war/terrorism. While these forces (Black Swans) can to some degree be defined and considered at the beginning of the execution process (Outer Ring), they are largely uncontrollable and can present themselves to varying degrees and effects at any time during the execution process.

    To mitigate the impact of these unforeseeable events teams must work to gain strategic foresight by engaging in periodic scenario planning exercises, and/or ensure outside perspectives and broad thinkers are actively involved on the core execution team. Contingency plans for such events should be developed early in the process to align with continuity of operations principles.

    In the middle ring, risk and uncertainty can become more tactical in nature at times relating directly to organizational factors that are preexisting or that arise due to the execution effort. Although they may be tactical in nature, these uncertainties must be addressed at the appropriate level by the execution team to avoid affecting the entire effort.

3. Mission Enabling Processes (under development)

4. Leadership – In the Middle Ring effective Leadership at all levels of the execution process is essential. This foundational requirement is made more difficult for many reasons, including leaders are often transient, creating an inherent challenge to accomplish any strategy; a large percentage of leaders are appointed so they serve at the pleasure of the President/Governor/Mayor; and most have laws or regulations governing their behavior and output. These constraints make it more difficult for political leaders to achieve or execute the stated outcomes of their strategies.

    Senior leadership must set the tone at the beginning of the execution effort that will be consistent throughout the process. For that reason, the leadership must completely understand and communicate the nuances of political influences and the associated risk & uncertainty caused.

    In addition to leading the execution of the strategy, leadership is accountable for ensuring that the right things are being done in the right way and at the right time by the right people, thus ensuring that team and material resources are not wasted on inefficient or inappropriate activities. This may pose tension as prioritization of tasks may be needed to safeguard the right resources are dedicated to the prioritized efforts. Often, this will entail some difficult discussions with external stakeholders, vendors, or organizational employees. Leadership is responsible, in partnership with the team, for deciding "what not to do" despite political pressures or because of cultural influences.

Another underlying responsibility of leadership during ALL aspects of the execution is to ensure that goals are broken down into manageable and achievable milestones with realistic target completion dates. This step is key to having small successes throughout the execution process and in building agility into execution. It also allows employees of the organization to see progress and to keep the messaging of the initiative fresh. It also affords the organization the opportunity to acknowledge and reinforce improvements. These small accomplishments not only demonstrate movement and progress, but they also serve as inspiration to the organization.

Given this context execution team and organizational leaders must effectively, consistently, and intentionally lead their personnel through these realities. Clear engagement of the execution teams and mid-level leadership engagement are key to organizational changes and achievement of the strategic outcomes. The role of senior management at this stage is to support and enable leadership below them while continuing to support the overall strategy through constant, clear, and consistent communications, reinforced messaging, and removal of organizational barriers.

5. <u>People</u> – Research indicates that if the people do not buy into the "why" change is required then achievement of what is desired will be difficult. Understanding this reality, the capabilities of the organization, and how the people will react to change is key to the execution process. This same understanding should also be used to ensure that the right people, i.e., competent ones that support the new strategy, are involved from the beginning to serve as "The Igniters" of execution performance.

To have this effect, leadership is not just a position but a mindset and must come from ALL levels of the organization. Leaders need to be capable of leaving their biases and territorial influences that were a part of the organizational "Silo" in which they represent or have come from. The process of people from different "Silos" working together is not accidental. It must be intentionally planned for and managed with a good dose of engagement, professional development, and authorization. Since people are the difference between effective execution and failure, it is important that team members are selected and enlisted as advocates for the execution effort from the onset.

Execution team members will serve as the "bridge"/connectivity that carries the strategic messaging from department to department in the organization. Leveraging the organizational hierarchy can be the most effective vehicle for the dissemination of the critical execution messaging required. This messaging should, especially focus on how the strategy relates to their job and the 'what's in it for me.' This way employees are not blindsided by the changes that may affect them while understanding the potential benefits.

Leadership and their people are synchronized when leadership ensures that employees are provided the opportunities and resources to support the execution.

At the onset of the execution process it will be important to develop the internal processes such as rewards and recognition and career development processes that can complement the execution process. Addressing these extrinsic issues in the beginning along with messaging and addressing intrinsic benefits of the outcomes of the strategy will set the stage for alignment and buy in through the execution process.

6. <u>Communications</u> – In all cases an essential element of improved strategy execution is effective communications between leaders, managers, employees, and key partners or external stakeholders. Effective communications mean more than the infrastructure required to send/ receive or disseminate messages to targeted audiences. Effective communication during execution requires clear and persistent messaging...bounce-back messaging. Bounce-back messaging means the message received and interpreted by the target audience at the execution level Is what was meant when it was originally sent, with no distortion.

   In addition, in this model of communication the term top-down/bottom up-communication implies that the message that originated at the highest level of the organization is understood and can be explained by the lowest level of the organization. Incumbent in this communication style is transparency that includes authentic communication, where bad news is delivered as well as those messages that are perceived as good news.

   The communication processes need to use mediums that fit the intended audiences, for example videos imbedded into organizational intranet communications may appeal to audiences that typically use headsets as they are working or using social media for reinforcing messages to the public or external stakeholders. One of the most impactful communication processes is to identify audiences and use the messaging mechanisms that best serve their needs and preferences as well as achieve the communications objectives that the organization seeks to attain.

   Timing of messaging is also an important element for leaders to consider. Not only should communications begin when the effort begins but also timed to coincide with significant milestones. In the beginning, members of the leadership team must begin messaging to explain the nature of the strategy and the expected outcomes. This should also include how the new strategy relates to the organization, individual or function in the organization. This messaging can be gradual at first but reinforced as the execution process unfolds.

   The communication process will experience some lag time, especially if the nature of the change is planned over a period. Maintaining the momentum of strategy execution requires a pulse on the organization as well as with external stakeholders. Emphasis should be on timely and effective messaging in support of the execution effort.

7. <u>Culture</u> – When an organization is making large-scale changes, addressing organizational culture will become crucial for behaviors to shift and organizational changes to stick. Prior to taking action to develop or change an organization's culture, a detailed assessment of the desirable and undesirable features of the existing culture must be done at the onset of the execution process. Leaders can use this data to develop steps necessary to refine the existing culture. When leaders build trust and lead their people with effective engagement and communications, an "accountable" and "adaptive" culture can evolve. Leadership actions and communication must be sincere, authentic and in alignment with the anticipated results.

   One of the essential lynchpins in developing the desired culture required for successful execution is openness in interpersonal communications at all levels of the organization. This facilitates communicating honestly and accurately when leaders pass positive and potentially negative information. For the culture competency transparency and authenticity reinforce the concept that the people involved are

Appendix 10

acknowledged, voices are felt heard, and that leaders are there to support the organization as they move through the execution.

Just as important is the need for the organization to promote open communications among all levels of employees and prohibit "Stove Piping," a practice in the Public Sector where parts of the same organization have <u>developed artificial boundaries</u> within their larger organizational boundaries by either budgeting or other bureaucratic practices such as protecting their organizational turfs and/or budget dollars. Organizational silos are difficult to penetrate however, through continued and deliberate engagement as well as establishing practices that promote cross-organizational behaviors including rewards and recognition programs, breaking down silos will become less of a barrier and more about creating organizational value through innovation and knowledge sharing.

As mentioned earlier the people and culture aspects will interact throughout the execution process. One of the major responsibilities of "The Igniters" mentioned in the People Competency is to "ignite" and sustain the alignment process into the culture and in every action and activity in execution.

Cultural characteristics too, must be examined by leadership teams to determine their ability to support the execution process by supporting employee buy in. The results of this analysis can then be used to determine which aspects of the culture need to be refined or modified so that the engagement and change processes can be started early enough to be supported in the organization.

When leaders build trust and lead their people with effective engagement and communications, an "accountable" and "adaptive" culture can evolve.

8. <u>Agility -</u> To be accountable and adaptive in today's disruptive environment requires broad team understanding of what it takes to be agile and resilient. The intersection of "Leadership," "Culture" and "People" key drivers of the model are critical to ensuring that the culture promotes risk taking, that people have the right skill sets and that resources available so that execution teams can make the decisions and take the steps necessary to change direction (be Agile) as the situation warrants.

   Another essential facet of the intersection between Culture, Leadership and People that ignites Agility is Trust. Leadership and the Culture must promote an environment of psychological safety and trust that encourages people to take risks that are essential for Agility.

   In the Outer Ring of the process, external factors (political influences and risk & uncertainty) can still change the course or nature of the strategy that might affect the execution process. Senior leaders and the execution teams must remain alert to indicators that the strategy execution process should be changed or refined.

   At this stage of strategy execution, agility is essential in responding to factors that may impede the execution effort. Close alignment between organizational design, communications and performance measurement will help the execution process to respond with agility to any last-minute issues that may arise.

   To be accountable and adaptive in today's disruptive environment requires execution team understanding of what it takes to be agile and resilient.

9. <u>Measure</u> – To guide the journey there must be a discipline and capability to accurately measure, and communicate, performance (strategic outcomes and mission execution) on a timely basis, i.e., a fundamental set of measures that answer the questions, "Are we making progress toward our intended

outcomes?" What have we accomplished?" "Do we need to make changes?" It is important that measures are balanced to reflect what the organization values (related to mission and outcomes) in addition to traditional project management measures that monitor completion of activities and milestones.

Measurement and reporting of the results of the measurement should be continual based on the needs of each execution phase and the department/team involved in the execution. While quarterly reporting may be sufficient for senior level executives, the timing of the measurement processes and related reporting must match the needs and capabilities of the elements and individuals involved in the execution with the resulting reporting shared across the organization. Leadership's critical role in measurement is to ensure only essential data collection and reporting takes place and needless or outdated data collection processes discontinued.

Measurement in the Outer Ring can take the form of monitoring and tracking stakeholder buy in as the effort progresses. Measure should be developed to monitor the effect and success of influencing efforts designed to educate the organization and encourage organizational buy in. Overall performance measures will be leading as well as lagging. Using performance measures from the beginning of the process will alert execution teams to deviations from the execution schedule or processes sooner rather than later in the process. This will provide execution teams the opportunity to make changes that reduce any negative impact on the execution process.

In the Middle Ring high impact measurement that can provide indications of disruption to the overall execution are particularly essential. The nature of the measures themselves can be shifted as appropriate to provide more leading indicators to provide insights on the progress of the Execution effort.

Appendix 11 – Robust Strategy Management Calendar

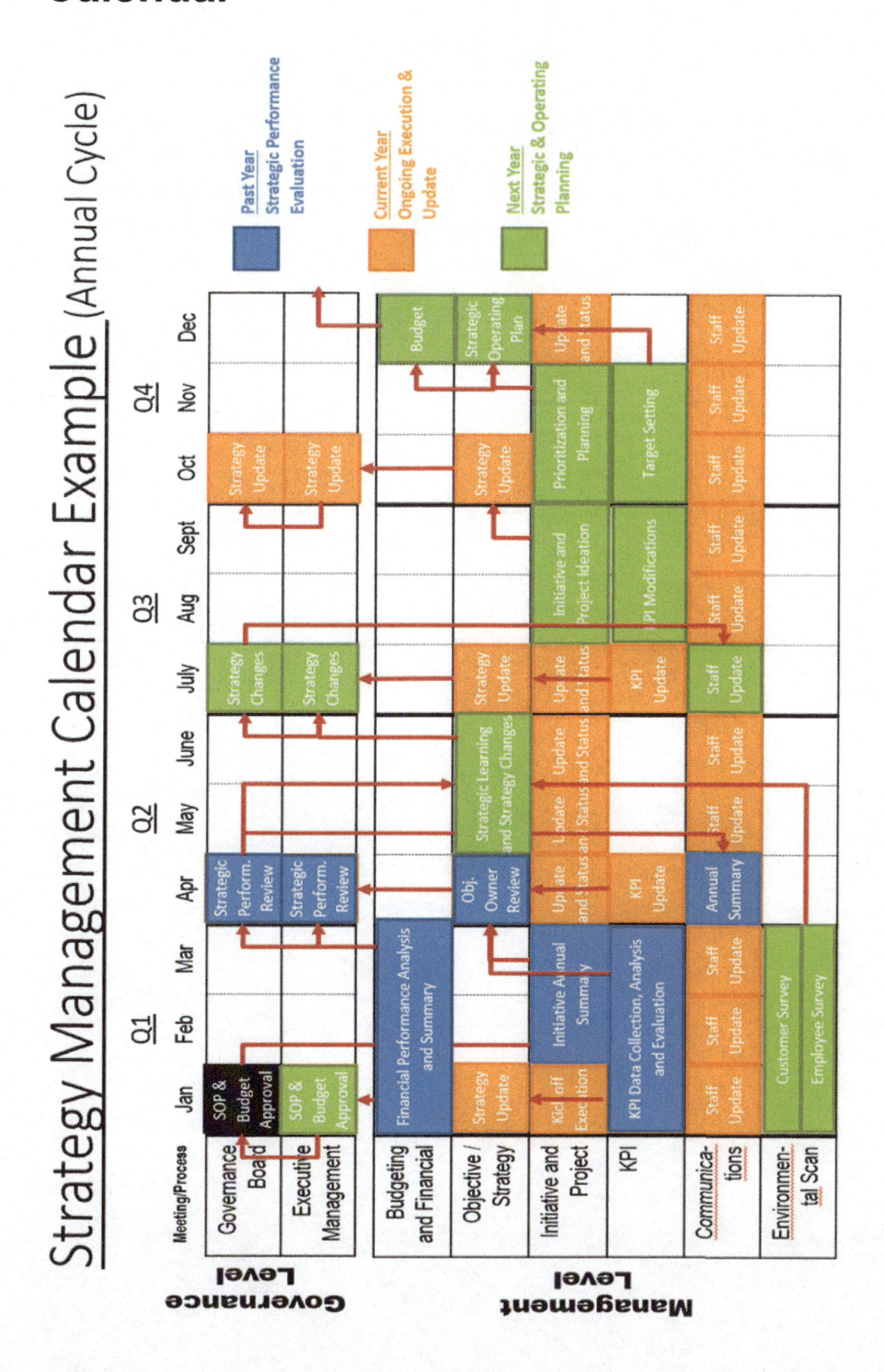

Strategy Management Calendar Example (Annual Cycle)

Legend:
- Past Year — Strategic Performance Evaluation (blue)
- Current Year — Ongoing Execution & Update (orange)
- Next Year — Strategic & Operating Planning (green)

Governance Level

Meeting/Process	Jan	Feb	Mar	Apr	May	June	July	Aug	Sept	Oct	Nov	Dec
Governance Board	SOP & Budget Approval			Strategic Perform. Review			Strategy Changes			Strategy Update		
Executive Management	SOP & Budget Approval			Strategic Perform. Review			Strategy Changes			Strategy Update		

Management Level

Meeting/Process	Jan	Feb	Mar	Apr	May	June	July	Aug	Sept	Oct	Nov	Dec
Budgeting and Financial		Financial Performance Analysis and Summary										Budget
Objective / Strategy	Strategy Update			Obj. Owner Review	Strategic Learning and Strategy Changes		Strategy Update			Strategy Update		Strategic Operating Plan
Initiative and Project	Kick off Execution	Initiative Annual Summary		Update and Status	Update and Status	Update and Status	Update and Status		Initiative and Project Ideation	Prioritization and Planning		Update and Status
KPI	KPI Data Collection, Analysis and Evaluation			KPI Update			KPI Update		PI Modifications	Target Setting		
Communications	Staff Update	Staff Update	Staff Update	Annual Summary	Staff Update	Staff Update	Staff Update	Staff Update	Staff Update	Staff Update	Staff Update	Staff Update
Environmental Scan	Customer Survey / Employee Survey											

357

Glossary of Strategic Management Terms

Activity – One of the steps required to complete a process.

ADLI Cycle – Integration as a factor used while evaluating Processes: Four factors used to evaluate process are approach, deployment, learning, and integration.

Agile – An integrative approach to strategic management emphasizing customer outcomes, iterative work, cross-functional self-managed teams, rigorous accountabilities, and decision-making at the levels with the needed information.

Agility – Agility is the ability of an organization to adapt, change quickly, and succeed in volatile, uncertain, complex, and ambiguous environment.

Agile design thinking – A process to solve complex problems by approaching the challenge from the user's perspective and turning the insights and innovations that follow into products and services as soon as possible. It deploys non-linear human-centered methods which integrate emotional intelligence into structured experimentation, to rapidly release innovation and creativity, and deliver unexpected solutions to previously unsolvable challenges. Agile design thinking enables adaptive organizational design.

Agile Manifesto – An integrated approach to facilitate rapid software development. Its 12 principles emphasize customer outcomes, iterative work, cross-functional self-managed teams, rigorous accountabilities, and encourage decision making at appropriate levels.

Alignment or organizational alignment – In the broadest sense, organizational alignment is the process of building individual and collective accountability throughout the organization for strategy implementation.

Analysis – Refers to an examination of data and information to understand its content, meaning, and significance for some purpose, in this case the strategic management of an organization.

Ansoff's grid – A tool to help a team categorize opportunities. It can also be used to help a team in mapping product/market growth alternative strategies with market opportunities.

Assessment – Analysis plus evaluation = assessment.

Balanced scorecard – A Balanced Scorecard bridges the gap between vision and strategy and execution, based on the premise that financial performance depends on satisfying customers, which results from having effective business processes, which in turn requires necessary organizational competencies. It includes a set of linked and aligned and deployed performance measurements that are deployed across four organizational dimensions: financial, customer, internal processes, and learning and growth. Their primary purpose is to provide management with an integrated and comprehensive approach to the implementation of a given set of strategies and derived operational objectives.

Baldrige Criteria – Malcolm Baldrige Criteria are part of the **Malcolm Baldrige National Quality Award** which recognizes U.S. organizations for performance excellence. Recipients are selected based on achievement and improvement in seven areas, known as the *Baldrige Criteria for Performance Excellence*

Baseline – A baseline is the organization's actual performance for the most recent reporting period.

Benchmark – A benchmark is an external comparison point, for example, an industry-wide statistic.

Board of Directors – An elected group of individuals that represent the owners (or constituents) of an organization.

Blue ocean strategy – A strategy to make the competition irrelevant by serving an untapped market space and creating new demand.

Business capability framework – The *Business Capability Framework* is at the heart of the enterprise architecture approach to organizational design. This novel approach encompasses three complementary components: (1) the target enterprise architecture (TEA); (2) the transformation plan; and (3) the enterprise architecture team.

Business ecosystem – An economic community supported by a foundation of interacting organizations and individuals — the organisms of the business world. In a business ecosystem, companies coevolve capabilities around an innovation: they work cooperatively and competitively to support new products, satisfy customer needs, and eventually incorporate the next round of innovations."

Business model canvas – A strategic management tool to define and communicate a business idea or concept quickly and easily. It describes how a system's components w work together to generate flow.

Cascading – The process of aligning enterprise and department level objectives with the work employees do on a day-to-day basis.

Cash cow – A business unit that has a large market share in a mature, slow-growing industry. Cash cows require little investment and generate cash that can be used to invest in other business units.

Change management – The process of moving an organization, function, or process through a transformation process to a new and/or improved level of performance.

Chief strategy officer – A member of the senior leadership team who provides high level and operational oversight to the entire strategic management process.

Co-creation – Co-creation is the process of accessing the inherent wisdom in an organizational system. An essential ingredient for co-creation to be effective is the inclusion of diverse thinking perspectives and work-life experience.

Glossary

Communications plan – A regularly updated plan to engage stakeholders in the strategic management process. It communicates the intent and desired benefit of the plan. The communications effort should inform "win hearts and minds" and ultimately change behaviors.

Competitive advantage – Competitive advantages provide an edge over rivals and an ability to generate greater value for an organization. In general, there are two types of competitive advantage: cost leadership and differentiation.

Consensus – A group decision or action that all members agree to support, even though it may not exactly reflect an individual's preferred choice. Consensus is possible when diverse points of view have been heard thoroughly and openly.

Contingency plans – The process of proactively evaluating alternative courses of action if performance falters or the environment changes in a significant manner. It includes consideration of contingencies with respect to size, scope, cost, and duration of strategic initiatives.

Continuous improvement – A mindset and a practice of constantly re-examining and improving products, services, or processes.

Core competency – Any area, factor, or consideration perceived by the customer to differentiate the organization by providing a sustainable competitive edge over its rivals.

Cost leadership – When you achieve parity of value at a lower cost than your competitors.

Critical friend – A critical friend can be defined as a trusted person who asks provocative questions, provides data to be examined through another lens, and offers critiques of a person's work as a friend. A critical friend takes the time to fully understand the context of the work presented and the outcomes that the person or team is working toward. The friend is an advocate for the success of that work.

Cross-functional – A process or activity that includes portions of the process or activity from two or more functions within an organization.

Culture (or Organizational Culture) – The set of expressed or implied norms, customs, beliefs, assumptions, and expectations that govern actions of employees, board members, and other contributors in the organization.

Current operations – The organization's day-to-day activities with respect to all functions, processes, and departments of the organization.

Current operating model – How the organization functions today.

Customer – The person(s), or organizations who use your output—the next in line to receive it. Whether your customers are internal or external to your organization, they use your output as an input to their work processes. Customers are the direct beneficiary of the organization's products or services. Customers can be segmented into "primary" and "secondary" customers.

Customer perspective – The customer perspective examines business success through the lens of the customer. Objectives in this perspective focus on those customer needs, desires, and expectations the organization must meet in order to meet its' financial expectations.

Customer requirements – What a customer needs, wants, and expects of an organization's output. Customers generally express requirements around the characteristics of timeliness, quantity, fitness for use, ease of use, expectations, and perceptions of value.

Customer value proposition – The value the organization wants to provide its customers in exchange for purchasing/utilizing its products/services.

Data Governance – Everything an organization does to ensure that its' data is secure, private, accurate, available, and usable.

Decision rights – Identify what business decisions need to be made, who is involved in making them, and define the framework for how they will be made through operating processes and support tool

Delta – The delta is where change occurs. It is where people stop operating in the old way, learn new ways, make mistakes, mourn the loss of the old, test the new way and integrate it into ongoing operations.

Development – The results of systematic efforts to bring about structural, operational, and performance improvements, in a set of capabilities in order to enhance and/or increase outputs.

Differentiation— When an organization adds more value (real or perceived) than competitors, evidenced by higher prices or discounts avoided.

Digital transformation – Information technology (IT) enables organizational transformation. A digital transformation is the application of digital technologies to enhance efficiency, increase customer satisfaction and explore opportunities for growth.

Diversification strategy – A strategy to introduce new products or services into new markets.

Dog – A business unit that has a small market share in a mature industry. A dog may not require substantial cash, but it ties up capital that could be better deployed elsewhere. Unless a dog has some strategic purpose, it should be liquidated if there is little prospect for it to gain market share.

Double loop learning – The process of incorporating feedback from actions taken by management, and their consequences, into the strategy execution processes (i.e., management control loop) and the governing variables and assumptions used to develop the strategies in the first place (i.e., strategic learning loop.)

Ecosystem – An economic community supported by a foundation of interacting organizations and individuals.

Employee value proposition – the value the organization wants to provide its employees in exchange for its employees' work, skills, and experience.

Glossary

Engage stakeholders – The set of activities and processes necessary to get key participants to commit themselves to making the new strategy work.

Engagement operating model – The capabilities, organizational structures, roles, and activities that enable the organization to foster change and properly engage employees throughout the organization in the formulation, organizational transformation, and execution of the strategy.

Enterprise architecture team – A team responsible for creating the TEA and the transformation plan as well as aligning the work of all stakeholders (e.g., program managers, solution architects, project managers and process experts) throughout the transform organization group of activity.

Environmental influences – Internal and external factors that have an impact on an industry and/or an organization.

Environmental scan - A systematic review of current and/or emerging trends, events, situations, problems, and issues that are or might impact the organization, its operation, and/or its performance. A scan may be focused on either external or internal factors.

Evaluation – Refers to the process of comparing the information that has been analyzed in terms of some evaluation criteria, whether qualitative or quantitative.

Execute strategy – The set of activities and processes to deliver value to the organization's stakeholders, as defined by the strategy.

External analyses – An examination of the dimensions of an organization's external environment, including the close scrutiny of those trends, events, that are having, or might have an impact on the performance capabilities of the management, resources, structure, processes, and operation of an organization.

Facilitation – The act of moving a team through a divergent thinking and priority setting process.

Financial perspective – Desired financial performance outcomes. Objectives in this perspective define the desired financial outcomes the organization must achieve to satisfy stockholders and/or other key stakeholders.

Focus – When you narrow your competitive strategy to concentrate only on your target customers and their specific need and potentially also only on your product range.

Forecast – A statement about the future intended to be logical, though not necessarily accurate.

Foresight – Insight into how and why the future may be different from the present.

Formulate strategy – The set of activities and processes to devise the strategy.

Function – Specialized area of related activities within an organization that are grouped together in order to manage them effectively and efficiently, for example, finance, marketing, and operations.

Functional management – A level of management below general management that is in charge of a given function.

Gantt chart – A graphic which visualizes an initiative or project schedule. Gantt charts illustrate the start and finish dates of the critical elements of an initiative or project.

Gap Analysis – The process of identifying all the major components of a robust strategic management system and assessing which components are in place and those in need of development.

Globalization – A process of interaction and integration among the people, companies, and governments of different nations, driven by international trade and investment and aided by information technology.

Goals (or Overarching goal) – A generally stated long-term target or fixed purpose to be achieved in accordance with the organization's vision and mission.

Good governance – Oversight of the structures, systems and practices an organization puts in place, including defining ground rules and assigning decision rights for decision-making; aligning strategy setting with relevant regulations, policies, and guidelines; overseeing delivery of service, including all matters related to Diversity, Equity, and Inclusion (DEI), and reporting on performance, often by committee. Although the board of directors is the guardian of organizational governance, for alignment and consistency, governance occurs at every level of an organization with decision-making authority delegated to the appropriate layer of management.

Govern strategy – The set of activities and processes necessary for overseeing the entire strategic management system.

Growth – The measurable increase in the input, throughput, or output of an organization, process, or activity.

Heat Map – A Heatmap Exposure is a chart that plots the severity of impact of an event occurring on one axis, and the probability of it occurring on the other.

Hoshin Kanri – A method for ensuring strategic goals of an organization drive progress and action at each level within the organization by eliminating waste that comes from inconsistent direction and poor communication. It is a systems approach to the management of change in critical business processes.

Implementation – The set of management and operational processes required to add to, or modify, an existing strategy, organization structure, process, or operating system, such that the change is accepted by the organization as the new strategic and operational norm.

Improvement – The enhanced capability and/or performance or an organization, its functions, processes, or activities made possible by changes in their design, management, and/or operation.

Initiative – A key enterprise undertaking to support the strategy and move the organization forward toward attaining its strategic objectives.

Innovation – Introduction and adaptation of a new idea, concept, or invention to an activity or process.

Glossary

Input – The materials, equipment, information, people, money, or environmental conditions that are needed beforehand.

Input measures – Measures used to track items that are used in production or workflow processes.

Intended results – The predominant outcome sought for each key driver of success.

Internal analyses – Critical examination of the internal dimensions and performance capabilities of the management, resources, structure, processes, and operation of an organization.

Internal perspective – The Internal or Process perspective helps organizations identify and monitor outcomes related to their internal operations. Often these objectives include improvements around quality, process effectiveness and efficiency.

Key driver of success – An explicitly stated area where tangible results must be realized to achieve a desired goal(s).

Key performance indicator – A significant and quantifiable measure to gauge and compare performance.

Lagging indicator – A measurable economic activity that changes after the economy has established a pattern or trend. They have no predictive value, but they are useful in confirming changes that have taken place in economic activity.

Leadership (or Role of leadership) – The ability of leaders, either formally or informally, to influence others to achieve a common goal. Success requires emotionally intelligent leaders to embrace a "stakeholder focused mindset" expressed via active listening, continuous learning, and agile navigating.

Leading indicator – A measurable economic activity that changes before the economy has established a pattern or trend. Useful in predicting changes in economic activity.

Learning and growth perspective – This perspective is often labeled as the capacity building perspective. It identifies where the organization must learn and grow as people and as a team to operate efficiently, satisfy customers, and meet financial expectations.

Logic model – A graphic representation of the logical relationships between the resources/inputs, activities, outputs, and outcomes of a program.

Long-term strategic plans – A small set of actionable strategies that will be implemented at some point over the life of the organization's planning horizon.

Line Manager – Person who heads a department or sub-function and is responsible for collaborating with his team to achieve a specific objective(s) via listening, learning, policy making, target setting, decision making.

Macro environment – Forces at work in the external operating environment that can affect an organization's ability to serve its customers and make a profit, e.g., technology developments, political and legal changes, demographic changes, and economic trends.

Strategy in the 21st Century, Second Edition

Malcolm Baldrige Criteria – The Malcolm Baldrige Criteria are part of the Malcolm Baldrige National Quality Award which recognizes U.S. organizations for performance excellence. Recipients are selected based on achievement and improvement in seven areas, known as the *Baldrige Criteria for Performance Excellence.*

Management – Management is how businesses and organizations organize and direct workflow, operations, and employees to meet company goals. The primary goal of management is to create an environment that lets employees work efficiently and productively.

Market development strategy – A strategy for launching existing products or services into new markets.

Market penetration strategy – A high-level strategy to go deeper into their existing markets with their existing products or services.

Market positioning – The process of identifying and occupying a distinct niche or place in the market for products and services in order to achieve an advantage over competing products and services.

Measure – A quantifiable value used to track and manage operations or assess strategic performance.

Microenvironment – Forces close to an organization that affects its ability to serve its customers and make a profit, e.g., regulatory changes, competition, and stakeholder perceptions.

Middle management – Middle management is the leadership level between senior or executive managers and the lower-level managers responsible for the daily operations.

Milestone – A key activity, whether a deliverable or a decision, being completed in a project or in the development or in the operations of the organization.

Mission – Actionable statement that identifies the organization's purpose and reason for existence.

Nominal Group Technique – The nominal group technique is a decision-making and prioritization method that delivers an efficient well-structured voting process that enables full participation of the planning team in a nonthreatening way.

North star – An organization's North Star supplies a clear identity that defines who the organization is and is not. It enables its members at all levels to constantly rethink how to deliver unique value. An organization's identity includes its strategic direction: mission, vision, values, and goals.

Objectives – An outcome or set of outcomes the organization must achieve to meet its strategic goals and to have its' strategy succeed.

Objective commentary – The documented essence of the team's discussion about strategic objectives.

OKRs – An agile implementation process where "O" or Objectives" refers to where the organization wants to go – specific outcomes for a set period of time; and KRs refers to the "Key Results" or how far the organization has progressed in pursuit of achieving their stated objectives.

Glossary

Operational excellence – A mindset that embraces certain principles and tools to create a culture of excellence within an organization.

Operations – The value-added activities of an organization directly related to providing its goods and/or services to the market.

Operating model – An operating model is "how" an organization works to create value for its customers and builds trust amongst its stakeholders. It includes everything from how the organization sources its products and services to how it structures its business, program areas, departments, and teams. An operating model serves as a schematic for executing the organization's strategic operating plan.

Operating plan – A balanced set of objectives and related projects designed to meet the organization's primary goals.

Opportunities (O) – Unlike strengths and weaknesses that are derived from the internal dimension of the organization, opportunities exist in the external dimension, that is, in the marketplace itself where customers make purchasing and/or other strategic decisions. They frequently emerge from changes in industry dynamics, customer buying behavior, new technologies, or from any other change that can give rise to a new business opportunity. Opportunities may exist in the "here and now," or they may relate to some future time frame.

Organizational alignment – The process of building individual and collective accountability throughout the organization for strategy implementation.

Organizational capability – A set of resources that work together to enable the organization to produce a particular result.

Organization culture – The specific collection of values and norms that are shared by people and groups in an organization, and that control the way they interact with each other and with stakeholders outside the organization.

Organizational design – The process of configuring the key components to achieve an organization purpose and strategy while delivering high-quality customer and employee experience effectively and efficiently.

Organizational learning – A process of detecting and correcting errors. Strategic learning occurs when organizations integrate valid data and evaluative thinking into their work and, in doing so, adapt their strategies and tactics in response to what they learn.

Organization life cycle – The continuous cycles of change and adaptation go through, with each cycle having four phases of development: inventing or renewal, birthing and growing, maturing, and releasing. This is true for individuals, teams, departments, entire organizations, and even for business ecosystems.

Organizational transformation – Aligning an operating model, including processes, policies, unit roles, and individual roles, to an organization's strategy. It is a final determinant of overall successful alignment with the strategy and the strategic operating plan.

OTSW evaluation (sometimes known as SWOT analysis) – An evaluation of the external environmental scan to determine opportunities or threats, followed by an evaluation of internal scan to determine strengths and weaknesses.

Outcome – The desired end result. Outcomes are the difference made by the outputs.

Outcome measures – Measures used to monitor what is accomplished.

Output – Outputs are the tangible or direct results of a process, task, or activity.

Output measures – Measures used to monitor what is produced.

Owner value proposition – the value the organization wants to provide its owners to justify their participation in its ownership.

Paired comparison scoring – A way of prioritizing a list of items where evaluation criteria are subjective, or where they are competing in importance.

Partner value proposition – the value the organization wants to provide its partners who contribute to the organization's customer value proposition, to justify the time and money they invest to build and maintain a relationship with the organization. Partners can include suppliers, distributors, wholesalers, complementors, etc.

Performance culture – A culture centered on performance. This level of strategic maturity requires a systematic, agile, and empowering approach to managing the organization at all levels.

Performance evaluation – Tracking and analysis of key performance indicators linked to specific objectives of the strategic operating plan, in order to measure success or failure in achieving stated outcomes and evaluate how successful the organization is in achieving its goals and objectives.

Performance improvement zone – When management compares an organization's *actual results* to its *desired results*, any discrepancy, where *actual* is less than *desired*, constitutes (by definition) a performance improvement zone requiring attention.

Performance management – The process of achieving desired organizational outcomes. It includes all organizational activities aimed at ensuring that the organization's strategic goal(s) and objectives are met in an effective and efficient manner.

Performance measurement – The process of collecting, analyzing, and reporting information specific to performance of a component of the strategic operating plan.

Performance measures – Key performance indicators comprised of variables configured into formulas to calculate and report measurable results used to help an organization define and evaluate how successful it is in achieving its goals and objectives.

PESTLE or STEEPLE – A "traditional approach" to macro-analysis is sometimes referred to as a PESTLE or STEEPLE analysis.

Planning horizon – the period of time covered by a strategic plan or the organization's planning cycle.

Playing to Win – An integrative approach to competitive positioning and strategy setting.

Policies – Requirement or guidelines developed for use in an organization to influence, instruct, and specify how leaders should act and govern when making decisions in given circumstances.

Porter's Five Forces – A framework to help leaders understand the forces driving industry competition and the attractiveness of a particular market.

Porter's three generic strategies – A business can choose one of two types of *competitive advantage*; having lower costs than its competitors or differentiating itself in ways valued by customers to command a higher price. A business also chooses one of two types of *market scope*, a narrow focus by offering its value proposition to a niche segment or a mass market approach, offering its value across many market segments.

Prioritization matrix – A graphic tool to display the strategic importance of a particular initiative and the expected Return on Investment (ROI).

Process – A sequence of steps, tasks, or activities that converts inputs to outputs.

Process measures – Measures used to monitor quality and efficiency of processes.

Product or service development strategy – A strategy to develop new products or services for existing markets.

Project – An undertaking with a defined starting point and ending point.

Psychological safety – Staff members feel safe and free to openly discuss their concerns and ideas without fear of reprisal or a belief that their communications will be ignored.

Question mark – A business unit that has a small market share in a high growth market.

RACI matrix – A responsibility assignment matrix (called a RACI matrix or a RAPID matrix) is a helpful tool which describes the participation of various roles in completing initiatives or deliverables for a strategic plan.

Readiness Assessment – A process to determine to where the organization is weakest and where implementation should initially focus.

Red ocean strategy – A strategy to outperform competitors to gain a larger share of the market by aligning organization resources and activities to be the low-cost provider or by offering a different value proposition.

Rising star – A business unit that has a large share in a fast-growing industry.

Risk appetite – The amount of risk that an organization is willing to seek or accept in pursuit of its long-term objectives.

Strategy in the 21st Century, Second Edition

Risk tolerance – The boundary of risk taking, outside of which the organization is not prepared to go in pursuit of its long-term objectives.

SBU – A Strategic Business Unit of an organization. An internal profit center composed of discrete and independent product or market segments. An SBU may be any size, but it must have a unique mission, identifiable competitors, an external market focus, and significant control over its business functions and processes.

Scenarios – Scenarios are carefully constructed, data driven stories about how an industry or sector might develop in the future.

Scenario planning – Scenario-based planning is a creative approach for engaging key stakeholders in evaluating the external environment for the purpose of gaining strategic foresight throughout an organization.

Segmentation – a narrow focus value proposition to a niche segment or a mass market approach, offering its value across many market segments.

SMART Objectives – **S** stands for Specific; **M** is Measurable; **A** is Attainable, Aspirational, or Appropriate, depending on the context; **R** is Relevant, Realistic, or Responsibility, again developing on the context; and **T** means Time frame for achievement or Timely.

Stakeholder – Individual person, group, association, or external organization that has a significant interest in, and/or impact on an organization.

Stakeholder engagement – The process of getting various stakeholder groups, particularly employees, to commit themselves to make the new strategy work.

Stakeholder focused mindset – The ability of leaders, either formally or informally, to influence others to achieve a common goal. Success here requires emotionally intelligent leaders to embrace a "stakeholder-focused mindset" expressed via active listening, continuous learning, and agile navigating.

Standard – Rule, norm, regulation, custom, or principle that is used as a basis for measurement, evaluation, comparison, or judgment.

Strategic agility – The capacity to sense change in the environment and adapt in a way that continuously builds value for stakeholders.

Strategic alternatives – Potentially actionable options for achieving the direction of the organization.

Strategic altitude – A hierarchy of strategy elements from the organization's high level, longer-term strategic direction down through the elements of its near term strategic operating plan.

Strategic capability – Capabilities that deliver on one or more of the four value propositions (customers, owners, partners, and employees), and provides a competitive advantage for commercial organizations.

Glossary

Strategic development program – A specific undertaking based on an understanding of the current situation with respect to strategy, organizational capabilities, and resources.

Strategic direction – The vision, mission, values, policies, and primary goal statements of an organization. The strategic direction is a selection filter that allows for removal of strategic alternatives that do not meet the leadership's consensus thinking.

Strategic governance – To oversee the (entire) strategic management process. It entails, amongst other things, monitoring the external environment, setting group and individual performance objectives, tracking, and evaluating deliverables and results throughout the organization, as well as learning from these activities and adapting whenever needed.

Strategic information system – A system established to maintain an organization's strategic focus through ongoing management and communication of information related to the development, implementation, and performance evaluation of strategy.

Strategic learning – The process of using data and insights to inform decision making about strategy.

Strategic management – The continuous cycle of all strategy-related activities, (i.e., strategy system activities) for an organization to succeed in the long-term.

Strategic management maturity model – This model was designed by the Strategy Management Group, aka the Balanced Scorecard Institute. It was designed for busy managers who need a quick assessment of where their organization stands in terms of level of strategic management maturity across eight fundamental dimensions. The tool can also be used to monitor progress in improving maturity of strategic management and to allow benchmarking across organizations, or departments within one organization.

Strategic operating plan – The strategic operating plan is an integrated and deployable set of marching orders detailing exactly *what* will be done to transform strategies into operational level activities with measurable results. It includes implementation of selected and approved strategies into operations level activities. It is tactically focused, including objectives, responsibilities, measures, and initiatives/projects.

Strategic performance – The process of assessing and reporting of achievement outcomes at the objective level, through the analysis of key performance indicators to keep the organization on track or to take corrective action.

Strategic planning – The process of converting the results of strategic thinking as a set of potentially actionable strategies into an integrated plan of action that can be implemented.

Strategic thinking – The synthesis of analytic, creative, and action-oriented thinking applied in a specific organizational context.

Strategos – A compound of two Greek words: *Stratos* which means "army" and *Agos* which means "leader", i.e., A military commander in histories of fifth-century B.C. Greek city-states.

Strategy – High-level guidelines an organization adopts to provide value to its stakeholders and gain advantages over competitors.

Strategy alternatives – High-level strategy choices to be evaluated and prioritized.

Strategy canvas – A central analytic and action structure for identifying and building a Blue Ocean Strategy. It graphically depicts key competitive factors of an organization's value proposition to customers compared to other organizations operating in the same market space.

Strategy deployment – Cascading an organizational strategy through linked initiatives/projects in all functional areas and their derived objectives, down to the lowest operating level of the organization.

Strategy execution gap – A failure at execution because leaders/managers lack understanding of, and appreciation for, the importance of alignment of strategy with the organization's operating model. Leaders often lack necessary strategy implementation (i.e., organizational transformation) knowledge, skills, and attitudes to be effective.

Strategy map or strategy deployment map – A graphical representation of the deployment of a strategy to provide a comprehensive overview of the cause-and-effect relationships amongst strategic objectives. A strategy map serves as a powerful visual communications tool. It is a versatile tool that communicates in different ways to different audiences in your organization.

Strategy development champion – A senior member of the management team responsible for leading development and execution of strategy.

Strategy formulation – The processes required to articulate the overall strategic direction of the organization, to compile a set of feasible strategies, and to evaluate and select those strategic options that are to be included in the strategic plan.

Strategy implementation – Strategy implementation is the process of turning plans into action to reach a desired outcome. Essentially, it's the art of getting stuff done. The success of every organization rests on its capacity to implement decisions and execute key processes efficiently, effectively, and consistently.

Strategy management calendar – A physical calendar used to maintain alignment and integrate strategic planning, operational planning, budgeting, and other key organizational processes.

Strategy management information system – A repository of strategic management data and information, often in an electronic format.

Strategy management office – A separate office which establishes, manages, and coordinates the entire strategy management process.

Strategy selection filters – An approach to narrowing the number of choices to the vital few strategies that will best move the organization forward.

Strengths (S) – The primary internal strengths of the organization. These attributes are essentially resources the organization can build on and/or draw upon to move forward.

Sub process – Group of related tasks that are designed to accomplish a significant portion or stage of a process.

Sub task – Activity required to carry out a particular task.

Supplier – The people (functions, departments, or organizations) who supply a process with its necessary inputs.

SWOT – See OTSW.

Tactic – The term tactics refers to the means by which a strategy is conducted to achieve a particular goal

Target – A target is the specific performance level the organization seeks for a particular indicator.

Target enterprise architecture – The TEA describes how the organization, and its assets will need to function as a whole to support the execution of the new strategy. TEA is thus synonymous with target operating model.

Tasks – One of the steps required to accomplish a particular process or project.

Threats (T) – Essentially storm clouds on the near-term or long-term horizon that could stand in the way of the organization moving forward.

Transformation plan – The process of regrouping all the building block transformations to be made to the operating model into projects. It orders the timing sequence of their execution so that the benefits the transformation projects will collectively generate are maximized.

Transform organization – The set of activities to change the organization to align its operating model to the new strategy.

Transformation project – A particular type of project, included in the transformation plan, that contributes to the transformation of the organization so it can execute its new strategy.

Trend – Direction in which something is changing. Trend is a general tendency or direction evident from past events increasing or decreasing in strength of frequency of observation. It usually suggests a pattern.

Trend cards – A set of cards depicting a particular set of drivers of change used to create future scenarios.

Trust (and organizational trust) – A confident belief in the safety, fortitude, integrity or reliability, truth, ability, or strength of someone or something. Organizational Trust is the positive expectation individuals have about the intent and behaviors of multiple organizational members based on organizational roles, relationships, experiences, and interdependencies.

Values (or Core Values) – The fundamental beliefs, philosophies, principles, or standards that dictate correct behavior and guide decisions and actions of an organization's leaders and workforce.

Value chain – The various activities and processes involved in developing a product or performing a service. A value chain can consist of the many stages of a product or service's lifecycle.

Variable – A variable is a quantity that may take on any of a set of values, for example, total number of customers served in one year.

Vision – Inspirational statement that articulates the desired future state of an organization in terms of its strategic direction.

VUCA – An acronym for volatile, uncertain, complex, and ambiguous.

Weaknesses (W) – The primary internal weaknesses the organization has that may interfere with the organization moving forward.

Weak signals – Early signs of currently small change. What is coming down the pike could be a huge disruptor/surprise. Not an established trend yet. They often are "not necessarily important things" which do not seem to have a strong impact in the present, but which could be the trigger for major events in the future.

Weighted criteria scoring – A tool that provides a systematic process for selecting projects based on many criteria.

Bibliography

Aguilar, F.J. *Scanning the Business Environment*, The Macmillan Company, 1967.

Anderson, J. C., Narus, J. A., & Van Rossum, W. *Customer Value Propositions in Business Markets*. Harvard Business Review, 84(3), 2006.

Andrews, Kenneth. *The Concept of Corporate Strategy, 2nd edition.* Homewood, IL: Dow-Jones Irwin Inc., 1980.

Ansoff, Igor H. *Corporate Strategy: An Analytical Approach to Business Policy for Growth and Expansion*, New York: McGraw Hill, 1965.

Argyris, Chris. *Knowledge for Action: A Guide to Overcoming Barriers to Organizational Change.* San Francisco: Jossey Bass, 1993.

Axelrod R. *Getting Everyone Involved: How One Organization Involved its Employees, Supervisors, and Managers in Redesigning the Organization*, The Journal of Applied Behavioral Science, 1992.

Baldrige Performance Excellence Program. *2023–2024 Baldrige Excellence Builder*®. Gaithersburg, MD: U.S. Department of Commerce, National Institute of Standards and Technology, 2023.

Beck K., et al. *The Agile Manifesto*. Agile Alliance, 2001.

Below, Patrick J. and George L. Morrisey, and Betty L. Acomb. *The Executive Guide to Strategic Planning*, San Francisco: Jossey- Bass, 1987.

Bossidy, Larry, and Ram Charan with Charles Burck. *Execution: The Discipline of Getting Things Done*. New York: Crown Business, 2002.

Campbell, Donald T. *Assessing the impact of planned social change. Evaluation and Program Planning*. 2 (1), 1979.

Chandler, Alfred. *Strategy and Structure.* Cambridge, MA: MIT Press, 1962.

Strategy in the 21st Century, Second Edition

Christensen, C. M. *The Innovator's Dilemma: When New Technologies Cause Great Firms to Fail*. Boston, MA: Harvard Business School Press, 1997.

Chugh J. *Bringing Agility to Strategy: Is Misalignment silently eroding your company's success?* Emergence, The Journal of Business Agility, Conference Special Edition, 2022.

Collins, Jim. *Good to Great: Why Some Companies Make the Leap... and Others Don't.* New York: Harper Collins Publishers, 2001.

Crumbaugh, Lee. *Big Decisions*, 2022.

Diggle, J. *The Cambridge Greek Lexicon*, Cambridge University Press, 2021.

Doerr, J., *Measure What Matters: How Google, Bono, and the Gates Foundation Rock the World with OKRs*, 2018.

Drucker, Peter. *The Practice of Management*. New York: Harper Collins Publishers, 1954.

Drucker, Peter. *Management for Results*. New York: Harper Collins Publishers, 1964.

Emery F. & Trist E. *The Causal Texture of Organizational Environments*. Human Relations v. 18, 1965.

Emery M. *The Current Version of Emery's Open Systems Theory,* Springer Publishing, 2000.

Endenburg, G. *Sociocratie: Een Redelijk Ideal [Sociocracy: A Reasonable Ideal],* Zaandijk, Woudt, 1975.

Farneworth, Ellis. *The Art of War by Niccolo Machiavelli.* Cambridge, MA: Da Capo Press, 2001.

Fry, Fred, and Charles Stoner. *Strategic Planning in the Small Business*, Chicago, Illinois: Upstart Publishing, 1995.

Galbraith, J.R. *Organization Design*. In Handbook of Organization Development (Ed. Cummings T.G.), 2008.

Von Ghyczy, T., Bassford, C., & and Von Oetinger, B (editor), *Clausewitz on Strategy: Inspiration and Insight from a Master Strategist.* New York: John Wiley and Sons, Inc., 2001.

Grant, R.M., *Contemporary Strategy Analysis – Text and Cases*, 9th Edition, 1991.

Grove, Andy. *High Output Management,* 1983, updated in 1995.

Grundy, Tony. *Gurus on Business Strategy*. London, UK: Thorogood, 2004.

Hackman, J. Richard, ed. *Groups That Work (and Those that Don't). Creating Conditions for Effective Teamwork)* San Francisco: Jossey-Bass, 1990.

Hadaya, P. and Gagnon, B. *Business Architecture: The Missing Link in Strategy Formulation, Implementation and Execution*. Montreal: ASATE Publishing, 2017.

Hadaya, P. and Gagnon, B. Making the Promise of Strategy a Reality with the Enterprise Architecture Approach. *Strategy Magazine*, 36(May), 2021.

Hadaya P. and Gagnon, B. Mapping an Agile Future. *Strategy Magazine*, 35 (May), 2020.

Hadaya, P. *Govern Your Strategy to Success*. ASP 2021 Annual Conference, 2021.

Hamel, Gary and C.K. Prahalad. Strategic Intent. *Harvard Business Review* 67, no. 3, 1989.

Haines, S.G. *The Complete Guide to Systems Thinking and Learning*. HRD Press, 2000.

Hamel, Gary and Prahalad, C.K. "The Core Competence of the Organization." *Harvard Business Review* 68, no. 3, 1990.

Hamel, Gary and Prahalad, C.K. "Strategy as Stretch and Leverage." *Harvard Business Review* 71, no. 2, 1993.

Hamel, Gary and Prahalad, C.K. *Competing for the Future*. Boston, MA: Harvard Business School Press, 1994.

Heffelfinger, L. & Parker, S. *Transformation Through Adaptive Leadership*, in *The Secret Sauce of Leading Transformational Change* by Ziskin I., Routledge Publishing, 2022.

Horwath, R. *Storm Rider: Becoming a Strategic Thinker*. Chicago, IL: Sculptura Consulting, Inc., 2004.

Hoskin, K. and Macve, R. and Stone, J. "The Historical Genesis of Modern Business and Military Strategy: 1850-1950." Paper, UMIST, LSE and University of Wales, Aberystwyth. As submitted to Interdisciplinary Perspectives on Accounting Conference, Manchester, July 1997.

Hughes, Marcia and Terrell, James Bradford. *The Emotionally Intelligent Team: Understanding and Developing the Behaviors of Success*. San Francisco: Jossey-Bass, A Wiley Imprint, 2007.

Humphrey, Albert. MBO Turned Upside Down. *Management Review*, 68(8), 1974.

Katzenbach, Jon R. *Teams at the Top: Unleashing the Potential of Both Teams and Individual Leaders*. Boston: Harvard Business School Press, 1998.

Katzenbach, Jon R. and Douglas K. Smith. *The Wisdom of Teams: Creating the High-Performance Organization*. New York: Harper Business: A Division of Harper Collins Publishers, 1993.

Katzenbach, J. R. *The Discipline of Teams: A Mindbook -Workbook for Delivering Small Group Performance*. New York: John Wiley and Sons, Inc., 2001.

Kanter, R.M. *The Change Masters: Innovation for Productivity in the American Corporation*. New York: Simon & Schuster, 1983.

Kanter, R.M. "Collaborative Advantage: The Art of Alliances." *Harvard Business Review* 72, no. 4 (July-August 1994): 96-108.

Kanter, R.M. *When Giants Learn to Dance: Mastering the Challenges of Strategy, Management, and Careers in the 1990s*. New York: Simon & Schuster, 1989.

Kaplan, R. and Norton, D. The Balanced Scorecard: Measures that Drive Performance. *Harvard Business Review* 70, no.1 (January-February 1992): 71-79.

Kaplan, R. and Norton D. *The Balanced Scorecard: Translating Strategy into Action*, Boston, Harvard Business School Press, 1996.

Kaplan, R. and Norton, D. *The Strategy-Focused Organization: How Balanced Scorecard Companies Thrive in the New Business Environment*. Boston, MA: Harvard Business School Press, 2000.

Kaplan, R.S. and Norton, D. *Strategy Maps - Converting Intangible Assets Into Tangible Outcomes*, Boston, MA: Harvard Business School Press, 2004.

Kaplan, R. and Norton. D., The Office of Strategy Management, *HBR Magazine*, October 2009.

Kaplan, R. and Norton D. *Double-Loop Management System*, HBR, January 2011.

Kenney, S. *Creating Adaptive Organizations*, American Management Association, Summer 2019

Kesler, G. and Kates. A. *Leading Organization Design: How to Make Organization Design Decisions to Drive the Results You Want*. Jossey-Bass Publishing, 2010.

Kesterson, R.K., *The Basics of Hoshin Kanri,* 2015.

Bibliography

Kiechel, W. III, *The Lords of Strategy – The Secret Intellectual History of the New Corporate World*, Harvard Business Press, 2010.

Kim, W.C., and Mauborgne, R. *Blue Ocean Strategy: How to Create Uncontested Market Space and Make the Competition Irrelevant*. Boston, MA: Harvard Business School Publishing Corporation, 2005.

Kim, W.C. and Mauborgne, R. *Blue Ocean Shift: Beyond Competing – Proven Seps to Inspire Confidence and Seize New Growth*, 2017.

Kippenberger, T. "Do Value Constellations Supersede Value Chains?" *The Antidote*, no. 2, Issue 5, 1997.

Kippenberger, T. Strategy according to Michael Porter, *The Antidote*, Vol. 3, Issue 6, 1998.

Lafley, A.G. and Martin, R.L., *Playing to Win*, Harvard Business Review Press, 2013.

LaMarsh, Jeanenne. *Changing the Way, We Change: Gaining Control of Major Operational Change*. Reading, MA: Addison-Wesley Publishing Company, 1995.

Learned, E.P. *Business Policy: Text and Cases*. Homewood, IL, Richard D. Irwin, 1969.

Lanning, J.J. Interview on Value Proposition (& Value Delivery), *Journal of Creating Value*, V5(2), 2019.

Mackin, Deborah. *The Team Building Tool Kit: Tips and Tactics for Effective Workplace Teams*. Chicago: American Management Association, 2007.

MacMillan, Pat. *The Performance Factor: Unlocking the Secrets of Teamwork*. Nashville, TN: Broadman and Holman Publishers, 2001.

Malcolm Baldrige Criteria. *2009-2010 Criteria for Performance Excellence,* the Baldrige National Quality Program at the National Institute of Standards and Technology in Gaithersburg, MD.

Maxwell, John C. *The 17 Indisputable Laws of Teamwork Workbook: Embrace Them and Empower Your Team*. Nashville, TN: Nelson Impact, A Division of Thomas Nelson Publishers, 2003.

McGrath, R., *Seeing Around Corners: How to Spot Inflection Points in Business Before They Happen*, Houghton Mifflin Harcourt, 2019.

McLaughlin, J.A. and Jordan, G.B. Logic Models: A Tool for Telling Your Program's Performance Story. *Evaluation and Program Planning*, 22(1), 1999.

Strategy in the 21st Century, Second Edition

McNeilly, M.R. *Sun Tzu and the Art of Business: Six Strategic Principles for Managers.* New York: Oxford University Press, 1996.

Michealson, Gerald A. *Sun Tzu—The Art of War for Managers: Fifty Strategic Rules.* Avon, MA: Adams Media Corporation, 2001.

Miller, S.C. and Kirkpatrick, S.A. *The Government Leader's Field Guide to Organizational Agility: How to Navigate Complex and Turbulent Times.* Oakland, CA: Berrett-Koehler, 2021.

Mintzberg, Henry. *The Nature of Management Work.* New York: Harper and Row, 1973.

Mintzberg, Henry. *The Structuring of Organizations.* Englewood Cliffs, New Jersey: Prentice Hall, 1979.

Mintzberg, Henry. *The Rise and Fall of Strategic Planning.* London: Prentice Hall, 1994.

Mintzberg, Henry, Quinn, J.B. and Voyer, J. *The Strategy Process*. Englewood Cliffs, New Jersey: Prentice Hall, 1995.

Montanari, J.R. and Bracker, J.S., *Strategic Management Journal*, V7, no. 3, 1986.

Montgomery, D. *Start Less, Finish More: Building Strategic Agility with Objectives and Key Results*, 2018.

Moore, J.F. *The Death of Competition: Leadership & Strategy in the Age of Business Ecosystems*. Harper Business, 1996.

Nadler, D. and Tushman, M. *A Model for Diagnosing Organizational Behavior.* Organizational Dynamics v9, #2, 1980.

Niven, P. and Lamorte, B. *OKR Field Book: A Step-by-Step Guide for Objectives and Key Results*, 2022.

Niven, P. and Lamorte, B. *Objectives and Key Results,* 2016.

Osterwalder, A. and Pigneur Y. *Business Model Generation,* John Wiley & Sons, 2010.

Owen, H. *Open Space Technology: A User's Guide (3rd ed.).* Berrett-Koehler Publishing, 2008.

Paret, Peter (ed.), *Makers of Modern Strategy, from Machiavelli to the Nuclear Age.* Princeton, New Jersey: Princeton University Press, 1986.

Parker, Glenn M. *Team Players and Teamwork: The New Competitive Business Strategy*. San Francisco: Jossey-Bass Publishers, 1990.

Parker, S. *Designing Living Organizations: Tapping and Unleashing Implementation and Execution.* ASATE Publishing, Montreal, 2023.

Pasmore W. A. and Winby S. and Mohrman S. A. and Vanasse R. (in press). *Sociotechnical Systems design: A reflection and look ahead.* Journal of Change Management, 2018.

Peters, Tom and Waterman, R.H. *In Search of Excellence: Lessons from America's Best-Run Companies.* New York: Harper and Row, 1982.

Project Management Institute, *Guide to the Project Management Body of Knowledge*, Seventh Edition, 2021.

Porter, M. E. *Competitive Strategy: Techniques for Analyzing Industries and Competitors.* New York: Free Press, 1980. (Republished with a new introduction, 1998)

Porter, M. E. *The Competitive Advantage: Creating and Sustaining Superior Performance.* New York: Free Press, 1985.

Porter, M. E. *Competitive Strategy: Techniques for Analyzing Industries and Competitors.* New York: Free Press, 1998.

Powers, Thomas L; Steward, Jocelyn L. Journal of Historical Research in Marketing; Bingley Vol. 2, 4, (2010)

Prahalad, C.K. and Hamel, G. (1993) Stretch and Leverage. Harvard Business Review, 1993.

Prahalad, C.K. and Ramaswamy, V. The Future of Competition: Co-Creating Unique Value With Customers, 2004.

Quinn, J.B. *Strategies for Change: Logical Incrementalism.* Homewood, IL: Richard D. Irwin Inc., 1980.

Robertson, B. *Holacracy: The New Management System for a Rapidly Changing World.* Henry Holt & Co, 2015.

Rohm, H., Wilsey, D., Perry, G.S., Montgomery, D. *The Institute Way: Simplify Strategic Planning and Management with the Balanced Scorecard, 2013*

Rollinson, R. and Young, E. *Strategy in the 21st Century*, Edition #1, 2010.

Ross, Jeanne, MIT expert recaps 30-plus years of enterprise architecture, MIT Management, August 10, 2020.

Sanderson, S. New Approaches to Strategy: New Ways of Thinking for the Millennium, *Management Decision*, Vol. 36, Issue 1, 1998.

Schein, E.H. *Organizational Culture and Leadership*, 2010.

Schwartz, P. *The Art of the Longview*, Doubleday, 1991

Senge, Peter. *The Fifth Discipline: The Art and Practice of the Learning Organization*. New York: Doubleday, 1990.

Snowden, D.J. and Boone, M.E. *A Leader's Framework for Decision Making*, HBR, November 2007.

Speculand, R. *Excellence in Execution: How to Implement Your Strategy, 2017.*

Stanford N. *Organization Design: The Practitioners Guide*. Routledge, London, (3rd ed) 2018.

Stoner, C. and Fry, F. *Strategic Planning in the Small Business*, South-Western, 1987.

Strauss, David. *How to Make Collaboration Work: Powerful Ways to Build Consensus, Solve Problems, and Make Decisions*. San Francisco: Berrett-Koehler Publishers, Inc., 2002.

Stern, C.W. and Deimler, M.S. (editors), *The Boston Consulting Group on Strategy: Classic Concepts and New Perspectives*. Hoboken, New Jersey: John Wiley and Sons, Inc., 2006.

Taylor F. *The Principles of Scientific Management*, Harper & Brothers Publishers, 1919.

Thayer, R. and Carnino, M. and Zybach, W. *Syngineering: Building Agility into Any Organization*. United Kingdom: Changemakers Books, 2021.

Tracy, Brian, *Victory! Applying the Proven Principles of Military Strategy to Achieve Greater Success in your Business and Personal Life*. New York: AMACOM, a division of American Management Association, 2002.

Treacy, M. and Wiersma, F. *The Discipline of Market Leaders*, 1995.

Wheelen, T.L. and Hunger, J.D. *Strategic Management Business Policy: Concepts and Cases*, 2014.

Weber, M. *Wirtschaft und Gesellschaft*. Mohr Siebeck Verlag, Tübingen, 1922.

Wholey, J.S. *Evaluation and Effective Public Management*. Boston: Little, Brown, 1983

Willeke, E. *Fit-for-Purpose Agility: There Is No "One True Agile"*. Cutter Business Technology J., v33, #4, 2020.

Worley, C. and Williams T. and Lawler E. *The Agility Factor: Building Adaptable Organizations for Superior Performance,* Jossey-Bass Publishing, 2014.

Wouter, A., et. al. *The Five Trademarks of Agile Organizations*, McKinsey & Co., 2018.

Wren, D.A. and Bedeian, A.G. *The Evolution of Management Thought*. (6th ed.), New York: Wiley, 2009.

Index

A.G. Lafley, 41
accountability, 223
action plan, 237
agile, 205
agile or adaptive design, 202
agile organization design cycle, 213
Agile Organization Design Framework, 206
agility, 230
AGILITY, 97
Albert Einstein, 93
Alexander Osterwalder, 139
Alfred Chandler, 27
Alfred Sloane, 24
ALIGNING INDIVIDUAL ROLES, 227
   Tier 3, 227
Alignment, 167
alternative strategies, 130
AMAZON, 96, 209
Analysis, 53
Andy Grove, 42
ANSOFF'S GRID, 105, 136
ANSOFF'S GRID, 29
Antonio Nieto Rodriguez, 41
Artificial Intelligence, ix, xi
assessment, 102

balanced scorecard, 157
BALANCED SCORECARD, 168
BALANCED SCORECARD, 37
Balanced Scorecard Institute, 225
Baldrige Criteria for Performance Excellence, 108
Baldrige Excellence Builder, 108
Baldrige Excellence Framework, 2, 11
baseline, 178
BCG Growth Share Matrix, 30, 58
benchmark, 178
Bernard Gagnon
   Pierre Hadaya, 206
BLUE OCEAN, 39
Blue Ocean Strategy, 88
Board of Directors, 259
Boston Consulting Group, 58
   BCG, 30
Brand, 216
building block, 216
building blocks, 201
bureaucracy, 198
Business capability, 216
Business Capability Framework, 206, 217
   Hadaya and Gagnon, 216
Business ecosystems, 201

385

Business Model Canvas
   Osterwalder, 138
C. K. Prahalad, 95
C. Roland Christensen, 26
Campbell's Law, 247
Cascading, 225
<u>Cash Cow</u>, 31
cause and effect
   Perspectives, 158
Change, 202
Charter, 186
Chicagoland Gas, 167
Chief Strategy Officer, 261
Chris Argyris, 249
Clausewitz, 22
Co-Creation, 209
Communication, 221
communications plan, 192
Communications Plan, 75
competitive advantage, 132
competitive advantages, 106
Competitive positioning, 132
Competitor, 91
competitors, 86, 90
COMPONENTS OF STRATEGIC DIRECTION, 114
CONCEPTUAL MODELS, 75
CONE OF POSSIBILITIES, 92
Conscious Capitalism, 43
contingencies, 150
contingency plans, 163
core competencies, 46, 106

Core competencies, 38, 95
core competency, 48
core process, 109
Cost leadership, 35
Cross-functional coordination, 187
culture, 215
Customer, 90
Customer perspective, 159
Customer Value Proposition, 134
Customers, 109
Cut before you add, 235
Daniel Taylor, 23
Data visualization, 243
Data-based decision making, 247
data-driven decisions, 247
DESIGN THINKING PROCESS, 210
Differentiation, 35
dimensions, 90
DIMENSIONS, 80
diversification, 105
Dog, 31
double-loop learning
   Chris Argyris, 249
Dr. Pierre Hadaya, 259
ecosystem, 211
ecosystem maps, 211
emotionally intelligent leaders, 254
Employee development, 224
engage stakeholders, 253
Engage stakeholders, 9, 10
Engage Stakeholders, 15, 220

Index

Engagement Operating Model, 256
ENTERPRISE ARCHITECTURE TEAM, 219
Environmental Assessment, 79
ESPOUSED ORGANIZATIONAL VALUES, 122
Evaluation, 53
Execute Strategy, 15
Executing Strategy, 48
execution planning guidelines, 168
external assistance, 54
External contracts, 189
external scan, 104
facilitate, 131
Financial perspective, 159
Focus, 35
Focus Group, 86
foresight, 79
Formulate Strategy, 15
Frederick Taylor, 198
function, 109
Function, 216
FUNCTIONS, 98
funding
 Resources, 163
Future of Strategy Implementation, 231
Gail Stout Perry, 134
 CVP, 134
Galbraith's Star Model, 199
GANTT CHART
 TIME PHASE INITIATIVES, 185
gap analysis, 61
Gary Hamel., 95

GE McKinsey Matrix, 32
Generative AI, 87
GENERIC BUSINESS CULTURES, 213
GENERIC BUSINESS ECOSYSTEMS, 212
George Albert Smith, 26
George Whistler, 23
Goal, 56
goal achievement, 143
Good to Great, 234
Google, 209
govern strategy, 10
Govern Strategy, 15
governance, 165, 191
GOVERNANCE AND ENGAGEMENT OPERATING MODEL, 260
Hamel and Prahalad, 36, 38
Heatmap Exposure Matrix, 106
Hedgehog Concept, 40
Henry Gantt, 186
Heritage College of Osteopathic Medicine, 128
Herman Kahn, 32
high-impact activities, 140
Hoshin Kanri, 172
IASP Body of Knowledge 3.0, 2, 14
IASP BOK 3.0, 17
IASP Competencies, iv, 17
IASP COMPETENCY DOMAINS, 16
IASP Competency Model, 2, 11, 14
Igor Ansoff, 28
Implement, 231
implementation, 167

387

Strategy in the 21st Century, Second Edition

Implementation, 175

implementation budget, 191

IMPLEMENTATION GUIDELINES, 169

implementation plans, 187

incentive, 224

Incentives, 256

Information, 216

information base, 51

information technology (IT) assets, 217

Innovation, 38

Input measures, 241

INTEGRATED ORGANIZATIONAL SYSTEMS, 208

intended results, 152, 156

INTERNAL ANALYSIS, 94

Internal Process perspective, 159

International Association for Strategy Professionals, 1

Interview, 86

James Brian Quinn, 43

James Stockmal, 14

Jim Collins, 39, 234

Jim Stockmal, 219

John Doerr, 42, 172

John Mackey, 43

Joseph S. Wholey
  Logic Model, 173

Kaplan and Norton, 36

Kaplan and Norton's, 162

Kenneth Andrews, 27

key drivers of revenue and profit growth, 192

key drivers of success, 152

key leaders, 60

key performance indicator, 175

key performance indicators, 178

Key Performance Indicators
  Targets, 240

Key Results
  OKRs, 230

Kiechel, 20

Knowledge, 216

Larry Bossidy, 41

leadership, 69, 139

Leadership, 109

leadership characteristics, 256

leadership perceptions, 142

leadership team, 72

leading indicators, 246

leading or lagging indicator, 176

Learning and Growth perspective, 159

line of sight, 224, 228
  Strategy, 224

listening, 69, 254

Logic Model, 173

longer-term strategic plan, 163
  Format, 163

long-term strategic plans, 149

Machiavelli, 22

MacMillian Matrix, 236

Macroenvironment, 81

Malcolm Baldrige National Quality Award, 108

Management, 169, 259

management approval, 191

388

Management by Objectives
  Peter Drucker, 25
Management Control Loop, 250
management feedback, 165
Management Systems, 170
market development, 105
market penetration, 105
market scope, 132
Mastering Strategy: Strategic Management Performance System (SMPS) Certification Program, 2
Max Weber, 198
measure, 239
Measure, 10
Measurement, 109
measurement of performance, 224
Medellin, 89
  Blue Ocean Strategy, 89
Michael Porter, 33, 43, 87, 132
Micro-level analysis, 85
Middle managers, 237
Military, 22
Mintzberg, 27, 28, 43, 44
Mission, 56
mission statement, 119
Nadler and Tushman's Congruence Model, 199
Napoleon, 22
Netflix, 209
nichijo kanri, 173
non-IT technology assets, 217
North Star, 207

Objective Commentary, 157
Objectives
  OKRs, 230
offerings, 58
OKR, 230
OKRs, 42, 171
operating model, 144, 196
Operating Model Canvas, 207
Operating models, 200
Operating plan, 150
operational planning, 145
Opportunities, 27
opportunities and threats, 105
Organization, 169
organizational alignment, 224
Organizational Capabilities, 51
organizational design, 198
organizational learning, 10, 248
ORGANIZATIONAL LIFE CYCLE, 212
ORGANIZATIONAL POLARITIES, 211
Organizational unit, 216
Organizational values
  Core Values, 121
Organizations as systems, 199
organization's identity, 207
Origins of Strategy, 22
OSTERWALDER'S OPERATING MODEL CANVAS, 200
OTSW, 6, 103
Outcome measures, 241
Output measures, 241

389

Overarching Goal, 124
   Goal, 124
Paired Comparison, 182
percent to target, 244
performance culture, 223
Performance management, 240
Performance Management, 9
PERFORMANCE MANAGEMENT, 239
Performance measurement, 240
PERFORMANCE MEASUREMENT, 177
PERFORMANCE MEASUREMENT CATEGORIES, 240
PERFORMANCE REVIEW, 246
PESTLE
   STEEPLE, 81
Peter Drucker, 18, 25, 42, 171, 173, 234, 239
Peter Senge, 37
Peters and Waterman, 36
Pierre Hadaya, 14, 206
Pierre Wack, 32
planning horizon, 72
planning process, 74
Playing to Win, 41, 137
Policies, 122
Policy Deployment
   Hoshin Kanri, 172
PORTER'S FIVE FORCES, 33
Porter's three generic strategies, 132
Preston McAfee, 35
PRIORITIZE, 103
Process, 216

Process measures, 241
Product and Process Results, 109
Product life cycles, 90
product/service development, 105
Professional Development, 223
project management, 186
Project Management Institute, 186, 232
projects, 180
psychological safety, 96
psychologically safe, 256
PUBLIC SECTOR, 59
Question Mark, 31
R. M. Kanter, 37
RACI matrix, 184
Raj Sisodia
   Conscious Capitalism, 43
Ram Charan, 41
readiness assessment
   Implementation, 235
Real Reasons to Believe, 136
   Jeff Varney, 136
RED OCEAN, 39
Report, 171
resource, 224, 262
resources, 98, 207
   Funding, 192
Resources
   Funding, 170
risk, 70
Robert F. Stewart, 26
Robert Kaplan and David Norton, 158

Index

two management loops, 250
Robert Waterman, 36
Robin Champ, 93
Robin Speculand, 41
Roger Martin, 41
role of leaders
    Strategy Implementation, 232
ROLES AND RESPONSIBILITIES OF THE STRATEGY MANAGEMENT OFFICE, 263
roll-out the strategy, 220
Scaled Agile Framework, 205
Scenario-based planning, 32, 91
Scientific management, 198
Self-Directed Teams, 253
Skills, 99
SMART, 228
SMPS Framework, iv, 11, 17
SMPS, Baldrige Builder Crosswalk, 13
SMPS, Full Baldrige Criterion Crosswalk, 13
Social Media, 86
Staffing, 170
Stakeholder Engagement, 253
stakeholder-focused mindset, 254
Stakeholders, 86
Star, 31
Stephen Haines, 1
Strategic alignment, 200
Strategic Alternatives, 47
strategic altitude, 166
strategic direction, 7, 52
Strategic Direction, 113

strategic foresight, 91
Strategic Governance, 253
strategic initiatives, 180
Strategic initiatives, 163, 224
Strategic learning, 249
Strategic Learning Loop, 250
strategic management, xi, 18, 100
Strategic management, 19
strategic management competencies, 61
Strategic Management Competencies, 44
Strategic Management Performance System Framework, 3
strategic management process, xii
strategic management processes, 111
Strategic Management Professional, 14
STRATEGIC MANAGEMENT ROLES AND RESPONSIBILITIES, 258
strategic management system, 110
strategic objectives, 156
strategic operating plan, 193
Strategic Operating Plan, 147
strategic operating plans, 151
strategic perspectives, 158
Strategic Plan, 147
strategic planning, 18, 146
Strategic Planning, 7, 145
Strategic Planning Professional, 14
Strategic Policy, 56
strategic thinking, 18, 23, 146
Strategic Thinking, 46
strategies, 141

391

Strategy in the 21st Century, Second Edition

strategos, 22

strategy, 19, 130

Strategy, 109

strategy cadence, 235

strategy canvas, 88

Strategy Canvas, 39, 133

Strategy Execution, 8, 195

Strategy Execution Gap, 195

strategy formulation, 146

Strategy Formulation, 113

Strategy Implementation Institute, 234

STRATEGY IMPLEMENTATION ROAD MAP, 233

Strategy management calendar, 261

Strategy management information system, 264

Strategy management office, 263

Strategy Management Office, 261

STRATEGY MAP, 161

STRATEGY MAPPING RULES, 162

strategy selection filters, 142

Strategy-Operating Model Cycle, 197

Strengths, 27

Sun Tzu, 23, 265

Supplier chain, 91

Survey, 86

SWOT, 6

SWOT analysis, 26

Sylvanus Thayer, 23

synergy, 143

Syngineering, 206

Syngineering Solutions, 206

SYNGINEERING SOLUTIONS DESIGN CYCLE, 214

tactical guidelines, 179

tactics, 180

Tamera Fields Parsons, 12

target, 178

target business architecture, 217

TAYLOR'S SCIENTIFIC MANAGEMENT, 198

Teamwork, 48

Technology assets, 216

The Agile Manifesto, 203

The Practice of Management
   Peter Drucker, 25

Threats, 27

THREE LEVELS OF PERFORMANCE MEASURES, 241

Tier 1, 226

Tier 2, 226

Tier 3, 227

Time phase initiatives, 185

Tom Peters, 36

Transform Organization, 15

transform the operating model, 8

Transform the Operating model, 196

Transform the Operating Model, 220

transformation plan, 218

transparency, 223

United States Coast Guard, 93

validity of data, 242

VALUE CHAIN, 36

value creation, 97

Value Propositions

392

Customer, Owner, Employee, Partner, 133

Values, 56

variable, 178

Vision, 56

vision statement, 115

Visioning, 46

Visualize performance data, 242

VUCA, 6, 202

W. C. Kim and Renee Mauborgne, 38

W. Edward Deming, 173

Walter Kiechel, 30

Weaknesses, 27

WEBER'S BUREAUCRACY THEORY, 199

West Point, 23

What's in it for me, 228

Windy City Shoes, 252

Workforce, 109

World War II, 25

X MATRIX, 173

About the Authors

Randall Rollinson is the Co-Founder and President of LBL Strategies, a federally certified veteran-owned business and internationally recognized leader in the practical application of strategic management principles, tools, and techniques. LBL Strategies is based in Chicago, IL.

Since 1985, Randall has served over 3,000 organizations across sectors with a focused range of strategic management education, training, consulting, and certification preparation services.

Randall is a certified Strategic Management Professional (SMP), a pioneer in the International Association for Strategy Professionals (IASP) certification program, a member of the IASP Hall of Fame, and an active participant in the IASP Government Community of Practice. He co-founded and previously served as president of the IASP – Chicago Chapter.

Throughout his career, Randall has specialized in the study and practice of strategic management. He is responsible for leading, designing, and instructing the *Mastering Strategy: Strategic Management Performance System Certification Program*, in partnership with George Washington University, Center for Excellence in Public Leadership and the Baldrige Foundation. This program won the 2001 Exemplar Award from the International Association for Continuing Education and Training for its exceptional results-oriented program.

Randall holds an MBA in Management from DePaul University, a master's degree in rehabilitation counseling, and a bachelor's degree in psychology from Southern Illinois University.

He is a US Army Veteran having served in Vietnam from 1970 -1971.

Earl Young was Professor Emeritus at DePaul University, where he taught in the Department of Management and in the Center for Professional Education. Prior to that he taught in the departments of management at the Illinois Institute of Technology, and the University of New York at Albany.

His primary teaching and consulting activities were focused on operations management, strategic management, and international development. In these areas he designed, developed, and administered programs in continuing and professional education, and small business management and entrepreneurship.

He conducted research on the technological development of firms in Mexico, and on small business development in both the United States and Mexico.

He received his MBA from the University of Chicago and his PhD in Industrial Engineering and Management Sciences from Northwestern University.

Made in the USA
Monee, IL
03 September 2025